150 Best Jobs™ Through Military Training

Part of JIST's Best Jobs™ Series

The Editors @ JIST **and Laurence Shatkin, Ph.D.**

Foreword by Janet E. Wall, Ed.D., President, Sage Solutions consulting firm, and Former Manager, ASVAB Career Exploration Program

Also in JIST's Best Jobs Series

- *Best Jobs for the 21st Century*
- *200 Best Jobs for College Graduates*
- *300 Best Jobs Without a Four-Year Degree*
- *250 Best Jobs Through Apprenticeships*
- *50 Best Jobs for Your Personality*
- *40 Best Fields for Your Career*
- *225 Best Jobs for Baby Boomers*
- *250 Best-Paying Jobs*
- *175 Best Jobs Not Behind a Desk*
- *150 Best Jobs for Your Skills*

150 Best Jobs Through Military Training

Published by JIST Works, an imprint of JIST Publishing
7321 Shadeland Station, Suite 200
Indianapolis, IN 46256-3923

Phone: 800-648-JIST
Fax: 877-454-7839
E-mail: info@jist.com
Web site: www.jist.com

Some Other Books by the Authors

The Editors at JIST

EZ Occupational Outlook Handbook
Salary Facts Handbook
Enhanced Occupational Outlook Handbook
Guide to America's Federal Jobs
Health-Care CareerVision Book and DVD

Laurence Shatkin

The 90-Minute College Major Matcher

Acquisitions Editor: Susan Pines
Development Editor: Stephanie Koutek
Cover and Interior Designer: Aleata Howard
Interior Layout: Toi Davis
Proofreaders: Paula Lowell, Jeanne Clark
Indexer: Kelly D. Henthorne

Printed in the United States of America

12 11 10 09 9 8 7 6 5 4 3 2

Library of Congress Cataloging-in-Publication Data

150 best jobs through military training / the editors at JIST and Laurence Shatkin.
p. cm. -- (Best jobs series)
Includes index.
ISBN-13: 978-1-59357-462-8 (alk. paper)
1. Career changes--United States. 2. Veterans--Employment--United States. 3. Vocational qualifications--United States. 4. Veterans--Vocational guidance--United States. 5. Job hunting--United States. I. Shatkin, Laurence. II. JIST Works, Inc. III. Title: One hundred fifty best jobs through military training.
HF5384.A15 2008
331.7020973--dc22

2007024876

ISBN 978-1-59357-462-8

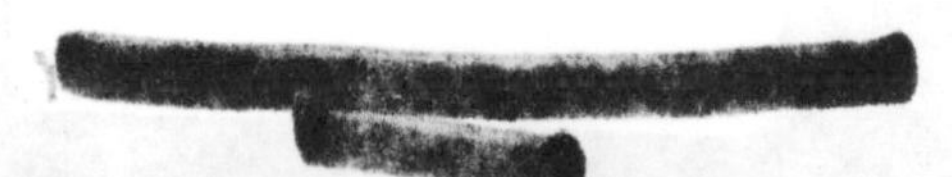

This Is a Big Book, But It Is Very Easy to Use

Attention! Listen up! Do you think the main skill you learn in the military is how to throw a salute? The armed forces have a lot more to offer. You can learn skills that put you ahead of the competition for civilian jobs. If you're already in the military, you know you have acquired a lot of skills, but you may not know which civilian jobs can make best use of those skills.

Every year the military swears in more than one-third of a million people and trains them for more than 4,000 different jobs. Through military training you may become experienced with high technology, health care, or other careers that are in high demand. You'll learn a lot of general work habits and attitudes that employers are looking for. And you'll gain the pride that comes from serving your country.

After your period of service you'll be ready to take your skills into the civilian job market. But what are *the best civilian jobs* that the military can prepare you for? That's what this book is about. It selects civilian jobs with a military training route and orders them to emphasize those with the highest earnings and the highest demand for workers. Specialized lists arrange these jobs by interest fields and personality types. You can also see lists of jobs that have high percentages of part-time, self-employed, female, or male workers.

Every civilian job is described in detail later in the book, so you can explore the jobs that interest you the most. You'll learn the major work tasks, all the important skills, the work conditions, and many other informative facts.

You'll also find detailed descriptions of all the related military jobs, plus a helpful discussion of how to navigate the recruiting process and improve your chances of getting the job assignment you want.

Using this book, you'll be surprised how quickly you'll get new ideas for civilian career goals that can benefit from military service and can suit you in many other ways. At ease!

Some Things You Can Do with This Book

- Develop long-term career plans for jobs that you can enter by getting military training.
- Identify jobs that can make use of military training you already have.
- Prepare for discussing your military and civilian career goals with a military recruiter.
- Prepare for interviews by learning how to connect your military-acquired skills to your career goal.

(continued)

(continued)

These are a few of the many ways you can use this book. We hope you find it as interesting to browse as we did to put together. We have tried to make it easy to use and as interesting as occupational information can be.

When you are done with this book, pass it along or tell someone else about it. We wish you well in your career and in your life.

Credits and Acknowledgments: While the authors created this book, it is based on the work of many others. The occupational information is based on data obtained from the U.S. Department of Labor and the U.S. Census Bureau. These sources provide the most authoritative occupational information available. The job titles and their related descriptions are from the O*NET database, which was developed by researchers and developers under the direction of the U.S. Department of Labor. They, in turn, were assisted by thousands of employers who provided details on the nature of work in the many thousands of job samplings used in the database's development. We used the most recent version of the O*NET database, release 11.0. We appreciate and thank the staff of the U.S. Department of Labor for their efforts and expertise in providing such a rich source of data.

Table of Contents

Summary of Major Sections

Detailed Table of Contents

Foreword

Serving your country by joining the military is one of the most honorable professions available to an American, and it can be an excellent way to prepare for a career. If you have picked up this book and leafed through its pages, you may be wondering whether military service is for you, and, if so, what your best options are.

Why should you consider joining the military? Serving in the military can provide opportunities to obtain excellent job and personal skills, and chances to advance in your education and career.

- The Armed Forces is the largest employer for entry-level workers. Each year more than 180,000 young men and women volunteer for active duty in the military. Here they get training that leads to improved technical and job skills, as well as a job.
- Joining the military as an enlisted person is a wonderful way to start your career. The military provides some of the best job training in the world. Full- and part-time training is available for more than 4,100 different military jobs.
- Military pay and benefits have improved greatly over the years and in many cases exceed what is paid for similar jobs in the civilian sector.
- The military offers many opportunities to continue your education. Military members can obtain education leading to degrees while on the job through programs offered on base or through distance education. In addition, members of the military can earn more than $70,000 in educational benefits to use after transitioning out of the military.
- People who join the military have extraordinary opportunities to take on leadership roles and handle far more responsibilities than their friends who start jobs in the civilian sector. Employers value individuals who have the skills learned in the military and the personal characteristics to be a loyal and productive employee.

Who joins the military? Military enlistees represent the best of American youth, and they come from various parts of the country, with academic smarts, and with diverse economic backgrounds.

- It is not true that the military is a last-chance option for young people who have no better alternatives. In reality, more than 90 percent of military recruits hold a high school diploma, while that is true of only 75 percent of their peers. About two-thirds of enlistees score above the national average in verbal and math tests, clearly outscoring their peers.
- It's a myth that the military draws only from a pool of poor, disadvantaged youth. Most military recruits come from the economic middle class, but individuals from economically advantaged and disadvantaged do sign up to serve their country.
- Military recruits come from all parts of the United States, nearly in proportion to available youth, although the South is slightly overrepresented.

- Not just anyone can get into the military. Wanting to serve is not enough. You have to meet physical standards, behavioral standards, and aptitude standards. You need self-discipline, willingness to do physical work, and a dedication to excellence in everything you do.
- People who care about protecting their friends and families join the military. They want to preserve the many freedoms we have as American citizens.

So if military service seems like a good choice for you, you can use this book to learn about the best civilian jobs available through military training. You will be able to find helpful details about these civilian jobs and about the military jobs that help prepare for them. Read the facts about these jobs and then make the best choice for your career.

Janet E. Wall, Ed.D.
President, Sage Solutions consulting firm
Former Manager, ASVAB Career Exploration Program

Introduction

The active-duty military employs close to one million enlisted or commissioned workers, making it one of the biggest employers in the United States. It has a remarkable record for encouraging achievement of women, people from minority groups, and recent immigrants. It also serves as the entry ramp to success for numerous young people in regions of the country with few other opportunities for career advancement and higher education. People may enter the military to serve their country; to gain military benefits, such as the G.I. Bill; or to learn job skills.

The military can be a lifetime career, but most recruits serve only a few years in uniform. They get training in specific job skills and in military work-related attitudes and then leave active duty to pursue a civilian career immediately. If you are thinking about being one of those people, this book is aimed at you.

The military can teach you a lot more than how to throw a salute, march in time, and shoot straight. It covers a range of jobs almost as diverse as those found in the civilian workplace. Here's the breakdown of where active-duty personnel are assigned:

Occupational Categories of Active-Duty Personnel

Category	Examples	Percent
Low Skills	Infantry, crafts, supply handling	30
Medium Skills	Medical support, mechanical repair	43
High Skills	Electronic equipment repair, communications	21
Nonoccupational	Trainees, prisoners, patients	6

The training and work experience you gain in the military can prepare you to enter a good-paying, high-growth job—either by providing all the qualifications you'll need for job entry or by giving you a significant head start on the formal qualifications.

Where the Information Came From

The information we used for developing the occupational information in this book came mostly from databases created by the U.S. Department of Labor, the U.S. Census Bureau, and the U.S. Department of Defense:

- We started with the civilian jobs included in the Department of Labor's O*NET (Occupational Information Network) database, which is now the primary source of detailed information on occupations. The Labor Department updates the O*NET on a regular basis, and we used the most recent one available—O*NET release 11.
- Because we wanted to include earnings, growth, number of openings, and other data about civilian jobs not in the O*NET, we cross-referenced information on earnings developed by the U.S. Bureau of Labor Statistics (BLS) and the U.S. Census Bureau. This information on earnings is the most reliable data we could obtain. For data on earnings, projected growth, and number of openings, the BLS uses a slightly different set of job titles than the O*NET uses, so we had to match similar titles. Data about part-time workers and the male-female breakdown of workers was derived from the Census Bureau, which also uses a slightly different set of job titles. By linking the BLS and Census data to the O*NET job titles in this book, we tied information about growth, earnings, and characteristics of workers to all the civilian job titles in this book.
- The detailed information about military occupations came from a Web site called www.todaysmilitary.com, created for the Department of Defense. This is the same site that you have seen referenced in television commercials and magazine advertisements about the military. The Defense Manpower Data Center developed the information for this site and provided a crosswalk from military to civilian occupations.

Of course, information in a database format can be boring and even confusing, so we did many things to help make the data useful and present it to you in a form that is easy to understand.

How the Best Jobs Through Military Training Were Selected

The only jobs that you *must* have military training to enter are military jobs. For some civilian jobs, however, military training is an accepted, common, or even preferred route, and those are the jobs that we wanted to focus on in this book. There is no official list of these civilian jobs, so to extract these jobs from the nearly 950 jobs in the O*NET database we applied the following criteria:

- Because this book is aimed primarily at people who are considering military training as an alternative to long years of college, we selected civilian jobs that require **less education than a bachelor's degree**.

- We made exceptions for a handful of jobs, such as Computer Programmers and Graphic Designers, that normally require a bachelor's but that are very **flexible about their requirements**, especially when a job candidate has relevant training and work experience.
- We made exceptions for three other civilian occupations because for them **military training is by far the most practical entry route**: Airline Pilots, Copilots, and Flight Engineers; Commercial Pilots; and Pilots, Ship, and Ship and Boat Captains. Private flying lessons are very expensive, and the civilian route to becoming captain or pilot of a ship requires years of experience in other maritime roles. Therefore we included these three occupations even though you need to have a bachelor's *before* you enter the military training programs for them.
- Apart from these three exceptions, we considered only jobs for which **enlisted-level military jobs are the entry route.** To become an officer, you need either to have a bachelor's degree or to be close enough to it that you can complete the degree while in the service. Therefore, civilian jobs that require officer-level military experience are not appropriate career goals for people who want to avoid many years of college.
- Military training needs to be able to **serve as some or all of the training** needed to enter the job. For this reason we excluded Air Traffic Controller, which requires all candidates to complete the same training program even if they have already been trained for the related job in the military. For many jobs that we did include, the military provides *partial* qualifications for job entry, but additional education or training is required for certification or licensing.
- The jobs had to have the **full set of O*NET data topics.** We had to eliminate 201 jobs for this reason alone, including several for which military training would be useful preparation, such as Emergency Management Specialists and Pharmacy Aides.

Based on these criteria, we assembled a preliminary list of 203 civilian jobs through military training. Next we created our own database from the O*NET, the Census Bureau, and other sources so we could evaluate the economic rewards of these jobs and select which to include in this book. We followed these procedures for creating our list of best jobs:

1. We eliminated two jobs because annual average income figures are not available. We also had to drop another three because they are both shrinking in size and taking on fewer than 500 new workers per year, so they cannot be considered best jobs.
2. We created three lists that ranked the remaining 198 jobs based on three major criteria: median annual earnings, projected growth through 2014, and number of job openings projected per year.
3. We then added the numerical ranks for each job from all three lists to calculate its overall score.
4. To emphasize jobs that tend to pay more, are likely to grow more rapidly, and have more job openings, we selected the 150 job titles with the best numerical scores for our final list. These civilian jobs are the focus of this book.

For example, Dental Hygienists has the best combined score for earnings, growth, and number of job openings, so Dental Hygienists is listed first in our "150 Best Civilian Jobs Overall Through Military Training" list even though it is not the best-paying job (which is Airline Pilots, Copilots, and Flight Engineers), the fastest-growing job (which is Medical Assistants), or the job with the most openings (which is Retail Salespersons).

Understand the Limits of the Data in This Book

In this book we use the most reliable and up-to-date information available on earnings, projected growth, number of openings, and other topics. The earnings data came from the U.S. Department of Labor's Bureau of Labor Statistics. As you look at the figures, keep in mind that they are estimates. They give you a general idea about the number of workers employed, annual earnings, rate of job growth, and annual job openings.

Understand that a problem with such data is that it describes an average. Just as there is no precisely average person, there is no such thing as a statistically average example of a particular job. We say this because data, while helpful, can also be misleading.

Take, for example, the yearly earnings information in this book for civilian jobs. This is highly reliable data obtained from a very large U.S. working population sample by the Bureau of Labor Statistics. It tells us the average annual pay received in May 2005 by people in various job titles (actually, it is the median annual pay, which means that half earned more and half less).

This sounds great, except that half of all people in that occupation earned less than that amount. For example, people who are new to the occupation or who have only a few years of work experience often earn much less than the median amount. People who live in rural areas or who work for smaller employers typically earn less than those who do similar work in cities (where the cost of living is higher) or for bigger employers. People in certain areas of the country earn less than those in others. Other factors also influence how much you are likely to earn in a given job in your area. For example, Aircraft Mechanics and Service Technicians in the Detroit-Warren-Livonia, Michigan, metropolitan area have median earnings of $73,070, probably because Northwest Airlines has its hub at Detroit and their mechanics are unionized. By comparison, the New Haven, Connecticut, metropolitan area has no major airline hub and only a small aircraft service facility with nonunionized workers; Aircraft Mechanics and Service Technicians there earn only a median of $26,280.

Also keep in mind that the figures for job growth and number of openings are projections by labor economists—their best guesses about what we can expect between now and 2014. They are not guarantees. A major economic downturn, war, or technological breakthrough could change the actual outcome.

Finally, don't forget that the job market consists of both job openings and job *seekers*. The figures on job growth and openings don't tell you how many people will be competing with you to be hired. The Department of Labor does not publish figures on the supply of job candidates, so we are unable to tell you about the level of competition you can expect. Competition is an important issue that you should research for any tentative career goal. In some cases, the *Occupational Outlook Handbook* provides informative statements. You should speak to civilian people who educate or train tomorrow's workers; they probably have a good idea of how many people with military training find rewarding employment and how quickly. People in the workforce, especially those who have been in the military, also can provide insights into this issue. Use your critical thinking skills to evaluate what people tell you. For example, military recruiters are highly motivated to get you to sign up, whereas people in the workforce may be trying to discourage you from competing. Get a variety of opinions to balance out possible biases.

So, in reviewing the information in this book, please understand the limitations of the data. You need to use common sense in career decision making as in most other things in life. We hope that, using that approach, you find the information helpful and interesting.

The Data Complexities

For those of you who like details, we present some of the complexities inherent in our sources of information and what we did to make sense of them here. You don't need to know this to use the book, so jump to the next section of the introduction if you are bored with details.

We include information on earnings, projected growth, and number of job openings for each civilian job throughout this book.

Earnings

The employment security agency of each state gathers information on earnings for various jobs and forwards it to the U.S. Bureau of Labor Statistics. This information is organized in standardized ways by a BLS program called Occupational Employment Statistics, or OES. To keep the earnings for the various jobs and regions comparable, the OES screens out certain types of earnings and includes others, so the OES earnings we use in this book represent straight-time gross pay exclusive of premium pay. More specifically, the OES earnings include the job's base rate; cost-of-living allowances; guaranteed pay; hazardous-duty pay; incentive pay, including commissions and production bonuses; on-call pay; and tips but do not include back pay, jury duty pay, overtime pay, severance pay, shift differentials, nonproduction bonuses, or tuition reimbursements. Also, self-employed workers are not included in the estimates, and they can be a significant segment in certain occupations. When data on earnings for an occupation is highly unreliable, OES does not report a figure, which meant that we reluctantly had to exclude from this book a few occupations such as Musicians and Singers. The median earnings for all workers in all occupations were $29,430 in May 2005. The jobs in this book were chosen partly on the basis of their earnings, so they average $30,097.

The OES reports job titles using an organization called the Standard Occupational Classification system, or SOC. We cross-referenced these titles to the O*NET job titles we use in this book so we could rank the jobs by their earnings and include earnings information in the job descriptions. In some cases, an SOC title cross-references to more than one O*NET job title. For example, the O*NET has separate information for Construction Carpenters and Rough Carpenters, but the SOC reports earnings for a single occupation called Carpenters. Therefore you may notice that we report the identical salaries for Construction Carpenters and Rough Carpenters: $35,580. In reality there probably is a difference, but this is the best information that is available.

Projected Growth and Number of Job Openings

This information comes from the Office of Occupational Statistics and Employment Projections, a program within the Bureau of Labor Statistics that develops information about projected trends in the nation's labor market for the next ten years. The most recent projections available cover the years from 2004 to 2014. The projections are based on information about people moving into and out of occupations. The BLS uses data from various sources in projecting the growth and number of openings for each job title—some data comes from the Census Bureau's Current Population Survey and some comes from an OES survey. The projections assume that there will be no major war, depression, or other economic upheaval.

Like the earnings figures, the figures on projected growth and job openings are reported according to the SOC classification, so again you will find that some of the SOC jobs crosswalk to more than one O*NET job. To continue the example we used earlier, the BLS reports growth (13.8%) and openings (210,000) for one SOC occupation called Carpenters, but in this book we report these figures separately for the occupation Construction Carpenters and for the occupation Rough Carpenters. When you see Construction Carpenters with 13.8% projected growth and 210,000 projected job openings and Rough Carpenters with the same two numbers, you should realize that the 13.8% rate of projected growth represents the *average* of these two occupations—one may actually experience higher growth than the other—and that these two occupations will *share* the 210,000 projected openings.

While salary figures are fairly straightforward, you may not know what to make of job-growth figures. For example, is projected growth of 15% good or bad? You should keep in mind that the average (mean) growth projected for all occupations by the Bureau of Labor Statistics is 13.0%. One-quarter of the occupations have a growth projection of 3.2% or lower. Growth of 12.2% is the median, meaning that half of the occupations have more, half less. Only one-quarter of the occupations have growth projected at 17.4% or higher.

Remember, however, that the jobs in this book were selected as "best" partly on the basis of high growth, so their median growth is better than the median for all jobs: 14.2%. Among these 150 outstanding jobs, the job ranked 38th by projected growth has a figure of 17.3%, and the job ranked 113th has a projected growth of 9.2%.

The news about job openings for jobs with military training is even better than the news about job growth: The figures are *almost double* the national average for all occupations. The Bureau of Labor statistics projects an average of about 35,000 job openings per year for each of the 750 occupations that it studies, but for each of the 150 occupations included in this book, the average is 69,500 openings. The job ranked 37th for job openings has a figure of 52,000 annual openings, the job ranked 75th (the median) has 17,000 openings projected, and the job ranked 113th has 6,000 openings projected.

Perhaps you're wondering why we present figures on both job growth *and* number of openings. Aren't these two ways of saying the same thing? Actually, you need to know both. Consider the occupation Occupational Therapist Assistants, which is projected to grow at the astounding rate of 34.1%. There should be lots of opportunities in such a fast-growing job, right? Not exactly. This is a very small occupation, with only about 21,000 people currently employed, so even though it is growing rapidly, it is expected to create only 2,000 job openings per year. Now consider First-Line Supervisors/Managers of Retail Sales Workers. This occupation is growing at the anemic rate of 3.8%, largely because computer sales-tracking systems have eliminated the need for many of these workers. Nevertheless, this is a huge occupation that employs more than 1.6 million workers, so even though its growth rate is unimpressive, it is expected to take on 229,000 new workers each year. That's why we base our selection of the best jobs on both of these economic indicators and why you should pay attention to both when you scan our lists of best jobs.

How This Book Is Organized

The information about job options through military training in this book moves from the general to the highly specific.

Part I. Overview of Military Training

Part I is an overview of the military as a route for job training—why it can be a good way to acquire job-related skills; the educational benefits of military service; what to expect from the recruitment process and from military life; factors to consider when you choose a job; and limitations on job choice in the military.

Part II. Descriptions of the Military Jobs That Provide Training for the 150 Best Jobs

This section of the book provides descriptions of the 75 military jobs that provide training for the 150 civilian jobs covered by this book. Here are the topics covered in each military job description:

Job Title

Photographic Specialists

Summary Definition

The military uses photographs for many purposes, such as intelligence gathering and news reporting. The services operate photographic laboratories to develop the numerous photos taken by the military. Photographic specialists take and develop still color or black-and-white photographs.

Officer/ Enlisted

Officer/Enlisted: Enlisted

Personality Type

Personality Type: Realistic. Realistic occupations frequently involve work activities that include practical, hands-on problems and solutions. They often deal with plants, animals, and real-world materials like wood, tools, and machinery. Many of the occupations require working outside and do not involve a lot of paperwork or working closely with others.

Services That Offer the Job

Services That Offer the Job: Air Force, Army, Marines, Navy

What They Do

What They Do. Photographic specialists in the military perform some or all of the following duties:

- Select camera, film, and other equipment needed for assignments
- Determine camera angles, lighting, and any special effects needed
- Take still photos of people, events, military equipment, land areas, and other subjects
- Develop, duplicate, or retouch film negatives, photos, or slides
- Maintain photographic equipment

Helpful Attributes

Helpful Attributes. Helpful school subjects include photography, chemistry, art, and mathematics. Helpful attributes include the following:

- Ability to recognize and arrange interesting photo subjects
- Accuracy and attention to detail

Training Provided

Training Provided. Job training consists of classroom instruction, including practice in taking and developing photographs. Length of training varies depending on the specialty. Further training occurs on the job and through advanced courses. Course content typically includes the following:

- Photographic processing and reproduction
- Principles of photojournalism
- Operation and maintenance of photographic equipment

Physical Demands

Physical Demands. Normal color vision is required to produce accurate color prints.

Work Environment

Work Environment. Photographic specialists work both indoors and outdoors while photographing their subjects. They may take photos from aircraft or ships. They process photographs in photographic laboratories on bases or aboard ships.

Opportunities in the Military

Opportunities in the Military. The services have about 1,500 photographic specialists. Each year, the services need new specialists because of changes in personnel and the demands of the field. After job training, specialists work under supervision. With experience, they are given more responsibility and, eventually, may supervise other photographic specialists.

Civilian Occupations It Provides Training For

Civilian Occupations It Provides Training For (those with stars are described in Part IV): Camera Operators, Television, Video, and Motion Picture*; Photographers*; Photographic Process Workers; Photographic Processing Machine Operators.

- **Job Title:** This is the job title that is used to summarize several specific military jobs, often in different service branches.
- **Summary Definition:** This paragraph gives a brief definition of the job and the role it plays in the military.
- **Officer/Enlisted:** Most of the jobs in this book are for enlisted personnel, but a few are open only to officers.
- **Personality Type:** This is the name of the related personality type from the Holland (RIASEC) classification. You can find more information on the personality types in Part I. The personality type identified here is based on O*NET information about the civilian job or jobs for which this military job prepares.
- **Services That Offer the Job:** This indicates where the job is available: Air Force, Army, Coast Guard, Marines, Navy, or more than one of these.
- **What They Do:** This is a listing of tasks that are generally performed by people who work in this job.
- **Helpful Attributes:** This topic opens with a summary of school subjects that would be helpful preparation for this job, followed by a list of skills, work habits, and preferences that would help you do the job well and feel comfortable in the work environment.
- **Training Provided:** The heading for this topic outlines the kind of training you would get for this job in the military. This is followed by a list of topics that are covered in the training period.
- **Physical Demands:** All military jobs require basic physical fitness, but if the job requires particular physical abilities, they are mentioned here.
- **Special Requirements:** This topic is included only when the job has additional nonphysical requirements. For example, some jobs require you to have certain prior coursework or skills. Also, some jobs are not open to women.
- **Work Environment:** This topic mentions aspects of the work setting, which may be anything from an aircraft hanger to an office to a ship at sea.
- **Opportunities in the Military:** This statement gives an estimate of how many of these workers are serving in the military at any given time. This can give you a rough idea of how many job openings may be expected, which affects your chances of getting the job.
- **Civilian Occupations It Provides Training For:** This list of job titles covers all the jobs in the O*NET database for which this military job provides appropriate training. Starred jobs are included in the 150 best jobs and are described in Part III. Do not assume that all unstarred jobs lack good economic rewards; in some cases they are not counted among the 150 best jobs because information about them is incomplete.

Part III. The Best Jobs Lists: Civilian Jobs Through Military Training

For many people, the 47 lists in Part III are the most interesting information in the book. Here you can see titles of civilian jobs that are commonly entered through military training and that have the best combination of high salaries, fast growth, and plentiful job openings. You can see which jobs are best in terms of each of these factors combined or considered separately. The list of high performers is broken out further according to the interest fields and several other features of the jobs. Look in the Table of Contents for a complete list of lists. Although there are a lot of lists, they are not difficult to understand because they have clear titles and are organized into groupings of related lists.

People who prefer to think about careers in terms of personality types will want to browse the lists that show the best civilian jobs through military training with Realistic, Investigative, Artistic, Social, Enterprising, and Conventional personality types. On the other hand, some people think first in terms of interest fields, and these people will prefer the lists that show the best jobs through military training using the interest categories of the *New Guide for Occupational Exploration.*

We suggest that you use the lists that make the most sense for you. Following are the names of each group of lists along with short comments on each group. You will find additional information in a brief introduction provided at the beginning of each group of lists in Part III.

Best Civilian Jobs Overall Through Military Training: Lists of Jobs with the Highest Pay, Fastest Growth, and Most Openings

This group has four lists, and they are the ones that most people want to see first. The first list presents all 150 jobs that are included in this book in order of their combined scores for earnings, growth, and number of job openings. These jobs are used in the more-specialized lists that follow and in the descriptions in Part IV. Three more lists in this group present specialized lists of jobs through military training: the 50 best-paying jobs through military training, the 50 fastest-growing jobs through military training, and the 50 jobs through military training with the most openings.

Best Civilian Jobs Through Military Training: Lists of Jobs by Demographic

This group of lists recognizes the diversity of civilian jobs through military training by presenting interesting information for a variety of types of workers based on data from the U.S. Census Bureau. The lists are arranged into groups for part-time workers, self-employed workers, women, and men. We created five lists for each group, basing the last four on the information in the first list:

- The jobs having the highest percentage of people of each type
- The 25 jobs with the best combined scores for earnings, growth, and number of openings
- The 25 jobs with the highest earnings
- The 25 jobs with the highest growth rates
- The 25 jobs with the largest number of openings

Best Civilian Jobs Through Military Training: Lists Based on Interests

These lists organize the 150 jobs into groups based on interests. Within each list, jobs are presented in order of their combined scores for earnings, growth, and number of openings. Here are the 15 interest areas used in these lists: Agriculture and Natural Resources; Architecture and Construction; Arts and Communication; Business and Administration; Finance and Insurance; Government and Public Administration; Health Science; Hospitality, Tourism, and Recreation; Human Service; Information Technology; Law and Public Safety; Manufacturing; Retail and Wholesale Sales and Service; Scientific Research, Engineering, and Mathematics; and Transportation, Distribution, and Logistics. (This classification of interest areas includes one additional area, Education and Training, but none of the 150 jobs falls into that category.)

Best Civilian Jobs Through Military Training: Lists Based on Personality Types

These lists organize the 150 civilian jobs into six personality types, which are described in the introduction to the lists: Realistic, Investigative, Artistic, Social, Enterprising, and Conventional. The jobs within each list are presented in order of their combined scores for earnings, growth, and number of openings.

Bonus Lists: Civilian Work Experiences of Veterans

These two lists show the kinds of work that veterans are *actually doing,* based on a sample of 12,502 veterans who were surveyed in August 2005. One list ranks the 20 jobs held by the largest number of veterans; the other ranks the 20 fields (or industries) in which the most veterans are working.

Part IV: Descriptions of the Best Civilian Jobs Through Military Training

This part describes each of the best civilian jobs through military training, using a format that is informative yet compact and easy to read. The descriptions contain statistics such as earnings and projected percent of growth; lists such as major work tasks, skills, and work environment; and key descriptors such as personality type and interest area. Because the jobs in this section are arranged in alphabetical order, you can easily find a job that you've identified from Part III and that you want to learn more about.

We used the most current information from a variety of government sources to create the descriptions. Although we've tried to make the descriptions easy to understand, the sample that follows—with an explanation of each of its parts—may help you better understand and use the descriptions.

Job Title →

Chemical Technicians

Data Elements →

- Annual Earnings: $38,500
- Growth: 4.4%
- Annual Job Openings: 7,000
- Self-Employed: 0.0%
- Part-Time: 5.6%
- Civilian Training Route: Associate degree

Summary Description and Tasks →

Conduct chemical and physical laboratory tests to assist scientists in making qualitative and quantitative analyses of solids, liquids, and gaseous materials for purposes such as research and development of new products or processes; quality control; maintenance of environmental standards; and other work involving experimental, theoretical, or practical application of chemistry and related sciences. Monitor product quality to ensure compliance to standards and specifications. Set up and conduct chemical experiments, tests, and analyses using techniques such as chromatography, spectroscopy, physical and chemical separation techniques, and microscopy. Conduct chemical and physical laboratory tests to assist scientists in making qualitative and quantitative analyses of solids, liquids, and gaseous materials. Compile and interpret results of tests and analyses. Provide technical support and assistance to chemists and engineers. Prepare chemical solutions for products and processes following standardized formulas or create experimental formulas. Maintain, clean, and sterilize laboratory instruments and equipment. Write technical reports or prepare graphs and charts to document experimental results. Order and inventory materials to maintain supplies. Develop and conduct programs of sampling and analysis to maintain quality standards of raw materials, chemical intermediates, and products. Direct or monitor other workers producing chemical products. Operate experimental pilot plants, assisting with experimental design. Develop new chemical engineering processes or production techniques. Design and fabricate experimental apparatus to develop new products and processes.

Military Jobs That Provide Training for It →

Military Jobs That Provide Training for It (see the descriptions in Part II): Medical Laboratory Technicians; Non-Destructive Testers

Personality Type →

Personality Type: Realistic. Realistic occupations frequently involve work activities that include practical, hands-on problems and solutions. They often deal with plants, animals, and real-world materials like wood, tools, and machinery. Many of the occupations require working outside and do not involve a lot of paperwork or working closely with others.

GOE Information →

GOE—Interest Area: 15. Scientific Research, Engineering, and Mathematics. **Work Group:** 15.05. Physical Science Laboratory Technology. **Other Civilian Jobs in This Work Group:** Nuclear Equipment Operation Technicians; Nuclear Technicians.

Skills →

Skills—Operation Monitoring: Watching gauges, dials, or other indicators to make sure a machine is working properly. **Science:** Using scientific rules and methods to solve problems. **Quality Control Analysis:** Conducting tests and inspections of products, services, or processes to evaluate quality or performance. **Equipment Maintenance:** Performing routine maintenance on equipment and determining when and what kind of maintenance is needed. **Operation and Control:** Controlling operations of equipment or systems. **Repairing:** Repairing machines or systems, using the needed tools. **Mathematics:** Using mathematics to solve problems. **Troubleshooting:** Determining causes of operating errors and deciding what to do about them.

Work Environment →

Work Environment: Indoors; noisy; contaminants; hazardous conditions; standing.

Here are some details on each of the major parts of the job descriptions you will find in Part IV:

- **Job Title:** This is the job title for the job as defined by the U.S. Department of Labor and used in its O*NET database.
- **Data Elements:** The information comes from various U.S. Department of Labor and Census Bureau databases, as explained elsewhere in this introduction. Bullet points tell you some important economic characteristics of the workers, plus the conventional civilian training route (for example, an associate degree).
- **Summary Description and Tasks:** The bold sentences provide a summary description of the occupation. It is followed by a listing of tasks that are generally performed by people who work in this job. This information comes from the O*NET database but where necessary has been edited to avoid exceeding 2,200 characters.
- **Military Job That Provides Training for It:** This military job is a common training route for this civilian job and is described in Part II.
- **Personality Type:** Each job description includes the name of the principal personality type that O*NET links to the job. You can find more information on the personality types in Part I.
- **GOE Information:** This information cross-references the Guide for Occupational Exploration (or the GOE), a system developed by the U.S. Department of Labor that organizes jobs based on interests. We use the groups from the *New Guide for Occupational Exploration*, as published by JIST. This book uses a set of interest areas based on the 16 career clusters developed by the U.S. Department of Education and used in a variety of career information systems. The description includes the major Interest Area the job fits into, its more-specific Work Group, and a list of related O*NET civilian job titles that are in this same GOE Work Group. This information will help you identify other job titles that have similar interests or require similar skills. You can find more information on the GOE and its Interest Areas in the introduction to the lists of jobs based on interests in Part III.
- **Skills:** The O*NET database provides data on many skills; we decided to list only those that were most important for each job rather than list pages of unhelpful details. For each job, we identified any skill with a rating at a level higher than the average rating for that skill for all jobs and that also is not rated as an unimportant skill. If there were more than eight, we included only those eight with the highest ratings, and we present them from highest to lowest score (that is, in terms of by how much its score exceeds the average score). If no skill has a rating higher than the average for all jobs, we say "None met the criteria." Each listed skill is followed by a brief description of that skill.

- **Work Environment:** This entry in the job description mentions aspects of the work setting that some people may want to avoid, such as exposure to loud noises or the necessity of standing for long periods of time. The ordering of the environmental factors is not significant.

Getting all the information we used in the job descriptions was not a simple process, and it is not always perfect. Even so, we used the best and most recent sources of data we could find, and we think that our efforts will be helpful to many people.

PART I

Overview of Military Training

Military service can jump-start your career, but it is not something to decide on in a casual way. It's a big commitment. Before you sign up, even before you talk to a recruiter, you need to know what military service is like, what it requires of you, what it can offer you, and how to get the most out of it. This part of the book answers several important questions about military service—including some that you might not have thought to ask. What you learn here can help you make better choices about your military service. If you're already in uniform, information here can help you with the transition to a good civilian career.

Why is the military a good place to start a career?

Although the military was created to defend our nation, it's also one of our nation's major educational and training institutions. The armed forces devote enormous resources to transforming unskilled recruits into highly skilled workers. You can take advantage of a military training program to gain the skills you'll need for a good start to your career.

The military has a large number of jobs that are equivalent to civilian occupations, which means that the skills you learn in the military may qualify you for employment in a good job after you hang up your uniform—for example, as a dental hygienist, a fire fighter, a dispensing optician, a plumber, or a truck driver, to name just a few.

The military teaches more than just the technical skills that are necessary to get the job done. People who have served in the military often mention several other skills and work-related attitudes they learn that serve them well throughout their career:

- **Teamwork** is essential in many careers, and it is part of military training from the very beginning. You learn how to work for the good of the team, how to divide up tasks, and how to draw on the diverse talents of each member of the team.

- **A sense of responsibility** and **pride in a job well done** are two attitudes every employer wants. In the military, every work assignment is viewed as a mission. You understand that others are depending on you to do the job right, and you gain satisfaction from achieving the goals that have been set for you.
- **A positive attitude toward authority** is another trait that employers value. The military experience is a lot more than the shouted orders of boot camp. You learn that your commanders are looking out for you, developing you into the best person you can be. You can carry over that relationship to a civilian job and find a mentor who will help you develop your career.
- Employers look for workers with **initiative,** and the military teaches that, too. The specifics of military orders go only so far; beyond that, you need to decide how best to accomplish the mission.
- **Stress management** is a skill that employers want. In the armed forces, you learn how to keep stress from interfering with your work and your leisure.
- **Diversity** is an important part of the workforce these days, and military experience exposes you to people from backgrounds very different from yours, both as members of your team and as commanders. You also will find military women working in nontraditional roles.
- **Global awareness** is constantly growing in the business world as American enterprises look for new markets and suppliers. The military has bases all over the world, so there is a good chance your experience in uniform will expose you to foreign cultures and make you feel more comfortable interacting with them.
- A **security clearance** is needed for some jobs, especially those that do a lot of government work. Many veterans already have this clearance, saving employers time and expense.
- **Physical fitness** is something that employers appreciate—even though *they* may be out of shape. Military service will get you in excellent physical shape, probably better than you've ever been before, and it will teach you habits of healthy living that you can use for the rest of your life.
- **Service to country** is at the core of military values, and it's something that many employers appreciate.
- A **college degree** or **certification** from a vocational training program is required or helpful for many careers, and the G.I. bill can pay for your education or training after you leave the service. Better yet, you can get tuition assistance to take college courses while you're still in uniform. Finally, your experience in the military may be accepted as equivalent to college coursework.

One employer gives special recognition for military service: the federal government. If you get a federal civil service job after you leave the military, your time in uniform will count toward your seniority on the job. This will boost your pay and allow you to take retirement earlier. Some state civil service rules also offer this benefit. Even better, if you served during an armed conflict, your score on the Federal civil service exam will be awarded additional points, giving you an edge over other job candidates.

One measure of the work-related value of military service is the employment rate, which in recent years has consistently been higher for veterans of active duty than for nonveterans. Although this difference has not been true for every age bracket, it seems likely that the all-volunteer military will continue to turn out veterans who have better work-related skills than the general population.

Another measure of the payoff of military service is the relative earnings of veterans versus nonveterans. In the sample obtained by the Current Population Survey in August 2005, veterans working in the same occupations as nonveterans earned an average of about $4,800 more per year. Again, this has not been true of every cohort of veterans in the past, but today's veterans probably have skill advantages that will lead to better pay.

If the military will train me, why do I need the G.I. Bill or tuition assistance?

The G.I. Bill and tuition assistance are such important benefits that they deserve further discussion here.

The G.I. Bill pays for a wide variety of programs: college, business school, vocational courses, correspondence courses (partial payment), degree-related independent study, and apprenticeships. It can be particularly helpful if your military training doesn't provide all the qualifications you need for the career you want or if you decide to pursue a career different from your military job. It also can be useful to help you advance in a career once you are employed—for example, to get a college degree that boosts you from an entry-level job to the management track. Employers sometimes pay for employees to get additional education or training, but they certainly will appreciate letting the G.I. Bill pick up the tab for you.

You are eligible to use G.I. bill benefits while on active duty and during the 10 years after honorable discharge. If you sign up for the benefit during basic training—it's your only chance to do so—your pay will be reduced slightly during your first year of service, but you'll qualify for payments worth more than 30 times the amount of earnings you set aside. After you leave the service, the benefit will pay a specified amount that may exceed tuition costs and thus also can function as a stipend. In addition, some branches of service offer a college fund that pays money beyond the G.I. Bill. On the other hand, if you use the benefit while still on active duty, it will pay only for tuition. For that reason, people in uniform tend to use the tuition assistance program instead.

Recently, many people in the National Guard and reserve services have been serving on active duty for longer than the normal 12-month call-up, and in some cases they are eligible for the benefits described in the previous paragraph. Usually a different set of G.I. Bill benefits is available for people in the selected reserve—that is, reservists in jobs of highest priority at times of mobilization. These benefits do not require any reduction in pay, and they are available for the 14 years after boot camp and military job training. However, this program pays only about one-third as much as the program for veterans of active duty.

Tuition assistance is offered by all of the active-duty services and by many of the National Guard and reserve services. It pays for college courses while you're serving and pays 100% of tuition within certain limits. Many states offer additional education benefits for members of their National Guard.

The **College Loan Repayment Program** is yet another educational benefit that is offered by all the active services (except the Marine Corps and Coast Guard) and by some of the reserve and National Guard services. If you have *already* attended college and have run up debt in some particular college loan programs, this benefit will pay off part or all of the loan.

Can I get college credit for my military training?

Much of the learning that takes place during military training is considered to be at college level, so you may be able to get college credit for it. This means that you can enter college after the service and have some of your course requirements already completed. You may even be able to earn a degree while still in uniform.

The American Council on Education has determined the course credits that are appropriate for various training programs, and most colleges grant this credit. The Air Force has its own program for granting credit and degrees. You may also get college credit by demonstrating your knowledge through a testing program—either DSST (the DANTES Subject Standardized Tests, formerly called DANTES, for Defense Activity for Non-Traditional Education Support) or CLEP (College Level Examination Program). Finally, some "colleges without walls" grant college credit on the basis of portfolios showing work outcomes. Appendix A has details about where to find out about these programs.

Can I take college courses while I'm in uniform?

Your options for taking college courses depend partly on your work schedule and partly on what is made available by the education office of your base. However, even if you work irregular hours and don't have access to on-base classes in the subjects you want, you may be able to take distance education classes. There are also limited opportunities to go to college full-time while in the service, but only a few candidates with outstanding military and prior college records are selected for this privilege.

Will the military help with my transition to a civilian career?

Each service branch provides a Transition Assistance Office, although the name varies; for example, the Army calls it an Army Career and Alumni Program (ACAP) office. This office can provide valuable help with the transition process, but because you need to include so many considerations in your post-service planning—your career goal, your health benefits, your education benefits—you should make your first visit there well in advance of leaving the service.

What's the difference between active duty, Reserves, and National Guard?

Active duty is a full-time commitment to one of the service branches, whereas in the Drilling Guard or reserves you may perform as few as 39 days of military duty per year during weekends and two-week drills, and in the Individual Ready Reserves you do no drilling at all (and receive no pay). In times of conflict, however, these distinctions can fall by the wayside as reservists (including those in the National Guard) may be activated. When National Guard units are not activated by presidential order, they serve their state and may be called by their governor to handle emergencies such as floods or civil unrest.

What are the entrance requirements for the military?

The military doesn't accept everybody who shows up. Recruits must meet certain requirements:

- **Citizenship.** Only United States citizens can become commissioned officers, but noncitizens can enlist if they are living in the U.S. with a valid visa (green card), they have established residence here, and their green card will not expire during their term of service.
- **Age.** Minimum age is 17 (with parental consent); maximum age is 42, in general, but some service branches set a younger maximum.
- **Dependents.** You may not be able to enlist if you have dependents under the age of 18, especially if your spouse is in the military. In some cases a spouse is considered a dependent. In general, single parents are not allowed to enlist, except in the Army National Guard. Rules on dependents vary among the different services and may be waived when eligible recruits are hard to find, so ask the recruiter for the specifics.
- **Education.** The military prefers recruits who have at least a high school diploma. A certain number of people with credentials from the GED, home schooling, or a vocational-technical school—and sometimes people with *no* formal equivalency credentials—may

also enlist, provided they score sufficiently high on the ASVAB test (discussed in detail elsewhere in Part I).

- **Mental aptitude.** The ASVAB test is also used to measure whether you meet the intelligence requirements.
- **Drugs and alcohol.** The recruiter will ask you about your use of alcohol and illegal drugs, and your urine will be tested at the Military Entrance Processing Station. Although some limited past drug use may be tolerated, any indication of substance *dependency,* actual or potential, will disqualify you.
- **Morality.** The armed forces will reject recruits who have a criminal record. Even legal judgments that put you on probation and avoid the normal criminal process may count against you, as may a series of minor traffic offenses. Records that are considered expunged or sealed are accessible by the military, so be completely truthful about any past run-ins with the law.
- **Financial obligations.** You may be rejected if you have a history of bankruptcy or will be unable to pay your debts while you're in uniform.
- **Sexual orientation.** Under the "don't ask, don't tell" policy, the recruiter will not ask about your sexual orientation. However, the military will reject you if you mention past or intended homosexual conduct.
- **Height, weight, and medical condition.** Being too tall or too short, having too much body fat, or having certain medical conditions (including a history of mental illness) will disqualify you. The service branches differ on the details of these requirements.
- **Various other issues.** You may be rejected for a variety of other reasons, such as conspicuous tattoos.

If I sign up for the military, how long is my commitment?

Your commitment to the military is for eight years. Your contract may specify only a portion of that time as active duty—as little as two years in some jobs and service branches. Theoretically, after this period of active duty you could ride out the remainder of your eight-year commitment in the Individual Ready Reserves, wearing a uniform only for annual inspections. However, if the military needs you, they have the right to keep you on active duty or in the drilling reserves or, having released you, to recall you to one of those roles at any time during your eight-year commitment.

Besides the military's need for you, another issue is the amount of training they have invested in you, for which they may expect a proportionate amount of active-duty service in return. The extreme example of this is Airplane Pilots, who get a full year or two of training and then are required to serve an additional 10 years in the Air Force—slightly less in other services.

Normally you will be free to hold a civilian job during any periods of inactivity within your eight-year commitment, but of course that career may be interrupted if you are called up again. Federal law prohibits your employer from discriminating against you because of your military obligations. In reality, however, a military call-up can be either a trivial or a serious interference with your career, depending on what type of job you hold. For example, if you are self-employed as a civilian, a military call-up can mean a significant cut in your income.

How does military life differ from civilian life?

When you enlist, you take an oath to uphold the Constitution of the United States and to obey your commanders. In practical terms, that means that you don't have the right to disobey lawful orders, tell your boss to take a hike, show up late for work, or quit. You could be jailed for serious or repeated acts of disobedience, or you could receive a less-than-honorable discharge and thus lose many benefits.

Although the military has pioneered the placement of women and minorities in work roles where they have been underrepresented in the past, some combat-related jobs are closed to women. (These are identified in the military job descriptions in Part IV.) You also lose control over some aspects of what you normally consider to be your private life. Adultery and homosexual activity are not tolerated. You are not allowed to possess pornography or hate literature. You also can expect routine random drug testing.

During active duty you are likely to be moved around a great deal, perhaps to foreign countries. If you would like a change of scene, you may enjoy these moves, but they can be stressful, especially for married personnel and their spouses.

On the other hand, many of the basic requirements of life are provided for you while you are on active duty. You get a place to live, all your meals, complete health care, recreation, worship services—and a salary that, although it is not outstanding, is not low when received on top of all these other benefits.

Most important for this book, you not only get a job, but all the training you need for the job, and you are encouraged to get additional training to build your skills.

It can't be emphasized too much that the military *wants you to succeed.* Although drill sergeants in boot camp are famous for being tough taskmasters, they are not trying to make their raw recruits give up. And once you get past the first few weeks of toughening up, the tone changes considerably.

You may know people who struggled to keep up with classmates in college. (Maybe this has happened to you.) You may have heard of highly competitive careers that permit success to very few people. Most military jobs are much more welcoming. It's true that the military has some basic entry requirements, but most people qualify. And it's also true that there is competition for some jobs in the military, such as Special Forces and Airplane Pilots. But in most military training programs you get a lot of encouragement and support.

In fact, the military runs the nation's biggest literacy-training program. They are committed to helping even the lowest-skilled recruits gain the learning skills they'll need to succeed.

Although the military does a lot of training, its core business is defense, and that sometimes can require combat. Even training exercises can involve big, fast, and dangerous equipment. The risks to life and limb are real. Don't let anyone tell you that military life is no more dangerous than life in an American city. On the other hand, these risks are part of the package called "serving your country." There aren't many civilian jobs that give you a chance for service as basic as this: putting your own safety on the line for the safety and freedom of your fellow citizens.

Why are some jobs open only to officers, and how do I become one?

As a general rule, the jobs that are open only to officers are those that involve management or a level of technical knowledge equivalent to a bachelor's or professional degree. For example, enlisted personnel may be trained to work as Transportation Specialists, but only an officer can be a Transportation Manager. Similarly, enlisted personnel may be trained as Dental Specialists, but Dentists must have a degree from a dentistry school and hold the rank of officers.

There are five main ways to become an officer:

- Graduate from a service academy, such as West Point or Annapolis.
- Attend Officer Candidate or Officer Training School—an option for college graduates who are under age 29.
- Complete a Reserve Officers' Training Corps (ROTC) program while in college.
- Be appointed after completing professional education or training—usually the route for being assigned to a professional-level job such as Pharmacist, Nuclear Engineer, or Chaplain.
- Complete an enlisted commissioning program—a training program that prepares promising enlisted personnel to complete college and become officers. Because the military doesn't want to wait four years for you to finish your bachelor's, you generally need to have some college coursework under your belt already. Opportunities are limited, but are best in areas where officers are in short supply, such as in health-care jobs.

What is the ASVAB test and what is it for?

The Armed Services Vocational Aptitude Battery (ASVAB) is a multiple-choice test that determines whether you are qualified to enter the military and in which military jobs you are most likely to be successful. It has eight sections:

- Word Knowledge (WK)
- Paragraph Comprehension (PC)
- Mathematics Knowledge (MK)
- Arithmetic Reasoning (AR)
- General Science (GS)
- Mechanical Comprehension (MC)
- Electronics Information (EI)
- Auto and Shop Information (AS)

The scores from the first four sections are combined according to a formula that produces a score called the Armed Forces Qualification Test (AFQT), which determines whether you have the basic literacy skills needed to be in the military.

Other combinations of scores—called line scores—are used to determine how well you will do in various categories of military jobs. For example, if you add your scores on GS, AR, MK, and EI you get a line score called Electronics (EL) that the Army uses. To qualify for training as a Fire Control System Repairer (described in this book as a Weapons Maintenance Technician) in the Army, you need an EL line score of at least 95.

Most recruits take the ASVAB as part of the enlistment process at the same place where they get their physical exam—the Military Entrance Processing Station (MEPS). But you may take the ASVAB in 11th grade or in a local military location, such as a National Guard armory. If the scores are less than two years old and are high enough, you can use them in the enlistment process.

Although the word "aptitude" suggests something that's inborn, ASVAB really measures developed skills, and that means that you can study to improve your ASVAB scores and get into a better military job. Several publishers have created ASVAB study guides that include practice tests, and you can probably find one at your local public library. Keep in mind that the practice tests do not contain the same questions as the actual test, so don't try to memorize the answers. Use the practice test to figure out which *areas* are your weakest, and then study to improve your understanding of those problem areas. Remember, usually the higher your test scores, the more jobs will be open to you, so studying for the test can be to your advantage.

What else should I consider when I decide on a military job?

One important consideration is learning a lot of job-specific skills that you can carry over to a civilian career. For example, if you work as an Avionics Technician, most of the skills you learn will be useful for the civilian job of the same name. By comparison, fewer of the skills you learn as an Armored Assault Vehicle Crew Member will carry over to civilian jobs, although some definitely will.

Another factor to consider is how interesting you find the job. If you take the ASVAB in high school, the test will include an interest measure and you will receive materials to help you interpret your scores. You can determine both military and civilian jobs that might be a good fit for you. Unfortunately, the ASVAB that you'll take at an enlistment center will cover only your abilities, and you'll have to decide for yourself what your interests are.

One useful way to focus on your interests is to learn about the six Holland personality types (explained next) and decide which type or types come closest to describing you. These same six personality types are used in the high school version of ASVAB and by lots of career counselors.

The theory developed by John L. Holland rests on the principle that people tend to be happier and more successful in jobs where they feel comfortable with the work tasks and problems, the physical environment, and the kinds of people who are co-workers. Holland identified six personality types that describe basic aspects of work situations. He called them Realistic, Investigative, Artistic, Social, Enterprising, and Conventional. (Some of these labels are difficult to grasp at first glance, but you'll gain a clearer understanding after you read the definitions in the sidebar.) The initials for these personality types spell RIASEC, so that is often used to refer to these types.

Holland argued that most people can be described by one of the RIASEC personality types—the type that dominates—and that likewise each of the various occupations that make up our economy can be described as having work situations and settings compatible with one of these personality types. Therefore, if you understand your dominant personality type and then identify which jobs are consistent with that type, you will have a clearer idea of which jobs will suit you best. Holland recognized that many people and jobs also tend toward a second or third personality type, so you may want to consider more than one type.

Read the definitions of the six personality types in the sidebar and decide which one or two describe you best. Compare these definitions to common situations in your experiences at work, at school, and in leisure activities. You may want to ask for input from people who know you well.

Once you have an understanding of your dominant personality type, you can use it while browsing the job descriptions in this book. All the job descriptions—military jobs in Part II and civilian jobs in Part IV—include the RIASEC personality type that dominates so you can easily see which jobs may be a good fit for your personality.

The Six Holland Personality Types: Which Describes You Best?

Realistic. *Realistic personalities like work activities that include practical, hands-on problems and solutions. They enjoy dealing with plants; animals; and real-world materials such as wood, tools, and machinery. They enjoy outside work. They often do not like occupations that mainly involve doing paperwork or working closely with others.*

Investigative. *Investigative personalities like work activities that have to do with ideas and thinking more than with physical activity. They like to search for facts and figure out problems mentally rather than to persuade or lead people.*

Artistic. *Artistic personalities like work activities that deal with the artistic side of things, such as forms, designs, and patterns. They like self-expression in their work. They prefer settings where work can be done without following a clear set of rules.*

Social. *Social personalities like work activities that assist others and promote learning and personal development. They prefer to communicate more than to work with objects, machines, or data. They like to teach, to give advice, to help, or otherwise to be of service to people.*

Enterprising. *Enterprising personalities like work activities having to do with starting up and carrying out projects, especially business ventures. They like persuading and leading people and making decisions. They like taking risks for profit. These personalities prefer action rather than thought.*

Conventional. *Conventional personalities like work activities that follow set procedures and routines. They prefer working with data and details rather than with ideas. They prefer work in which there are precise standards rather than work in which you have to judge things by yourself. These personalities like working where the lines of authority are clear.*

Will my training carry over to a civilian job?

Perhaps you've heard this old joke: There's the right way, the wrong way, and the Army way.

It's true that some jobs are done somewhat differently in the military than they are in civilian life. In some cases the military trains you on very high-tech equipment that civilian employers are not yet using, but these skills can eventually give you an advantage. In other cases, the military trains you on outmoded equipment that few civilian employers use anymore, but at least you learn the theory and general skills associated with the job. It's difficult to generalize about what you can expect.

One objective way to check on the relevance of the skills learned in a specific military training program is to see what kind of college credit the American Council on Education considers appropriate to award. This credit is accepted by most colleges and by many employers because it accurately reflects the quality of the training program. The appendix has information about how to access this resource under the topic "College Credit for Military Training."

Another strategy is to talk to workers or, better yet, to employers for the civilian job you have in mind. Ask them how well military training is respected and what specific military jobs seem to prepare workers best.

What can I do in the military to get the greatest benefit for my civilian career?

Even before you hang up the uniform, you can take some positive steps to make your military experience useful in civilian life.

When you first enlist, try to get a military job that will prepare you for a civilian job that appeals to you. This book can help you identify both kinds of jobs.

After enlistment, get as much training and education as possible. Take advantage of the educational benefits available to people in uniform (described elsewhere in this section) and sign up for GI Bill benefits that you will be able to use as a civilian.

Use this book to identify the most important skills for the civilian job you have in mind. Better yet, talk to employers for the civilian job and learn what specific skills they look for in people they hire—for example, what technologies are used on the job. Then try to get relevant training, education, or (ideally) work experience to prepare you for those specific skills.

It shouldn't be necessary to add this, but be sure to avoid breaking any military regulations that would cause you to receive a less-than-honorable discharge. Having that blot on your record not only can cause you to lose some military benefits, it can make it harder for you to get a good civilian job.

What should I say to the recruiter?

The most important consideration is to be honest with the recruiter, even if the recruiter seems willing to hear less than the truth. It is a felony to give untrue information to a recruiter or even to withhold important information.

Ask specific questions and don't accept vague answers. Take notes and, if the recruiter gives you literature that is meant to answer your questions, don't continue the enlistment process until you find the specific answers to all of your questions. It can be helpful to bring along a parent or friend, especially if that person has had military experience. Keep in mind that the recruiter will ask you some very personal questions, such as about drug use, so your companion should be someone you can confide in.

Depending on the service branch, you may be able to discuss job choice with the recruiter, or this discussion may have to wait until you report to the Military Entrance Processing Station (MEPS).

Can I get the military training program and job that I want?

You can choose a training program and job, but there are no ironclad guarantees that you'll get your choice.

To choose an assignment you must qualify for it, based on your scores on the ASVAB test and, for some assignments, your ability to meet security requirements and physical demands. Some jobs also require a prior college degree, perhaps in a specific subject, and some jobs are closed to women. In Part II, where military jobs are described, all such requirements are listed in the job descriptions under the headings "Physical Demands" and "Special Requirements."

Another factor is timing. The service branches forecast their needs for various kinds of workers, and the training programs are ready to take on a new batch of recruits at certain intervals. So the day you talk to the counselor at the MEPS may or may not be the ideal time to get the job you want. In many cases the counselor can tell you when openings can be expected, and you can enlist in a way that delays your arrival at boot camp until the appropriate date.

Some military jobs are never going to have many openings, and your odds of getting them are slim even if you qualify. For example, the Army is always going to need a lot more Vehicle Drivers than Meteorological Specialists. Of course, the Army also needs few Flight Operations Specialists, but the Air Force needs many, so you may find it helpful to talk to recruiters from different service branches to find current opportunities in the job or jobs that interest you. Keep in mind that a service branch with a lot of qualified applicants—the Marine Corps, Coast Guard, or Air Force—may not take you unless you are willing to be flexible about your job preferences. You may have to specify a training program that is available but is not your first choice; a broad occupational area, such as mechanical repair or medical support; or even an "undesignated" or "general" job target.

Even if your enlistment contract specifies a "guaranteed job" and you appear to be qualified, you still may fail to get the job for a number of reasons. For example, your security clearance may not go through, or you may not pass the training program. Also, the job may turn out to be unavailable even though the recruiter thought that it was. Remember, the whole purpose of the military is to defend the United States, and the role of people in uniform is to serve the military's needs, which sometimes change suddenly. You will be assigned where you're needed.

This can even mean that you end up doing work that has little or nothing to do with your job title. For example, if you are assigned to a war zone you may be given combat duties even though you are a Printing Specialist. (Everyone also gets combat training.)

If you get a military job that you dislike, you may be able to get retraining for another job, but usually you have to complete a certain number of years in the first job. You also may have to agree to re-enlist for active service. Finally, your ability to change jobs will always depend on the military's needs.

To sum up, it is certainly true that the military does not give you as much freedom of job choice as civilian life does. But be honest about your circumstances. Do you really have a lot of promising job options where you live? Do you have the education and training to open a lot of doors? Or would you simply be choosing among a lot of dead-end jobs?

Take another look at the first section of this chapter, where there is a list of positive, career-building skills and attitudes that you can get out of military service *no matter what your military job is.* You may decide that enlisting is a good career move even if you don't have total control over your job assignment.

PART II

Descriptions of the Military Jobs That Provide Training for the 150 Best Civilian Jobs

This section of the book provides descriptions of 75 military jobs. Each military job is formally known as an MOTD (from "Military Occupational Training Database") and represents a family of specialized job titles, often in several difference service branches. For example, the MOTD called Machinists lumps together the following specialized job titles: Machinist (Army and Marines), Machinery Repairman (Coast Guard and Navy), Advanced Machinery Repairman (Navy), Computer Numerically Controlled Machinist (Navy), plus three other specialized Navy jobs. Some MOTDs represent dozens of specialized job titles. In fact, the 75 MOTDs described in this part represent *more than 3,900* separate job titles.

The armed forces currently recognize 141 MOTDs, but the descriptions in this section cover only 75. As the introduction explains, we didn't want to include most officer-level jobs, for which you must almost always get considerable education and training *before* you enter the military, or military jobs such as Infantry that don't have an equivalent in civilian life. Appendix B gives a complete list of the 66 MOTDs that are not described in this book.

When you look at the job descriptions in this section, think about how much the job appeals to you. Consider aspects such as the personality type, work tasks, physical demands, any special requirements, and work environment. Because you're interested in the military as a source of training for a future career, be sure to note what kind of training is provided and what civilian careers it helps train for. In particular, note the starred civilian job titles—these are the "best 150"—and look at their descriptions in Part IV.

All of the information in these descriptions comes from the U.S. Department of Defense.

Administrative Support Specialists

The military must keep accurate information for planning and managing its operations. Paper and electronic records are kept on equipment, funds, personnel, supplies, and all other aspects of the military. Administrative support specialists record information, fill out reports, and maintain files to assist in the operation of military offices.

Officer/Enlisted: Enlisted

Personality Type: Conventional. Conventional occupations frequently involve following set procedures and routines. These occupations can include working with data and details more than with ideas. Usually there is a clear line of authority to follow.

Services That Offer the Job: Air Force, Army, Coast Guard, Marines, Navy

What They Do. Administrative support specialists in the military perform some or all of the following duties:

- Use a computer to type and prepare letters, reports, and other kinds of documents
- Proofread written material for spelling, punctuation, and grammatical errors
- Organize and maintain electronic and paper files and publications
- Order office supplies
- Greet and direct office visitors
- Sort and deliver mail to office workers
- Use office equipment such as fax machines, copiers, and computers
- Schedule training and leave for unit personnel
- Answer phones and provide general information
- Take meeting notes

Helpful Attributes. Helpful school subjects include English, math, and business administration. Helpful attributes include the following:

- Ability to organize and plan
- Interest in keeping organized and accurate records
- Interest in operating computers and other office machines
- Preference for office work

Training Provided. Job training consists of classroom instruction, including practice in various office functions. Further training occurs on the job. Course content typically includes the following:

- English grammar, spelling, and punctuation
- Keyboard and clerical skills

- Setting up and maintaining filing and publication systems
- Preparing forms and correspondence in military style

Physical Demands. No significant demands.

Work Environment. Administrative support specialists work in office settings, both on land and aboard ships.

Opportunities in the Military. The military has about 23,000 administrative support specialists. Each year, the services need new specialists because of changes in personnel and the demands of the field. After job training, administrative support specialists develop their skills under close supervision. As they gain experience, specialists are assigned more difficult tasks and work more independently. In time, they may supervise and eventually manage an office.

Civilian Occupations It Provides Training For (those with stars are described in Part IV): Business Operations Specialists, All Other; Computer Operators; Computer Systems Analysts; Couriers and Messengers; Desktop Publishers*; Executive Secretaries and Administrative Assistants*; First-Line Supervisors/Managers of Housekeeping and Janitorial Workers*; First-Line Supervisors/Managers of Office and Administrative Support Workers*; Historians; Human Resources, Training, and Labor Relations Specialists, All Other; Information and Record Clerks, All Other; Office and Administrative Support Workers, All Other; Office Clerks, General*; Postal Service Clerks*; Procurement Clerks; Purchasing Agents, Except Wholesale, Retail, and Farm Products*; Secretaries, Except Legal, Medical, and Executive*; Word Processors and Typists.

Aircraft Launch and Recovery Specialists

The military operates thousands of aircraft that take off and land on aircraft carriers all over the world. The successful launch and recovery of aircraft is important to the completion of air missions and the safety of flight crews. Aircraft launch and recovery specialists operate and maintain catapults, arresting gear, and other equipment used in aircraft carrier takeoff and landing operations.

Officer/Enlisted: Enlisted

Personality Type: Realistic. Realistic occupations frequently involve work activities that include practical, hands-on problems and solutions. They often deal with plants; animals; and real-world materials such as wood, tools, and machinery. Many of the occupations require working outside and do not involve a lot of paperwork or working closely with others.

Services That Offer the Job: Marines, Navy

What They Do. Aircraft launch and recovery specialists in the military perform some or all of the following duties:

- Operate consoles to control launch and recovery equipment, including catapults and arresting gear

- Operate elevators to transfer aircraft between flight and storage decks
- Install and maintain visual landing aids
- Test and adjust launch and recovery equipment
- Install airfield crash barriers and barricades
- Direct aircraft launch and recovery operations

Helpful Attributes. Helpful school subjects include shop mechanics. Helpful attributes include the following:

- Ability to use hand tools and test equipment
- Interest in aircraft flight operations
- Interest in working on hydraulic and mechanical equipment

Training Provided. Job training consists of classroom instruction, including practice in maintaining launch and recovery equipment. Course content typically includes the following:

- Operating and maintaining launch and recovery equipment
- Installing crash barriers and barricades

Physical Demands. Normal color vision is required to work with color-coded parts and the wiring of launch and recovery equipment.

Work Environment. Aircraft launch and recovery specialists work outdoors aboard ships while operating and maintaining launch and recovery equipment or holding visual landing aids for incoming aircraft. They are exposed to noise and fumes from jet and helicopter engines.

Opportunities in the Military. The services have about 2,500 aircraft launch and recovery specialists. Each year, they need new specialists because of changes in personnel and the demands of the field. After job training, specialists are assigned to an aircraft launch and recovery section aboard an aircraft carrier or at an airfield. Initially, they perform maintenance and repair on equipment, working under close supervision. With experience, they perform more complex activities. In time, they may train and supervise other specialists. Eventually, they may supervise activities on carrier flight and storage decks.

Civilian Occupation It Provides Training For (those with stars are described in Part IV): Municipal Fire Fighters*.

Aircraft Mechanics

Military aircraft are used to fly hundreds of missions each day for transport, patrol, and flight training. They need frequent servicing to remain safe and ready to fly. Aircraft mechanics inspect, service, and repair helicopters and airplanes.

Officer/Enlisted: Enlisted

Personality Type: Realistic. Realistic occupations frequently involve work activities that include practical, hands-on problems and solutions. They often deal with plants; animals; and real-world materials such as wood, tools, and machinery. Many of the occupations require working outside and do not involve a lot of paperwork or working closely with others.

Services That Offer the Job: Air Force, Army, Coast Guard, Marines, Navy

What They Do. Aircraft mechanics in the military perform some or all of the following duties:

- Service and repair helicopter, jet, and propeller aircraft engines
- Inspect and repair aircraft wings, fuselages, and tail assemblies
- Service and repair aircraft landing gear
- Repair or replace starters, lights, wiring, and other electrical parts

Helpful Attributes. Helpful school subjects include mathematics and shop mechanics. Helpful attributes include the following:

- Ability to use hand and power tools
- Interest in engine mechanics
- Interest in work involving aircraft

Training Provided. Job training consists of classroom instruction, including inspection and repair of aircraft engines and equipment. Training length varies depending upon the specialty. Further training occurs on the job and through advanced courses. Course content typically includes the following:

- Engine disassembly and repair
- Repair of hydraulic, fuel, and electrical systems
- Repair of aluminum, steel, and fiberglass airframes and coverings

Physical Demands. Some specialties require moderate to heavy lifting. Normal color vision is required to work with color-coded wiring.

Work Environment. Aircraft mechanics work in aircraft hangars and machine shops located on air bases or aboard aircraft carriers.

Opportunities in the Military. The services have about 70,000 aircraft mechanics. Each year, they need new mechanics because of changes in personnel and the demands of the field. After job training, mechanics are assigned to an aircraft maintenance unit, where they perform routine maintenance and simple repair jobs. In time, they may perform more difficult repairs and train and supervise new mechanics. Eventually, they may become inspectors, shop supervisors, or maintenance superintendents.

Civilian Occupations It Provides Training For (those with stars are described in Part IV): Aircraft Mechanics and Service Technicians*; Aircraft Structure, Surfaces, Rigging, and Systems Assemblers*; Avionics Technicians*; Electrical and Electronics Repairers, Commercial and Industrial Equipment*;

First-Line Supervisors/Managers of Mechanics, Installers, and Repairers*; Painters, Transportation Equipment*; Production, Planning, and Expediting Clerks*.

Airplane Navigators

Pilots rely on the precision and skill of the navigator to keep the aircraft on course. Airplane navigators use radar, radio, and other navigation equipment to determine position, direction of travel, intended course, and other information about their flights.

Officer/Enlisted: Officer

Personality Type: Realistic. Realistic occupations frequently involve work activities that include practical, hands-on problems and solutions. They often deal with plants; animals; and real-world materials such as wood, tools, and machinery. Many of the occupations require working outside and do not involve a lot of paperwork or working closely with others.

Services That Offer the Job: Air Force, Marines, Navy

What They Do. Airplane navigators in the military perform some or all of the following duties:

- Guide tankers and other airplanes during in-flight refueling operations
- Provide pilots with instrument readings, fuel usage, and other flight information
- Direct aircraft course, using radar, sight, and other navigation methods
- Operate radios and other communication equipment to send and receive messages
- Locate other aircraft, using radar equipment
- Operate bombardier systems during bombing runs
- Inspect and test navigation and weapons systems before flights

Helpful Attributes. Helpful fields of study include cartography, geography, and surveying. Helpful attributes include the following:

- Ability to read maps and charts
- Ability to respond quickly to emergencies
- Interest in work requiring accuracy and attention to detail
- Strong desire to fly

Training Provided. Job training consists of classroom instruction. Practical experience in navigation is gained through training in aircraft simulators and through about 100 hours of actual flying time. Further training occurs on the job and through advanced courses. Course content typically includes the following:

- Principles and methods of navigation
- Operation of communication, weapon, and radar systems

- Inspection and testing of navigation equipment and systems
- Combat and bombing navigation procedures and tactics

Physical Demands. Airplane navigators, like pilots, have a physically and mentally demanding job. Navigators are required to have excellent vision and must be in top physical shape.

Work Environment. Airplane navigators perform their work in aircraft. They may be stationed at airbases or aboard aircraft carriers anywhere around the world.

Special Requirements. A 4-year college degree is required to enter this occupation. Although there are women airplane navigators, some specialties are open only to men.

Opportunities in the Military. The services have about 6,000 airplane navigators. Each year, they need new navigators because of changes in personnel and the demands of the field. After job training, airplane navigators are assigned to flying sections for duty. They work as officer crewmembers on bombers, tankers, fighters, or other airplanes. In time, they may advance to senior management or command positions.

Civilian Occupations It Provides Training For (those with stars are described in Part IV): Airline Pilots, Copilots, and Flight Engineers*; Commercial Pilots*.

Airplane Pilots

The military operates one of the largest fleets of specialized airplanes in the world. Supersonic fighters and bombers fly combat missions. Large transports carry troops and equipment. Intelligence-gathering airplanes take photographs from high altitudes. Military airplane pilots fly the thousands of jet and propeller airplanes operated by the services.

Officer/Enlisted: Officer

Personality Type: Realistic. Realistic occupations frequently involve work activities that include practical, hands-on problems and solutions. They often deal with plants; animals; and real-world materials such as wood, tools, and machinery. Many of the occupations require working outside and do not involve a lot of paperwork or working closely with others.

Services That Offer the Job: Air Force, Army, Coast Guard, Marines, Navy

What They Do. Airplane pilots in the military perform some or all of the following duties:

- Check weather reports to learn about flying conditions
- Develop flight plans showing air routes and schedules
- Contact air traffic controllers to obtain takeoff and landing instructions
- Fly airplanes by controlling engines, rudders, elevators, and other controls

- Monitor gauges and dials located on cockpit control panels
- Perform combat maneuvers, take photographs, transport equipment, and patrol areas to carry out flight missions

Helpful Attributes. Helpful fields of study include physics and aerospace, electrical, or mechanical engineering. Helpful attributes include the following:

- Determination to complete a very demanding training program
- Self-confidence and ability to remain calm in stressful situations
- Strong desire to fly airplanes

Training Provided. Pilot training is generally a 2-year program covering 1 year each in initial and advanced training. Initial training includes time spent in flight simulators, classroom training, officer training, and basic flight training. This is among the most challenging training given by the services; not everyone who attempts this training can meet the strict requirements for completion. Advanced training begins when pilots successfully complete initial training and are awarded their "wings." Advanced training consists of instruction in flying a particular type of aircraft. Course content typically includes the following:

- Aircraft aerodynamics
- Jet and propeller engine operation
- Operation of aircraft navigation systems
- Foul-weather flying
- Federal Aviation Administration (FAA) regulations

Physical Demands. Airplane pilots must pass the most demanding physical test of any job in the military. To be accepted for pilot training, applicants must have 20/20 vision and be in top physical condition. They must have very good eye-hand coordination and have extremely quick reaction times to maneuver at high speeds.

Work Environment. Airplane pilots may be stationed at airbases or aboard aircraft carriers anywhere in the world. They fly in all types of weather conditions. Military pilots take off and land on airport runways and aircraft carrier landing decks.

Special Requirements. A 4-year college degree is normally required to enter this occupation. Although the military has many women pilots, some specialties involving duty in combat airplanes are open only to men.

Opportunities in the Military. Civilian airplane pilots who work for passenger airlines and air cargo businesses are called commercial pilots. Other civilian pilots work as flight instructors at local airports, as crop dusters, or as pilots transporting business executives in company planes. Many commercial pilots began their career in the military.

Civilian Occupations It Provides Training For (those with stars are described in Part IV): Airline Pilots, Copilots, and Flight Engineers*; Commercial Pilots*.

Audiovisual and Broadcast Technicians

Television and film productions are an important part of military communications. Films are used for training in many military occupations. They are also used to record military operations, ceremonies, and news events. These productions require the teamwork of many technicians. Audiovisual and broadcast technicians perform many specialized tasks, ranging from filming to script editing to operating audio recording devices.

Officer/Enlisted: Enlisted

Personality Type: Artistic. Artistic occupations frequently involve working with forms, designs, and patterns. They often require self-expression, and the work can be done without following a clear set of rules.

Services That Offer the Job: Air Force, Army, Marines, Navy

What They Do. Audiovisual and broadcast technicians in the military perform some or all of the following duties:

- Work with writers, producers, and directors in preparing and interpreting scripts
- Plan and design production scenery, graphics, and special effects
- Operate media equipment and special effect devices, including cameras, sound recorders, and lighting
- Follow script and instructions of film or TV directors to move cameras, zoom, pan, or adjust focus

Helpful Attributes. Helpful school subjects include photography, graphics, art, speech, and drama. Helpful attributes include the following:

- Experience in school plays or making home movies
- Interest in creative and artistic work
- Preference for working as part of a team

Training Provided. Job training consists of instruction. Training length varies depending on specialty. Further training occurs on the job and through advanced courses. Course content typically includes the following:

- Motion picture equipment operation
- Audio recording
- Scripting and special effects techniques
- Maintenance of public address sound equipment

Physical Demands. Normal color vision and the ability to speak clearly are required for some specialties in this area.

Work Environment. Audiovisual and broadcast technicians work in studios or outdoors on location. They sometimes work from aircraft or ships. They travel and work in all climates.

Opportunities in the Military. The services have about 1,000 audiovisual and broadcast technicians. Each year, they need new technicians because of changes in personnel and the demands of the field. After job training, new technicians assist with various production processes. With experience, they work more independently and, in time, may direct audiovisual productions.

Civilian Occupations It Provides Training For (those with stars are described in Part IV): Audio and Video Equipment Technicians*; Broadcast News Analysts; Broadcast Technicians; Camera Operators, Television, Video, and Motion Picture*; Copy Writers; Directors—Stage, Motion Pictures, Television, and Radio; Electronic Home Entertainment Equipment Installers and Repairers; Film and Video Editors; Media and Communication Equipment Workers, All Other; Media and Communication Workers, All Other; Program Directors; Radio and Television Announcers; Reporters and Correspondents; Technical Directors/Managers*.

Automotive and Heavy Equipment Mechanics

Keeping automotive and heavy equipment in good working condition is vital to the success of military missions. Automotive and heavy equipment mechanics maintain and repair vehicles such as jeeps, cars, trucks, tanks, and other combat vehicles. They also repair bulldozers, power shovels, and other construction equipment.

Officer/Enlisted: Enlisted

Personality Type: Realistic. Realistic occupations frequently involve work activities that include practical, hands-on problems and solutions. They often deal with plants; animals; and real-world materials such as wood, tools, and machinery. Many of the occupations require working outside and do not involve a lot of paperwork or working closely with others.

Services That Offer the Job: Air Force, Army, Coast Guard, Marines, Navy

What They Do. Automotive and heavy equipment mechanics in the military perform some or all of the following duties:

- Troubleshoot problems in vehicle engines, electrical systems, steering, brakes, and suspensions
- Tune and repair engines
- Replace or repair damaged body parts, hydraulic arms or shovels, and grader blades
- Establish and follow schedules for maintaining vehicles

Helpful Attributes. Helpful school subjects include auto mechanics and industrial arts. Helpful attributes include the following:

- Interest in automotive engines and how they work
- Interest in troubleshooting and repairing mechanical problems
- Preference for physical work

Training Provided. Job training consists of classroom instruction. Training length varies depending on specialty. Further training occurs on the job and through advanced courses. Course content typically includes the following:

- Engine repair and tune-up
- Troubleshooting mechanical and electrical problems
- Repairing and replacing body panels, fenders, and radiators

Physical Demands. Automotive and heavy equipment mechanics have to lift heavy parts and tools. They sometimes have to work in cramped positions. Normal color vision is required for some specialties to work with color-coded wiring and to read diagrams.

Work Environment. Automotive and heavy equipment mechanics usually work inside large repair garages. They work outdoors when making emergency repairs in the field.

Opportunities in the Military. The services have about 45,000 automotive and heavy equipment mechanics. Each year, they need new mechanics because of changes in personnel and the demands of the field. After job training, mechanics begin repairing equipment under the direction of a supervisor. In time, they have the opportunity to supervise other workers and possibly manage repair shops, motor pools, or maintenance units.

Civilian Occupations It Provides Training For (those with stars are described in Part IV): Automotive Body and Related Repairers*; Automotive Master Mechanics*; Automotive Specialty Technicians*; Bus and Truck Mechanics and Diesel Engine Specialists*; Electrical and Electronics Installers and Repairers, Transportation Equipment*; Electrical and Electronics Repairers, Commercial and Industrial Equipment*; Electronic Equipment Installers and Repairers, Motor Vehicles; Elevator Installers and Repairers*; First-Line Supervisors/Managers of Construction Trades and Extraction Workers*; First-Line Supervisors/Managers of Mechanics, Installers, and Repairers*; Industrial Machinery Mechanics*; Maintenance and Repair Workers, General*; Mobile Heavy Equipment Mechanics, Except Engines*; Rail Car Repairers.

Avionics Technicians

Airplanes and helicopters have complex electrical and electronic systems for communication, navigation, and radar. Instruments, lights, weapons, landing gear, sensors, and many other aircraft parts are also controlled by electronics. Avionics technicians install, maintain, and repair electronic and electrical systems on all types of aircraft.

Officer/Enlisted: Enlisted

Personality Type: Realistic. Realistic occupations frequently involve work activities that include practical, hands-on problems and solutions. They often deal with plants; animals; and real-world materials such as wood, tools, and machinery. Many of the occupations require working outside and do not involve a lot of paperwork or working closely with others.

Services That Offer the Job: Air Force, Army, Coast Guard, Marines, Navy

What They Do. Avionics technicians in the military perform some or all of the following duties:

- Troubleshoot aircraft electronics and electrical systems, using test equipment
- Repair or replace defective components
- Inspect and maintain electronics and electrical systems
- Replace faulty wiring
- Install electronic components
- Repair or replace instruments, such as tachometers, temperature gauges, and altimeters
- Read electronic and electrical diagrams

Helpful Attributes. Helpful school courses include math and shop mechanics. Helpful attributes include the following:

- Ability to work with tools
- Interest in electronics and electrical equipment
- Interest in solving problems

Training Provided. Job training consists of classroom instruction, including practice in repairing avionics systems. Training length varies depending on specialty. Further training occurs on the job and through advanced courses. Course content typically includes the following:

- Electronics and electrical theory
- Troubleshooting procedures
- Installation techniques
- Avionics and electrical system maintenance

Physical Demands. Normal color vision is required to work with color-coded wiring.

Work Environment. Avionics technicians usually work indoors in aircraft hangars, airplanes, and repair shops. They may also work on aircraft parked outdoors.

Opportunities in the Military. The military has more than 25,000 avionics technicians. Each year, the services need new technicians because of changes in personnel and the demands of the field. After job training, avionics technicians perform maintenance and routine repairs under close supervision. With experience, they are assigned more complicated troubleshooting and repairs and may supervise other technicians. In time, they may become supervisors of aircraft maintenance shops.

Civilian Occupations It Provides Training For (those with stars are described in Part IV): Aircraft Mechanics and Service Technicians*; Aircraft Structure, Surfaces, Rigging, and Systems Assemblers*; Avionics Technicians*; Computer, Automated Teller, and Office Machine Repairers*; Electrical and Electronics Repairers, Commercial and Industrial Equipment*; First-Line Supervisors/Managers of Mechanics, Installers, and Repairers*; Radio Mechanics.

Broadcast Journalists and Newswriters

The military publishes newspapers and broadcasts television and radio programs for its personnel and the public. These services are an important source of general information about people and events in the military. Broadcast journalists and newswriters write and present news programs, music programs, and radio talk shows.

Officer/Enlisted: Enlisted

Personality Type: Artistic. Artistic occupations frequently involve working with forms, designs, and patterns. They often require self-expression, and the work can be done without following a clear set of rules.

Services That Offer the Job: Air Force, Army, Coast Guard, Marines, Navy

What They Do. Broadcast journalists and newswriters in the military perform some or all of the following duties:

- Gather information for military news programs and publications
- Write radio and TV scripts
- Develop ideas for news articles
- Arrange and conduct interviews
- Collect information for commercial media use
- Select photographs and write captions for news articles
- Write news releases, feature articles, and editorials

Helpful Attributes. Helpful school subjects include English, journalism, speech, and media communications. Helpful attributes include the following:

- Ability to keep detailed and accurate records
- Ability to write clearly and concisely
- Interest in researching facts and issues for news stories
- Strong, clear speaking voice

Training Provided. Job training consists of classroom instruction. Course content typically includes the following:

- Newswriting and research
- Newspaper format and layout
- Photojournalism (writing news stories featuring pictures)
- Radio and television programming and production

Physical Demands. Normal color vision and the passing of a voice audition are required for some specialties in this area.

Work Environment. Broadcast journalists and newswriters work in broadcasting studios on land or aboard ships or sometimes outdoors, depending upon the research needed for their articles.

Opportunities in the Military. The military has about 2,000 broadcast journalists and newswriters. Each year, the services need new journalists and newswriters because of changes in personnel and the demands of the field. After job training, they research and announce news stories and music programs. Eventually, they may become editors or editorial assistants or managers of broadcasting stations.

Civilian Occupations It Provides Training For (those with stars are described in Part IV): Broadcast News Analysts; Copy Writers; Court Reporters*; Editors; Photographers*; Poets, Lyricists, and Creative Writers; Public Relations Specialists; Radio and Television Announcers; Reporters and Correspondents.

Building Electricians

The military uses electricity to do many jobs, including lighting hospitals, running power tools, and operating computers. Building electricians install and repair electrical wiring systems in offices, repair shops, airplane hangars, and other buildings on military bases.

Officer/Enlisted: Enlisted

Personality Type: Realistic. Realistic occupations frequently involve work activities that include practical, hands-on problems and solutions. They often deal with plants; animals; and real-world materials such as wood, tools, and machinery. Many of the occupations require working outside and do not involve a lot of paperwork or working closely with others.

Services That Offer the Job: Air Force, Army, Marines, Navy

What They Do. Building electricians in the military perform some or all of the following duties:

- Install and wire transformers, junction boxes, and circuit breakers, using wire cutters, insulation strippers, and other hand tools
- Read blueprints, wiring plans, and repair orders to determine wiring layouts or repair needs
- Cut, bend, and string wires and conduits (pipe or tubing)

- Inspect power distribution systems, shorts in wires, and faulty equipment, using test meters
- Repair and replace faulty wiring and lighting fixtures
- Install lightning rods to protect electrical systems

Helpful Attributes. Helpful school subjects include science and math. Helpful attributes include the following:

- Ability to use hand tools
- Interest in electricity
- Preference for doing physical work

Training Provided. Job training consists of classroom instruction, including practice in the installation and repair of electrical wiring systems. Further training occurs on the job and through advanced courses. Course content typically includes the following:

- Fundamentals of electricity
- Electrical circuit troubleshooting
- Safety procedures
- Techniques for wiring switches, outlets, and junction boxes

Physical Demands. Normal color vision is required for working with color-coded wiring and circuits.

Work Environment. Building electricians usually work indoors while installing wiring systems. They work outdoors while installing transformers and lightning rods.

Opportunities in the Military. The military has about 3,000 building electricians. Each year, the services need new electricians because of changes in personnel and the demands of the field. After job training, building electricians work under close supervision. As they gain experience, building electricians work more independently. In time, they may be promoted to supervisors of one or more work crews. Eventually, they may become construction superintendents.

Civilian Occupations It Provides Training For (those with stars are described in Part IV): Electricians*; First-Line Supervisors/Managers of Construction Trades and Extraction Workers*; First-Line Supervisors/Managers of Mechanics, Installers, and Repairers*.

Cardiopulmonary and EEG Technicians

Military health care includes medical treatment for heart, lung, and brain disorders. Physicians need sophisticated tests to help diagnose and treat these problems. Cardiopulmonary and EEG (electroencephalograph) technicians administer a variety of diagnostic tests of the heart, lungs, blood, and brain, using complex electronic testing equipment.

Officer/Enlisted: Enlisted

Personality Type: Social. Social occupations frequently involve working with, communicating with, and teaching people. These occupations often involve helping or providing service to others.

Services That Offer the Job: Air Force, Army, Navy

What They Do. Cardiopulmonary and EEG technicians in the military perform some or all of the following duties:

- Take patients' blood pressure readings
- Attach electrodes or other test equipment to patients' bodies
- Help physicians revive heart attack victims
- Adjust settings and operate test equipment
- Monitor graphs and screens during tests
- Talk to physicians to learn what tests or treatments are needed
- Keep records of test results and discuss them with medical staff
- Operate electrocardiographs and other test equipment

Helpful Attributes. Helpful school subjects include algebra, chemistry, biology, or related courses. Helpful attributes include the following:

- Ability to follow strict standards and procedures
- Ability to keep accurate records
- Interest in electronic equipment
- Interest in learning how the heart, lungs, and blood work together

Training Provided. Job training consists of classroom instruction. Further training occurs on the job and through advanced courses. Course content typically includes the following:

- Diagnostic procedures
- Operation and maintenance of diagnostic equipment
- Preparation of patients for testing
- Methods of resuscitation

Physical Demands. No significant demands.

Work Environment. Cardiopulmonary and EEG technicians usually work in hospitals and clinics. In combat situations, they may work in mobile field hospitals.

Opportunities in the Military. The services have about 6,000 cardiopulmonary and EEG technicians. Each year, they need new technicians because of changes in personnel and the demands of the field. After job training, new technicians are assigned to hospitals and clinics, where they work under the supervision of physicians and senior technicians. With experience, they may supervise others and assist in managing clinics.

Civilian Occupations It Provides Training For (those with stars are described in Part IV): Cardiovascular Technologists and Technicians*; Health Technologists and Technicians, All Other; Medical Assistants*; Respiratory Therapy Technicians.

Cargo Specialists

The military delivers supplies, weapons, equipment, and mail to United States forces in many parts of the world. Military cargo travels by ship, truck, or airplane. It must be handled carefully to ensure safe arrival at the correct destination. Cargo specialists load and unload military supplies and material, using equipment such as forklifts and cranes. They also plan and organize loading schedules.

Officer/Enlisted: Enlisted

Personality Type: Conventional. Conventional occupations frequently involve following set procedures and routines. These occupations can include working with data and details more than with ideas. Usually there is a clear line of authority to follow.

Services That Offer the Job: Air Force, Army, Coast Guard, Marines, Navy

What They Do. Cargo specialists in the military perform some or all of the following duties:

- Load supplies into trucks, transport planes, and railroad cars, using forklifts
- Load equipment such as jeeps, trucks, and weapons aboard ships, using dockyard cranes
- Pack and crate boxes of supplies for shipping
- Inspect cargo for damage
- Plan and inspect loads for balance and safety
- Check cargo against invoices to make sure the amount and destination of material are correct

Helpful Attributes. Helpful school subjects include general office and business mathematics. Helpful attributes include the following:

- Interest in working with forklifts and cranes
- Preference for physical work

Training Provided. Job training consists of classroom instruction, including practice in loading cargo. Further training occurs on the job. Course content typically includes the following:

- Operation and care of forklifts, power winches, and cranes
- Techniques for loading and storing cargo

- Techniques for planning and scheduling cargo shipments
- Safety procedures for handling potentially dangerous cargo

Physical Demands. Cargo specialists must lift and carry heavy cargo.

Work Environment. Cargo specialists work outdoors on loading docks and indoors in warehouses.

Opportunities in the Military. The services have about 6,000 cargo specialists. Each year, they need new cargo specialists because of changes in personnel and the demands of the field. After job training, cargo specialists work in teams preparing and loading cargo for shipment under the direction of supervisors. In time, they may advance to become team leaders or supervisors of other cargo specialists. Eventually, they may become warehouse managers.

Civilian Occupations It Provides Training For (those with stars are described in Part IV): Aircraft Cargo Handling Supervisors; Cargo and Freight Agents*; Material Moving Workers, All Other; Order Fillers, Wholesale and Retail Sales; Packers and Packagers, Hand*; Postal Service Clerks*; Sailors and Marine Oilers; Shipping, Receiving, and Traffic Clerks*; Storage and Distribution Managers*.

Caseworkers and Counselors

C

Just like some civilians, some military personnel need assistance with various problems or concerns, including career decisions, family issues, substance abuse, or emotional problems. Caseworkers and counselors work with military personnel and their families to help them with their particular concerns. They may specialize by the type of counseling that they do, such as career guidance or alcohol and drug abuse prevention. They normally work as part of a team that may include social workers, psychologists, medical officers, chaplains, personnel specialists, and commanders.

Officer/Enlisted: Enlisted

Personality Type: Social. Social occupations frequently involve working with, communicating with, and teaching people. These occupations often involve helping or providing service to others.

Services That Offer the Job: Air Force, Army, Marines, Navy

What They Do. Caseworkers and counselors in the military perform some or all of the following duties:

- Interview personnel who request help or are referred by their commanders
- Identify problems and determine the need for professional help
- Counsel personnel and their families
- Administer and score psychological tests
- Help personnel evaluate and explore career opportunities

- Teach classes on human relations
- Keep records of counseling sessions

Helpful Attributes. Helpful school subjects include health, biology, psychology, sociology, social science, and speech. Helpful attributes include the following:

- Interest in working with people
- Patience in dealing with problems that take time and effort to overcome
- Sensitivity to the needs of others

Training Provided. Job training consists of classroom instruction, including practice in counseling. Further training occurs on the job and through advanced courses. Course content typically includes the following:

- Orientation to counseling and social service programs
- Interviewing and counseling methods
- Treatments for drug and alcohol abuse
- Psychological testing techniques

Physical Demands. Caseworkers and counselors need to speak clearly and distinctly in order to teach classes and work with personnel who have problems.

Work Environment. Caseworkers and counselors usually work in offices or clinics.

Opportunities in the Military. The services have about 1,000 caseworkers and counselors. Each year, they need new caseworkers and counselors because of changes in personnel and the demands of the field. After job training, they work under close supervision. With experience, they work more independently and may supervise other caseworkers.

Civilian Occupations It Provides Training For (those with stars are described in Part IV): Mental Health and Substance Abuse Social Workers; Probation Officers and Correctional Treatment Specialists; Psychiatric Technicians; Social and Human Service Assistants*; Social Workers, All Other.

Combat Mission Support Officers

Military combat operations require careful planning and coordination of combat resources. Combat mission support officers ensure that everything is in the right place at the right time during military operations. They provide battle management from specialized aircraft, ground locations, and ships. Combat mission support officers normally specialize according to their area of expertise.

Officer/Enlisted: Officer

Personality Type: Enterprising. Enterprising occupations frequently involve starting up and carrying out projects. These occupations can involve leading people and making many decisions. They sometimes require risk taking and often deal with business.

Services That Offer the Job: Air Force, Army, Coast Guard, Marines, Navy

What They Do. Combat mission support officers in the military perform some or all of the following duties:

- Develop plans, policies, and procedures for battle management
- Train, establish standards, and conduct evaluations of unit personnel
- Advise commanders of ground, air, and naval units on deployment of combat forces
- Assist in the planning and execution of combat operations
- Direct the movement of resources within the combat zone

Helpful Attributes. Helpful attributes include the following:

- Ability to absorb large amounts of data in a short period of time
- Ability to coordinate with others
- Ability to make decisions in stressful situations
- Ability to manage a large staff

Training Provided. Job training consists of classroom instruction and field training under simulated combat situations. Training length varies depending on position. Course content typically includes the following:

- Battle tactics and management
- Relationships among air, ground, and naval forces
- Capabilities of weapon systems
- Communications systems

Physical Demands. No significant demands.

Work Environment. Combat mission support officers work in a variety of settings. Some work in offices or command and control centers. Others work primarily outdoors in the field during training exercises and actual combat situations. Depending on the service branch and specialty, combat mission support officers may work in aircraft and aboard ships.

Opportunities in the Military. The services have about 2,000 combat mission support officers. Each year, they need new officers because of changes in personnel and the demands of the field. After job training, combat mission support officers typically assist commanders in battle management activities. Based on performance and demonstrated leadership ability, they may become responsible for larger forces.

Civilian Occupation It Provides Training For (those with stars are described in Part IV): Airline Pilots, Copilots, and Flight Engineers*.

Communications Equipment Operators

The ability to relay information between air, sea, and ground forces is critical in the military. The military has sophisticated communications systems that use a variety of technologies and telecommunications equipment such as radios, telephones, antennas, satellites, and complex security and network devices. Communications equipment operators use these systems to transmit, receive, and decode messages at military locations throughout the world.

Officer/Enlisted: Enlisted

Personality Type: Realistic. Realistic occupations frequently involve work activities that include practical, hands-on problems and solutions. They often deal with plants; animals; and real-world materials such as wood, tools, and machinery. Many of the occupations require working outside and do not involve a lot of paperwork or working closely with others.

Services That Offer the Job: Air Force, Army, Coast Guard, Marines, Navy

What They Do. Communications equipment operators in the military perform some or all of the following duties:

- Transmit, receive, and log messages according to military procedures
- Encode and decode classified messages
- Operate different types of telephone switchboards, satellite communications terminals, and network switches
- Set up and operate communications equipment and security equipment
- Monitor and respond to emergency calls
- Run state-of-the-art command, control, communications, and computer and signals intelligence/electronic warfare equipment
- Install, operate, and repair communications and security equipment

Helpful Attributes. Helpful school subjects include English and speech. Helpful attributes include the following:

- Ability to remain calm in an emergency
- Interest in working with codes
- Interest in working with communications equipment

Training Provided. Job training consists of instruction, including practice with equipment. Further training occurs on the job and through advanced courses. Course content typically includes the following:

- Installation and usage of various types of communications equipment
- Communications security
- Message encoding and decoding

Physical Demands. No significant demands.

Work Environment. Communications equipment operators may work either indoors or outdoors, depending on the specialty. They may be assigned to ships, aircraft, land bases, or mobile field units.

Opportunities in the Military. The military has about 40,000 communications equipment operators. Each year, the services need new operators because of changes in personnel and the demands of the field. After job training, they prepare and send messages under supervision. With experience, they work more independently. In time, they may become supervisors of communications centers.

Civilian Occupations It Provides Training For (those with stars are described in Part IV): Broadcast Technicians; Camera Operators, Television, Video, and Motion Picture*; Communications Equipment Operators, All Other; Electrical and Electronics Repairers, Commercial and Industrial Equipment*; First-Line Supervisors/Managers of Mechanics, Installers, and Repairers*; Radio Mechanics; Radio Operators; Telecommunications Equipment Installers and Repairers, Except Line Installers*; Telecommunications Line Installers and Repairers*.

Computer Systems Specialists

The military uses computers to store and process data on personnel, weather, communications, finances, and many other areas, as well as to operate sophisticated equipment during combat and peacetime maneuvers.

Officer/Enlisted: Enlisted

Personality Type: Realistic. Realistic occupations frequently involve work activities that include practical, hands-on problems and solutions. They often deal with plants; animals; and real-world materials such as wood, tools, and machinery. Many of the occupations require working outside and do not involve a lot of paperwork or working closely with others.

Services That Offer the Job: Air Force, Army, Marines, Navy

What They Do. Computer systems specialists in the military perform some or all of the following duties:

- Install, configure, and monitor local and wide area networks, hardware, and software
- Collect, enter, and process information, using computers
- Provide customer and network administration services, such as electronic mail accounts, user training, security, virus protection, and troubleshooting
- Use computer programs to solve problems
- Determine and analyze computer systems requirements

- Program information into languages that computers can read
- Develop, test, and debug computer programs
- Provide system analysis and maintenance
- Implement procedures to ensure computer and network security

Helpful Attributes. Helpful school subjects include computer science, math, and typing. Helpful attributes include the following:

- Ability to communicate effectively
- Ability to understand and apply math concepts
- Interest in solving problems
- Interest in work requiring accuracy and attention to detail

Training Provided. Job training consists of classroom instruction, depending upon the specialty area. Further training occurs on the job and through advanced courses in specific computer systems and languages. Course content typically includes the following:

- Use of computers and peripheral equipment
- Computer systems concepts
- Planning, designing, and testing computer systems
- Program structuring, coding, and debugging
- Use of current programming languages
- Computer security issues
- Network management

Physical Demands. No significant demands.

Work Environment. Computer systems specialists in the military work in offices or at computer sites on military bases or aboard ships.

Opportunities in the Military. The services have about 24,000 computer systems specialists. Each year, they need new specialists to meet the changing demands in the field. After training, computer systems specialists work under the direction of experienced computer systems officers. With experience, they may manage other computer systems specialists.

Civilian Occupations It Provides Training For (those with stars are described in Part IV): Communications Equipment Operators, All Other; Computer Operators; Computer Programmers*; Computer Security Specialists; Computer Support Specialists*; Computer Systems Analysts; Computer, Automated Teller, and Office Machine Repairers*; Database Administrators; Electrical and Electronics Repairers, Commercial and Industrial Equipment*; First-Line Supervisors/Managers of Office and Administrative Support Workers*; Life, Physical, and Social Science Technicians, All Other; Network and Computer Systems Administrators; Network Systems and Data Communications Analysts.

Construction Equipment Operators

Each year the military completes hundreds of construction projects. Tons of earth and building materials must be moved to build airfields, roads, dams, and buildings. Construction equipment operators use bulldozers, cranes, graders, and other heavy equipment in military construction.

Officer/Enlisted: Enlisted

Personality Type: Realistic. Realistic occupations frequently involve work activities that include practical, hands-on problems and solutions. They often deal with plants; animals; and real-world materials such as wood, tools, and machinery. Many of the occupations require working outside and do not involve a lot of paperwork or working closely with others.

Services That Offer the Job: Air Force, Army, Coast Guard, Marines, Navy

What They Do. Construction equipment operators in the military perform some or all of the following duties:

- Drive bulldozers, roadgraders, and other heavy equipment to cut and level earth for runways and roadbeds
- Lift and move steel and other heavy building materials, using winches, cranes, and hoists
- Dig holes and trenches, using power shovels
- Operate mixing plants to make concrete and asphalt
- Spread asphalt and concrete with paving machines
- Drill wells, using drilling rigs
- Place and detonate explosives
- Remove ice and snow from runways, roads, and other areas, using scrapers and snowblowers

Helpful Attributes. Helpful school subjects include shop mechanics. Helpful attributes include the following:

- Interest in operating heavy construction equipment
- Preference for working outdoors

Training Provided. Job training consists of classroom instruction, including practice operating construction equipment. Further training occurs on the job and through advanced courses. Course content typically includes the following:

- Operation of different types of construction equipment
- Maintenance and repair of equipment

Physical Demands. Some specialties require normal hearing, color vision, and heavy lifting.

C

Work Environment. Construction equipment operators work outdoors in all kinds of weather conditions. They often sit for long periods and are subject to loud noise and vibrations. They may work indoors while repairing equipment.

Opportunities in the Military. The services have about 10,000 construction equipment operators. Each year, they need new equipment operators because of changes in personnel and the demands of the field. With time, they have the opportunity to become construction supervisors or construction superintendents.

Civilian Occupations It Provides Training For (those with stars are described in Part IV): Crane and Tower Operators*; Earth Drillers, Except Oil and Gas; Explosives Workers, Ordnance Handling Experts, and Blasters; First-Line Supervisors/Managers of Construction Trades and Extraction Workers*; Highway Maintenance Workers*; Operating Engineers and Other Construction Equipment Operators*; Paving, Surfacing, and Tamping Equipment Operators*; Rock Splitters, Quarry.

Construction Specialists

The military builds many temporary and permanent structures each year. Lumber, plywood, plasterboard, and concrete and masonry (bricks, stone, and concrete blocks) are the basic building materials for many of these projects. Construction specialists build and repair buildings, bridges, foundations, dams, and bunkers. They work with engineers and other building specialists as part of military construction teams.

Officer/Enlisted: Enlisted

Personality Type: Realistic. Realistic occupations frequently involve work activities that include practical, hands-on problems and solutions. They often deal with plants; animals; and real-world materials such as wood, tools, and machinery. Many of the occupations require working outside and do not involve a lot of paperwork or working closely with others.

Services That Offer the Job: Air Force, Army, Coast Guard, Marines, Navy

What They Do. Construction specialists in the military perform some or all of the following duties:

- Build foundations, floor slabs, and walls with brick, cement block, mortar, or stone
- Erect wood framing for buildings, using hand and power tools such as hammers, saws, levels, and drills
- Lay roofing materials such as asphalt, tile, and wooden shingles
- Install plasterboard, plaster, and paneling to form interior walls and ceilings
- Lay wood and ceramic tile floors and build steps, staircases, and porches
- Build temporary shelters for storing supplies and equipment while on training maneuvers

Helpful Attributes. Helpful school subjects include math, woodworking, and industrial arts. Helpful attributes include the following:

- Ability to work with blueprints
- Interest in using power tools
- Preference for physical work

Training Provided. Job training consists of instruction, including practice with carpentry and masonry tools. Further training occurs on the job and through advanced courses. Course content typically includes the following:

- Building construction
- Masonry construction methods
- Types and uses of construction joints and braces
- Interpretation of blueprints and drawings
- How to mix and set concrete, mortar, and plaster

Physical Demands. Construction specialists may have to lift and carry heavy building materials, such as lumber, plasterboard, and concrete. Sometimes they climb and work from ladders and scaffolding.

Work Environment. Construction specialists work indoors and outdoors on construction sites.

Opportunities in the Military. The military has about 5,000 construction specialists. Each year, the services need new specialists because of changes in personnel and the demands of the field. After job training, construction specialists work in teams under close supervision. Initially, they perform simple work, such as form building and rough framing. With experience, they perform more difficult tasks. In time, they may supervise and train other specialists. They may become construction superintendents.

Civilian Occupations It Provides Training For (those with stars are described in Part IV): Architectural Drafters*; Brickmasons and Blockmasons*; Cabinetmakers and Bench Carpenters; Carpenters; Cement Masons and Concrete Finishers*; Civil Drafters*; Civil Engineering Technicians*; Compliance Officers, Except Agriculture, Construction, Health and Safety, and Transportation; Construction and Building Inspectors*; Construction and Related Workers, All Other; Construction Carpenters*; Drywall and Ceiling Tile Installers*; Elevator Installers and Repairers*; Explosives Workers, Ordnance Handling Experts, and Blasters; First-Line Supervisors/Managers of Construction Trades and Extraction Workers*; Mapping Technicians*; Rail-Track Laying and Maintenance Equipment Operators; Roofers*; Rough Carpenters*; Stonemasons; Structural Iron and Steel Workers*; Surveying Technicians*.

Dental Specialists

Dental care is one of the health services provided to all military personnel. It is available in military dental clinics all over the world. Dental specialists assist military dentists in examining and treating patients. They also help manage dental offices.

Officer/Enlisted: Enlisted

Personality Type: Social. Social occupations frequently involve working with, communicating with, and teaching people. These occupations often involve helping or providing service to others.

Services That Offer the Job: Air Force, Army, Coast Guard, Navy

What They Do. Dental specialists in the military perform some or all of the following duties:

- Help dentists perform oral surgery
- Prepare for patient examinations by selecting and arranging instruments and medications
- Help dentists during examinations by preparing dental compounds and operating dental equipment
- Clean patients' teeth, using scaling and polishing instruments and equipment
- Operate dental X-ray equipment and process X rays of patients' teeth, gums, and jaws
- Provide guidance to patients on daily care of their teeth
- Perform administrative duties, such as scheduling office visits, keeping patient records, and ordering dental supplies

Helpful Attributes. Helpful school subjects include biology and chemistry. Helpful attributes include the following:

- Ability to follow spoken instructions and detailed procedures
- Good eye-hand coordination
- Interest in working with people

Training Provided. Job training consists of classroom instruction, including practice in dental care tasks. Further training occurs on the job and through advanced courses. Course content typically includes the following:

- Preventive dentistry
- Radiology (X-ray) techniques
- Dental office procedures
- Dental hygiene procedures

Physical Demands. No significant demands.

Work Environment. Dental specialists in the military usually work indoors in dental offices or clinics. Some specialists may be assigned to duty aboard ships.

Opportunities in the Military. The military has about 6,000 dental specialists. Each year, the services need new specialists because of changes in personnel and the demands of the field. After job training, new specialists are assigned to dental offices or clinics, where they work under the supervision of dentists. With experience, dental specialists perform more difficult tasks involving patient care. In time, they may become responsible for assisting dental officers in the management of dental programs.

Civilian Occupations It Provides Training For (those with stars are described in Part IV): Dental Assistants*; Dental Hygienists*; Healthcare Practitioners and Technical Workers, All Other; Surgical Technologists*.

Electrical Products Repairers

Much of the military's equipment is electrically powered. Electric motors, electric tools, and medical equipment require careful maintenance and repair. Electrical products repairers maintain and repair electrical equipment. They specialize by type of equipment.

Officer/Enlisted: Enlisted

Personality Type: Realistic. Realistic occupations frequently involve work activities that include practical, hands-on problems and solutions. They often deal with plants; animals; and real-world materials such as wood, tools, and machinery. Many of the occupations require working outside and do not involve a lot of paperwork or working closely with others.

Services That Offer the Job: Air Force, Army, Marines, Navy

What They Do. Electrical products repairers in the military perform some or all of the following duties:

- Maintain, test, and repair electric motors in many kinds of machines, such as lathes, pumps, office machines, and appliances
- Inspect and repair electrical, medical, and dental equipment
- Inspect and repair electric instruments, such as voltmeters
- Maintain and repair portable electric tools, such as saws and drills

Helpful Attributes. Helpful school subjects include math, electricity, and shop mechanics. Helpful attributes include the following:

- Ability to use tools
- Interest in electric motors and appliances
- Interest in solving problems

E

Training Provided. Job training consists of classroom instruction, including practice in repairing electrical products. Training length varies depending on specialty. Further training occurs on the job and through advanced courses. Course content typically includes the following:

- Maintenance and repair procedures
- Use of electrical test equipment

Physical Demands. Normal color vision is required to work with color-coded wiring.

Work Environment. Electrical products repairers usually work in repair shops on land or aboard ships.

Opportunities in the Military. The military has about 4,000 electrical products repairers. Each year, the services need new repairers because of changes in personnel and the demands of the field. After job training, they normally make simple repairs under the direction of more experienced workers. With experience, they perform more complicated repairs. In time, repairers may become electrical repair shop supervisors.

Civilian Occupations It Provides Training For (those with stars are described in Part IV): Electric Motor, Power Tool, and Related Repairers; Electrical and Electronics Repairers, Commercial and Industrial Equipment*; Electronic Equipment Installers and Repairers, Motor Vehicles; Electronic Home Entertainment Equipment Installers and Repairers; First-Line Supervisors/Managers of Mechanics, Installers, and Repairers*; Home Appliance Repairers; Medical Equipment Repairers*; Precision Instrument and Equipment Repairers, All Other; Radio Mechanics; Security and Fire Alarm Systems Installers; Tool Grinders, Filers, and Sharpeners.

Electronic Instrument and Equipment Repairers

The military uses electronic instruments and equipment in many different areas, including health care, weather forecasting, and combat, to name a few. Electronics repairers maintain and repair instruments and equipment such as computers, communications equipment, radar and sonar systems, precision measuring equipment, and biomedical instruments. Electronic instrument and equipment repairers normally specialize by type of equipment or instrument being repaired.

Officer/Enlisted: Enlisted

Personality Type: Realistic. Realistic occupations frequently involve work activities that include practical, hands-on problems and solutions. They often deal with plants; animals; and real-world materials such as wood, tools, and machinery. Many of the occupations require working outside and do not involve a lot of paperwork or working closely with others.

Services That Offer the Job: Air Force, Army, Coast Guard, Marines, Navy

What They Do. Electronic instrument and equipment repairers in the military perform some or all of the following duties:

- Maintain, test, adjust, and repair electronic equipment, using frequency meters, circuit analyzers, and other specialized test equipment.
- Install and repair circuits and wiring, using soldering iron and hand tools
- Install computers and other data-processing equipment
- Use technical guides and diagrams to locate defective parts and components of equipment
- String overhead communications and electric cables between utility polls
- Monitor the operation of air traffic control, missile tracking, air defense, and other radar systems to make sure there are no problems

Helpful Attributes. Helpful school subjects include math, electricity or electronic repair, shop mechanics, and physics. Helpful attributes include the following:

- Ability to apply electronic principles and concepts
- Interest in solving problems
- Interest in working with electrical, electronic, and electrochemical equipment

Training Provided. Job training consists of classroom instruction, including practice in repairing electronic instruments and equipment. Training length varies depending on specialty. Course content typically includes the following:

- Mechanical, electronic, and electrical principles
- Maintenance and repair procedures
- Line installation and wiring techniques
- Use of test equipment

Physical Demands. Normal color vision is required to work with color-coded wires. Some repairers may work from ladders or tall utility poles.

Work Environment. Electronic instrument and equipment repairers usually work in repair shops and laboratories on land or aboard ships.

Opportunities in the Military. The services have about 58,000 electronic instrument and equipment repairers. Each year, they need new repairers because of changes in personnel and the demands of the field. After job training, they are assigned to an operations or equipment maintenance unit, where they perform routine repair jobs. In time, they may perform more difficult repairs and supervise other repair personnel. Eventually, they may become supervisors or managers of electronic equipment maintenance units.

Civilian Occupations It Provides Training For (those with stars are described in Part IV): Aircraft Mechanics and Service Technicians*; Avionics Technicians*; Communications Equipment Operators, All Other; Computer Operators; Computer Security Specialists; Computer, Automated Teller, and Office Machine Repairers*; Electrical and Electronics Installers and Repairers, Transportation Equipment*; Electrical and Electronics Repairers, Commercial and Industrial Equipment*;

Electronic Equipment Installers and Repairers, Motor Vehicles; Electronic Home Entertainment Equipment Installers and Repairers; First-Line Supervisors/Managers of Mechanics, Installers, and Repairers*; First-Line Supervisors/Managers of Office and Administrative Support Workers*; Network and Computer Systems Administrators; Precision Instrument and Equipment Repairers, All Other; Radio Mechanics; Radio Operators; Telecommunications Equipment Installers and Repairers, Except Line Installers*; Telecommunications Line Installers and Repairers*.

Environmental Health and Safety Specialists

Each military base is a small community. The health and well-being of the residents and surrounding land is a major concern of the services. Keeping military workplaces and living areas sanitary helps to prevent illness. Environmental health and safety specialists inspect military facilities and food supplies for the presence of disease, germs, or other conditions hazardous to health and the environment.

Officer/Enlisted: Enlisted

Personality Type: Realistic. Realistic occupations frequently involve work activities that include practical, hands-on problems and solutions. They often deal with plants; animals; and real-world materials such as wood, tools, and machinery. Many of the occupations require working outside and do not involve a lot of paperwork or working closely with others.

Services That Offer the Job: Air Force, Army, Marines, Navy

What They Do. Environmental health and safety specialists in the military perform some or all of the following duties:

- Monitor storage, transportation, and disposal of hazardous waste
- Analyze food and water samples to ensure quality
- Conduct health and safety investigations of living quarters and base facilities
- Provide training on industrial hygiene, environmental health, and occupational health issues
- Monitor noise and radiation levels at job sites

Helpful Attributes. Helpful school subjects include algebra, biology, chemistry, and general science. Helpful attributes include the following:

- Interest in gathering information
- Interest in protecting the environment
- Preference for work requiring attention to detail

Training Provided. Job training consists of classroom instruction, including practice in making health and sanitation inspections. Further training occurs on the job and through advanced courses. Training length varies depending on specialty. Course content typically includes the following:

- Identification of health hazards
- Inspection of food products and food service operations
- Inspection of wastewater and waste disposal facilities

Physical Demands. No significant demands.

Work Environment. Environmental health specialists work indoors while inspecting food facilities and buildings. They work outdoors while inspecting waste disposal facilities and field camps.

Opportunities in the Military. The services have about 5,500 environmental health and safety specialists. Each year, they need new specialists because of changes in personnel and the demands of the field. After job training, environmental health and safety specialists help to make inspections. With experience, they work more independently and may supervise other environmental health and safety specialists. Eventually, they may become superintendents of environmental health programs at large military bases.

Civilian Occupations It Provides Training For (those with stars are described in Part IV): Agricultural Inspectors; Hazardous Materials Removal Workers*; Occupational Health and Safety Specialists; Occupational Health and Safety Technicians; Pest Control Workers*; Veterinary Assistants and Laboratory Animal Caretakers; Veterinary Technologists and Technicians.

Finance and Accounting Specialists

Millions of paychecks are issued and large amounts of materials are purchased by the services each year. To account for military spending, exact financial records must be kept of these transactions. Finance and accounting specialists organize and keep track of financial records. They also compute payrolls and other allowances, audit accounting records, and prepare payments for military personnel.

Officer/Enlisted: Enlisted

Personality Type: Conventional. Conventional occupations frequently involve following set procedures and routines. These occupations can include working with data and details more than with ideas. Usually there is a clear line of authority to follow.

Services That Offer the Job: Air Force, Army, Coast Guard, Marines, Navy

What They Do. Finance and accounting specialists in the military perform some or all of the following duties:

- Use computers to perform calculations, record details of financial transactions, and maintain accounting records
- Review or audit financial records to check the accuracy of figures and calculations
- Prepare paychecks, earnings statements, bills, and financial accounts and reports

- Disburse cash, checks, advance pay, and bonds
- Organize information on past expenses to help plan budgets for future expenses

Helpful Attributes. Helpful school subjects include mathematics, statistics, bookkeeping, and accounting. Helpful attributes include the following:

- Ability to work with numbers
- Interest in using office machines such as computers and calculators
- Interest in work requiring accuracy and attention to detail

Training Provided. Job training consists of classroom instruction, including practice in accounting techniques. Course content typically includes the following:

- Accounting principles and procedures
- Preparation and maintenance of financial reports and budgets
- Statistical analyses to interpret financial data
- Computation of pay and deductions

Physical Demands. No significant demands.

Work Environment. Finance and accounting specialists work in offices on land or aboard ships.

Special Requirements. Depending on the specialty, entry into this occupation may require courses in mathematics, bookkeeping, or accounting.

Opportunities in the Military. The services have over 10,000 finance and accounting specialists. Each year, they need new specialists because of changes in personnel and the demands of the field. After job training, finance and accounting specialists typically perform routine financial recording activities under the direction of supervisors. With experience, they are given more difficult tasks, such as auditing, and may become responsible for checking the work of others. In time, finance and accounting specialists may become supervisors or managers of accounting units or pay and finance centers.

Civilian Occupations It Provides Training For (those with stars are described in Part IV): Bookkeeping, Accounting, and Auditing Clerks*; First-Line Supervisors/Managers of Office and Administrative Support Workers*; Information and Record Clerks, All Other; Payroll and Timekeeping Clerks*; Procurement Clerks; Purchasing Agents, Except Wholesale, Retail, and Farm Products*; Tellers*.

Firefighters

Military bases have their own fire departments. Military firefighting units are responsible for protecting lives and property on base from fire. Firefighters put out, control, and help prevent fires in buildings, aircraft, and aboard ships.

Officer/Enlisted: Enlisted

Personality Type: Realistic. Realistic occupations frequently involve work activities that include practical, hands-on problems and solutions. They often deal with plants; animals; and real-world materials such as wood, tools, and machinery. Many of the occupations require working outside and do not involve a lot of paperwork or working closely with others.

Services That Offer the Job: Air Force, Army, Marines, Navy

What They Do. Firefighters in the military perform some or all of the following duties:

- Operate pumps, hoses, and extinguishers
- Force entry into aircraft, vehicles, and buildings in order to fight fires and rescue personnel
- Drive firefighting trucks and emergency rescue vehicles
- Give first aid to injured personnel
- Inspect aircraft, buildings, and equipment for fire hazards
- Teach fire protection procedures
- Repair firefighting equipment and fill fire extinguishers

Helpful Attributes. Helpful school subjects include health and general science. Helpful attributes include the following:

- Ability to remain calm under stress
- Ability to think and act decisively
- Willingness to risk injury to help others

Training Provided. Job training consists of classroom training, including practice in fighting fires. Further training occurs on the job. Course content typically includes the following:

- Types of fires
- Firefighting equipment operations
- Firefighting procedures
- First aid procedures
- Rescue procedures

Physical Demands. Good vision without glasses and a clear speaking voice are required to enter some specialties in this occupation. Firefighters have to climb ladders and stairs. They must also be able to lift and carry injured personnel.

Work Environment. Firefighters work indoors and outdoors while fighting fires. They are exposed to the smoke, heat, and flames of the fires they fight.

Opportunities in the Military. The services have about 8,000 firefighters. Each year, they need new firefighters because of changes in personnel and the demands of the field. After training, new firefighters perform work under close supervision. With experience, they work more independently and may supervise others. Eventually, they may become chiefs of base fire departments or similar units.

Civilian Occupations It Provides Training For (those with stars are described in Part IV): Emergency Management Specialists; Municipal Fire Fighters*; Municipal Fire Fighting and Prevention Supervisors*.

Flight Engineers

The military operates thousands of airplanes and helicopters. Pilots and air crew members rely upon trained personnel to keep aircraft ready to fly. Flight engineers inspect airplanes and helicopters before, during, and after flights to ensure safe and efficient operations. They also serve as crew members aboard military aircraft.

Officer/Enlisted: Enlisted

Personality Type: Realistic. Realistic occupations frequently involve work activities that include practical, hands-on problems and solutions. They often deal with plants; animals; and real-world materials such as wood, tools, and machinery. Many of the occupations require working outside and do not involve a lot of paperwork or working closely with others.

Services That Offer the Job: Air Force, Coast Guard, Marines, Navy

What They Do. Flight engineers in the military perform some or all of the following duties:

- Inspect aircraft before and after flights
- Plan and monitor the loading of passengers, cargo, and fuel
- Assist pilots in engine startup and shutdown
- Compute aircraft load weights and fuel distribution and consumption
- Monitor engine instruments and adjust controls, following pilot orders
- Check fuel, pressure, electrical, and other aircraft systems during flight
- Inform pilot of aircraft problems and recommend corrective action

Helpful Attributes. Helpful school subjects include general mathematics and shop mechanics. Helpful attributes include the following:

- Ability to work as a member of a team
- Interest in working with mechanical systems and equipment
- Skill in using wiring diagrams and maintenance manuals
- Strong desire to fly

Training Provided. Job training consists of classroom instruction and practical experience in aircraft inspection. Further training occurs on the job during flight operations. Course content typically includes the following:

- Operation of aircraft systems
- Inspection of aircraft engines, structures, and systems
- Preparation of records and logs

Physical Demands. Flight engineers, like pilots and navigators, have to be mentally alert and physically fit to perform their job. They must pass a special physical exam to qualify for flight duty.

Work Environment. Flight engineers live and work on air bases or aboard ships in all areas of the world. They fly in hot and cold climates and in all types of weather.

Opportunities in the Military. The services have about 3,000 flight engineers. Each year, they need new flight engineers because of changes in personnel and the demands of the field. After receiving their "air crew qualified" rating, they are assigned to an airplane or helicopter flying unit. With experience, they work more independently and may supervise or train others. They may become flight engineer chiefs or air crew chiefs.

Civilian Occupations It Provides Training For (those with stars are described in Part IV): Airline Pilots, Copilots, and Flight Engineers*; Commercial Pilots*.

Food Service Specialists

Every day, more than one million meals are prepared in military kitchens. Some kitchens prepare thousands of meals at one time, while others prepare food for small groups of people. Food service specialists prepare all types of food according to standard and dietetic recipes. They also order and inspect food supplies and prepare meats for cooking.

Officer/Enlisted: Enlisted

Personality Type: Realistic. Realistic occupations frequently involve work activities that include practical, hands-on problems and solutions. They often deal with plants; animals; and real-world materials such as wood, tools, and machinery. Many of the occupations require working outside and do not involve a lot of paperwork or working closely with others.

Services That Offer the Job: Air Force, Army, Coast Guard, Marines, Navy

What They Do. Food service specialists in the military perform some or all of the following duties:

- Order, receive, and inspect meat, fish, fruit, and vegetables
- Prepare standard cuts of meat, using cleavers, knives, and band saws
- Cook steaks, chops, and roasts

- Bake or fry chicken, turkey, and fish
- Prepare gravies and sauces
- Bake breads, cakes, pies, and pastries
- Serve food in dining halls, hospitals, or field kitchens or aboard ship
- Clean ovens, stoves, mixers, pots, and utensils

Helpful Attributes. Helpful school subjects include home economics, health, mathematics, accounting, and chemistry. Helpful attributes include the following:

- Interest in cooking
- Interest in working with the hands

Training Provided. Job training consists of classroom instruction, including practice in food preparation. Training length varies depending on specialty. Further training occurs on the job and through advanced courses. Course content typically includes the following:

- Standard and dietetic menus and recipes
- Preparation and cooking of various foodstuffs and bakery products
- Food and supply ordering
- Storage of meats, poultry, and other perishable items

Physical Demands. Food service specialists may have to lift and carry heavy containers of foodstuffs and large cooking utensils.

Work Environment. Food service specialists normally work in clean, sanitary kitchens and dining facilities. They may sometimes work in refrigerated meat lockers. Sometimes they work outdoors in tents while preparing and serving food under field conditions.

Opportunities in the Military. The services have about 28,000 food service specialists. Each year, they need new specialists because of changes in personnel and the demands of the field. After job training, food service specialists help prepare and serve food under close supervision. Some food service specialists specialize as bakers, cooks, butchers, or meat cutters. With experience, they work more independently and may train new food service specialists. Eventually, they may become head cooks, chefs, or food service supervisors.

Civilian Occupations It Provides Training For (those with stars are described in Part IV): Chefs and Head Cooks*; Combined Food Preparation and Serving Workers, Including Fast Food*; Cooks, Institution and Cafeteria; Cooks, Restaurant*; Cooks, Short Order*; First-Line Supervisors/Managers of Food Preparation and Serving Workers*; Food Preparation Workers*.

Graphic Designers and Illustrators

The military produces many publications, such as training manuals, newspapers, reports, and promotional materials. Graphic artwork is used in these publications and for signs, charts, posters, and TV and motion picture productions. Graphic designers and illustrators produce graphic artwork, drawings, and other visual displays.

Officer/Enlisted: Enlisted

Personality Type: Artistic. Artistic occupations frequently involve working with forms, designs, and patterns. They often require self-expression, and the work can be done without following a clear set of rules.

Services That Offer the Job: Air Force, Army, Marines, Navy

What They Do. Graphic designers and illustrators in the military perform some or all of the following duties:

- Produce computer-generated graphics
- Draw graphs and charts to represent budgets, numbers of troops, supply levels, and office organization
- Develop ideas and design posters and signs
- Help instructors design artwork for training courses
- Draw illustrations and cartoons for filmstrips and animation for films
- Make silkscreen prints
- Work with TV and film producers to design backdrops and props for film sets

Helpful Attributes. Helpful school subjects include art, drafting, and geometry. Helpful attributes include the following:

- Ability to convert ideas into visual presentations
- Interest in artwork or lettering
- Neatness and an eye for detail

Training Provided. Job training consists of classroom instruction, including practice in preparing graphic designs and illustrations. Further training occurs on the job. Course content typically includes the following:

- Introduction to graphics, lettering, drawing, and layout techniques
- Illustration and television graphic techniques
- Theory and use of color

Physical Demands. Coordination of eyes, hands, and fingers is needed to draw sketches. Normal color vision is required to work with paints and other art materials.

Work Environment. Graphic designers and illustrators usually work in offices on land or aboard ships.

Opportunities in the Military. The services have about 1,000 graphic designers and illustrators. Each year, they need new designers and illustrators because of changes in personnel and the demands of the field. After job training, graphic designers prepare tables, signs, and graphics under close supervision. With experience, they help formulate and produce more complex designs. In time, they may supervise others and lead large projects. Eventually, they may manage graphics departments.

Civilian Occupations It Provides Training For (those with stars are described in Part IV): Art Directors; Craft Artists; Desktop Publishers*; Fine Artists, Including Painters, Sculptors, and Illustrators; Graphic Designers*; Media and Communication Equipment Workers, All Other; Multi-Media Artists and Animators.

Heating and Cooling Mechanics

Air conditioning and heating equipment is used to maintain comfortable temperatures in military buildings, airplanes, and ships. Refrigeration equipment is used to keep food cold and to keep some missile fuels at sub-zero storage temperatures. Heating and cooling mechanics install and repair air conditioning, refrigeration, and heating equipment.

Officer/Enlisted: Enlisted

Personality Type: Realistic. Realistic occupations frequently involve work activities that include practical, hands-on problems and solutions. They often deal with plants; animals; and real-world materials such as wood, tools, and machinery. Many of the occupations require working outside and do not involve a lot of paperwork or working closely with others.

Services That Offer the Job: Air Force, Army, Coast Guard, Marines, Navy

What They Do. Heating and cooling mechanics in the military perform some or all of the following duties:

- Install and repair furnaces, boilers, and air conditioners
- Recharge cooling systems with refrigerant gases
- Install copper tubing systems that circulate water or cooling gases
- Replace compressor parts such as valves, pistons, bearings, and electrical motors on refrigeration units
- Repair thermostats and electrical circuits

Helpful Attributes. Helpful school subjects include science, math, and shop mechanics. Helpful attributes include the following:

- Ability to use hand and power tools
- Interest in solving problems
- Interest in working on machines

Training Provided. Job training consists of classroom instruction, including practice in repair work. Training length varies depending on specialty. Additional training is available on the job and in advanced courses. Course content typically includes the following:

- Refrigeration theory
- Installation and repair of refrigeration and air conditioning units
- Installation and repair of furnaces and boilers
- Use of diagrams and blueprints

Physical Demands. Heating and cooling mechanics may have to lift or move heavy equipment. They are often required to stoop, kneel, and work in cramped positions. Normal color vision is required for locating and repairing color-coded wiring.

Work Environment. Heating and cooling mechanics may work inside repair shops. Frequently, they work wherever equipment is to be installed or repaired.

Opportunities in the Military. The military has about 7,000 heating and cooling mechanics. Each year, the services need new mechanics because of changes in personnel and the demands of the field. After job training, mechanics maintain and repair equipment under supervision. With experience, they may learn to diagnose mechanical problems and perform complicated repairs. Eventually, they may become superintendents of utilities for large bases.

Civilian Occupations It Provides Training For (those with stars are described in Part IV): First-Line Supervisors/Managers of Mechanics, Installers, and Repairers*; Heating and Air Conditioning Mechanics and Installers*; Industrial Machinery Mechanics*; Pipelayers; Plumbers*; Refrigeration Mechanics and Installers*.

Helicopter Pilots

Helicopters can take off from and land on small areas. They can also hover in one spot in the air. The military uses these versatile aircraft to transport troops and cargo, perform search and rescue missions, and provide close combat support for ground troops. Helicopter pilots fly the many helicopters operated by the services.

Officer/Enlisted: Officer

Personality Type: Realistic. Realistic occupations frequently involve work activities that include practical, hands-on problems and solutions. They often deal with plants; animals; and real-world materials such as wood, tools, and machinery. Many of the occupations require working outside and do not involve a lot of paperwork or working closely with others.

Services That Offer the Job: Air Force, Army, Marines

What They Do. Helicopter pilots in the military perform some or all of the following duties:

- Prepare flight plans showing air routes and schedules
- Fly helicopters by controlling engines, flight controls, and other systems
- Monitor gauges and dials located on cockpit control panels
- Perform combat maneuvers, spot and observe enemy positions, transport troops and equipment, and evacuate wounded troops
- Check weather reports to learn about flying conditions

Helpful Attributes. Helpful fields of study include physics and aerospace, electrical, or mechanical engineering. Helpful attributes include the following:

- Determination to complete a very demanding training program
- Self-confidence and ability to remain calm under stress
- Strong desire to fly aircraft

Training Provided. Job training consists of academic and flight instruction. Flight training consists of at least 80 hours of flying time. Training length varies depending on specialty. Course content typically includes the following:

- Principles of helicopter operation
- Principles of helicopter inspection
- Flying techniques and emergency procedures
- Combat skills and tactics

Physical Demands. Helicopter pilots must pass some of the most demanding physical tests of any job in the military. To be accepted for pilot training, applicants must have excellent vision and be in top physical condition. They must have very good eye-hand-foot coordination and have quick reflexes.

Work Environment. Helicopter pilots are stationed at military bases or aboard aircraft carriers around the world. They fly in all types of weather conditions. Helicopter pilots take off and land from airports, forward landing areas, and ship landing decks.

Special Requirements. A 4-year college degree is normally required to enter this occupation. Some specialties in the Army do not require a 4-year college degree, but are only open to personnel who have been in the service for several years and who are selected for a special pilot training program. Although there are women helicopter pilots, some specialties are open only to men.

Opportunities in the Military. The military has about 6,500 helicopter pilots. The services need new pilots each year because of changes in personnel and the demands of the field. After receiving their pilot rating, helicopter pilots are assigned to flying units. With experience, they may become group leaders or flight instructors. Helicopter pilots may advance to senior management and command positions.

Civilian Occupations It Provides Training For (those with stars are described in Part IV): Airline Pilots, Copilots, and Flight Engineers*; Commercial Pilots*.

Intelligence Specialists

Military intelligence is information needed to plan for our national defense. Knowledge of the number, location, and tactics of enemy forces and potential battle areas is needed to develop military plans. To gather information, the services rely on aerial photographs; electronic monitoring, using radar and sensitive radios; and human observation. Intelligence specialists gather and study the information required to design defense plans and tactics.

Officer/Enlisted: Enlisted

Personality Type: Investigative. Investigative occupations frequently involve working with ideas and require an extensive amount of thinking. These occupations can involve searching for facts and figuring out problems mentally.

Services That Offer the Job: Air Force, Army, Coast Guard, Marines, Navy

What They Do. Intelligence specialists in the military perform some or all of the following duties:

- Study aerial photographs of foreign ships, bases, and missile sites
- Study foreign troop movements
- Operate sensitive radios to intercept foreign military communications
- Study land and sea areas that could become battlegrounds in time of war
- Store and retrieve intelligence data, using computers
- Study foreign military codes
- Prepare intelligence reports, maps, and charts
- Install, operate, and conduct preventive maintenance of associated equipment and facilities
- Conduct investigations to detect, identify, assess, counter, exploit, and neutralize threats to national security
- Collect human intelligence (HUMINT) by interviewing, interrogating, or otherwise interacting directly with human sources of information

Helpful Attributes. Helpful school subjects include algebra, geometry, trigonometry, and geography. Helpful attributes include the following:

- Ability to organize information
- Ability to think and write clearly
- Interest in gathering information and studying its meaning
- Interest in reading maps and charts

Training Provided. Job training consists of classroom instruction, including practice in intelligence gathering. Training length varies depending on specialty. Further training occurs on the job and through advanced courses. Course content typically includes the following:

- Planning aerial and satellite observations
- Preparing intelligence reports, maps, and charts
- Analyzing aerial photographs
- Using computer systems

Physical Demands. No significant demands.

Work Environment. Intelligence specialists work in offices on land and aboard ships and in tents when in the field.

Opportunities in the Military. The services have more than 26,000 intelligence specialists. Each year, they need new specialists because of changes in personnel and the demands of the field. After job training, they collect information and prepare maps and charts under close supervision. With experience, they are given more responsibility for organizing intelligence data. Eventually, they may become chiefs of intelligence units.

Civilian Occupations It Provides Training For (those with stars are described in Part IV): Cartographers and Photogrammetrists; Communications Equipment Operators, All Other; Computer Security Specialists; Interpreters and Translators*; Management Analysts; Mapping Technicians*; Mathematicians; Network and Computer Systems Administrators; Social Scientists and Related Workers, All Other; Surveyors.

Interpreters and Translators

Some members of the military must be able to read and understand the many languages of the world. Information from foreign language newspapers, magazines, and radio broadcasts is important to the nation's defense. Interpreters and translators convert written or spoken foreign languages into English or other languages. They usually specialize in a particular foreign language.

Officer/Enlisted: Enlisted

Personality Type: Conventional. Conventional occupations frequently involve following set procedures and routines. These occupations can include working with data and details more than with ideas. Usually there is a clear line of authority to follow.

Services That Offer the Job: Air Force, Army, Marines, Navy

What They Do. Interpreters and translators in the military perform some or all of the following duties:

- Translate written and spoken foreign-language material to and from English, making sure to preserve the original meaning
- Interview prisoners of war, enemy deserters, and civilian informers in their native languages
- Record foreign radio transmissions, using sensitive communications equipment
- Prepare written reports about the information obtained
- Translate foreign documents, such as battle plans and personnel records
- Translate foreign books and articles describing foreign equipment and construction techniques
- Install, operate, and maintain electronic equipment used to intercept foreign communications

Helpful Attributes. Helpful school subjects include speech, communications, and foreign languages. Helpful attributes include the following:

- Interest in reading and writing
- Interest in working with people
- Talent for foreign languages

Training Provided. Job training consists of classroom instruction, including practice in interpretation. Training length varies depending on specialty. Longer training is necessary for specialties that do not require foreign language fluency prior to entry. For these specialties, foreign language training for 6 to 12 months is provided. Further training occurs on the job and through advanced courses. Course content typically includes the following:

- Interrogation (questioning) methods
- Use and care of communications equipment
- Procedures for preparing reports

Physical Demands. Normal hearing and the ability to speak clearly and distinctly are usually required to enter this occupation.

Work Environment. Interpreters and translators normally work on military bases, aboard ships, or in airplanes.

Special Requirements. Fluency in a foreign language is required to enter most specialties within this occupation.

Opportunities in the Military. The military has about 8,000 interpreters and translators. Each year, the services need new interpreters and translators because of changes in personnel and the demands of the field. After job training, interpreters and translators work under the direction of more experienced workers and supervisors. With experience, they work more independently. In time, interpreters and translators may become directors of translation for large bases.

Civilian Occupations It Provides Training For (those with stars are described in Part IV): Interpreters and Translators*; Office Clerks, General*.

Law Enforcement and Security Specialists

The military services have their own law enforcement and police forces. These specialists investigate crimes committed on military property or that involve military personnel. Military police do many of the same things as civilian officers—control traffic, prevent crime, and respond to emergencies. They also guard military bases and inmates in military correctional facilities.

Officer/Enlisted: Enlisted

Personality Type: Enterprising. Enterprising occupations frequently involve starting up and carrying out projects. These occupations can involve leading people and making many decisions. They sometimes require risk taking and often deal with business.

Services That Offer the Job: Air Force, Army, Coast Guard, Marines, Navy

What They Do. Law enforcement and security specialists in the military perform some or all of the following duties:

- Investigate criminal activities and activities related to espionage, treason, and terrorism
- Interview witnesses and arrest suspects
- Guard correctional facilities and other military installations
- Patrol areas on foot, by car, or by boat
- Perform fire and riot control duties

Helpful Attributes. Helpful school subjects include government and speech. Helpful attributes include the following:

- Ability to remain calm under pressure
- Interest in law enforcement and crime prevention
- Willingness to perform potentially dangerous work

Training Provided. Job training consists of classroom instruction. Training length varies depending on specialty. Course content typically includes the following:

- Civil and military laws
- Investigation and evidence collection procedures and techniques
- Prisoner control and discipline

- Use of firearms and hand-to-hand defense techniques
- Traffic and crowd control procedures

Physical Demands. Normal color vision is necessary to enter some specialties in this area. Some specialties have minimum age and height requirements.

Work Environment. Law enforcement and security specialists in the military work both indoors and outdoors depending on their assignment. They may work outdoors while conducting investigations or patrolling facilities.

Opportunities in the Military. The military has about 30,000 law enforcement and security specialists. Each year, the services need new specialists because of changes in personnel and the demands of the field. After job training, they work under the direction of more experienced specialists. In time, they may supervise and train new workers or lead investigations. Eventually, they may become chiefs of detectives, chiefs of police, or superintendents of correctional facilities.

Civilian Occupations It Provides Training For (those with stars are described in Part IV): Correctional Officers and Jailers*; Criminal Investigators and Special Agents*; First-Line Supervisors/Managers of Police and Detectives*; Lifeguards, Ski Patrol, and Other Recreational Protective Service Workers*; Police and Sheriff's Patrol Officers; Police Detectives*; Police Patrol Officers*; Security Guards*; Sheriffs and Deputy Sheriffs*; Transit and Railroad Police*.

Legal Specialists and Court Reporters

The military has its own judicial system for prosecuting lawbreakers and handling disputes. Legal specialists and court reporters assist military lawyers and judges in the performance of legal and judicial work. They perform legal research, prepare legal documents, and record legal proceedings.

Officer/Enlisted: Enlisted

Personality Type: Conventional. Conventional occupations frequently involve following set procedures and routines. These occupations can include working with data and details more than with ideas. Usually there is a clear line of authority to follow.

Services That Offer the Job: Air Force, Army, Marines, Navy

What They Do. Legal specialists and court reporters in the military perform some or all of the following duties:

- Research court decisions and military regulations
- Process legal claims and appeals
- Interview clients and take statements
- Prepare trial requests and make arrangements for courtrooms
- Maintain law libraries and trial case files

- Use a variety of methods and equipment to record and transcribe court proceedings
- Prepare records of hearings, investigations, court-martials, and courts of inquiry

Helpful Attributes. Helpful school subjects include business mathematics, typing, speech, and shorthand. Helpful attributes include the following:

- Ability to keep organized and accurate records
- Ability to listen carefully
- Interest in the law and legal proceedings

Training Provided. Job training consists of classroom instruction. Course content typically includes the following:

- Legal terminology and research techniques
- How to prepare legal documents
- High-speed transcription
- Military judicial processes

Physical Demands. Good hearing and clear speech are needed to record and read aloud court proceedings. A clear speaking ability is necessary to interview clients.

Work Environment. Legal specialists and court reporters work in military law offices and courtrooms.

Special Requirements. Some specialties require the ability to type at a rate of 25–50 words per minute.

Opportunities in the Military. The services have about 3,000 legal specialists and court reporters. Each year, they need new specialists and court reporters because of changes in personnel and the demands of the field. After training, they normally work under an attorney or in a legal office. With experience, legal specialists and court reporters perform more demanding activities and may supervise other specialists.

Civilian Occupations It Provides Training For (those with stars are described in Part IV): Court Reporters*; Law Clerks; Legal Secretaries*; Paralegals and Legal Assistants*.

Machinists

Sometimes when engines or machines break down, the parts needed to repair them are not available. In these cases, the broken parts must be repaired or new ones made. Machinists make and repair metal parts for engines and all types of machines. They operate lathes, drill presses, grinders, and other machine shop equipment.

Officer/Enlisted: Enlisted

Personality Type: Realistic. Realistic occupations frequently involve work activities that include practical, hands-on problems and solutions. They often deal with plants; animals; and real-world materials such as wood, tools, and machinery. Many of the occupations require working outside and do not involve a lot of paperwork or working closely with others.

Services That Offer the Job: Army, Coast Guard, Marines, Navy

What They Do. Machinists in the military perform some or all of the following duties:

- Study blueprints or written plans of the parts to be made
- Set up and operate lathes to make parts such as shafts and gears
- Cut metal stock, using power hacksaws and band saws
- Bore holes, using drill presses
- Shape and smooth parts, using grinders
- Measure work, using micrometers, calipers, and depth gauges

Helpful Attributes. Helpful school subjects include math, general science, metalworking, and mechanical drawing. Helpful attributes include the following:

- Ability to apply mathematical formulas
- Interest in making things and finding solutions to mechanical problems
- Preference for working with the hands

Training Provided. Job training consists of classroom instruction, including practice in machine operation. Further training occurs on the job and through advanced courses. Course content typically includes the following:

- Machine types and uses
- Machine setup and operation
- Uses of different metals
- Safety procedures

Physical Demands. No significant demands.

Work Environment. Machinists work in machine shops, which are often noisy.

Opportunities in the Military. The services have about 2,000 machinists. Each year, they need new machinists because of changes in personnel and the demands of the field. After job training, machinists perform routine repairs under close supervision. In time, they perform more difficult repairs and may train others. Eventually, they may become managers of one or more machine shops.

Civilian Occupations It Provides Training For (those with stars are described in Part IV): Computer-Controlled Machine Tool Operators, Metal and Plastic; Industrial Machinery Mechanics*;

Machinists*; Numerical Tool and Process Control Programmers; Structural Metal Fabricators and Fitters.

Marine Engine Mechanics

The military operates many types of watercraft, from small motor launches to large ships. Many of these vessels are powered by gasoline or diesel engines. Marine engine mechanics repair and maintain gasoline and diesel engines on ships, boats, and other watercraft. They also repair shipboard mechanical and electrical equipment.

Officer/Enlisted: Enlisted

Personality Type: Realistic. Realistic occupations frequently involve work activities that include practical, hands-on problems and solutions. They often deal with plants; animals; and real-world materials such as wood, tools, and machinery. Many of the occupations require working outside and do not involve a lot of paperwork or working closely with others.

Services That Offer the Job: Army, Coast Guard, Marines, Navy

What They Do. Marine engine mechanics in the military perform some or all of the following duties:

- Repair and maintain shipboard gasoline and diesel engines
- Locate and repair machinery parts, including valves and piping systems
- Repair ship propulsion machinery
- Repair and service hoisting machinery and ship elevators
- Repair refrigeration and air conditioning equipment on ships
- Repair engine-related electrical systems

Helpful Attributes. Helpful school subjects include shop mechanics. Helpful attributes include the following:

- Ability to use hand and power tools
- Interest in fixing engines and machinery
- Preference for doing physical work

Training Provided. Job training consists of classroom instruction, including practice in marine engine maintenance and repair. Training length varies depending on specialty. Further training occurs on the job and through advanced courses. Course content typically includes the following:

- Internal combustion engine theory
- Repair of shipboard electronic and electrical machinery systems
- Service and repair of fuel injection systems
- Use and care of hand and power tools

Physical Demands. Normal color vision is required to work with color-coded diagrams and wiring.

Work Environment. Marine engine mechanics work aboard ships, normally in the engine or power rooms. Sometimes they work in repair centers on land bases. Working conditions in engine rooms tend to be noisy and hot.

Opportunities in the Military. The military has about 7,000 marine engine mechanics. Each year, the services need new mechanics because of changes in personnel and the demands of the field. After job training, they work under close supervision in repair centers or shipboard engine rooms. With experience, they work more independently and may supervise other mechanics. In time, marine engine mechanics may become supervisors of marine engine repair centers or shipboard maintenance sections.

Civilian Occupations It Provides Training For (those with stars are described in Part IV): Bus and Truck Mechanics and Diesel Engine Specialists*; Electrical and Electronics Repairers, Commercial and Industrial Equipment*; Elevator Installers and Repairers*; Industrial Machinery Mechanics*; Maintenance and Repair Workers, General*; Mobile Heavy Equipment Mechanics, Except Engines*; Motorboat Mechanics*; Power Plant Operators*; Ship Engineers.

Medical Care Technicians

The military provides medical care to all men and women in the services. Medical care technicians work with teams of physicians, nurses, and other health care professionals to provide treatment to patients. They help give patients the care and treatment required to help them recover from illness or injury. They also prepare rooms, equipment, and supplies in hospitals and medical clinics.

Officer/Enlisted: Enlisted

Personality Type: Realistic. Realistic occupations frequently involve work activities that include practical, hands-on problems and solutions. They often deal with plants; animals; and real-world materials such as wood, tools, and machinery. Many of the occupations require working outside and do not involve a lot of paperwork or working closely with others.

Services That Offer the Job: Air Force, Army, Coast Guard, Navy

What They Do. Medical care technicians in the military perform some or all of the following duties:

- Provide bedside care in hospitals, including taking the body temperature, pulse, and respiration rate of patients
- Feed, bathe, and dress patients
- Prepare patients, operating rooms, equipment, and supplies for surgery
- Make casts, traction devices, and splints according to physicians' instructions
- Give medication to patients under the direction of physicians and nurses

Helpful Attributes. Helpful school subjects include general science, biology, and psychology. Helpful attributes include the following:

- Ability to follow directions precisely
- Ability to work under stressful or emergency conditions
- Interest in helping others

Training Provided. Job training consists of classroom instruction, including practice in patient care. Training length varies depending on specialty. Further training occurs on the job and through advanced courses. Course content may include

- Patient care techniques
- Emergency medical techniques
- Methods of sterilizing surgical equipment
- Plaster casting techniques

Physical Demands. No significant demands.

Work Environment. Medical care technicians work in hospitals and clinics on land or aboard ships. In combat situations, they may work in mobile field hospitals.

Opportunities in the Military. The services have about 10,000 medical care technicians. Each year, they need new technicians because of changes in personnel and the demands of the field. After job training, new technicians are assigned to hospitals or medical units, where they work under close supervision. In time, they may advance to supervisory positions and help train others.

Civilian Occupations It Provides Training For (those with stars are described in Part IV): Diagnostic Medical Sonographers; Health Technologists and Technicians, All Other; Licensed Practical and Licensed Vocational Nurses*; Medical Appliance Technicians; Medical Assistants*; Medical Equipment Preparers*; Medical Equipment Repairers*; Medical Records and Health Information Technicians*; Nuclear Medicine Technologists; Nursing Aides, Orderlies, and Attendants*; Orthotists and Prosthetists*; Psychiatric Technicians; Respiratory Therapy Technicians; Surgical Technologists*.

Medical Laboratory Technicians

Medical laboratories are an important part of the military health care system. The staffs of medical laboratories perform clinical tests required to detect and identify diseases in patients. Medical laboratory technicians conduct tests on the tissue, blood, and body fluids of medical patients.

Officer/Enlisted: Enlisted

Personality Type: Realistic. Realistic occupations frequently involve work activities that include practical, hands-on problems and solutions. They often deal with plants; animals; and real-world materials such as wood, tools, and machinery. Many of the occupations require working outside and do not involve a lot of paperwork or working closely with others.

Services That Offer the Job: Air Force, Army, Navy

What They Do. Medical laboratory technicians in the military perform some or all of the following duties:

- Use lab equipment to analyze specimens (samples) of tissue, blood, and body fluids
- Examine blood and bone marrow under microscopes
- Test specimens for bacteria or viruses
- Draw blood from patients
- Assist in collecting specimens at autopsies (medical examinations of the dead)
- Record and file results of laboratory tests

Helpful Attributes. Helpful school subjects include biology, chemistry, and algebra. Helpful attributes include the following:

- Ability to follow detailed procedures precisely
- Interest in scientific and technical work

Training Provided. Job training consists of classroom and on-the-job instruction, including practice in testing specimens. Training length varies depending on specialty. Course content typically includes the following:

- Medical laboratory procedures
- Study of human parasites and diseases
- Laboratory administration and record keeping

Physical Demands. No significant demands.

Work Environment. Medical laboratory technicians work in medical centers, clinics, and hospitals on land or aboard ships.

Opportunities in the Military. The military has about 5,000 medical laboratory technicians. Each year, the services need new technicians because of changes in personnel and the demands of the field. After job training, technicians perform routine laboratory tests under close supervision. With experience, they do more complex testing and analysis and work more independently. After demonstrating job proficiency, medical laboratory technicians help train new technicians and supervise laboratory personnel. In time, they may advance to laboratory management positions.

Civilian Occupations It Provides Training For (those with stars are described in Part IV): Biological Technicians*; Chemical Technicians*; Medical and Clinical Laboratory Technicians*; Medical and Clinical Laboratory Technologists.

Medical Record Technicians

Medical records are important for health care delivery. To provide proper treatment, physicians need complete and accurate information about patient symptoms, test results, illnesses, and prior treatments. Medical record technicians prepare and maintain patient records, reports, and correspondence.

Officer/Enlisted: Enlisted

Personality Type: Conventional. Conventional occupations frequently involve following set procedures and routines. These occupations can include working with data and details more than with ideas. Usually there is a clear line of authority to follow.

Services That Offer the Job: Air Force, Army, Navy

What They Do. Medical record technicians in the military perform some or all of the following duties:

- Fill out admission and discharge records for patients entering and leaving military hospitals
- Assign patients to hospital rooms
- Prepare daily reports about patients admitted and discharged
- Organize, file, and maintain medical records
- Prepare reports about physical examinations, illnesses, and treatments
- Prepare tables of medical statistics
- Maintain libraries of medical publications

Helpful Attributes. Helpful school subjects include general science and business administration. Helpful attributes include the following:

- Ability to communicate well
- Interest in using computers and other office machines
- Interest in work requiring accuracy and attention to detail

Training Provided. Job training consists of classroom instruction. Training length varies depending on specialty. Course content typically includes the following:

- Basic computer skills
- Medical terminology
- Medical records preparation and maintenance
- Maintenance of medical libraries

Physical Demands. No significant demands.

Work Environment. Medical record technicians work in admissions or medical records sections of hospitals and clinics. They work in land-based facilities and aboard ships.

Opportunities in the Military. The services have about 5,000 medical record technicians. Each year, they need new technicians because of changes in personnel and the demands of the field. After training, new technicians are assigned to hospitals or clinics, where they work under close supervision. With experience, they may assume supervisory positions and may manage medical record units or admission or discharge units.

Civilian Occupations It Provides Training For (those with stars are described in Part IV): First-Line Supervisors/Managers of Office and Administrative Support Workers*; Medical Records and Health Information Technicians*; Physician Assistants.

Medical Service Technicians

In emergencies or in combat, physicians are not always immediately available to treat the injured or wounded. When a physician is not available, medical service technicians provide basic and emergency medical treatment. They also assist medical officers in caring for sick and injured patients.

Officer/Enlisted: Enlisted

Personality Type: Social. Social occupations frequently involve working with, communicating with, and teaching people. These occupations often involve helping or providing service to others.

Services That Offer the Job: Air Force, Army, Coast Guard, Navy

What They Do. Medical service technicians in the military perform some or all of the following duties:

- Examine and treat emergency or battlefield patients
- Interview patients and record their medical histories
- Take patients' temperature, pulse, and blood pressure
- Prepare blood samples for laboratory analysis
- Keep health records and clinical files up to date
- Give shots and medicines to patients

Helpful Attributes. Helpful school subjects include chemistry, biology, psychology, general science, and algebra. Helpful attributes include the following:

- Ability to communicate effectively
- Ability to work under stressful conditions
- Interest in helping others

Training Provided. Job training consists of classroom instruction, depending on specialty. Further training occurs on the job and through advanced courses. Course content typically includes the following:

- Emergency medical treatment
- Basic nursing care
- Study of the human body
- Minor surgical procedures
- Clinical laboratory procedures
- Methods for diagnosing diseases

Physical Demands. No significant demands.

Work Environment. Medical service technicians usually work in hospitals and clinics on land or aboard ships. Medical service technicians may give emergency medical treatment in the field.

Opportunities in the Military. The services have about 27,000 medical service technicians. Each year, they need new technicians because of changes in personnel and the demands of the field. After job training, technicians are assigned to serve in their medical specialty. They work under the direction and supervision of medical officers and experienced medical service technicians. Eventually, they may advance to supervisory positions and help manage a medical facility.

Civilian Occupations It Provides Training For (those with stars are described in Part IV): Emergency Medical Technicians and Paramedics*; Healthcare Practitioners and Technical Workers, All Other; Human Resources, Training, and Labor Relations Specialists, All Other; Medical and Health Services Managers; Medical Assistants*; Medical Equipment Preparers*; Occupational Health and Safety Specialists; Occupational Therapist Assistants*.

Musicians

Music is an important part of military life. Service bands and vocal groups have a strong tradition of performing at ceremonies, parades, concerts, festivals, and dances. Musicians and singers perform in service bands, orchestras, and small groups. They perform many types of music, including marches, classics, jazz, and popular music.

Officer/Enlisted: Enlisted

Personality Type: Artistic. Artistic occupations frequently involve working with forms, designs, and patterns. They often require self-expression, and the work can be done without following a clear set of rules.

Services That Offer the Job: Air Force, Army, Coast Guard, Marines, Navy

What They Do. Musicians in the military perform some or all of the following duties:

- Play in or lead bands, orchestras, combos, and jazz groups
- Sing in choral groups or as soloists
- Perform for ceremonies, parades, concerts, festivals, and dances
- Rehearse and learn new music when not performing
- Play brass, percussion, woodwind, or string instruments

Helpful Attributes. Helpful school subjects include band, music theory, harmony, and other music courses. Helpful attributes include the following:

- Ability to play more than one instrument
- Ability to sing
- Poise when performing in public

Training Provided. Although musicians must be musically proficient to enter the service, music training is given to new band members. Job training consists of classroom instruction, including practice playing instruments. Training length varies depending on musical specialty. Further training occurs on the job through regular rehearsals and individual practice. Course content typically includes the following:

- Music theory
- Group instrumental techniques
- Sight-reading musical scores
- Dance band techniques

Physical Demands. No significant demands.

Work Environment. Musicians play indoors in theaters, concert halls, and at dances and outdoors at parades and open-air concerts. They also travel regularly.

Special Requirements. To qualify for a service band, applicants must pass one or more auditions. They must be fairly accomplished musicians and be able to sight-read musical notations.

Opportunities in the Military. The services have more than 4,000 musicians. Each year, they need new musicians because of changes in personnel and the demands of the field. After job training, musicians are assigned to band units located with U.S. forces around the world. They perform as members of bands and vocal groups. In time, they may become heads of their instrument sections and, possibly, bandleaders or orchestra conductors. The most outstanding performers are selected for the official service bands or orchestras of their service.

Civilian Occupations It Provides Training For (those with stars are described in Part IV): Music Composers and Arrangers*; Music Directors; Musicians and Singers; Musicians, Instrumental; Singers.

Non-Destructive Testers

Military equipment is often placed under heavy stress. An airplane's landing gear absorbs heavy runway impact. Submarine hulls withstand tremendous pressure in the ocean depths. In time, stress may cause structural weakening or damage. Non-destructive testers examine metal parts for stress damage. They use X rays, ultrasonics, and other testing methods that do not damage (are non-destructive to) the parts tested.

Officer/Enlisted: Enlisted

Personality Type: Realistic. Realistic occupations frequently involve work activities that include practical, hands-on problems and solutions. They often deal with plants; animals; and real-world materials such as wood, tools, and machinery. Many of the occupations require working outside and do not involve a lot of paperwork or working closely with others.

Services That Offer the Job: Air Force, Army, Marines, Navy

What They Do. Non-destructive testers in the military perform some or all of the following duties:

- Inspect metal parts and joints for wear and damage
- Take X rays of aircraft and ship parts
- Examine X-ray film to detect cracks and flaws in metal parts and welds
- Operate ultrasonic, atomic absorption, and other kinds of test equipment
- Conduct oil analysis and heat damage tests to detect engine wear
- Prepare inspection reports

Helpful Attributes. Helpful school subjects include math and metal shop. Helpful attributes include the following:

- Interest in machines and how they work
- Thoroughness and dependability
- Interest in operating test equipment

Training Provided. Job training consists of classroom instruction, including practice in testing metal parts. Course content typically includes the following:

- Methods for inspecting parts and welds
- Operation of X-ray and film processing equipment
- Operation of ultrasonic test equipment
- Preparation of test reports

Physical Demands. No significant demands.

Work Environment. Non-destructive testers work indoors in laboratories and aircraft hangars. They also work outdoors in shipyards and in the field.

Opportunities in the Military. The military has about 1,500 non-destructive testers. Each year, the services need new testers because of changes in personnel and the demands of the field. After job training, testers are assigned to testing units, where they perform tests under supervision. With experience, they work more independently. In time, non-destructive testers may become supervisors of testing laboratories or maintenance units.

Civilian Occupations It Provides Training For (those with stars are described in Part IV): Aerospace Engineering and Operations Technicians*; Aircraft Mechanics and Service Technicians*; Chemical Technicians*; Electrical and Electronics Repairers, Commercial and Industrial Equipment*; Engineering Technicians, Except Drafters, All Other; Inspectors, Testers, Sorters, Samplers, and Weighers*; Mechanical Engineering Technicians*; Nuclear Equipment Operation Technicians*; Petroleum Pump System Operators, Refinery Operators, and Gaugers*; Precision Instrument and Equipment Repairers, All Other.

Optometric Technicians

Optometry, or vision care, is one of the many health benefits available to military personnel. The military operates its own clinics to examine eyes and fit glasses or contact lenses. Optometric technicians assist optometrists in providing vision care. They work with patients and manage clinic offices.

Officer/Enlisted: Enlisted

Personality Type: Realistic. Realistic occupations frequently involve work activities that include practical, hands-on problems and solutions. They often deal with plants; animals; and real-world materials such as wood, tools, and machinery. Many of the occupations require working outside and do not involve a lot of paperwork or working closely with others.

Services That Offer the Job: Air Force, Army, Navy

What They Do. Optometric technicians in the military perform some or all of the following duties:

- Use and maintain ophthalmic instruments and equipment
- Perform screening tests
- Order eyeglasses and contact lenses from prescriptions
- Fit eyeglasses to patients
- Make minor repairs to glasses
- Place eye drops and ointment into patients' eyes
- Keep records in optometry offices

Helpful Attributes. Helpful school subjects include algebra, geometry, biology, and related courses. Helpful attributes include the following:

- Ability to communicate effectively
- Interest in work requiring accuracy and attention to detail

Training Provided. Job training consists of classroom instruction, including practice in optometric procedures. Further training occurs on the job. Course content typically includes the following:

- Preparing and fitting glasses and contact lenses
- Vision testing
- Maintenance of optometric instruments

Physical Demands. No significant demands.

Work Environment. Optometric technicians normally work in optometric clinics.

Opportunities in the Military. The services have more than 500 optometric technicians. Each year, they need new technicians because of changes in personnel and the demands of the field. After training, new technicians give simple vision tests under close supervision and perform office duties. As they gain experience, they work with less supervision and perform more difficult tasks. In time, they may help to manage optometric clinics.

Civilian Occupations It Provides Training For (those with stars are described in Part IV): Medical Assistants*; Medical Equipment Preparers*; Ophthalmic Laboratory Technicians; Opticians, Dispensing.

Ordnance Specialists

Ordnance is a military term for ammunition and weapons. Ordnance includes all types of ammunition, missiles, toxic chemicals, and nuclear weapons. Ammunition and weapons must be handled carefully and stored properly. Ordnance specialists transport, store, inspect, prepare, and dispose of weapons and ammunition.

Officer/Enlisted: Enlisted

Personality Type: Realistic. Realistic occupations frequently involve work activities that include practical, hands-on problems and solutions. They often deal with plants; animals; and real-world materials such as wood, tools, and machinery. Many of the occupations require working outside and do not involve a lot of paperwork or working closely with others.

Services That Offer the Job: Air Force, Army, Marines, Navy

What They Do. Ordnance specialists in the military perform some or all of the following duties:

- Load nuclear and conventional explosives and ammunition on aircraft, ships, and submarines
- Inspect mounted guns, bomb release systems, and missile launchers

- Assemble and load explosives
- Defuse unexploded bombs
- Locate, identify, and dispose of chemical munitions

Helpful Attributes. Helpful school subjects include general science and shop mechanics. Helpful attributes include the following:

- Ability to remain calm under stress
- Interest in working with guns and explosives

Training Provided. Job training consists of classroom instruction, including practice in ordnance maintenance. Training length varies depending on specialty. Further training occurs on the job and through advanced courses. Course content typically includes the following:

- Maintenance of nuclear weapons
- Handling, testing, and maintenance of missiles and rockets

Physical Demands. No significant demands.

Work Environment. Ordnance specialists work indoors and outdoors. They work in repair shops while assembling explosives and repairing weapons. They work outdoors while repairing equipment in the field and loading weapons on tanks, ships, or aircraft.

Opportunities in the Military. The services have about 16,000 ordnance specialists. Each year, they need new ordnance specialists because of changes in personnel and the demands of the field. After job training, ordnance specialists work under close supervision. With experience, they perform more complex duties. In time, they may become trainers or supervisors. Eventually, they may become managers of weapons maintenance units.

Civilian Occupations It Provides Training For (those with stars are described in Part IV): Commercial Divers; Earth Drillers, Except Oil and Gas; Electrical and Electronics Repairers, Commercial and Industrial Equipment*; Emergency Management Specialists; Explosives Workers, Ordnance Handling Experts, and Blasters; First-Line Supervisors/Managers of Mechanics, Installers, and Repairers*; Installation, Maintenance, and Repair Workers, All Other; Maintenance and Repair Workers, General*; Rock Splitters, Quarry.

Personnel Specialists

Personnel management helps individuals develop their military careers. It also serves the military's need to fill jobs with qualified workers. Personnel specialists collect and store information about the people in the military, such as training, job assignment, promotion, and health information. They work directly with service personnel and their families.

Officer/Enlisted: Enlisted

Personality Type: Conventional. Conventional occupations frequently involve following set procedures and routines. These occupations can include working with data and details more than with ideas. Usually there is a clear line of authority to follow.

Services That Offer the Job: Air Force, Army, Coast Guard, Marines, Navy

What They Do. Personnel specialists in the military perform some or all of the following duties:

- Organize, maintain, and review personnel records
- Enter and retrieve personnel information, using computer terminals
- Assign personnel to jobs
- Prepare correspondence, organizational charts, and reports
- Provide career guidance
- Assist personnel and their families who have special needs

Helpful Attributes. Helpful school subjects include English, speech, and business administration. Helpful attributes include the following:

- Ability to compose clear instructions or correspondence
- Ability to follow detailed procedures and instructions
- Interest in working closely with others

Training Provided. Job training consists of classroom instruction. Further training occurs on the job and through advanced courses. Course content typically includes the following:

- Preparation of military correspondence and forms
- Personnel records management
- Computer update and retrieval procedures

Physical Demands. No significant demands.

Work Environment. Personnel specialists normally work in office settings on land or aboard ships.

Opportunities in the Military. The services have about 20,000 personnel specialists. Each year, they need new specialists because of changes in personnel and the demands of the field. After job training, specialists process personnel actions and add information to records. In time, they may supervise other personnel specialists and eventually may manage personnel offices.

Civilian Occupations It Provides Training For (those with stars are described in Part IV): Compensation, Benefits, and Job Analysis Specialists; Computer Operators; Employment, Recruitment, and Placement Specialists; First-Line Supervisors/Managers of Office and Administrative Support Workers*; Human Resources Assistants, Except Payroll and Timekeeping*; Human Resources, Training, and Labor Relations Specialists, All Other; Management Analysts; Office Clerks, General*; Personnel Recruiters; Training and Development Specialists.

Petroleum Supply Specialists

Ships, airplanes, trucks, tanks, and other military vehicles require large amounts of fuel and lubricants. These and other petroleum products require special storage and handling. Petroleum supply specialists store, handle, and ship petroleum products, such as oil, fuel, compressed gas, and lubricants.

Officer/Enlisted: Enlisted

Personality Type: Realistic. Realistic occupations frequently involve work activities that include practical, hands-on problems and solutions. They often deal with plants; animals; and real-world materials such as wood, tools, and machinery. Many of the occupations require working outside and do not involve a lot of paperwork or working closely with others.

Services That Offer the Job: Air Force, Army, Marines, Navy

What They Do. Petroleum supply specialists in the military perform some or all of the following duties:

- Connect hoses and valves and operate pumps to load petroleum products into tanker trucks, airplanes, ships, and railroad cars
- Test oils and fuels for pollutants
- Repair pipeline systems, hoses, valves, and pumps
- Check the volume and temperature of petroleum and gases in tankers, barges, and storage tanks
- Prepare storage and shipping records
- Store and move packaged petroleum products, using forklifts

Helpful Attributes. Helpful school subjects include shop mechanics and business math. Helpful attributes include the following:

- Ability to follow spoken instructions
- Interest in working with machines and equipment
- Preference for physical work

Training Provided. Job training consists of classroom instruction, including practice in using petroleum pumping equipment. Further training occurs on the job and through advanced courses. Course content typically includes the following:

- Testing oil and fuels
- Operating airplane refueling systems and equipment
- Operating pumps, pipelines, and tanker equipment
- Planning and scheduling petroleum transport
- Safety regulations and procedures for handling dangerous materials

Physical Demands. Petroleum supply specialists may have to perform moderate to heavy lifting.

Work Environment. Petroleum supply specialists work outdoors in all types of weather while filling storage tanks and refueling airplanes, ships, and tankers.

Opportunities in the Military. The services have about 13,000 petroleum supply specialists. Each year, they need new specialists because of changes in personnel and the demands of the field. After training, specialists work in teams while performing oil and fuel pumping operations. Each team works under the direction of a supervisor. With experience, petroleum supply specialists may become team leaders, pipeline or pump station supervisors, or petroleum storage supervisors.

Civilian Occupations It Provides Training For (those with stars are described in Part IV): Chemical Technicians*; First-Line Supervisors/Managers of Production and Operating Workers*; Inspectors, Testers, Sorters, Samplers, and Weighers*; Installation, Maintenance, and Repair Workers, All Other; Petroleum Pump System Operators, Refinery Operators, and Gaugers*; Pump Operators, Except Wellhead Pumpers; Service Station Attendants; Storage and Distribution Managers*.

Pharmacy Technicians

Prescription drugs and medicines are important to medical treatment. Patients and physicians depend on military pharmacies to fill their prescriptions accurately. Pharmacy technicians prepare and dispense prescribed drugs and medicines under the supervision of pharmacists or physicians. They also maintain pharmacy supplies and records.

Officer/Enlisted: Enlisted

Personality Type: Conventional. Conventional occupations frequently involve following set procedures and routines. These occupations can include working with data and details more than with ideas. Usually there is a clear line of authority to follow.

Services That Offer the Job: Air Force, Army, Navy

What They Do. Pharmacy technicians in the military perform some or all of the following duties:

- Read physicians' prescriptions to determine the types and amount of drugs to prepare
- Weigh and measure drugs and chemicals
- Mix ingredients to produce prescription medications
- Prepare labels for prescriptions
- Dispense medications to patients
- Store shipments of drugs and medications

Helpful Attributes. Helpful school subjects include algebra, chemistry, biology, physiology, and anatomy. Helpful attributes include the following:

- Ability to follow strict procedures and directions
- Ability to work using precise measurements and standards
- Interest in body chemistry

Training Provided. Job training consists of classroom instruction. Course content typically includes the following:

- Pharmacy laws and regulations
- Drug types and uses
- Mixing and dispensing drugs

Physical Demands. No significant demands.

Work Environment. Pharmacy technicians usually work in hospitals and clinics on land or aboard ships. They may also work in field hospitals.

Opportunities in the Military. The services have more than 2,000 pharmacy technicians. Each year, they need new technicians because of changes in personnel and the demands of the field. After job training, new technicians work under the supervision of experienced pharmacy technicians and pharmacists. With experience, they work more independently. Eventually, they may supervise other technicians and may manage military pharmacies.

Civilian Occupation It Provides Training For (those with stars are described in Part IV): Pharmacy Technicians*.

Photographic Specialists

The military uses photographs for many purposes, such as intelligence gathering and news reporting. The services operate photographic laboratories to develop the numerous photos taken by the military. Photographic specialists take and develop still color or black-and-white photographs.

Officer/Enlisted: Enlisted

Personality Type: Realistic. Realistic occupations frequently involve work activities that include practical, hands-on problems and solutions. They often deal with plants; animals; and real-world materials such as wood, tools, and machinery. Many of the occupations require working outside and do not involve a lot of paperwork or working closely with others.

Services That Offer the Job: Air Force, Army, Marines, Navy

What They Do. Photographic specialists in the military perform some or all of the following duties:

- Select camera, film, and other equipment needed for assignments
- Determine camera angles, lighting, and any special effects needed
- Take still photos of people, events, military equipment, land areas, and other subjects

- Develop, duplicate, or retouch film negatives, photos, or slides
- Maintain photographic equipment

Helpful Attributes. Helpful school subjects include photography, chemistry, art, and mathematics. Helpful attributes include the following:

- Ability to recognize and arrange interesting photo subjects
- Accuracy and attention to detail

Training Provided. Job training consists of classroom instruction, including practice in taking and developing photographs. Length of training varies depending on the specialty. Further training occurs on the job and through advanced courses. Course content typically includes the following:

- Photographic processing and reproduction
- Principles of photojournalism
- Operation and maintenance of photographic equipment

Physical Demands. Normal color vision is required to produce accurate color prints.

Work Environment. Photographic specialists work both indoors and outdoors while photographing their subjects. They may take photos from aircraft or ships. They process photographs in photographic laboratories on bases or aboard ships.

Opportunities in the Military. The services have about 1,500 photographic specialists. Each year, the services need new specialists because of changes in personnel and the demands of the field. After job training, specialists work under supervision. With experience, they are given more responsibility and, eventually, may supervise other photographic specialists.

Civilian Occupations It Provides Training For (those with stars are described in Part IV): Camera Operators, Television, Video, and Motion Picture*; Photographers*; Photographic Process Workers; Photographic Processing Machine Operators.

Physical and Occupational Therapy Specialists

Physical and occupational therapy consists of treatment and exercise for patients disabled by illness or injury. Physical and occupational therapy specialists assist in administering treatment aimed at helping disabled patients regain strength and mobility and preparing them to return to work.

Officer/Enlisted: Enlisted

Personality Type: Social. Social occupations frequently involve working with, communicating with, and teaching people. These occupations often involve helping or providing service to others.

Services That Offer the Job: Air Force, Army, Navy

What They Do. Physical and occupational therapy specialists in the military perform some or all of the following duties:

- Test and interview patients to determine their physical and mental abilities
- Assist physical and occupational therapists in planning therapy programs and exercise schedules
- Fit artificial limbs (prostheses) and train patients in their use
- Provide massages and heat treatments to patients
- Teach patients new mobility skills
- Set up and maintain therapeutic equipment such as exercise machines and whirlpools

Helpful Attributes. Helpful school subjects include general science, biology, physiology, and psychology. Helpful attributes include the following:

- Ability to communicate effectively
- Interest in working with and helping people
- Patience to work with people whose injuries heal slowly

Training Provided. Job training consists of classroom instruction, including practice in applying therapy techniques. Further training occurs on the job and through advanced courses. Course content typically includes the following:

- Anatomy, physiology, and psychology (the study of the body, body functions, and the mind)
- Methods of therapy, including massage, electric therapy, and radiation therapy
- Handling and positioning of patients
- Principles of rehabilitation

Physical Demands. No significant demands.

Work Environment. Therapy specialists work in hospitals, clinics, and rehabilitation centers.

Opportunities in the Military. The services have more than 500 physical and occupational therapy specialists. Each year, they need new specialists because of changes in personnel and the demands of the field. After job training, therapy specialists provide routine therapy care under the direction of supervisors. With experience, they work with patients with more serious problems. Eventually they may advance to supervisory positions.

Civilian Occupations It Provides Training For (those with stars are described in Part IV): Occupational Therapist Assistants*; Orthotists and Prosthetists*; Physical Therapist Assistants*.

Plumbers and Pipe Fitters

Military buildings and equipment require pipe systems for water, steam, gas, and waste. Pipe systems are also needed on aircraft, missiles, and ships for hydraulic (fluid pressure) and pneumatic (air pressure) systems. Plumbers and pipe fitters install and repair plumbing and pipe systems.

Officer/Enlisted: Enlisted

Personality Type: Realistic. Realistic occupations frequently involve work activities that include practical, hands-on problems and solutions. They often deal with plants; animals; and real-world materials such as wood, tools, and machinery. Many of the occupations require working outside and do not involve a lot of paperwork or working closely with others.

Services That Offer the Job: Army, Coast Guard, Navy

What They Do. Plumbers and pipe fitters in the military perform some or all of the following duties:

- Plan layouts of pipe systems, using blueprints and drawings
- Bend, cut, and thread pipes made of lead, copper, and plastic
- Install connectors, fittings, and joints
- Solder or braze pipe and tubing to join them
- Install sinks, toilets, and other plumbing fixtures
- Troubleshoot, test, and calibrate hydraulic and pneumatic systems

Helpful Attributes. Helpful school subjects include math and shop mechanics. Helpful attributes include the following:

- Ability to work with detailed plans
- Preference for doing physical work

Training Provided. Job training consists of classroom instruction, including practice in repairing plumbing systems. Course content typically includes the following:

- Installation, operation, and repair of pipe systems
- Installation and repair of plumbing fixtures and boiler controls
- Maintenance and repair of hydraulic and pneumatic systems
- Methods of soldering, welding, silver brazing, and cutting

Physical Demands. Plumbers and pipe fitters have to lift and carry heavy pipes and tubes.

Work Environment. Plumbers and pipe fitters work both indoors and outdoors on land and aboard ships.

Opportunities in the Military. The military has more than 1,000 plumbers and pipe fitters. Each year, the services need new plumbers and pipe fitters because of changes in personnel and the demands of the field. After job training, plumbers and pipe fitters work under close supervision. With experience, they work more independently and may supervise others. Eventually, they may advance to become managers of utilities departments, construction units, or missile maintenance units.

Civilian Occupations It Provides Training For (those with stars are described in Part IV): Boilermakers*; Pipe Fitters and Steamfitters*; Pipelayers; Plumbers*; Plumbers, Pipefitters, and Steamfitters.

P

Power Plant Electricians

Each military base—anywhere in the world—must have its own electricity. Power plant electricians maintain and repair electricity-generating equipment in mobile and stationary power plants.

Officer/Enlisted: Enlisted

Personality Type: Realistic. Realistic occupations frequently involve work activities that include practical, hands-on problems and solutions. They often deal with plants; animals; and real-world materials such as wood, tools, and machinery. Many of the occupations require working outside and do not involve a lot of paperwork or working closely with others.

Services That Offer the Job: Army, Navy

What They Do. Power plant electricians perform some or all of the following duties:

- Maintain and repair motors, generators, switchboards, and control equipment
- Maintain and repair power and lighting circuits, electrical fixtures, and other electrical equipment
- Detect and locate grounds, open circuits, and short circuits in power distribution cables
- Read technical guides and diagrams to locate damaged parts of generators and control equipment

Helpful Attributes. Helpful school subjects include electrical and electronic theory, math, and technical drawing. Helpful attributes include the following:

- Ability to use hand and power tools
- Interest in electricity
- Interest in working with machinery

Training Provided. Job training consists of classroom instruction, including practice in maintaining electrical power systems. Course length varies depending on specialty. Further training occurs on the job and through advanced courses. Course content typically includes the following:

- Generator and power plant operations
- Electrical generation and distribution
- Diesel generator operation, disassembly, inspection, and maintenance
- Principles of electrical and electronic circuitry

Physical Demands. Normal color vision is required to work with color-coded wiring.

Work Environment. Power plant electricians work in repair shops on land, aboard ships, or wherever generating equipment needing repair is located.

Opportunities in the Military. The services have about 3,000 power plant electricians. Each year, they need new electricians because of changes in personnel and the demands of the field. After job training, power plant electricians perform routine maintenance and repairs under supervision. In time, they perform more complex tasks and may help train others. Eventually, they may become supervisors of power plant operations.

Civilian Occupations It Provides Training For (those with stars are described in Part IV): Control and Valve Installers and Repairers, Except Mechanical Door*; Electrical and Electronics Installers and Repairers, Transportation Equipment*; Electrical and Electronics Repairers, Commercial and Industrial Equipment*; Electrical and Electronics Repairers, Powerhouse, Substation, and Relay*; Electrical Power-Line Installers and Repairers*; Electricians*; Industrial Machinery Mechanics*; Stationary Engineers and Boiler Operators*.

Power Plant Operators

Power plants generate electricity for ships, submarines, and military bases. The military uses many different types of power plants. Many ships and submarines have nuclear power plants. Power plant operators control power-generating plants on land and aboard ships and submarines. They operate boilers, turbines, nuclear reactors, and portable generators.

Officer/Enlisted: Enlisted

Personality Type: Realistic. Realistic occupations frequently involve work activities that include practical, hands-on problems and solutions. They often deal with plants; animals; and real-world materials such as wood, tools, and machinery. Many of the occupations require working outside and do not involve a lot of paperwork or working closely with others.

Services That Offer the Job: Air Force, Army, Coast Guard, Marines, Navy

What They Do. Power plant operators in the military perform some or all of the following duties:

- Monitor and operate control boards to regulate power plants
- Operate and maintain diesel generating units

- Monitor and control nuclear reactors that produce electricity and power ships and submarines
- Operate and maintain stationary engines, such as steam engines, air compressors, and generators
- Operate and maintain auxiliary equipment
- Inspect equipment for malfunctions
- Operate the steam turbines that generate power for ships

Helpful Attributes. Helpful school subjects include math and shop mechanics. Helpful attributes include the following:

- Interest in nuclear power
- Interest in working with large machinery

Training Provided. Job training consists of classroom instruction, including practice in operating power plants. Nuclear specialties have training programs that last 1 year or more, covering all aspects of nuclear power plant operations. Course content typically includes the following:

- Operation of pressure boilers
- Operation and maintenance of reactor control systems
- Operation and maintenance of mechanical systems on nuclear-powered ships and submarines

Physical Demands. Power plant operators lift heavy parts or tools when maintaining power plants. They may also have to stoop and kneel and work in awkward positions while repairing.

Work Environment. Power plant operators usually work indoors. They are subject to high temperatures and noise.

Opportunities in the Military. The services have about 13,000 power plant operators. Each year, they need new power plant operators because of changes in personnel and the demands of the field. After job training, power plant operators work under the close direction of supervisors. With experience, they may gain greater responsibility for plant operations and supervise other operators. Eventually, they may become superintendents of utilities for large bases or chiefs of ships' engineering departments.

Civilian Occupations It Provides Training For (those with stars are described in Part IV): Electrical and Electronics Repairers, Powerhouse, Substation, and Relay*; First-Line Supervisors/Managers of Mechanics, Installers, and Repairers*; First-Line Supervisors/Managers of Production and Operating Workers*; Gas Plant Operators*; Industrial Machinery Mechanics*; Nuclear Equipment Operation Technicians*; Nuclear Power Reactor Operators*; Plant and System Operators, All Other; Power Plant Operators*; Stationary Engineers and Boiler Operators*.

Powerhouse Mechanics

Power-generating stations (powerhouses) provide electric power for military bases, ships, and field camps. There are many types of powerhouses, from small gas generators to large nuclear reactors. Powerhouse mechanics install, maintain, and repair electrical and mechanical equipment in power-generating stations.

Officer/Enlisted: Enlisted

Personality Type: Realistic. Realistic occupations frequently involve work activities that include practical, hands-on problems and solutions. They often deal with plants; animals; and real-world materials such as wood, tools, and machinery. Many of the occupations require working outside and do not involve a lot of paperwork or working closely with others.

Services That Offer the Job: Army, Navy

What They Do. Powerhouse mechanics in the military perform some or all of the following duties:

- Install generating equipment, such as gasoline and diesel engines, turbines, and air compressors
- Repair and maintain nuclear power plants
- Inspect and service pumps, generators, batteries, and cables
- Tune engines, using hand tools, timing lights, and combustion pressure gauges
- Diagnose (troubleshoot) engine and electrical system problems
- Replace damaged parts, such as fuel injectors, valves, and pistons

Helpful Attributes. Helpful school subjects include shop mechanics and math. Helpful attributes include the following:

- Interest in nuclear power
- Interest in repairing machines and equipment
- Preference for doing physical work

Training Provided. Job training for non-nuclear specialties consists of classroom instruction, including practice in repairing power generating equipment. Nuclear specialties have training programs that last 1 year or more, covering all aspects of nuclear power plant operations. Further training occurs on the job and through advanced courses. Training length varies depending on the specialty. Course content typically includes the following:

- Principles of electricity
- Gas and diesel engine theories
- Hydraulic (fluid pressure) and pneumatic (air pressure) system maintenance

Physical Demands. Powerhouse mechanics may have to lift and move heavy electrical generators or batteries. Normal color vision is required to work with color-coded wiring and cables.

Work Environment. Powerhouse mechanics work in equipment repair shops, power plant stations, or power-generating rooms aboard ships. Sometimes they work outdoors while repairing substation generating equipment.

Opportunities in the Military. The services have about 12,000 powerhouse mechanics. Each year, they need new mechanics because of changes in personnel and the demands of the field. After job training, mechanics perform routine maintenance tasks under close supervision. With experience, they perform more complex repair work. In time, they may become powerhouse repair crew supervisors or power plant operations managers.

Civilian Occupations It Provides Training For (those with stars are described in Part IV): Control and Valve Installers and Repairers, Except Mechanical Door*; Electrical and Electronics Repairers, Powerhouse, Substation, and Relay*; First-Line Supervisors/Managers of Mechanics, Installers, and Repairers*; Industrial Machinery Mechanics*; Maintenance and Repair Workers, General*; Mobile Heavy Equipment Mechanics, Except Engines*; Outdoor Power Equipment and Other Small Engine Mechanics*; Power Plant Operators*; Stationary Engineers and Boiler Operators*.

Precision Instrument and Equipment Repairers

The military uses precision instruments and equipment to perform a variety of functions. Some precision instruments are used to measure distance, pressure, altitude, temperature, underwater depth, and other physical properties. Other types of precision equipment include photographic and imaging equipment such as cameras, projectors, and film-processing equipment. All of these items have many sensitive mechanisms that require regular attention to stay in good working order. Precision instrument and equipment repairers maintain and adjust these delicate items. They may specialize by the type of equipment that they work on.

Officer/Enlisted: Enlisted

Personality Type: Realistic. Realistic occupations frequently involve work activities that include practical, hands-on problems and solutions. They often deal with plants; animals; and real-world materials such as wood, tools, and machinery. Many of the occupations require working outside and do not involve a lot of paperwork or working closely with others.

Services That Offer the Job: Air Force, Army, Marines, Navy

What They Do. Precision instrument and equipment repairers in the military perform some or all of the following duties:

- Calibrate and repair instruments used in aircraft
- Calibrate measuring instruments such as barometers, thermometers, and telemeters

- Adjust and repair weapon-aiming devices such as range finders, telescopes, and periscopes
- Diagnose and repair problems in all types of cameras and photo-processing equipment
- Repair watches, clocks, and timers
- Calibrate electrical test instruments

Helpful Attributes. Helpful school subjects include math, science, electronics, and shop mechanics. Helpful attributes include the following:

- Ability to solve mechanical problems
- Ability to use repair tools

Training Provided. Job training consists of classroom instruction, including practice in repairing precision instruments and equipment. Training length varies depending upon specialty. Further training occurs on the job and through advanced courses. Course content typically includes the following:

- Calibration and repair of precision measuring instruments
- Use of blueprints and schematics
- Test and repair of cameras and darkroom equipment
- Test and repair of aerial sensor equipment

Physical Demands. Normal color vision is required to work with color-coded wiring.

Work Environment. Precision instrument and equipment repairers usually work in repair shops on land or aboard ships.

Opportunities in the Military. The services have about 7,000 precision instrument and equipment repairers. Each year, they need new repairers because of changes in personnel and the demands of the field. After job training, precision instrument and equipment repairers make routine adjustments and simple repairs under close supervision. With experience, they perform more complicated repairs and may supervise others. They may eventually become managers of repair shops.

Civilian Occupations It Provides Training For (those with stars are described in Part IV): Camera and Photographic Equipment Repairers; Computer, Automated Teller, and Office Machine Repairers*; Electrical and Electronics Repairers, Commercial and Industrial Equipment*; First-Line Supervisors/Managers of Mechanics, Installers, and Repairers*; First-Line Supervisors/Managers of Production and Operating Workers*; Industrial Machinery Mechanics*; Inspectors, Testers, Sorters, Samplers, and Weighers*; Locksmiths and Safe Repairers*; Medical Equipment Repairers*; Musical Instrument Repairers and Tuners; Precision Instrument and Equipment Repairers, All Other; Watch Repairers.

Preventive Maintenance Analysts

Regular maintenance extends the time aircraft, vehicles, and machinery can be used. To make sure military equipment is well maintained, the services prepare detailed maintenance schedules. Preventive maintenance analysts promote equipment maintenance. They watch schedules and notify mechanics about upcoming maintenance needs.

Officer/Enlisted: Enlisted

Personality Type: Conventional. Conventional occupations frequently involve following set procedures and routines. These occupations can include working with data and details more than with ideas. Usually there is a clear line of authority to follow.

Services That Offer the Job: Air Force, Marines, Navy

What They Do. Preventive maintenance analysts in the military perform some or all of the following duties:

- Review maintenance schedules and notify mechanics about the types of service needed
- Compare schedules to records of maintenance work actually performed
- Prepare charts and reports on maintenance activities
- Calculate how many mechanics and spare parts are needed to maintain equipment
- Operate computers and calculators to enter or retrieve maintenance data

Helpful Attributes. Helpful school subjects include general mathematics and algebra. Helpful attributes include the following:

- Ability to use mathematical formulas
- Interest in working with computers
- Interest in working with numbers and statistics
- Preference for work requiring attention to detail

Training Provided. Job training consists of classroom instruction. Training length varies depending on specialty. Course content typically includes the following:

- Equipment maintenance management concepts
- Accounting procedures
- Statistical reporting methods
- Parts and supply inventory control procedures

Physical Demands. Normal color vision is required to read and interpret maintenance charts and graphs in some specialties. Some specialties require the ability to speak clearly.

Work Environment. Preventive maintenance analysts usually work in office settings.

Opportunities in the Military. The services have about 9,000 preventive maintenance analysts. Each year, they need new analysts because of changes in personnel and the demands of the field. After job training, new analysts work under close supervision. As they gain experience, they are given more responsibility and more difficult work assignments. Eventually, they may become supervisors of maintenance control units.

Civilian Occupations It Provides Training For (those with stars are described in Part IV): First-Line Supervisors/Managers of Office and Administrative Support Workers*; Information and Record Clerks, All Other; Logisticians; Maintenance and Repair Workers, General*; Production, Planning, and Expediting Clerks*.

Printing Specialists

The military produces many printed publications each year, including newspapers, booklets, training manuals, maps, and charts. Printing specialists operate printing presses and binding machines to make finished copies of printed material.

Officer/Enlisted: Enlisted

Personality Type: Realistic. Realistic occupations frequently involve work activities that include practical, hands-on problems and solutions. They often deal with plants; animals; and real-world materials such as wood, tools, and machinery. Many of the occupations require working outside and do not involve a lot of paperwork or working closely with others.

Services That Offer the Job: Army, Marines, Navy

What They Do. Printing specialists in the military perform some or all of the following duties:

- Reproduce printed matter, using offset lithographic printing processes
- Prepare photographic negatives and transfer them to printing plates, using copy cameras and enlargers
- Prepare layouts of artwork, photographs, and text for lithographic plates
- Produce brochures, newspapers, maps, and charts
- Bind printed material into hardback or paperback books, using binding machines
- Maintain printing presses

Helpful Attributes. Helpful school subjects include shop mechanics and photography. Helpful attributes include the following:

- Interest in learning about printing
- Preference for doing physical work

Training Provided. Job training consists of classroom instruction, including practice in operating printing presses. Training length varies by specialty. Further training occurs on the job and through advanced courses. Course content typically includes the following:

- Photolithography techniques
- Operation of offset presses
- Techniques for making printing plates
- Binding techniques

Physical Demands. Normal color vision is required to enter some specialties in this occupation.

Work Environment. Printing specialists work indoors in print shops and offices located on land or aboard ships.

Opportunities in the Military. The military has about 500 printing specialists. Each year, the services need new specialists because of changes in personnel and the demands of the field. After job training, specialists normally operate printing and binding machines under direct supervision. With experience, they work more independently, setting up and operating machines. In time, printing specialists may become supervisors of printing plants.

Civilian Occupations It Provides Training For (those with stars are described in Part IV): Bindery Workers; Job Printers; Prepress Technicians and Workers; Printing Machine Operators*.

Quartermasters and Boat Operators

The military operates many small boats for amphibious troop landings, harbor patrols, and transportation over short distances. Quartermasters and boat operators navigate and pilot many types of small watercraft, including tugboats, gunboats, and barges.

Officer/Enlisted: Enlisted

Personality Type: Realistic. Realistic occupations frequently involve work activities that include practical, hands-on problems and solutions. They often deal with plants; animals; and real-world materials such as wood, tools, and machinery. Many of the occupations require working outside and do not involve a lot of paperwork or working closely with others.

Services That Offer the Job: Army, Coast Guard, Marines, Navy

What They Do. Quartermasters and boat operators in the military perform some or all of the following duties:

- Direct the course and speed of boats
- Consult maps, charts, weather reports, and navigation equipment
- Pilot tugboats when towing and docking barges and large ships

- Operate amphibious craft during troop landings
- Maintain boats and deck equipment
- Operate ship-to-shore radios
- Keep ship logs

Helpful Attributes. Helpful school subjects include mathematics. Helpful attributes include the following:

- Ability to follow detailed instructions and read maps
- Ability to work with mathematical formulas
- Interest in sailing and navigation

Training Provided. Job training consists of classroom instruction, including practice in boat operations. Course content typically includes the following:

- Boat-handling procedures
- Log- and message-handling procedures
- Use of compasses, radar, charts, and other navigational aids
- Navigational mathematics

Physical Demands. Quartermasters and boat operators may have to stand for several hours at a time. They must be able to speak clearly. Some specialties require normal depth perception and hearing.

Work Environment. Quartermasters and boat operators work aboard all types of boats and in all types of weather conditions. When not piloting boats, they may work on or below deck repairing boats and equipment or overseeing cargo storage. When ashore, they may work in offices that make nautical maps or in harbor management offices. Some boats are operated in combat situations.

Opportunities in the Military. The services have more than 2,000 quartermasters and boat operators. Each year, they need new quartermasters and boat operators because of changes in personnel and the demands of the field. After job training, they assist more experienced operators in maintaining logs and charts and operating navigational equipment. After gaining experience, they perform more difficult tasks, such as operating navigational equipment and calculating ship position. In time, they pilot boats and help train new quartermasters and boat operators.

Civilian Occupations It Provides Training For (those with stars are described in Part IV): Mates—Ship, Boat, and Barge*; Motorboat Operators; Pilots, Ship*; Sailors and Marine Oilers; Ship and Boat Captains*.

Radar and Sonar Operators

Radar and sonar devices work by bouncing radio or sound waves off objects to determine their location and measure distance. They have many uses, such as tracking aircraft and missiles, determining positions of ships and submarines, directing artillery fire, forecasting weather, and aiding navigation. Radar and sonar operators monitor sophisticated equipment. They normally specialize in either radar or sonar.

Officer/Enlisted: Enlisted

Personality Type: Realistic. Realistic occupations frequently involve work activities that include practical, hands-on problems and solutions. They often deal with plants; animals; and real-world materials such as wood, tools, and machinery. Many of the occupations require working outside and do not involve a lot of paperwork or working closely with others.

Services That Offer the Job: Air Force, Army, Coast Guard, Marines, Navy

What They Do. Radar and sonar operators in the military perform some or all of the following duties:

- Detect and track position, direction, and speed of aircraft, ships, submarines, and missiles
- Plot and record data on status charts and plotting boards
- Set up and operate radar equipment to direct artillery fire
- Monitor early warning air defense systems
- Send and receive messages, using electronic communication systems

Helpful Attributes. Helpful school subjects include geometry, algebra, and science. Helpful attributes include the following:

- Ability to concentrate for long periods
- Interest in working with electronic equipment

Training Provided. Job training consists of classroom instruction and practice operating radar or sonar equipment. Training length varies by specialty. Further training occurs on the job and through advanced courses. Course content typically includes the following:

- Operation and maintenance of radar and sonar equipment
- Identification of ships, submarines, aircraft, and missiles
- Computation of aircraft or missile speed, direction, and altitude

Physical Demands. No significant demands.

Work Environment. Radar and sonar operators in the military primarily work indoors in security-controlled areas. They work in operations centers and command posts either on land or aboard aircraft, ships, or submarines. Some may work in a mobile field radar unit.

Opportunities in the Military. The services have more than 11,000 radar and sonar operators. Each year, they need new operators because of changes in personnel and the demands of the field. After job training, new operators use radar or sonar equipment under close supervision. With experience, they work more independently and may eventually become supervisors of ground, airborne, or shipboard radar or sonar units.

Civilian Occupations It Provides Training For (those with stars are described in Part IV): Computer Operators; Electrical and Electronics Repairers, Commercial and Industrial Equipment*.

Radiologic (X-Ray) Technicians

Radiology (the use of X rays) is important in the diagnosis and treatment of medical conditions. X rays and other diagnostic techniques, such as ultrasound and magnetic resonance imaging (MRI), help physicians detect injuries and illnesses. Radiology is also used to treat some diseases, such as cancer. Radiologic technicians operate X-ray and other imaging related equipment used in diagnosing and treating injuries and diseases. They work as part of a medical team of physicians and specialists to provide health care to patients. Radiologic technicians may specialize by the type of equipment they operate.

Officer/Enlisted: Enlisted

Personality Type: Realistic. Realistic occupations frequently involve work activities that include practical, hands-on problems and solutions. They often deal with plants; animals; and real-world materials such as wood, tools, and machinery. Many of the occupations require working outside and do not involve a lot of paperwork or working closely with others.

Services That Offer the Job: Air Force, Army, Navy

What They Do. Radiologic technicians in the military perform some or all of the following duties:

- Read requests or instructions from physicians to determine each patient's X-ray or imaging needs
- Position patients under radiologic equipment
- Operate imaging equipment
- Adjust equipment to the correct time and power of exposure
- Process X-ray pictures
- Prepare and administer radioactive solutions to patients
- Keep records of patient treatment

Helpful Attributes. Helpful school subjects include algebra, biology, and other science courses. Helpful attributes include the following:

- Ability to follow strict standards and procedures
- Interest in activities requiring accuracy and attention to detail
- Interest in helping others

Training Provided. Job training consists of classroom instruction, including practice with radiologic equipment. Extensive on-the-job training is also provided. Additional training occurs through advanced courses. Training length varies depending on specialty. Course content typically includes the following:

- Operation of diagnostic imaging equipment
- Radioactive isotope therapy
- X-ray film processing
- Anatomy and physiology

Physical Demands. No significant demands.

Work Environment. Radiologic technicians work in hospitals and clinics. In combat situations, they may work in mobile field hospitals. They follow strict safety procedures to minimize exposure to radiation.

Opportunities in the Military. The military has about 3,500 radiologic technicians. Each year, the services need new technicians because of changes in personnel and the demands of the field. After job training, technicians start operating routine imaging equipment. With experience, they may specialize in nuclear medicine and administer radiation and radioisotopic treatment and therapy. In time, they may advance to become supervisors of radiologic units.

Civilian Occupations It Provides Training For (those with stars are described in Part IV): Diagnostic Medical Sonographers; Health Technologists and Technicians, All Other; Nuclear Medicine Technologists; Radiologic Technicians*; Radiologic Technologists*; Radiologic Technologists and Technicians.

Recreation, Welfare, and Morale Specialists

The military has an obligation to provide for the overall well-being of its service members and their families, not only in peacetime, but especially during times of war or crisis. In peacetime, programs are designed to maintain mission readiness, promote fitness and esprit de corps, and create a strong sense of military community that enhances the quality of life. During conflict, high morale is critical for those personnel who are deployed, as well as for the families that remain behind. In order to withstand the physical and emotional stresses endured, particularly during deployment situations, the military community depends upon a strong support system. This system is comprised of programs designed to encourage positive individual values; aid in recruitment and retention of personnel; provide for physical, mental, cultural, and social needs and the general well-being of service members and their families; and establish a core sense of community for its transient population. Without providing these kinds of support services, including physical fitness facilities, libraries, youth and outdoor recreation activities, arts and crafts, and unit-level sports, the military would have difficulty accomplishing its basic missions.

Officer/Enlisted: Enlisted

Personality Type: Enterprising. Enterprising occupations frequently involve starting up and carrying out projects. These occupations can involve leading people and making many decisions. They sometimes require risk taking and often deal with business.

Services That Offer the Job: Air Force, Marines, Navy

What They Do. Recreation, welfare, and morale specialists in the military perform some or all of the following duties:

- Plan, prepare, and direct social functions, meetings, or recreational activities
- Prepare daily activity reports
- Track inventory, purchasing, receiving, and storage of equipment and goods for club and entertainment services
- Direct operation of clubs, open messes, recreational buildings, and libraries
- Arrange publicity for social or recreational events, such as plays, concerts, and tournaments
- Issue and maintain recreation gear and resources, such as sports equipment and movies
- Conduct surveys to determine interests and attitudes of the military population and their dependents
- Schedule facility or property maintenance

Helpful Attributes. Helpful school subjects include psychology, speech communications, business, and physical education. Helpful attributes include the following:

- Interest in working with people
- Interest in physical fitness, athletics, arts and crafts, and other recreational activities
- Ability to plan and organize group and individual events, programs, and activities
- Enjoy helping, teaching, and caring for others
- Ability to coordinate and prioritize the work and activities of others
- Ability to work with minimal supervision

Training Provided. No data available.

Physical Demands. No significant demands.

Work Environment. They typically work indoors when planning and organizing events or maintaining facilities and outdoors when conducting recreational activities.

Opportunities in the Military. No data available.

Civilian Occupations It Provides Training For (those with stars are described in Part IV): Business Operations Specialists, All Other; Cooks, Institution and Cafeteria; First-Line Supervisors/Managers of Food Preparation and Serving Workers*; First-Line Supervisors/Managers of Retail Sales Workers*;

Hotel, Motel, and Resort Desk Clerks*; Human Resources Managers, All Other; Order Fillers, Wholesale and Retail Sales; Public Relations Managers; Recreation Workers; Retail Salespersons*; Social Workers, All Other; Stock Clerks, Sales Floor.

Recruiting Specialists

Attracting young people with the kinds of talent needed to succeed in today's military is a large task. Recruiting specialists provide information about military careers to young people, parents, schools, and local communities. They explain service employment and training opportunities, pay and benefits, and service life.

Officer/Enlisted: Enlisted

Personality Type: Enterprising. Enterprising occupations frequently involve starting up and carrying out projects. These occupations can involve leading people and making many decisions. They sometimes require risk taking and often deal with business.

Services That Offer the Job: Air Force, Army, Marines, Navy

What They Do. Recruiting specialists in the military perform some or all of the following duties:

- Interview civilians interested in military careers
- Describe military careers to groups of high school students
- Explain the purpose of the ASVAB (Armed Services Vocational Aptitude Battery) and test results to students and counselors
- Participate in local job fairs and career day programs
- Talk about the military to community groups
- Counsel military personnel about career opportunities and benefits

Helpful Attributes. Helpful school subjects include the social sciences, speech, psychology, and English. Helpful attributes include the following:

- Ability to speak before groups
- Ability to work independently
- Interest in working with youths

Training Provided. Job training consists of classroom instruction. Further training occurs on the job and through advanced courses. Course content typically includes the following:

- Recruiting procedures
- Interviewing techniques
- Public speaking techniques
- Community relations practices

Physical Demands. No significant demands.

Work Environment. Recruiting specialists work in local recruiting offices, on high school campuses and career centers, and in local communities. They may have to travel often.

Opportunities in the Military. The services have about 8,000 recruiting specialists. Normally, personnel must be in the service for several years before they are eligible to become recruiters. Each year, the services need new recruiters since some specialists spend only a few years in recruiting before returning to their primary occupational area. Those who choose to make a career of recruiting may, in time, supervise one or more recruiting offices.

Civilian Occupations It Provides Training For (those with stars are described in Part IV): Compensation, Benefits, and Job Analysis Specialists; Human Resources Assistants, Except Payroll and Timekeeping*; Personnel Recruiters.

Religious Program Specialists

The military has personnel from many religions and faiths. The military provides chaplains and religious program specialists to help meet the spiritual needs of its personnel. Religious program specialists assist chaplains with religious services, religious education programs, and related administrative duties.

Officer/Enlisted: Enlisted

Personality Type: Conventional. Conventional occupations frequently involve following set procedures and routines. These occupations can include working with data and details more than with ideas. Usually there is a clear line of authority to follow.

Services That Offer the Job: Air Force, Army, Navy

What They Do. Religious program specialists in the military perform some or all of the following duties:

- Assist chaplains in planning religious programs and activities
- Assist chaplains in conducting religious services
- Prepare religious, educational, and devotional materials
- Organize charitable and public service volunteer programs
- Maintain relations with religious communities and public service organizations
- Perform administrative duties for chaplains

Helpful Attributes. Helpful school subjects include English, public speaking, accounting, and typing. Helpful attributes include the following:

- Ability to express ideas clearly
- Interest in administrative work
- Interest in religious guidance
- Knowledge of various religious customs and beliefs
- Sensitivity to the needs of others

Training Provided. Job training consists of classroom instruction. Course content typically includes the following:

- Principles of religious support programs
- Guidance and counseling techniques
- Leadership skills
- Office procedures

Physical Demands. The ability to speak clearly and distinctly is required to enter this occupation.

Work Environment. Religious program specialists in the military usually work indoors. They also serve aboard ships or with land and air units in the field.

Opportunities in the Military. The services have about 1,000 religious program specialists. Each year, they need new specialists because of changes in personnel and the demands of the field. After job training, religious program specialists help chaplains and supervisors with administrative matters. With experience, they gain more responsibility for organizing activities and working in the local community. In time, they may supervise other specialists.

Civilian Occupations It Provides Training For (those with stars are described in Part IV): Directors, Religious Activities and Education*; Office Clerks, General*; Religious Workers, All Other.

Sales and Stock Specialists

The military operates retail stores that sell food and merchandise to make it easier for personnel to obtain whatever they need where they are stationed. Sales and stock specialists perform a variety of duties to support the operation of these stores, whether working aboard a ship or overseas in a remote location.

Officer/Enlisted: Enlisted

Personality Type: Conventional. Conventional occupations frequently involve following set procedures and routines. These occupations can include working with data and details more than with ideas. Usually there is a clear line of authority to follow.

Services That Offer the Job: Air Force, Coast Guard, Navy

What They Do. Sales and stock specialists in the military perform some or all of the following duties:

- Order and receive merchandise and food for retail sales
- Inspect food and merchandise for spoilage or damage
- Price retail sales items, using stamping machines
- Stock shelves and racks for the display of products
- Count merchandise and supplies during inventory checks
- Operate cash registers
- Record money received and prepare bank deposits

Helpful Attributes. Helpful school subjects include bookkeeping and mathematics. Helpful attributes include the following:

- Ability to use cash registers, and calculators
- Interest in working with people

Training Provided. Job training consists of classroom instruction for some specialties. For others, training occurs on the job. Further training occurs on the job. Course content includes the following:

- Stock procedures
- Recordkeeping and bookkeeping procedures

Physical Demands. The ability to speak clearly is required. Sales and stock specialists may have to lift and carry heavy objects.

Work Environment. Sales and stock specialists work on land and aboard ships in retail stores and storerooms.

Opportunities in the Military. The services have more than 1,500 sales and stock specialists. Each year, they need new specialists because of changes in personnel and the demands of the field. After job training, sales and stock specialists are assigned to retail stores and storerooms. Initially, they work under close supervision. With experience, they work more independently, train new workers, and assume more responsibility for sales and stock activities.

Civilian Occupations It Provides Training For (those with stars are described in Part IV): First-Line Supervisors/Managers of Retail Sales Workers*; Order Fillers, Wholesale and Retail Sales; Retail Salespersons*; Shipping, Receiving, and Traffic Clerks*; Stock Clerks, Sales Floor*; Stock Clerks—Stockroom, Warehouse, or Storage Yard.

Seamen

All ships must have teams of individuals with "jack-of-all-trades" skills who make things run smoothly above deck. Seamen perform many duties to help operate and maintain military ships, boats, and submarines.

Officer/Enlisted: Enlisted

Personality Type: Realistic. Realistic occupations frequently involve work activities that include practical, hands-on problems and solutions. They often deal with plants; animals; and real-world materials such as wood, tools, and machinery. Many of the occupations require working outside and do not involve a lot of paperwork or working closely with others.

Services That Offer the Job: Coast Guard, Navy

What They Do. Seamen in the military perform some or all of the following duties:

- Operate hoists, cranes, and winches to load cargo or set gangplanks
- Operate and maintain on-deck equipment and ship rigging
- Supervise firefighting and damage control exercises
- Handle lines to secure vessels to wharves or other ships
- Stand watch for security, navigation, or communications
- Supervise crews painting and maintaining decks and sides of ships

Helpful Attributes. Helpful school subjects include mathematics and shop mechanics. Helpful attributes include the following:

- Ability to work closely with others
- Interest in sailing and being at sea
- Preference for physical work

Training Provided. Although classroom training is provided to seamen, most training occurs on the job. Training programs vary depending on service and specialty.

Physical Demands. Seamen may have to climb ships' rigging and perform work at heights. Their work often involves moderate to heavy lifting.

Work Environment. Seamen and deckhands work aboard all types of ships and submarines. On ships, they often work outdoors on deck while servicing shipboard equipment.

Opportunities in the Military. The services have about 10,000 seamen. Each year, the services need new seamen because of changes in personnel and the demands of the field. New seamen work together on teams led by experienced supervisors. Through practice, they learn the many tasks they must perform. In time, seamen supervise one or more teams. Eventually, they may become managers responsible for planning and directing the work of many seamen. Often, seamen receive additional training that prepares them for other occupations in their service.

Civilian Occupations It Provides Training For (those with stars are described in Part IV): Mates—Ship, Boat, and Barge*; Sailors and Marine Oilers.

Ship and Submarine Officers

Ships and submarines are organized by departments, such as engineering, communications, weapons, and supply. Ship and submarine officers work as team members to manage the various departments aboard their vessels.

Officer/Enlisted: Officer

Personality Type: Realistic. Realistic occupations frequently involve work activities that include practical, hands-on problems and solutions. They often deal with plants; animals; and real-world materials such as wood, tools, and machinery. Many of the occupations require working outside and do not involve a lot of paperwork or working closely with others.

Services That Offer the Job: Army, Coast Guard, Navy

What They Do. Ship and submarine officers in the military perform some or all of the following duties:

- Command vessels of all sizes at sea or in coastal waters
- Plan and manage the operating departments under the captain's direction
- Plan and manage training exercises, such as target practice, aircraft operations, damage control drills, and searches for enemy submarines
- Evaluate subordinate personnel and recommend awards and promotions
- Direct search and rescue missions

Helpful Attributes. Helpful fields of study include engineering, oceanography, mathematics, and computer science. Helpful attributes include the following:

- Ability to organize and direct the work of others
- Interest in sailing and being at sea

Training Provided. Job training consists of classroom instruction and practical experience in one of the following departments: air, weapons, operations, communications, engineering, deck, administration, or supply. Training length varies depending on specialty. Further training occurs on the job and through advanced courses. Course content typically includes the following:

- Management and organization of ship or submarine operations
- Piloting and navigation of ships
- Interpretation of maritime laws and policies

Physical Demands. Good vision and normal color vision are required for reading color-coded charts and maps.

Work Environment. Ship and submarine officers work aboard their vessels. Engineering officers are subjected to hot, humid, and noisy environments. Submarine officers work in confined spaces for extended periods.

Special Requirements. A 4-year college degree is normally required to enter this occupation. Although there are women ship officers, some assignments, such as submarine duty, are open only to men.

Opportunities in the Military. The services have about 6,000 ship and submarine officers. Each year, they need officers because of changes in personnel and the demands of the field. After job training, officers are assigned to management positions in one of the ship's departments. With experience and demonstrated ability to lead, they assume greater responsibility. Depending on their specialty, ship and submarine officers gain experience in more than one department. Also, they are regularly reassigned to different ships or submarines, where they meet and work with new people. Between sea tours, they work and attend training at shore bases. Eventually, ship and submarine officers may be selected to command a vessel.

Civilian Occupations It Provides Training For (those with stars are described in Part IV): Commercial Divers; First-Line Supervisors/Managers of Mechanics, Installers, and Repairers*; General and Operations Managers; Managers, All Other; Pilots, Ship*; Ship and Boat Captains*.

Ship Electricians

Electrical systems supply power to operate ships and submarines. Lights, radar, weapons, and machinery all need electricity. Ship electricians operate and repair electrical systems on ships. They keep electrical power plants, wiring, and machinery in working order.

Officer/Enlisted: Enlisted

Personality Type: Realistic. Realistic occupations frequently involve work activities that include practical, hands-on problems and solutions. They often deal with plants; animals; and real-world materials such as wood, tools, and machinery. Many of the occupations require working outside and do not involve a lot of paperwork or working closely with others.

Services That Offer the Job: Coast Guard, Navy

What They Do. Ship electricians in the military perform some or all of the following duties:

- Install wiring for lights and equipment
- Troubleshoot electrical wiring and equipment, using test meters
- Inspect and maintain devices that distribute electricity throughout ships, such as circuits, transformers, and regulators
- Monitor and maintain electrical devices connected to the ship's main engines or nuclear reactors

Helpful Attributes. Helpful school courses include math and shop mechanics. Helpful attributes include the following:

- Ability to use tools
- Interest in electricity and how electrical machines work
- Interest in solving problems

Training Provided. Job training consists of classroom instruction, including practice repairing electrical systems. Further training occurs on the job and through advanced courses. Course content typically includes the following:

- Electrical theory
- Troubleshooting procedures
- Maintenance and repair procedures
- Reading diagrams and calculating amperage, voltage, and resistance levels

Physical Demands. Normal color vision is required to work with color-coded wiring.

Work Environment. Ship electricians usually work indoors, aboard ships or submarines. They also work in ship repair shops on land.

Opportunities in the Military. The military has more than 2,000 ship electricians. Each year, the services need new ship electricians because of changes in personnel and the demands of the field. After job training, ship electricians perform maintenance work and repair electrical problems. Eventually, they may become superintendents of electrical repair shops or of ship electrical systems.

Civilian Occupations It Provides Training For (those with stars are described in Part IV): Electric Motor, Power Tool, and Related Repairers; Electrical and Electronics Installers and Repairers, Transportation Equipment*; Electrical and Electronics Repairers, Commercial and Industrial Equipment*; Electrical and Electronics Repairers, Powerhouse, Substation, and Relay*; Electricians*; Elevator Installers and Repairers*; Home Appliance Repairers; Precision Instrument and Equipment Repairers, All Other; Security and Fire Alarm Systems Installers; Telecommunications Equipment Installers and Repairers, Except Line Installers*; Telecommunications Line Installers and Repairers*.

Space Operations Officers

Orbiting satellites and other space vehicles are used for national security, communications, weather forecasting, and space exploration. Space operations officers manage space flight planning, training, mission control, and other activities involved in launching and recovering spacecraft. They may also be astronauts who command space flights or who serve as crew members.

Officer/Enlisted: Officer

Personality Type: Investigative. Investigative occupations frequently involve working with ideas and require an extensive amount of thinking. These occupations can involve searching for facts and figuring out problems mentally.

Services That Offer the Job: Air Force, Army, Marines

What They Do. Space operations officers in the military perform some or all of the following duties:

- Manage activities of the flight control facility, including mission planning and training
- Manage operation of guidance, navigation, and propulsion systems for ground and space vehicles
- Develop space flight simulation exercises to train astronauts
- Plan space stations
- Direct space center launch and recovery activities
- Command and pilot space shuttles
- Perform in-orbit tasks and experiments aboard spacecraft
- Monitor foreign space flights and missile launches

Helpful Attributes. Helpful attributes include the following:

- Ability to work well as part of a team
- Decisiveness
- Interest in scientific research
- Interest in space travel

Training Provided. Job training for mission control officers consists of about 1 year of classroom instruction and practical experience. Further training occurs on the job and through academic courses. Astronauts must complete the NASA astronaut candidate training school. They also receive 1 year of practical training in space transport systems. Course content typically includes the following:

- Evaluation of space transport systems
- Development of space mission plans
- Methods for conducting space flight training programs
- Development of space flight simulation exercises

Physical Demands. No significant demands.

Work Environment. Launch and mission control space operations officers work in offices. Astronauts are required at times to work in a zero gravity environment in training as well as in space flight.

Opportunities in the Military. The services have fewer than 500 space operations officers. The field is very competitive because of the limited number of specialties in this area. The services sometimes need new space operations officers because of changes in personnel and changes in the demands of the field. After job training, new officers are assigned to space operations, launch and mission control centers, or research facilities. With experience and special training, they have the opportunity to work in various areas such as astronautics or space flight control. Eventually, they may manage a missile warning facility, a satellite command center, a space launch system, a space systems analysis facility, or a manned space flight.

Civilian Occupation It Provides Training For (those with stars are described in Part IV): Airline Pilots, Copilots, and Flight Engineers*.

Surveying, Mapping, and Drafting Technicians

The military builds and repairs many airstrips, docks, barracks, roads, and other projects each year. Surveying, mapping, and drafting technicians conduct land surveys, make maps, and prepare detailed plans and drawings for construction projects. Surveys and maps are also used to locate military targets and plot troop movements.

Officer/Enlisted: Enlisted

Personality Type: Realistic. Realistic occupations frequently involve work activities that include practical, hands-on problems and solutions. They often deal with plants; animals; and real-world materials such as wood, tools, and machinery. Many of the occupations require working outside and do not involve a lot of paperwork or working closely with others.

Services That Offer the Job: Air Force, Army, Coast Guard, Marines, Navy

What They Do. Surveying, mapping, and drafting technicians in the military perform some or all of the following duties:

- Draw maps and charts, using drafting tools and computers
- Make scale drawings of roads, airfields, buildings, and other military projects
- Conduct land surveys and compute survey results
- Draw diagrams for wiring and plumbing of structures
- Build scale models of land areas that show hills, lakes, roads, and buildings
- Piece together aerial photographs to form large photomaps
- Use global positioning systems to collect location information from satellites

Helpful Attributes. Helpful school subjects include algebra, geometry, and trigonometry. Helpful attributes include the following:

- Ability to convert ideas into drawings
- Interest in maps and charts
- Interest in working with drafting equipment and computers

Training Provided. Job training consists of classroom instruction, depending on specialty. Further training occurs on the job and through advanced courses. Course content typically includes the following:

- Surveying and drafting techniques
- Aerial photo interpretation
- Architectural and structural drawing

Physical Demands. No significant demands.

Work Environment. Surveying, mapping, and drafting technicians work both indoors and outdoors in all climates and weather conditions. Those assigned to engineering units sometimes work outdoors with survey teams. Those assigned to intelligence units may work on ships as well as on land.

Opportunities in the Military. The military has about 3,000 surveying, mapping, and drafting technicians. Each year, the services need new technicians because of changes in personnel and the demands of the field. After job training, technicians make simple drawings, trace photos, perform basic survey duties, or help make maps under close supervision. With experience, they work more independently. Eventually, they may supervise mapmaking facilities, surveying teams, or construction units.

Civilian Occupations It Provides Training For (those with stars are described in Part IV): Architectural Drafters*; Cartographers and Photogrammetrists; Civil Drafters*; Civil Engineering Technicians*; Engineering Technicians, Except Drafters, All Other; Mapping Technicians*; Surveying and Mapping Technicians; Surveying Technicians*; Surveyors.

Survival Equipment Specialists

Military personnel often have hazardous assignments. They depend on survival equipment to protect their lives in case of emergencies. Survival equipment specialists inspect, maintain, and repair survival equipment such as parachutes, aircraft life support equipment, and air-sea rescue equipment.

Officer/Enlisted: Enlisted

Personality Type: Realistic. Realistic occupations frequently involve work activities that include practical, hands-on problems and solutions. They often deal with plants; animals; and real-world materials such as wood, tools, and machinery. Many of the occupations require working outside and do not involve a lot of paperwork or working closely with others.

Services That Offer the Job: Air Force, Army, Coast Guard, Marines, Navy

What They Do. Survival equipment specialists in the military perform some or all of the following duties:

- Inspect parachutes for rips and tangled lines
- Pack parachutes for safe operation
- Repair life rafts and load them with emergency provisions
- Test emergency oxygen regulators on aircraft

- Stock aircraft with fire extinguishers, flares, and survival provisions
- Train crews in the use of survival equipment
- Assemble, maintain, and repair protective fabric components such as clothing and upholstery
- Train crews in the use of survival equipment

Helpful Attributes. Helpful school subjects include shop mechanics and science. Helpful attributes include the following:

- Ability to do work requiring accuracy and attention to detail
- Interest in working for the safety of others

Training Provided. Job training consists of classroom instruction, including practice in working with survival equipment. Further training occurs on the job and through additional courses. Course content typically includes the following:

- Parachute rigging techniques
- Repair of inflatable rafts and other survival equipment
- Maintenance of oxygen equipment
- Maintenance of air-sea rescue equipment

Physical Demands. Normal color vision is required to work with color-coded wiring and repair charts.

Work Environment. Survival equipment specialists in the military work in repair shops on land or aboard ships.

Opportunities in the Military. The military has about 5,000 survival equipment specialists. Each year, the services need new specialists because of changes in personnel and the demands of the field. After job training, survival equipment specialists work on survival equipment under the close direction of supervisors. With experience, they work with less supervision and perform more challenging tasks. In time, survival equipment specialists may become supervisors, assisting in the management of survival equipment repair facilities.

Civilian Occupations It Provides Training For (those with stars are described in Part IV): Aircraft Mechanics and Service Technicians*; Fabric Menders, Except Garment; First-Line Supervisors/Managers of Mechanics, Installers, and Repairers*; Industrial Machinery Mechanics*; Inspectors, Testers, Sorters, Samplers, and Weighers*; Installation, Maintenance, and Repair Workers, All Other; Maintenance and Repair Workers, General*; Maintenance Workers, Machinery; Riggers*.

T

Transportation Specialists

The military constantly moves passengers and cargo. Personnel often travel to meetings, training sessions, and new assignments. Supplies and equipment to support troops must be shipped regularly. Transportation specialists plan and assist in air, sea, and land transportation for people and cargo. Some assist passenger travel as gate agents and flight attendants.

Officer/Enlisted: Enlisted

Personality Type: Conventional. Conventional occupations frequently involve following set procedures and routines. These occupations can include working with data and details more than with ideas. Usually there is a clear line of authority to follow.

Services That Offer the Job: Air Force, Army, Marines, Navy

What They Do. Transportation specialists in the military perform some or all of the following duties:

- Arrange for passenger travel via plane, bus, train, or boat
- Arrange for shipment and delivery of household goods
- Determine which vehicles to use based on freight or passenger-movement requirements
- Determine transportation and shipping routes
- Prepare transportation requests and shipping documents
- Check in passengers and baggage for military transport flights
- Serve as military airplane flight attendants
- Inspect cargo for proper packing, loading, and marking

Helpful Attributes. Helpful school subjects include mathematics and English. Helpful attributes include the following:

- Interest in arranging travel schedules
- Interest in serving people
- Interest in using computers

Training Provided. Job training consists of classroom instruction, including practice in making transportation arrangements. Further training occurs on the job and through advanced courses. Course content typically includes the following:

- Planning transportation for personnel and cargo
- Proper cargo handling, shipping, and storing methods
- Analysis of transportation documents

Physical Demands. No significant demands.

Work Environment. Transportation specialists usually work in offices. They may work outdoors when escorting passengers or processing shipments. Flight attendants work on land and in airplanes.

Opportunities in the Military. The military has about 11,000 transportation specialists. Each year, the services need new specialists because of changes in personnel and the demands of the field. After job training, they make travel and shipping arrangements under direct supervision. Some may specialize as flight attendants and gate agents. With experience, they may become supervisors of other transportation specialists. In time, they may manage transportation offices.

Civilian Occupations It Provides Training For (those with stars are described in Part IV): Aircraft Cargo Handling Supervisors; Cargo and Freight Agents*; First-Line Supervisors/Managers of Office and Administrative Support Workers*; First-Line Supervisors/Managers of Personal Service Workers; First-Line Supervisors/Managers of Transportation and Material-Moving Machine and Vehicle Operators*; Flight Attendants; Industrial Truck and Tractor Operators; Logisticians; Production, Planning, and Expediting Clerks*; Railroad Brake, Signal, and Switch Operators; Reservation and Transportation Ticket Agents and Travel Clerks; Shipping, Receiving, and Traffic Clerks*; Travel Agents.

Unmanned Vehicle (UV) Operations Specialists

The military uses remotely piloted unmanned vehicles for a variety of purposes, such as deep sea exploration, intelligence gathering, remote surveillance, and target applications. These vehicles are used in the air, on land, and at sea in operations or missions that could be dangerous for human operators onboard the vehicle. The military requires skilled operators and technicians to maintain and control these vehicles. Personnel normally specialize by the type of vehicle they operate, such as unmanned aerial vehicles, ground vehicles, surface vehicles, and undersea vehicles.

Officer/Enlisted: Enlisted

Personality Type: Realistic. Realistic occupations frequently involve work activities that include practical, hands-on problems and solutions. They often deal with plants; animals; and real-world materials such as wood, tools, and machinery. Many of the occupations require working outside and do not involve a lot of paperwork or working closely with others.

Services That Offer the Job: Army, Marines, Navy

What They Do. Unmanned vehicle operations specialists in the military perform some or all of the following duties:

- Prepare and install equipment on or within the unmanned vehicle
- Operate, navigate, launch, track, and recover unmanned vehicles
- Operate equipment in remote receiving stations and ground control stations
- Coordinate with other personnel to complete the designated mission
- Inspect and maintain components in unmanned vehicles

Helpful Attributes. Helpful attributes include the following:

- Enjoy working with tools
- Knowledge of electronic theory and schematic drawing
- Superior adaptability to three-dimensional spatial relationships

Training Provided. Job training varies depending on the position. Course content typically includes the following:

- Unmanned vehicle concepts and capabilities
- Operation of unmanned vehicles
- Basic preventative maintenance

Physical Demands. No significant demands.

Work Environment. Unmanned vehicle operations specialists work under a variety of conditions depending upon the type of vehicle and mission. Some specialists work in control stations or receiving stations on land, while others work aboard ships.

Opportunities in the Military. The services have more than 500 unmanned vehicle operations specialists. Each year, they need new specialists because of changes in personnel and the growing use of this kind of technology. After job training, new unmanned vehicle operations specialists normally work under close supervision to prepare unmanned vehicles for their missions. With experience, they may perform more difficult duties, such as piloting, navigating, and recovering unmanned vehicles. In time, some operations specialists may plan and oversee unmanned vehicle missions.

Civilian Occupation It Provides Training For (those with stars are described in Part IV): Electro-Mechanical Technicians*.

Vehicle Drivers

The military uses numerous vehicles to transport its troops, equipment, and supplies. Together, the services own and operate about 50,000 heavy trucks and buses. Vehicle drivers operate all types of heavy military vehicles. They drive fuel or water tank trucks, semi-tractor trailers, heavy troop transports, and passenger buses.

Officer/Enlisted: Enlisted

Personality Type: Realistic. Realistic occupations frequently involve work activities that include practical, hands-on problems and solutions. They often deal with plants; animals; and real-world materials such as wood, tools, and machinery. Many of the occupations require working outside and do not involve a lot of paperwork or working closely with others.

Services That Offer the Job: Air Force, Army, Coast Guard, Marines

What They Do. Vehicle drivers in the military perform some or all of the following duties:

- Read travel instructions to determine travel routes, arrival dates, and types of cargo
- Make sure vehicles are loaded properly
- Check oil, fuel, and other fluid levels and tire pressure
- Drive vehicles over all types of roads, traveling alone or in convoys
- Keep records of mileage driven and fuel and oil used
- Wash vehicles and perform routine maintenance and repairs

Helpful Attributes. Helpful school courses include driver education. Helpful attributes include the following:

- Interest in driving
- Interest in mechanics

Training Provided. Job training consists of classroom instruction, including practice in driving heavy military vehicles. Course content typically includes the following:

- Accident prevention
- Safety check procedures
- International road signs
- Basic vehicle maintenance

Physical Demands. Normal color vision is required to read road maps. Drivers sometimes must change heavy tires.

Work Environment. Vehicle driving involves long periods of sitting.

Opportunities in the Military. The services have about 14,000 vehicle drivers. Each year, they need new vehicle drivers because of changes in personnel and the demands of the field. After job training, vehicle drivers are assigned to motor pools or motor transport units. They generally work without close supervision. In time, vehicle drivers may advance to supervisory positions assisting in the management of motor transport units.

Civilian Occupations It Provides Training For (those with stars are described in Part IV): Bus Drivers, Transit and Intercity*; First-Line Supervisors/Managers of Transportation and Material-Moving Machine and Vehicle Operators*; Motor Vehicle Operators, All Other; Operating Engineers and Other Construction Equipment Operators*; Taxi Drivers and Chauffeurs*; Truck Drivers, Heavy and Tractor-Trailer*; Truck Drivers, Light or Delivery Services*.

Warehousing and Distribution Specialists

The military maintains a large inventory of food, medicines, ammunition, spare parts, and other supplies. Keeping the military's supply system operating smoothly is an important job. The lives of combat troops in the field may depend on receiving the right supplies on time. Warehousing and distribution specialists receive, store, record, and issue military supplies.

Officer/Enlisted: Enlisted

Personality Type: Conventional. Conventional occupations frequently involve following set procedures and routines. These occupations can include working with data and details more than with ideas. Usually there is a clear line of authority to follow.

Services That Offer the Job: Air Force, Army, Coast Guard, Marines, Navy

What They Do. Warehousing and distribution specialists in the military perform some or all of the following duties:

- Perform inventory and financial management procedures, including ordering, receiving, and storing supplies
- Locate and catalog stock
- Give special handling to medicine, ammunition, and other delicate supplies
- Select the correct stock for issue
- Load, unload, and move stock, using equipment such as forklifts and hand trucks
- Keep records on incoming and outgoing stock

Helpful Attributes. Helpful school subjects include math, bookkeeping, accounting, and business administration. Helpful attributes include the following:

- Ability to keep accurate records
- Interest in operating forklifts and other warehouse equipment
- Preference for physical work
- Preference for work requiring attention to detail

Training Provided. Job training consists of classroom instruction, including practice in handling and storing stock. Further training occurs on the job and through advanced courses. Course content typically includes the following:

- Stock control and accounting procedures
- Procedures for shipping, receiving, storing, and issuing stock
- Procedures for handling medical and food supplies
- Movement, storage, and maintenance of ammunition

W

Physical Demands. Warehousing and distribution specialists may have to lift and carry heavy boxes of ammunition and other supplies. Normal color vision is required for specialties that handle color-coded parts, supplies, and ammunition.

Work Environment. Warehousing and distribution specialists work in large general supply centers, small specialized supply rooms, or ship storerooms.

Opportunities in the Military. The services have about 65,000 warehousing and distribution specialists. Each year, they need new specialists because of changes in personnel and the demands of the field. After job training, specialists stock shelves, learn about different parts and supplies, and fill supply requests. In time, they also estimate needs, order stock, and supervise others. Eventually, they may become superintendents of supply centers.

Civilian Occupations It Provides Training For (those with stars are described in Part IV): Bookkeeping, Accounting, and Auditing Clerks*; Computer Operators; Database Administrators; First-Line Supervisors/Managers of Office and Administrative Support Workers*; Laborers and Freight, Stock, and Material Movers, Hand*; Logisticians; Order Fillers, Wholesale and Retail Sales; Postal Service Clerks*; Procurement Clerks; Production, Planning, and Expediting Clerks*; Shipping, Receiving, and Traffic Clerks*; Stock Clerks—Stockroom, Warehouse, or Storage Yard.

Water and Sewage Treatment Plant Operators

Military bases operate their own water treatment plants when public facilities cannot be used. These plants provide drinking water and safely dispose of sewage. Water and sewage treatment plant operators maintain the systems that purify water and treat sewage.

Officer/Enlisted: Enlisted

Personality Type: Realistic. Realistic occupations frequently involve work activities that include practical, hands-on problems and solutions. They often deal with plants; animals; and real-world materials such as wood, tools, and machinery. Many of the occupations require working outside and do not involve a lot of paperwork or working closely with others.

Services That Offer the Job: Air Force, Army, Coast Guard, Navy

What They Do. Water and sewage treatment plant operators in the military perform some or all of the following duties:

- Operate pumps to transfer water from reservoirs and storage tanks to treatment plants
- Add chemicals and operate machinery that purifies water for drinking or cleans it for safe disposal
- Test water for chlorine content, acidity, oxygen demand, and impurities
- Regulate the flow of drinking water to meet demand

- Clean and maintain water treatment machinery
- Keep records of chemical treatments, water pressure, and maintenance

Helpful Attributes. Helpful school subjects include chemistry, math, and shop mechanics. Helpful attributes include the following:

- Interest in chemistry and pollution control
- Interest in working with mechanical equipment

Training Provided. Job training consists of classroom instruction, including practice operating water and sewage treatment equipment. Further training occurs on the job and through advanced courses. Course content typically includes the following:

- Operation of treatment systems
- Water testing and analysis
- Maintenance and repair of pumps, compressors, and other equipment

Physical Demands. Normal color vision is needed to examine water for acidity and impurities.

Work Environment. Water and sewage treatment plant operators work indoors and outdoors. They may be exposed to strong odors.

Opportunities in the Military. The services have more than 3,000 water and sewage plant operators. Each year, they need new plant operators because of changes in personnel and the demands of the field. After job training, new operators work under close supervision in water or sewage treatment plants. With experience, they may supervise plant operations. Eventually, they may become base utilities superintendents.

Civilian Occupations It Provides Training For (those with stars are described in Part IV): First-Line Supervisors/Managers of Mechanics, Installers, and Repairers*; First-Line Supervisors/Managers of Production and Operating Workers*; Industrial Machinery Mechanics*; Pipelayers; Water and Liquid Waste Treatment Plant and System Operators*.

Weapons Maintenance Technicians

Combat forces use many different types of weapons, from small field artillery to large ballistic missiles. Weapons may be fired from ships, planes, and ground stations. Most modern weapons have electronic components and systems that assist in locating targets and aiming and firing weapons. Weapons maintenance technicians maintain and repair weapons used by combat forces.

Officer/Enlisted: Enlisted

Personality Type: Realistic. Realistic occupations frequently involve work activities that include practical, hands-on problems and solutions. They often deal with plants; animals; and real-world materials such as wood, tools, and machinery. Many of the occupations require working outside and do not involve a lot of paperwork or working closely with others.

Services That Offer the Job: Air Force, Army, Coast Guard, Marines, Navy

What They Do. Weapons maintenance technicians in the military perform some or all of the following duties:

- Repair and maintain artillery, naval gun systems, and infantry weapons
- Clean and lubricate gyroscopes, sights, and other electro-optical fire control components
- Repair and maintain missile mounts, platforms, and launch mechanisms
- Test and adjust weapons firing, guidance, and launch systems
- Maintain, operate, service, and repair weapons support systems such as power generation and distribution systems, environmental control, loading equipment, and associated interfaces
- Operate and maintain automated data-processing equipment to perform munitions accounting, computations, and research

Helpful Attributes. Helpful school subjects include science and math. Helpful attributes include the following:

- Ability to do work requiring accuracy and attention to detail
- Interest in working with electronic or electrical equipment
- Interest in working with weapons

Training Provided. Job training consists of classroom instruction and practical experience. Training length varies depending on specialty. Further training occurs on the job and through advanced courses. Course content typically includes the following:

- Electronic and mechanical principles and concepts
- Use of schematics, drawings, blueprints, and wiring diagrams
- Operation, testing, and maintenance of weapons systems and fire control systems

Physical Demands. Some specialties involve moderate to heavy lifting. Normal color vision is required to read color-coded charts and diagrams.

Work Environment. Weapons maintenance technicians work in workshops when testing and repairing electronic components. They may work outdoors while inspecting and repairing combat vehicles, ships, artillery, aircraft, and missile silos.

Opportunities in the Military. The services have about 34,000 weapons maintenance technicians. Each year, they need new technicians because of changes in personnel and the demands of the field. After job training, they are assigned to weapons operations or maintenance units. They perform routine maintenance and work under close supervision. With experience, they may work more independently and train new personnel. Eventually, they may become managers of missile facilities or avionics or electronics maintenance units or shops.

Civilian Occupations It Provides Training For (those with stars are described in Part IV): Aircraft Mechanics and Service Technicians*; Aircraft Structure, Surfaces, Rigging, and Systems Assemblers*; Avionics Technicians*; Bus and Truck Mechanics and Diesel Engine Specialists*; Computer, Automated Teller, and Office Machine Repairers*; Electrical and Electronics Repairers, Commercial and Industrial Equipment*; Explosives Workers, Ordnance Handling Experts, and Blasters; First-Line Supervisors/Managers of Housekeeping and Janitorial Workers*; First-Line Supervisors/Managers of Mechanics, Installers, and Repairers*; Installation, Maintenance, and Repair Workers, All Other; Maintenance and Repair Workers, General*; Precision Instrument and Equipment Repairers, All Other; Radio Mechanics.

Welders and Metal Workers

Sheet metal is used as a building material in many military construction projects. Ships, tanks, and aircraft are made of heavy metal armor. Welders and metal workers make and install sheet metal products, such as roofs, air ducts, gutters, and vents. They also make custom parts to repair the structural parts of ships, submarines, landing craft, buildings, and equipment.

Officer/Enlisted: Enlisted

Personality Type: Realistic. Realistic occupations frequently involve work activities that include practical, hands-on problems and solutions. They often deal with plants; animals; and real-world materials such as wood, tools, and machinery. Many of the occupations require working outside and do not involve a lot of paperwork or working closely with others.

Services That Offer the Job: Air Force, Army, Coast Guard, Marines, Navy

What They Do. Welders and metal workers in the military perform some or all of the following duties:

- Weld, braze, or solder metal parts together
- Repair automotive and ship parts, using welding equipment
- Measure work with calipers, micrometers, and rulers

Helpful Attributes. Helpful school subjects include auto mechanics and industrial arts. Helpful attributes include the following:

- Interest in working with repair tools
- Preference for physical work

Training Provided. Job training consists of classroom instruction. Training length varies depending on specialty. Further training occurs on the job and through advanced courses. Course content typically includes the following:

- Sheet metal layout and duct work
- Procedures for cutting, brazing, and heat treating
- Operation and care of welding, soldering, and brazing equipment

Physical Demands. Welders and metal workers may have to lift heavy metal parts and work in crouching or kneeling positions. Good color vision is required for locating and marking reference points, setting and adjusting welding equipment, and matching paints.

Work Environment. Welders and metal workers work indoors in metalworking shops and aircraft hangars. They also work outdoors at construction sites, on ships, and in the field.

Opportunities in the Military. The services have more than 6,000 welders and metal workers. Each year, they need new welders and metal workers because of changes in personnel and the demands of the field. After job training, welders and metal workers begin to make and repair metal equipment under the direction of a supervisor. With experience, they may become managers of repair shops, maintenance depots, or shipyards.

Civilian Occupations It Provides Training For (those with stars are described in Part IV): Aircraft Mechanics and Service Technicians*; Computer-Controlled Machine Tool Operators, Metal and Plastic; First-Line Supervisors/Managers of Mechanics, Installers, and Repairers*; First-Line Supervisors/Managers of Production and Operating Workers*; Heat Treating Equipment Setters, Operators, and Tenders, Metal and Plastic; Lay-Out Workers, Metal and Plastic; Machinists*; Pipe Fitters and Steamfitters*; Plumbers*; Sheet Metal Workers*; Solderers and Brazers*; Structural Iron and Steel Workers*; Structural Metal Fabricators and Fitters; Welders, Cutters, and Welder Fitters*; Welders, Cutters, Solderers, and Brazers.

PART III

The Best Jobs Lists: Civilian Jobs Through Military Training

This part contains a lot of interesting lists, and it's a good place for you to start using the book. Here are some suggestions for using the lists to explore career options:

- The table of contents at the beginning of this book presents a complete listing of the list titles in this section. You can browse the lists or use the table of contents to find those that interest you most.
- We gave the lists clear titles, so most require little explanation. We provide comments for each group of lists.
- As you review the lists of civilian jobs, one or more of the jobs may appeal to you enough that you want to seek additional information. As this happens, mark that job (or, if someone else will be using this book, write it on a separate sheet of paper) so that you can look up the description of the job in Part IV. You should also look at the description of the related military job(s) in Part II.
- Keep in mind that all jobs in these lists meet our basic criteria for being included in this book. All lists, therefore, emphasize occupations with high pay, high growth, or large numbers of openings. These measures are easily quantified and are often presented in lists of best jobs in the newspapers and other media. While earnings, growth, and openings are important, there are other factors to consider in your career planning. For example, location, liking the people you work with, having an opportunity to serve others, and enjoying your work are a few of many factors that may define the ideal job for you. These measures are difficult or impossible to quantify and thus are not used in this book, so you will need to consider the importance of these issues yourself.
- All data used to create these lists comes from the U.S. Department of Labor and the Census Bureau. The earnings figures are based on the average annual pay received by full-time workers. Because the earnings represent the national averages, actual pay rates can vary greatly by location, amount of previous work experience, and other factors.

Some Details on the Lists

The sources of the information we used in constructing these lists are presented in this book's introduction. Here are some additional details on how we created the lists:

- Some jobs have the same scores for one or more data elements. For example, in the category of fastest-growing, two jobs (Desktop Publishers and Radiologic Technicians) are expected to grow at the same rate, 23.2 percent. Therefore we ordered these two jobs alphabetically, and their order has no other significance. There was no way to avoid these ties, so simply understand that the difference of several positions on a list may not mean as much as it seems.
- Some jobs share certain data elements. For example, in Part IV you will find separate descriptions of the jobs Automotive Master Mechanics and Automotive Specialty Technicians—so you will also find these as two separate jobs on the lists here in Part III. However, the U.S. Department of Labor provides data on earnings, job growth, and job openings only for the *single combined* job called Automotive Service Technicians and Mechanics, which means that on these lists we have to print the same information for both jobs. That can be misleading if you don't understand that these jobs share data. The earnings figure of $33,050 represents the *average* for the two jobs; probably there are differences in their earnings, but we don't have separate data. The figure of 15.7 percent for their job growth is also an *average*. It's especially important to understand that the figure of 93,000 job openings represents the *total number of job openings for the two jobs*. They share this figure—each job is projected to have *some fraction* of 93,000 job openings, but we don't know exactly how many. To remind you about how to read these figures, we identify all the jobs that share data in footnotes after each list that contains such jobs.

Best Jobs Overall Through Military Training: Lists of Jobs with the Highest Pay, Fastest Growth, and Most Openings

The four lists that follow are the most important lists in this book. To create these lists, we ranked 198 major civilian jobs for which military training is a common entry route according to a combination of their earnings, growth, and openings. We then selected the 150 jobs with the best combined scores for use in this book. (The process for ranking the jobs is explained in more detail in the introduction.)

The first list presents all 150 best jobs according to these combined scores for pay, growth, and number of openings. Three additional lists present the 50 jobs with the best scores for each of three measures: annual earnings, projected percentage growth through 2014, and number of annual openings. Descriptions for all the jobs in these lists are included in Part IV.

The 150 Best Civilian Jobs Through Military Training—Jobs with the Best Combination of Pay, Growth, and Openings

This is the list that most people want to see first. It includes the 150 jobs with a military training route that have the best overall combined ratings for earnings, projected growth, and number of openings. (The section in the introduction called "How the Best Jobs Through Military Training Were Selected" explains in detail how we rated jobs to assemble this list.)

You'll notice a wide variety of jobs on the list. Among the top 20 are jobs in health care, law enforcement, construction, and office support.

Dental Hygienists was the occupation with the best combined score, and it is on the top of the list. The other occupations follow in descending order based on their combined scores. Many jobs had tied scores and are simply listed one after another, so there are often only very small or even no differences between the scores of jobs that are near each other on the list. All other civilian job lists in this book use this list as their source. You can find descriptions for each of these jobs in Part IV.

The 150 Best Civilian Jobs Overall Through Military Training

Job	Annual Earnings	Percent Growth	Annual Openings
1. Dental Hygienists	$60,890	43.3%	17,000
2. Computer Support Specialists	$40,610	23.0%	87,000
3. Paralegals and Legal Assistants	$41,170	29.7%	28,000
4. Radiologic Technicians	$45,950	23.2%	17,000
5. Radiologic Technologists	$45,950	23.2%	17,000
6. Police Patrol Officers	$46,290	15.5%	47,000
7. Sheriffs and Deputy Sheriffs	$46,290	15.5%	47,000
8. Pipe Fitters and Steamfitters	$42,160	15.7%	61,000
9. Plumbers	$42,160	15.7%	61,000
10. First-Line Supervisors/Managers of Construction Trades and Extraction Workers	$51,970	10.9%	57,000
11. Legal Secretaries	$37,750	17.4%	41,000
12. Municipal Fire Fighters	$39,090	24.3%	21,000
13. First-Line Supervisors/Managers of Mechanics, Installers, and Repairers	$51,980	12.4%	33,000
14. Airline Pilots, Copilots, and Flight Engineers	$138,170	17.2%	7,000
15. Heating and Air Conditioning Mechanics and Installers	$37,040	19.0%	33,000
16. Refrigeration Mechanics and Installers	$37,040	19.0%	33,000

(continued)

(continued)

The 150 Best Civilian Jobs Overall Through Military Training

Job	Annual Earnings	Percent Growth	Annual Openings
17. Licensed Practical and Licensed Vocational Nurses	$35,230	17.1%	84,000
18. Technical Directors/Managers	$53,860	16.6%	11,000
19. First-Line Supervisors/Managers of Transportation and Material-Moving Machine and Vehicle Operators	$47,530	15.3%	22,000
20. Criminal Investigators and Special Agents	$55,790	16.3%	9,000
21. Police Detectives	$55,790	16.3%	9,000
22. Electricians	$42,790	11.8%	68,000
23. Storage and Distribution Managers	$69,120	12.7%	15,000
24. First-Line Supervisors/Managers of Police and Detectives	$65,570	15.5%	9,000
25. Construction Carpenters	$35,580	13.8%	210,000
26. Rough Carpenters	$35,580	13.8%	210,000
27. Municipal Fire Fighting and Prevention Supervisors	$60,840	21.1%	4,000
28. Executive Secretaries and Administrative Assistants	$35,960	12.4%	218,000
29. First-Line Supervisors/Managers of Office and Administrative Support Workers	$42,400	8.1%	167,000
30. Automotive Master Mechanics	$33,050	15.7%	93,000
31. Automotive Specialty Technicians	$33,050	15.7%	93,000
32. Graphic Designers	$38,390	15.2%	35,000
33. Construction and Building Inspectors	$44,720	22.3%	6,000
34. Dental Assistants	$29,520	42.7%	45,000
35. Medical Assistants	$25,350	52.1%	93,000
36. Truck Drivers, Heavy and Tractor-Trailer	$34,280	12.9%	274,000
37. Physical Therapist Assistants	$39,490	44.2%	7,000
38. Surgical Technologists	$34,830	29.5%	12,000
39. Cardiovascular Technologists and Technicians	$40,420	32.6%	5,000
40. Nursing Aides, Orderlies, and Attendants	$21,440	22.3%	307,000
41. Bus Drivers, Transit and Intercity	$31,010	21.7%	34,000
42. Hazardous Materials Removal Workers	$33,690	31.2%	11,000
43. Aircraft Mechanics and Service Technicians	$47,310	13.4%	11,000
44. Bus and Truck Mechanics and Diesel Engine Specialists	$36,620	14.4%	32,000
45. Social and Human Service Assistants	$25,030	29.7%	61,000
46. Payroll and Timekeeping Clerks	$31,360	17.3%	36,000
47. Sheet Metal Workers	$36,390	12.2%	50,000
48. Commercial Pilots	$55,810	16.8%	2,000
49. Maintenance and Repair Workers, General	$31,210	15.2%	154,000
50. Telecommunications Line Installers and Repairers	$42,410	10.8%	23,000

The 150 Best Civilian Jobs Overall Through Military Training

Job	Annual Earnings	Percent Growth	Annual Openings
51. First-Line Supervisors/Managers of Production and Operating Workers	$46,140	2.7%	89,000
52. Structural Iron and Steel Workers	$40,580	15.0%	13,000
53. Roofers	$31,230	16.8%	38,000
54. Purchasing Agents, Except Wholesale, Retail, and Farm Products	$49,030	8.1%	19,000
55. Highway Maintenance Workers	$30,250	23.3%	27,000
56. Medical and Clinical Laboratory Technicians	$31,700	25.0%	14,000
57. Retail Salespersons	$19,140	17.3%	1,350,000
58. Brickmasons and Blockmasons	$41,860	12.0%	17,000
59. Food Preparation Workers	$17,040	19.7%	294,000
60. Human Resources Assistants, Except Payroll and Timekeeping	$32,730	16.7%	28,000
61. Computer Programmers	$63,420	2.0%	28,000
62. First-Line Supervisors/Managers of Food Preparation and Serving Workers	$26,050	16.6%	187,000
63. Operating Engineers and Other Construction Equipment Operators	$35,830	11.6%	37,000
64. Pharmacy Technicians	$24,390	28.6%	35,000
65. Cement Masons and Concrete Finishers	$32,030	15.9%	32,000
66. Combined Food Preparation and Serving Workers, Including Fast Food	$14,790	17.1%	751,000
67. Elevator Installers and Repairers	$59,190	14.8%	3,000
68. Occupational Therapist Assistants	$39,750	34.1%	2,000
69. Orthotists and Prosthetists	$53,760	18.0%	fewer than 500
70. First-Line Supervisors/Managers of Housekeeping and Janitorial Workers	$30,330	19.0%	21,000
71. Civil Engineering Technicians	$39,210	14.1%	10,000
72. Taxi Drivers and Chauffeurs	$19,980	24.8%	43,000
73. Emergency Medical Technicians and Paramedics	$26,080	27.3%	21,000
74. Cooks, Restaurant	$19,840	16.6%	207,000
75. Truck Drivers, Light or Delivery Services	$24,790	15.7%	169,000
76. Desktop Publishers	$32,800	23.2%	8,000
77. Directors, Religious Activities and Education	$32,540	18.5%	10,000
78. Medical Records and Health Information Technicians	$26,690	28.9%	14,000
79. Biological Technicians	$34,270	17.2%	8,000
80. Lifeguards, Ski Patrol, and Other Recreational Protective Service Workers	$16,910	20.4%	49,000

(continued)

(continued)

The 150 Best Civilian Jobs Overall Through Military Training

Job	Annual Earnings	Percent Growth	Annual Openings
81. Chefs and Head Cooks	$32,330	16.7%	11,000
82. Hotel, Motel, and Resort Desk Clerks	$17,810	17.2%	62,000
83. Electrical and Electronics Repairers, Commercial and Industrial Equipment	$44,120	9.7%	8,000
84. Mechanical Engineering Technicians	$44,830	12.3%	5,000
85. Mobile Heavy Equipment Mechanics, Except Engines	$39,410	8.8%	14,000
86. Correctional Officers and Jailers	$34,090	6.7%	54,000
87. Interpreters and Translators	$34,800	19.9%	4,000
88. Nuclear Equipment Operation Technicians	$61,120	13.7%	1,000
89. Production, Planning, and Expediting Clerks	$37,590	7.7%	24,000
90. Automotive Body and Related Repairers	$34,810	10.3%	18,000
91. Camera Operators, Television, Video, and Motion Picture	$41,610	14.2%	4,000
92. Painters, Transportation Equipment	$34,840	14.1%	10,000
93. First-Line Supervisors/Managers of Retail Sales Workers	$32,840	3.8%	229,000
94. Security Guards	$20,760	12.6%	230,000
95. Court Reporters	$41,640	14.8%	3,000
96. Telecommunications Equipment Installers and Repairers, Except Line Installers	$50,620	–4.9%	21,000
97. Water and Liquid Waste Treatment Plant and System Operators	$34,930	16.2%	6,000
98. Audio and Video Equipment Technicians	$32,940	18.1%	5,000
99. Electrical Power-Line Installers and Repairers	$50,150	2.5%	11,000
100. Bookkeeping, Accounting, and Auditing Clerks	$29,490	5.9%	291,000
101. Laborers and Freight, Stock, and Material Movers, Hand	$20,610	10.2%	671,000
102. Medical Equipment Repairers	$39,570	14.8%	4,000
103. Computer, Automated Teller, and Office Machine Repairers	$36,060	3.8%	31,000
104. Drywall and Ceiling Tile Installers	$34,740	9.0%	17,000
105. Office Clerks, General	$23,070	8.4%	695,000
106. Music Composers and Arrangers	$34,810	10.4%	11,000
107. Machinists	$34,350	4.3%	33,000
108. Avionics Technicians	$46,630	9.1%	2,000
109. Solderers and Brazers	$30,990	5.0%	52,000
110. Welders, Cutters, and Welder Fitters	$30,990	5.0%	52,000
111. Aircraft Structure, Surfaces, Rigging, and Systems Assemblers	$43,990	7.8%	4,000
112. Boilermakers	$48,050	8.7%	2,000
113. Motorboat Mechanics	$32,780	15.1%	7,000

The 150 Best Civilian Jobs Overall Through Military Training

Job	Annual Earnings	Percent Growth	Annual Openings
114. Architectural Drafters	$40,390	4.6%	9,000
115. Civil Drafters	$40,390	4.6%	9,000
116. Packers and Packagers, Hand	$17,390	10.1%	194,000
117. Gas Plant Operators	$51,920	7.7%	2,000
118. Aerospace Engineering and Operations Technicians	$52,450	8.5%	1,000
119. Medical Equipment Preparers	$24,880	20.0%	8,000
120. Electro-Mechanical Technicians	$43,880	9.7%	2,000
121. Industrial Machinery Mechanics	$39,740	–0.2%	13,000
122. Control and Valve Installers and Repairers, Except Mechanical Door	$44,120	4.9%	4,000
123. Cooks, Short Order	$17,230	11.8%	58,000
124. Photographers	$26,100	12.3%	23,000
125. Power Plant Operators	$53,170	–0.4%	5,000
126. Paving, Surfacing, and Tamping Equipment Operators	$30,320	15.6%	7,000
127. Mates—Ship, Boat, and Barge	$50,940	4.8%	2,000
128. Pilots, Ship	$50,940	4.8%	2,000
129. Ship and Boat Captains	$50,940	4.8%	2,000
130. Locksmiths and Safe Repairers	$30,880	16.1%	5,000
131. Tellers	$21,300	6.8%	108,000
132. Transit and Railroad Police	$48,850	9.2%	fewer than 500
133. Riggers	$37,010	13.9%	2,000
134. Stationary Engineers and Boiler Operators	$44,600	3.4%	5,000
135. Crane and Tower Operators	$38,870	8.2%	4,000
136. Chemical Technicians	$38,500	4.4%	7,000
137. Shipping, Receiving, and Traffic Clerks	$25,180	3.7%	121,000
138. Pest Control Workers	$27,170	18.4%	4,000
139. Petroleum Pump System Operators, Refinery Operators, and Gaugers	$51,060	–8.6%	6,000
140. Secretaries, Except Legal, Medical, and Executive	$26,670	–2.5%	231,000
141. Electrical and Electronics Repairers, Powerhouse, Substation, and Relay	$54,970	–0.4%	2,000
142. Outdoor Power Equipment and Other Small Engine Mechanics	$25,810	14.0%	10,000
143. Postal Service Clerks	$48,310	0.0%	4,000
144. Mapping Technicians	$31,290	9.6%	9,000
145. Surveying Technicians	$31,290	9.6%	9,000

(continued)

(continued)

The 150 Best Civilian Jobs Overall Through Military Training

Job	Annual Earnings	Percent Growth	Annual Openings
146. Electrical and Electronics Installers and Repairers, Transportation Equipment	$41,490	6.6%	2,000
147. Inspectors, Testers, Sorters, Samplers, and Weighers	$29,200	–2.6%	85,000
148. Printing Machine Operators	$30,730	2.9%	26,000
149. Nuclear Power Reactor Operators	$66,230	–0.5%	1,000
150. Cargo and Freight Agents	$35,860	–5.6%	12,000

Jobs 4 and 5 share 17,000 openings. Jobs 6 and 7 share 47,000 openings. Jobs 8 and 9 share 61,000 openings. Job 12 shares 21,000 openings with another job not included in this list. Jobs 15 and 16 share 33,000 openings. Job 18 shares 11,000 openings with four other jobs not included in this list. Jobs 20 and 21 share 9,000 openings with each other and with two other jobs not included in this list. Job 23 shares 15,000 openings with another job not included in this list. Jobs 25 and 26 share 210,000 openings. Job 27 shares 4,000 openings with another job not included in this list. Jobs 30 and 31 share 93,000 openings. Job 88 shares 1,000 openings with another job not included in this list. Job 106 shares 11,000 openings with another job not included in this list. Jobs 109 and 110 share 52,000 openings. Jobs 114 and 115 share 9,000 openings. Jobs 127, 128, and 129 share 2,000 openings. Jobs 144 and 145 share 9,000 openings.

The 50 Best-Paying Civilian Jobs Through Military Training

Of the 150 jobs that met our criteria for this book, this list shows the 50 with the highest median earnings. (*Median earnings* means that half of all workers in these jobs earn more than that amount and half earn less. The median annual wage for all occupations in the workforce is $29,430.) This is a popular list for obvious reasons.

It's no accident that the job that tops this list—Airline Pilots, Copilots, and Flight Engineers—requires quite a bit more than military training. It requires a bachelor's degree *before* military training, unlike almost all the other jobs in this book. It also requires many years of military service to justify the time and money the military has invested in your training. But military training is a valuable entry route to this job, because civilian flying lessons can be an expensive way to get training and accumulate flying time, whereas the military *pays you* while you are earning your qualifications.

For the other jobs on this list, military training provides an attractive route for preparing or for reducing preparation time and expense.

Keep in mind that the earnings figures reflect the *national* median for *all* workers in the occupation. This is an important consideration, because starting pay in the job is usually a lot less than the pay that workers can earn with several years of experience. Earnings also vary significantly by region of the country, so actual pay in your area could be substantially different.

The 50 Best-Paying Civilian Jobs Through Military Training

Job	Annual Earnings
1. Airline Pilots, Copilots, and Flight Engineers	$138,170
2. Storage and Distribution Managers	$69,120
3. Nuclear Power Reactor Operators	$66,230
4. First-Line Supervisors/Managers of Police and Detectives	$65,570
5. Computer Programmers	$63,420
6. Nuclear Equipment Operation Technicians	$61,120
7. Dental Hygienists	$60,890
8. Municipal Fire Fighting and Prevention Supervisors	$60,840
9. Elevator Installers and Repairers	$59,190
10. Commercial Pilots	$55,810
11. Criminal Investigators and Special Agents	$55,790
12. Police Detectives	$55,790
13. Electrical and Electronics Repairers, Powerhouse, Substation, and Relay	$54,970
14. Technical Directors/Managers	$53,860
15. Orthotists and Prosthetists	$53,760
16. Power Plant Operators	$53,170
17. Aerospace Engineering and Operations Technicians	$52,450
18. First-Line Supervisors/Managers of Mechanics, Installers, and Repairers	$51,980
19. First-Line Supervisors/Managers of Construction Trades and Extraction Workers	$51,970
20. Gas Plant Operators	$51,920
21. Petroleum Pump System Operators, Refinery Operators, and Gaugers	$51,060
22. Mates—Ship, Boat, and Barge	$50,940
23. Pilots, Ship	$50,940
24. Ship and Boat Captains	$50,940
25. Telecommunications Equipment Installers and Repairers, Except Line Installers	$50,620
26. Electrical Power-Line Installers and Repairers	$50,150
27. Purchasing Agents, Except Wholesale, Retail, and Farm Products	$49,030
28. Transit and Railroad Police	$48,850
29. Postal Service Clerks	$48,310
30. Boilermakers	$48,050
31. First-Line Supervisors/Managers of Transportation and Material-Moving Machine and Vehicle Operators	$47,530
32. Aircraft Mechanics and Service Technicians	$47,310
33. Avionics Technicians	$46,630
34. Police Patrol Officers	$46,290
35. Sheriffs and Deputy Sheriffs	$46,290
36. First-Line Supervisors/Managers of Production and Operating Workers	$46,140

(continued)

(continued)

The 50 Best-Paying Civilian Jobs Through Military Training

Job	Annual Earnings
37. Radiologic Technicians	$45,950
38. Radiologic Technologists	$45,950
39. Mechanical Engineering Technicians	$44,830
40. Construction and Building Inspectors	$44,720
41. Stationary Engineers and Boiler Operators	$44,600
42. Control and Valve Installers and Repairers, Except Mechanical Door	$44,120
43. Electrical and Electronics Repairers, Commercial and Industrial Equipment	$44,120
44. Aircraft Structure, Surfaces, Rigging, and Systems Assemblers	$43,990
45. Electro-Mechanical Technicians	$43,880
46. Electricians	$42,790
47. Telecommunications Line Installers and Repairers	$42,410
48. First-Line Supervisors/Managers of Office and Administrative Support Workers	$42,400
49. Pipe Fitters and Steamfitters	$42,160
50. Plumbers	$42,160

The 50 Fastest-Growing Civilian Jobs Through Military Training

Of the 150 jobs that met our criteria for this book, this list shows the 50 that are projected to have the highest percentage increase in the number of people employed through 2014. (The average growth rate for *all* occupations in the workforce is 14.8 percent.)

Jobs in the health care fields dominate the top of this list of the 50 fastest-growing jobs. Medical Assistants is the job with the highest growth rate—the number employed is projected to grow by more than half during this time. You can find a wide range of rapidly growing jobs in a variety of fields among the jobs in the full list of 150 jobs.

The 50 Fastest-Growing Civilian Jobs Through Military Training

Job	Percent Growth
1. Medical Assistants	52.1%
2. Physical Therapist Assistants	44.2%
3. Dental Hygienists	43.3%
4. Dental Assistants	42.7%
5. Occupational Therapist Assistants	34.1%
6. Cardiovascular Technologists and Technicians	32.6%

The 50 Fastest-Growing Civilian Jobs Through Military Training

Job	Percent Growth
7. Hazardous Materials Removal Workers	31.2%
8. Paralegals and Legal Assistants	29.7%
9. Social and Human Service Assistants	29.7%
10. Surgical Technologists	29.5%
11. Medical Records and Health Information Technicians	28.9%
12. Pharmacy Technicians	28.6%
13. Emergency Medical Technicians and Paramedics	27.3%
14. Medical and Clinical Laboratory Technicians	25.0%
15. Taxi Drivers and Chauffeurs	24.8%
16. Municipal Fire Fighters	24.3%
17. Highway Maintenance Workers	23.3%
18. Desktop Publishers	23.2%
19. Radiologic Technicians	23.2%
20. Radiologic Technologists	23.2%
21. Computer Support Specialists	23.0%
22. Construction and Building Inspectors	22.3%
23. Nursing Aides, Orderlies, and Attendants	22.3%
24. Bus Drivers, Transit and Intercity	21.7%
25. Municipal Fire Fighting and Prevention Supervisors	21.1%
26. Lifeguards, Ski Patrol, and Other Recreational Protective Service Workers	20.4%
27. Medical Equipment Preparers	20.0%
28. Interpreters and Translators	19.9%
29. Food Preparation Workers	19.7%
30. First-Line Supervisors/Managers of Housekeeping and Janitorial Workers	19.0%
31. Heating and Air Conditioning Mechanics and Installers	19.0%
32. Refrigeration Mechanics and Installers	19.0%
33. Directors, Religious Activities and Education	18.5%
34. Pest Control Workers	18.4%
35. Audio and Video Equipment Technicians	18.1%
36. Orthotists and Prosthetists	18.0%
37. Legal Secretaries	17.4%
38. Payroll and Timekeeping Clerks	17.3%
39. Retail Salespersons	17.3%
40. Airline Pilots, Copilots, and Flight Engineers	17.2%
41. Biological Technicians	17.2%
42. Hotel, Motel, and Resort Desk Clerks	17.2%
43. Combined Food Preparation and Serving Workers, Including Fast Food	17.1%

(continued)

(continued)

The 50 Fastest-Growing Civilian Jobs Through Military Training	
Job	**Percent Growth**
44. Licensed Practical and Licensed Vocational Nurses	17.1%
45. Commercial Pilots	16.8%
46. Roofers	16.8%
47. Chefs and Head Cooks	16.7%
48. Human Resources Assistants, Except Payroll and Timekeeping	16.7%
49. Cooks, Restaurant	16.6%
50. First-Line Supervisors/Managers of Food Preparation and Serving Workers	16.6%

The 50 Civilian Jobs Through Military Training with the Most Openings

Of the 150 jobs that met our criteria for this book, this list shows the 50 jobs that are projected to have the largest number of job openings per year.

Jobs with many openings present several advantages that may be attractive if you're planning on military service. Because there are many openings projected through 2014, you have a better chance of getting one of these jobs a few years from now, when you are ready to hang up your uniform. If part-time work is your goal, the odds of achieving that work arrangement are better when there are more openings. Though some of these jobs have average or below-average pay, some also pay quite well.

It is interesting to note that high technology does not play a large role among the jobs on this list. Therefore it is not really true that nowadays you must master high-tech skills to be employable. In fact, most of these jobs have so many openings precisely because they require hands-on work and workers cannot be replaced by technology. They also require on-site work, sometimes in-person work, and therefore cannot be exported overseas.

The 50 Civilian Jobs Through Military Training with the Most Openings	
Job	**Annual Openings**
1. Retail Salespersons	1,350,000
2. Combined Food Preparation and Serving Workers, Including Fast Food	751,000
3. Office Clerks, General	695,000
4. Laborers and Freight, Stock, and Material Movers, Hand	671,000
5. Nursing Aides, Orderlies, and Attendants	307,000
6. Food Preparation Workers	294,000
7. Bookkeeping, Accounting, and Auditing Clerks	291,000

The 50 Civilian Jobs Through Military Training with the Most Openings	
Job	**Annual Openings**
8. Truck Drivers, Heavy and Tractor-Trailer	274,000
9. Secretaries, Except Legal, Medical, and Executive	231,000
10. Security Guards	230,000
11. First-Line Supervisors/Managers of Retail Sales Workers	229,000
12. Executive Secretaries and Administrative Assistants	218,000
13. Construction Carpenters	210,000
14. Rough Carpenters	210,000
15. Cooks, Restaurant	207,000
16. Packers and Packagers, Hand	194,000
17. First-Line Supervisors/Managers of Food Preparation and Serving Workers	187,000
18. Truck Drivers, Light or Delivery Services	169,000
19. First-Line Supervisors/Managers of Office and Administrative Support Workers	167,000
20. Maintenance and Repair Workers, General	154,000
21. Shipping, Receiving, and Traffic Clerks	121,000
22. Tellers	108,000
23. Automotive Master Mechanics	93,000
24. Automotive Specialty Technicians	93,000
25. Medical Assistants	93,000
26. First-Line Supervisors/Managers of Production and Operating Workers	89,000
27. Computer Support Specialists	87,000
28. Inspectors, Testers, Sorters, Samplers, and Weighers	85,000
29. Licensed Practical and Licensed Vocational Nurses	84,000
30. Electricians	68,000
31. Hotel, Motel, and Resort Desk Clerks	62,000
32. Pipe Fitters and Steamfitters	61,000
33. Plumbers	61,000
34. Social and Human Service Assistants	61,000
35. Cooks, Short Order	58,000
36. First-Line Supervisors/Managers of Construction Trades and Extraction Workers	57,000
37. Correctional Officers and Jailers	54,000
38. Solderers and Brazers	52,000
39. Welders, Cutters, and Welder Fitters	52,000
40. Sheet Metal Workers	50,000
41. Lifeguards, Ski Patrol, and Other Recreational Protective Service Workers	49,000
42. Police Patrol Officers	47,000
43. Sheriffs and Deputy Sheriffs	47,000
44. Dental Assistants	45,000

(continued)

(continued)

The 50 Civilian Jobs Through Military Training with the Most Openings

Job	Annual Openings
45. Taxi Drivers and Chauffeurs	43,000
46. Legal Secretaries	41,000
47. Roofers	38,000
48. Operating Engineers and Other Construction Equipment Operators	37,000
49. Payroll and Timekeeping Clerks	36,000
50. Graphic Designers	35,000

Jobs 13 and 14 share 210,000 openings. Jobs 23 and 24 share 93,000 openings. Jobs 32 and 33 share 61,000 openings. Jobs 38 and 39 share 52,000 openings. Jobs 42 and 43 share 47,000 openings.

Best Civilian Jobs Lists Through Military Training by Demographic

Demographic statistics can provide some useful insights into the 150 jobs in this book. So we included lists that highlight jobs with a high percentage of part-time workers, self-employed workers, and male or female workers.

All of the lists in this section were created by using a similar process. We began with all 150 best jobs through military training and sorted those jobs in order of the primary criterion for each set of lists. Then, we selected the jobs with the highest percentage of workers fitting the primary criterion and listed them along with their earnings, growth, and number of openings data. (For example, we sorted all 150 jobs based on the percentage of part-time workers and then selected the jobs with more than 15 percent of these workers for inclusion in the first list for this group.) From the list of jobs with a high percentage of each type of worker, we created four more-specialized lists:

- 25 Best Jobs Overall (jobs with the best combined score for earnings, growth rate, and number of openings)
- 25 Best-Paying Jobs
- 25 Fastest-Growing Jobs
- 25 Jobs with the Most Openings

Again, each of these four lists includes only jobs from among those with the highest percentages of different types of workers. The same basic process was used to create all the lists in this section. The lists are interesting, and we hope you find them helpful.

Best Civilian Jobs Through Military Training with a High Percentage of Part-Time Workers

Full-time work is the norm for active-duty military personnel, but in civilian life about half of not-yet-retired veterans work in part-time jobs. Some of these vets are working part time while seeking full-time work, but others prefer part-time work—and so may you. For example, after you leave the service you may want to start a family and assume major child care duties. Or you may want to work part time while using your G.I. Bill benefits to pursue further education or training.

Look over the lists of civilian jobs with high percentages (more than 15 percent) of part-time workers and you will find some interesting things. For example, if you look at the top of the list of jobs with the *most* part-time workers, you will find a wide variety of fields represented: recreation, health care, food service, the arts, transportation, and clerical work. But next look at the *best jobs overall,* and a different picture emerges: The top twenty slots are almost monopolized by health-care jobs.

This is fortunate, because part-time workers in the health-care field tend to defy the rule of thumb that part-time workers can expect to earn an hourly rate of about 60 cents for every dollar that full-time workers earn. In fact, for a few jobs in health care, part-timers get a *better* hourly wage. This may be partly because the part-timers in these jobs tend to have good skills credentials and partly because much of the part-time work is on higher-paid late-night shifts.

If you want to work part time now or in the future, these lists will help you identify jobs that are more likely to provide that opportunity. If you want full-time work, the lists may also help you identify civilian jobs for which such opportunities are more difficult to find. In either case, it's good information to know in advance.

Best Civilian Jobs Through Military Training with the Highest Percentage of Part-Time Workers

Job	Percent Part-Time Workers
1. Lifeguards, Ski Patrol, and Other Recreational Protective Service Workers	63.8%
2. Dental Hygienists	56.0%
3. Combined Food Preparation and Serving Workers, Including Fast Food	54.3%
4. Food Preparation Workers	53.7%
5. Music Composers and Arrangers	46.1%
6. Dental Assistants	38.9%
7. Bus Drivers, Transit and Intercity	38.4%
8. Retail Salespersons	36.7%

(continued)

(continued)

Best Civilian Jobs Through Military Training with the Highest Percentage of Part-Time Workers

Job	Percent Part-Time Workers
9. Office Clerks, General	29.7%
10. Bookkeeping, Accounting, and Auditing Clerks	29.5%
11. Photographers	28.9%
12. Physical Therapist Assistants	28.6%
13. Nursing Aides, Orderlies, and Attendants	28.0%
14. Directors, Religious Activities and Education	27.9%
15. Camera Operators, Television, Video, and Motion Picture	27.6%
16. Medical Assistants	27.5%
17. Medical Equipment Preparers	27.5%
18. Tellers	26.6%
19. Laborers and Freight, Stock, and Material Movers, Hand	25.1%
20. Hotel, Motel, and Resort Desk Clerks	24.6%
21. Pharmacy Technicians	23.2%
22. Surgical Technologists	23.2%
23. Licensed Practical and Licensed Vocational Nurses	21.9%
24. Graphic Designers	21.3%
25. Taxi Drivers and Chauffeurs	21.0%
26. Executive Secretaries and Administrative Assistants	20.3%
27. Legal Secretaries	20.3%
28. Secretaries, Except Legal, Medical, and Executive	20.3%
29. Occupational Therapist Assistants	18.6%
30. Audio and Video Equipment Technicians	18.3%
31. Locksmiths and Safe Repairers	18.2%
32. Orthotists and Prosthetists	18.2%
33. Packers and Packagers, Hand	17.8%
34. Medical Records and Health Information Technicians	17.6%
35. Medical and Clinical Laboratory Technicians	17.3%
36. Cardiovascular Technologists and Technicians	17.2%
37. Radiologic Technicians	17.2%
38. Radiologic Technologists	17.2%
39. Security Guards	17.1%
40. Social and Human Service Assistants	16.0%
41. First-Line Supervisors/Managers of Food Preparation and Serving Workers	15.5%

The jobs in the following four lists are derived from the preceding list of the civilian jobs with the highest percentage of part-time workers.

Best Civilian Jobs Through Military Training Overall for Part-Time Workers

Job	Percent Part-Time Workers	Annual Earnings	Percent Growth	Annual Openings
1. Dental Hygienists	56.0%	$60,890	43.3%	17,000
2. Medical Assistants	27.5%	$25,350	52.1%	93,000
3. Radiologic Technicians	17.2%	$45,950	23.2%	17,000
4. Radiologic Technologists	17.2%	$45,950	23.2%	17,000
5. Dental Assistants	38.9%	$29,520	42.7%	45,000
6. Physical Therapist Assistants	28.6%	$39,490	44.2%	7,000
7. Cardiovascular Technologists and Technicians	17.2%	$40,420	32.6%	5,000
8. Nursing Aides, Orderlies, and Attendants	28.0%	$21,440	22.3%	307,000
9. Social and Human Service Assistants	16.0%	$25,030	29.7%	61,000
10. Occupational Therapist Assistants	18.6%	$39,750	34.1%	2,000
11. Surgical Technologists	23.2%	$34,830	29.5%	12,000
12. Licensed Practical and Licensed Vocational Nurses	21.9%	$35,230	17.1%	84,000
13. Executive Secretaries and Administrative Assistants	20.3%	$35,960	12.4%	218,000
14. Legal Secretaries	20.3%	$37,750	17.4%	41,000
15. Medical and Clinical Laboratory Technicians	17.3%	$31,700	25.0%	14,000
16. Bus Drivers, Transit and Intercity	38.4%	$31,010	21.7%	34,000
17. Medical Records and Health Information Technicians	17.6%	$26,690	28.9%	14,000
18. Graphic Designers	21.3%	$38,390	15.2%	35,000
19. Pharmacy Technicians	23.2%	$24,390	28.6%	35,000
20. Retail Salespersons	36.7%	$19,140	17.3%	1,350,000
21. Food Preparation Workers	53.7%	$17,040	19.7%	294,000
22. First-Line Supervisors/Managers of Food Preparation and Serving Workers	15.5%	$26,050	16.6%	187,000
23. Orthotists and Prosthetists	18.2%	$53,760	18.0%	fewer than 500
24. Taxi Drivers and Chauffeurs	21.0%	$19,980	24.8%	43,000
25. Bookkeeping, Accounting, and Auditing Clerks	29.5%	$29,490	5.9%	291,000

Jobs 3 and 4 share 17,000 openings.

Best-Paying Civilian Jobs Through Military Training for Part-Time Workers

Job	Percent Part-Time Workers	Annual Earnings
1. Dental Hygienists	56.0%	$60,890
2. Orthotists and Prosthetists	18.2%	$53,760
3. Radiologic Technicians	17.2%	$45,950
4. Radiologic Technologists	17.2%	$45,950
5. Camera Operators, Television, Video, and Motion Picture	27.6%	$41,610
6. Cardiovascular Technologists and Technicians	17.2%	$40,420
7. Occupational Therapist Assistants	18.6%	$39,750
8. Physical Therapist Assistants	28.6%	$39,490
9. Graphic Designers	21.3%	$38,390
10. Legal Secretaries	20.3%	$37,750
11. Executive Secretaries and Administrative Assistants	20.3%	$35,960
12. Licensed Practical and Licensed Vocational Nurses	21.9%	$35,230
13. Surgical Technologists	23.2%	$34,830
14. Music Composers and Arrangers	46.1%	$34,810
15. Audio and Video Equipment Technicians	18.3%	$32,940
16. Directors, Religious Activities and Education	27.9%	$32,540
17. Medical and Clinical Laboratory Technicians	17.3%	$31,700
18. Bus Drivers, Transit and Intercity	38.4%	$31,010
19. Locksmiths and Safe Repairers	18.2%	$30,880
20. Dental Assistants	38.9%	$29,520
21. Bookkeeping, Accounting, and Auditing Clerks	29.5%	$29,490
22. Medical Records and Health Information Technicians	17.6%	$26,690
23. Secretaries, Except Legal, Medical, and Executive	20.3%	$26,670
24. Photographers	28.9%	$26,100
25. First-Line Supervisors/Managers of Food Preparation and Serving Workers	15.5%	$26,050

Fastest-Growing Civilian Jobs Through Military Training for Part-Time Workers

Job	Percent Part-Time Workers	Percent Growth
1. Medical Assistants	27.5%	52.1%
2. Physical Therapist Assistants	28.6%	44.2%

Fastest-Growing Civilian Jobs Through Military Training for Part-Time Workers

Job	Percent Part-Time Workers	Percent Growth
3. Dental Hygienists	56.0%	43.3%
4. Dental Assistants	38.9%	42.7%
5. Occupational Therapist Assistants	18.6%	34.1%
6. Cardiovascular Technologists and Technicians	17.2%	32.6%
7. Social and Human Service Assistants	16.0%	29.7%
8. Surgical Technologists	23.2%	29.5%
9. Medical Records and Health Information Technicians	17.6%	28.9%
10. Pharmacy Technicians	23.2%	28.6%
11. Medical and Clinical Laboratory Technicians	17.3%	25.0%
12. Taxi Drivers and Chauffeurs	21.0%	24.8%
13. Radiologic Technicians	17.2%	23.2%
14. Radiologic Technologists	17.2%	23.2%
15. Nursing Aides, Orderlies, and Attendants	28.0%	22.3%
16. Bus Drivers, Transit and Intercity	38.4%	21.7%
17. Lifeguards, Ski Patrol, and Other Recreational Protective Service Workers	63.8%	20.4%
18. Medical Equipment Preparers	27.5%	20.0%
19. Food Preparation Workers	53.7%	19.7%
20. Directors, Religious Activities and Education	27.9%	18.5%
21. Audio and Video Equipment Technicians	18.3%	18.1%
22. Orthotists and Prosthetists	18.2%	18.0%
23. Legal Secretaries	20.3%	17.4%
24. Retail Salespersons	36.7%	17.3%
25. Hotel, Motel, and Resort Desk Clerks	24.6%	17.2%

Civilian Jobs Through Military Training for Part-Time Workers with the Most Openings

Job	Percent Part-Time Workers	Annual Openings
1. Retail Salespersons	36.7%	1,350,000
2. Combined Food Preparation and Serving Workers, Including Fast Food	54.3%	751,000
3. Office Clerks, General	29.7%	695,000
4. Laborers and Freight, Stock, and Material Movers, Hand	25.1%	671,000

(continued)

(continued)

Civilian Jobs Through Military Training for Part-Time Workers with the Most Openings

Job	Percent Part-Time Workers	Annual Openings
5. Nursing Aides, Orderlies, and Attendants	28.0%	307,000
6. Food Preparation Workers	53.7%	294,000
7. Bookkeeping, Accounting, and Auditing Clerks	29.5%	291,000
8. Secretaries, Except Legal, Medical, and Executive	20.3%	231,000
9. Security Guards	17.1%	230,000
10. Executive Secretaries and Administrative Assistants	20.3%	218,000
11. Packers and Packagers, Hand	17.8%	194,000
12. First-Line Supervisors/Managers of Food Preparation and Serving Workers	15.5%	187,000
13. Tellers	26.6%	108,000
14. Medical Assistants	27.5%	93,000
15. Licensed Practical and Licensed Vocational Nurses	21.9%	84,000
16. Hotel, Motel, and Resort Desk Clerks	24.6%	62,000
17. Social and Human Service Assistants	16.0%	61,000
18. Lifeguards, Ski Patrol, and Other Recreational Protective Service Workers	63.8%	49,000
19. Dental Assistants	38.9%	45,000
20. Taxi Drivers and Chauffeurs	21.0%	43,000
21. Legal Secretaries	20.3%	41,000
22. Graphic Designers	21.3%	35,000
23. Pharmacy Technicians	23.2%	35,000
24. Bus Drivers, Transit and Intercity	38.4%	34,000
25. Photographers	28.9%	23,000

Best Civilian Jobs Through Military Training with a High Percentage of Self-Employed Workers

More than 10 percent of the civilian workforce is self-employed, but among veterans the fraction is about 15 percent. Did you think that military experience teaches only how to follow orders? This statistic suggests otherwise.

Although you may think of the self-employed as having similar jobs, they actually work in an enormous range of situations, fields, and work environments that you may not have considered. Among the self-employed are people who own small or large businesses; professionals such as lawyers, psychologists, and medical doctors; part-time workers; people working on a contract basis for one or more employers; people running home consulting companies or other home-based businesses; and people in many other situations. They may go to the same office every day, as an attorney might; visit multiple employers during the course of a week; or do most of their work from home. Some work part time, others full time, some as a way to have fun, some so they can spend time with their children or go back to school.

The point is that there is an enormous range of situations, and one of them could make sense for you as a career that follows military training.

The following list contains civilian jobs in which more than 10 percent of the workers are self-employed.

Best Civilian Jobs Through Military Training with the Highest Percentage of Self-Employed Workers

Job	Percent Self-Employed Workers
1. Photographers	58.8%
2. Music Composers and Arrangers	44.8%
3. Locksmiths and Safe Repairers	37.6%
4. Construction Carpenters	32.4%
5. Rough Carpenters	32.4%
6. First-Line Supervisors/Managers of Retail Sales Workers	31.9%
7. Technical Directors/Managers	30.4%
8. Brickmasons and Blockmasons	28.6%
9. Taxi Drivers and Chauffeurs	25.7%
10. Graphic Designers	25.6%
11. First-Line Supervisors/Managers of Construction Trades and Extraction Workers	24.7%
12. Roofers	23.8%
13. Drywall and Ceiling Tile Installers	23.4%
14. Camera Operators, Television, Video, and Motion Picture	21.1%
15. Outdoor Power Equipment and Other Small Engine Mechanics	19.2%
16. Motorboat Mechanics	18.9%
17. Automotive Body and Related Repairers	17.6%
18. Medical Equipment Repairers	16.2%
19. Automotive Master Mechanics	14.8%
20. Automotive Specialty Technicians	14.8%
21. Orthotists and Prosthetists	14.4%
22. Computer, Automated Teller, and Office Machine Repairers	13.7%
23. Interpreters and Translators	13.5%
24. Pipe Fitters and Steamfitters	13.3%

(continued)

(continued)

Best Civilian Jobs Through Military Training with the Highest Percentage of Self-Employed Workers

Job	Percent Self-Employed Workers
25. Plumbers	13.3%
26. Heating and Air Conditioning Mechanics and Installers	13.1%
27. Refrigeration Mechanics and Installers	13.1%
28. Court Reporters	10.9%
29. Construction and Building Inspectors	10.2%

The jobs in the following four lists are derived from the preceding list of the civilian jobs with the highest percentage of self-employed workers. All of the following lists give earnings estimates, but keep in mind that these figures are based on a survey that *does not include self-employed workers*. The median earnings for self-employed workers may be significantly higher or lower.

Best Civilian Jobs Through Military Training Overall for Self-Employed Workers

Job	Percent Self-Employed Workers	Annual Earnings	Percent Growth	Annual Openings
1. Pipe Fitters and Steamfitters	13.3%	$42,160	15.7%	61,000
2. Plumbers	13.3%	$42,160	15.7%	61,000
3. Heating and Air Conditioning Mechanics and Installers	13.1%	$37,040	19.0%	33,000
4. Refrigeration Mechanics and Installers	13.1%	$37,040	19.0%	33,000
5. Technical Directors/Managers	30.4%	$53,860	16.6%	11,000
6. Construction and Building Inspectors	10.2%	$44,720	22.3%	6,000
7. Automotive Master Mechanics	14.8%	$33,050	15.7%	93,000
8. Automotive Specialty Technicians	14.8%	$33,050	15.7%	93,000
9. First-Line Supervisors/Managers of Construction Trades and Extraction Workers	24.7%	$51,970	10.9%	57,000
10. Graphic Designers	25.6%	$38,390	15.2%	35,000
11. Construction Carpenters	32.4%	$35,580	13.8%	210,000
12. Rough Carpenters	32.4%	$35,580	13.8%	210,000
13. Orthotists and Prosthetists	14.4%	$53,760	18.0%	fewer than 500
14. Taxi Drivers and Chauffeurs	25.7%	$19,980	24.8%	43,000
15. Roofers	23.8%	$31,230	16.8%	38,000

Best Civilian Jobs Through Military Training Overall for Self-Employed Workers

Job	Percent Self-Employed Workers	Annual Earnings	Percent Growth	Annual Openings
16. Brickmasons and Blockmasons	28.6%	$41,860	12.0%	17,000
17. Interpreters and Translators	13.5%	$34,800	19.9%	4,000
18. Medical Equipment Repairers	16.2%	$39,570	14.8%	4,000
19. Camera Operators, Television, Video, and Motion Picture	21.1%	$41,610	14.2%	4,000
20. Court Reporters	10.9%	$41,640	14.8%	3,000
21. First-Line Supervisors/Managers of Retail Sales Workers	31.9%	$32,840	3.8%	229,000
22. Computer, Automated Teller, and Office Machine Repairers	13.7%	$36,060	3.8%	31,000
23. Automotive Body and Related Repairers	17.6%	$34,810	10.3%	18,000
24. Locksmiths and Safe Repairers	37.6%	$30,880	16.1%	5,000
25. Motorboat Mechanics	18.9%	$32,780	15.1%	7,000

Jobs 1 and 2 share 61,000 openings. Jobs 3 and 4 share 33,000 openings. Job 5 shares 11,000 openings with four other jobs not included in this list. Jobs 7 and 8 share 93,000 openings. Jobs 11 and 12 share 210,000 openings.

Best-Paying Civilian Jobs Through Military Training for Self-Employed Workers

Job	Percent Self-Employed Workers	Annual Earnings
1. Technical Directors/Managers	30.4%	$53,860
2. Orthotists and Prosthetists	14.4%	$53,760
3. First-Line Supervisors/Managers of Construction Trades and Extraction Workers	24.7%	$51,970
4. Construction and Building Inspectors	10.2%	$44,720
5. Pipe Fitters and Steamfitters	13.3%	$42,160
6. Plumbers	13.3%	$42,160
7. Brickmasons and Blockmasons	28.6%	$41,860
8. Court Reporters	10.9%	$41,640
9. Camera Operators, Television, Video, and Motion Picture	21.1%	$41,610
10. Medical Equipment Repairers	16.2%	$39,570
11. Graphic Designers	25.6%	$38,390

(continued)

(continued)

Best-Paying Civilian Jobs Through Military Training for Self-Employed Workers

Job	Percent Self-Employed Workers	Annual Earnings
12. Heating and Air Conditioning Mechanics and Installers	13.1%	$37,040
13. Refrigeration Mechanics and Installers	13.1%	$37,040
14. Computer, Automated Teller, and Office Machine Repairers	13.7%	$36,060
15. Construction Carpenters	32.4%	$35,580
16. Rough Carpenters	32.4%	$35,580
17. Automotive Body and Related Repairers	17.6%	$34,810
18. Music Composers and Arrangers	44.8%	$34,810
19. Interpreters and Translators	13.5%	$34,800
20. Drywall and Ceiling Tile Installers	23.4%	$34,740
21. Automotive Master Mechanics	14.8%	$33,050
22. Automotive Specialty Technicians	14.8%	$33,050
23. First-Line Supervisors/Managers of Retail Sales Workers	31.9%	$32,840
24. Motorboat Mechanics	18.9%	$32,780
25. Roofers	23.8%	$31,230

Fastest-Growing Civilian Jobs Through Military Training for Self-Employed Workers

Job	Percent Self-Employed Workers	Percent Growth
1. Taxi Drivers and Chauffeurs	25.7%	24.8%
2. Construction and Building Inspectors	10.2%	22.3%
3. Interpreters and Translators	13.5%	19.9%
4. Heating and Air Conditioning Mechanics and Installers	13.1%	19.0%
5. Refrigeration Mechanics and Installers	13.1%	19.0%
6. Orthotists and Prosthetists	14.4%	18.0%
7. Roofers	23.8%	16.8%
8. Technical Directors/Managers	30.4%	16.6%
9. Locksmiths and Safe Repairers	37.6%	16.1%
10. Automotive Master Mechanics	14.8%	15.7%
11. Automotive Specialty Technicians	14.8%	15.7%
12. Pipe Fitters and Steamfitters	13.3%	15.7%

Fastest-Growing Civilian Jobs Through Military Training for Self-Employed Workers

Job	Percent Self-Employed Workers	Percent Growth
13. Plumbers	13.3%	15.7%
14. Graphic Designers	25.6%	15.2%
15. Motorboat Mechanics	18.9%	15.1%
16. Court Reporters	10.9%	14.8%
17. Medical Equipment Repairers	16.2%	14.8%
18. Camera Operators, Television, Video, and Motion Picture	21.1%	14.2%
19. Outdoor Power Equipment and Other Small Engine Mechanics	19.2%	14.0%
20. Construction Carpenters	32.4%	13.8%
21. Rough Carpenters	32.4%	13.8%
22. Photographers	58.8%	12.3%
23. Brickmasons and Blockmasons	28.6%	12.0%
24. First-Line Supervisors/Managers of Construction Trades and Extraction Workers	24.7%	10.9%
25. Music Composers and Arrangers	44.8%	10.4%

Civilian Jobs Through Military Training for Self-Employed Workers with the Most Openings

Job	Percent Self-Employed Workers	Annual Openings
1. First-Line Supervisors/Managers of Retail Sales Workers	31.9%	229,000
2. Construction Carpenters	32.4%	210,000
3. Rough Carpenters	32.4%	210,000
4. Automotive Master Mechanics	14.8%	93,000
5. Automotive Specialty Technicians	14.8%	93,000
6. Pipe Fitters and Steamfitters	13.3%	61,000
7. Plumbers	13.3%	61,000
8. First-Line Supervisors/Managers of Construction Trades and Extraction Workers	24.7%	57,000
9. Taxi Drivers and Chauffeurs	25.7%	43,000
10. Roofers	23.8%	38,000
11. Graphic Designers	25.6%	35,000
12. Heating and Air Conditioning Mechanics and Installers	13.1%	33,000

(continued)

(continued)

Civilian Jobs Through Military Training for Self-Employed Workers with the Most Openings

Job	Percent Self-Employed Workers	Annual Openings
13. Refrigeration Mechanics and Installers	13.1%	33,000
14. Computer, Automated Teller, and Office Machine Repairers	13.7%	31,000
15. Photographers	58.8%	23,000
16. Automotive Body and Related Repairers	17.6%	18,000
17. Brickmasons and Blockmasons	28.6%	17,000
18. Drywall and Ceiling Tile Installers	23.4%	17,000
19. Music Composers and Arrangers	44.8%	11,000
20. Technical Directors/Managers	30.4%	11,000
21. Outdoor Power Equipment and Other Small Engine Mechanics	19.2%	10,000
22. Motorboat Mechanics	18.9%	7,000
23. Construction and Building Inspectors	10.2%	6,000
24. Locksmiths and Safe Repairers	37.6%	5,000
25. Camera Operators, Television, Video, and Motion Picture	21.1%	4,000

Jobs 2 and 3 share 210,000 openings. Jobs 4 and 5 share 93,000 openings. Jobs 6 and 7 share 61,000 openings. Jobs 12 and 13 share 33,000 openings. Job 19 shares 11,000 openings with another job not included in this list. Job 20 shares 11,000 openings with four other jobs not included in this list.

Best Civilian Jobs Through Military Training Employing a High Percentage of Women

Military service offers many opportunities for women to be trained for and work in civilian jobs that have traditionally been dominated by men. Some combat-related jobs remain closed to women, and these are identified in the military job descriptions in Part II. But enlisted women are now are about as likely as men to be in service and supply jobs or communication and intelligence jobs, roles that used to be filled primarily by men.

The following table shows the percentages of men and women assigned to the major groups of military occupations.

Men and Women in Military Occupational Areas, 2004

Occupational Area	Percent Males	Percent Females
Infantry, Gun Crews, and Seamanship Specialists	19.1%	5.3%
Electronic Equipment Repairers	9.3%	5.2%
Communications and Intelligence Specialists	9.0%	10.0%
Medical and Dental Specialists	5.2%	15.6%
Other Allied Specialists	2.9%	3.3%
Functional Support and Administration	12.9%	33.2%
Electrical/Mechanical Equipment Repairers	22.8%	9.1%
Craftsmen	4.3%	1.8%
Service and Supply Handlers	8.7%	10.6%
Nonoccupational	5.8%	5.7%

Recent research suggests that women leaving the service transfer their skills more easily to a civilian job than men do. However, military experience gives less of a wage boost to women than it does to men.

Because men and women have different experiences in the workforce, we thought it would be interesting to look at what kinds of civilian jobs have a high percentage of male or female workers, regardless of where those workers received their training. We're not saying that men or women workers should consider these jobs over others, but it is interesting know what those jobs are and what their rewards are.

To create the two sets of five lists that follow, we sorted the 150 best jobs through military training according to the percentages of women and men in the civilian workforce and retained those that employ more than 70 percent of men or women. We knew we would create some controversy when we first included best jobs lists of this kind in an earlier book in this series. But these lists are not meant to restrict women or men from considering job options; one reason for including these lists is exactly the opposite. We hope the lists will help people see possibilities that they might not otherwise have considered. For example, perhaps women should consider some civilian jobs that traditionally have high percentages of men in them.

An interesting and unfortunate tidbit to bring up at your next party is that in the jobs listed here with the highest percentage of women, the weighted average earnings are $26,651, compared to $36,289 in the jobs with the highest percentage of men. But earnings don't tell the whole story. We computed the average growth and job openings of the jobs with the highest percentage of women and found statistics of 13.8% growth and 115,074 openings, compared to 12.2% growth and 39,150 openings for the jobs with the highest percentage of men. This discrepancy reinforces the idea that men have had more problems than women in adapting to a civilian economy dominated by service and information-based jobs. Many women may simply be better prepared for these jobs, possessing more appropriate skills for the civilian jobs that are now growing rapidly and have more job openings.

The fact is that civilian jobs with high percentages of women or high percentages of men offer good opportunities for both men and women if they want to do one of these jobs. So we suggest that women browse the lists of civilian jobs that employ high percentages of men and that men browse the lists of civilian jobs with high percentages of women. There are jobs among both lists that pay well, and women or men who are interested in them and who have or can obtain the necessary education and training (perhaps through the military) should consider them.

Best Civilian Jobs Through Military Training Employing the Highest Percentage of Women

Job	Percent Women
1. Executive Secretaries and Administrative Assistants	97.3%
2. Legal Secretaries	97.3%
3. Secretaries, Except Legal, Medical, and Executive	97.3%
4. Dental Hygienists	97.1%
5. Dental Assistants	96.1%
6. Licensed Practical and Licensed Vocational Nurses	93.4%
7. Payroll and Timekeeping Clerks	91.4%
8. Bookkeeping, Accounting, and Auditing Clerks	91.3%
9. Human Resources Assistants, Except Payroll and Timekeeping	89.3%
10. Medical Assistants	89.0%
11. Medical Equipment Preparers	89.0%
12. Orthotists and Prosthetists	89.0%
13. Nursing Aides, Orderlies, and Attendants	88.7%
14. Occupational Therapist Assistants	88.7%
15. Physical Therapist Assistants	88.7%
16. Tellers	87.3%
17. Medical Records and Health Information Technicians	86.6%
18. Paralegals and Legal Assistants	86.4%
19. Office Clerks, General	84.5%
20. Pharmacy Technicians	81.8%
21. Surgical Technologists	81.8%
22. Court Reporters	75.3%
23. Cardiovascular Technologists and Technicians	72.0%
24. Medical and Clinical Laboratory Technicians	72.0%
25. Radiologic Technicians	72.0%
26. Radiologic Technologists	72.0%
27. Combined Food Preparation and Serving Workers, Including Fast Food	71.5%

The jobs in the following four lists are derived from the preceding list of the jobs employing the highest percentage of women.

Best Civilian Jobs Through Military Training Overall Employing a High Percentage of Women

Job	Percent Women	Annual Earnings	Percent Growth	Annual Openings
1. Dental Hygienists	97.1%	$60,890	43.3%	17,000
2. Paralegals and Legal Assistants	86.4%	$41,170	29.7%	28,000
3. Medical Assistants	89.0%	$25,350	52.1%	93,000
4. Dental Assistants	96.1%	$29,520	42.7%	45,000
5. Radiologic Technicians	72.0%	$45,950	23.2%	17,000
6. Radiologic Technologists	72.0%	$45,950	23.2%	17,000
7. Physical Therapist Assistants	88.7%	$39,490	44.2%	7,000
8. Cardiovascular Technologists and Technicians	72.0%	$40,420	32.6%	5,000
9. Legal Secretaries	97.3%	$37,750	17.4%	41,000
10. Occupational Therapist Assistants	88.7%	$39,750	34.1%	2,000
11. Executive Secretaries and Administrative Assistants	97.3%	$35,960	12.4%	218,000
12. Licensed Practical and Licensed Vocational Nurses	93.4%	$35,230	17.1%	84,000
13. Nursing Aides, Orderlies, and Attendants	88.7%	$21,440	22.3%	307,000
14. Surgical Technologists	81.8%	$34,830	29.5%	12,000
15. Medical and Clinical Laboratory Technicians	72.0%	$31,700	25.0%	14,000
16. Orthotists and Prosthetists	89.0%	$53,760	18.0%	fewer than 500
17. Payroll and Timekeeping Clerks	91.4%	$31,360	17.3%	36,000
18. Pharmacy Technicians	81.8%	$24,390	28.6%	35,000
19. Combined Food Preparation and Serving Workers, Including Fast Food	71.5%	$14,790	17.1%	751,000
20. Medical Records and Health Information Technicians	86.6%	$26,690	28.9%	14,000
21. Bookkeeping, Accounting, and Auditing Clerks	91.3%	$29,490	5.9%	291,000
22. Human Resources Assistants, Except Payroll and Timekeeping	89.3%	$32,730	16.7%	28,000
23. Office Clerks, General	84.5%	$23,070	8.4%	695,000
24. Court Reporters	75.3%	$41,640	14.8%	3,000
25. Secretaries, Except Legal, Medical, and Executive	97.3%	$26,670	–2.5%	231,000

Jobs 5 and 6 share 17,000 openings.

Best-Paying Civilian Jobs Through Military Training Employing a High Percentage of Women

Job	Percent Women	Annual Earnings
1. Dental Hygienists	97.1%	$60,890
2. Orthotists and Prosthetists	89.0%	$53,760
3. Radiologic Technicians	72.0%	$45,950
4. Radiologic Technologists	72.0%	$45,950
5. Court Reporters	75.3%	$41,640
6. Paralegals and Legal Assistants	86.4%	$41,170
7. Cardiovascular Technologists and Technicians	72.0%	$40,420
8. Occupational Therapist Assistants	88.7%	$39,750
9. Physical Therapist Assistants	88.7%	$39,490
10. Legal Secretaries	97.3%	$37,750
11. Executive Secretaries and Administrative Assistants	97.3%	$35,960
12. Licensed Practical and Licensed Vocational Nurses	93.4%	$35,230
13. Surgical Technologists	81.8%	$34,830
14. Human Resources Assistants, Except Payroll and Timekeeping	89.3%	$32,730
15. Medical and Clinical Laboratory Technicians	72.0%	$31,700
16. Payroll and Timekeeping Clerks	91.4%	$31,360
17. Dental Assistants	96.1%	$29,520
18. Bookkeeping, Accounting, and Auditing Clerks	91.3%	$29,490
19. Medical Records and Health Information Technicians	86.6%	$26,690
20. Secretaries, Except Legal, Medical, and Executive	97.3%	$26,670
21. Medical Assistants	89.0%	$25,350
22. Medical Equipment Preparers	89.0%	$24,880
23. Pharmacy Technicians	81.8%	$24,390
24. Office Clerks, General	84.5%	$23,070
25. Nursing Aides, Orderlies, and Attendants	88.7%	$21,440

Fastest-Growing Civilian Jobs Through Military Training Employing a High Percentage of Women

Job	Percent Women	Percent Growth
1. Medical Assistants	89.0%	52.1%
2. Physical Therapist Assistants	88.7%	44.2%
3. Dental Hygienists	97.1%	43.3%
4. Dental Assistants	96.1%	42.7%

Fastest-Growing Civilian Jobs Through Military Training Employing a High Percentage of Women

Job	Percent Women	Percent Growth
5. Occupational Therapist Assistants	88.7%	34.1%
6. Cardiovascular Technologists and Technicians	72.0%	32.6%
7. Paralegals and Legal Assistants	86.4%	29.7%
8. Surgical Technologists	81.8%	29.5%
9. Medical Records and Health Information Technicians	86.6%	28.9%
10. Pharmacy Technicians	81.8%	28.6%
11. Medical and Clinical Laboratory Technicians	72.0%	25.0%
12. Radiologic Technicians	72.0%	23.2%
13. Radiologic Technologists	72.0%	23.2%
14. Nursing Aides, Orderlies, and Attendants	88.7%	22.3%
15. Medical Equipment Preparers	89.0%	20.0%
16. Orthotists and Prosthetists	89.0%	18.0%
17. Legal Secretaries	97.3%	17.4%
18. Payroll and Timekeeping Clerks	91.4%	17.3%
19. Combined Food Preparation and Serving Workers, Including Fast Food	71.5%	17.1%
20. Licensed Practical and Licensed Vocational Nurses	93.4%	17.1%
21. Human Resources Assistants, Except Payroll and Timekeeping	89.3%	16.7%
22. Court Reporters	75.3%	14.8%
23. Executive Secretaries and Administrative Assistants	97.3%	12.4%
24. Office Clerks, General	84.5%	8.4%
25. Tellers	87.3%	6.8%

Civilian Jobs Through Military Training with the Most Openings Employing a High Percentage of Women

Job	Percent Women	Annual Openings
1. Combined Food Preparation and Serving Workers, Including Fast Food	71.5%	751,000
2. Office Clerks, General	84.5%	695,000
3. Nursing Aides, Orderlies, and Attendants	88.7%	307,000
4. Bookkeeping, Accounting, and Auditing Clerks	91.3%	291,000
5. Secretaries, Except Legal, Medical, and Executive	97.3%	231,000
6. Executive Secretaries and Administrative Assistants	97.3%	218,000
7. Tellers	87.3%	108,000

(continued)

(continued)

Civilian Jobs Through Military Training with the Most Openings Employing a High Percentage of Women

Job	Percent Women	Annual Openings
8. Medical Assistants	89.0%	93,000
9. Licensed Practical and Licensed Vocational Nurses	93.4%	84,000
10. Dental Assistants	96.1%	45,000
11. Legal Secretaries	97.3%	41,000
12. Payroll and Timekeeping Clerks	91.4%	36,000
13. Pharmacy Technicians	81.8%	35,000
14. Human Resources Assistants, Except Payroll and Timekeeping	89.3%	28,000
15. Paralegals and Legal Assistants	86.4%	28,000
16. Dental Hygienists	97.1%	17,000
17. Radiologic Technicians	72.0%	17,000
18. Radiologic Technologists	72.0%	17,000
19. Medical and Clinical Laboratory Technicians	72.0%	14,000
20. Medical Records and Health Information Technicians	86.6%	14,000
21. Surgical Technologists	81.8%	12,000
22. Medical Equipment Preparers	89.0%	8,000
23. Physical Therapist Assistants	88.7%	7,000
24. Cardiovascular Technologists and Technicians	72.0%	5,000
25. Court Reporters	75.3%	3,000

Jobs 17 and 18 share 17,000 openings.

Best Civilian Jobs Through Military Training Employing a High Percentage of Men

If you have not already read the intro to the previous group of lists, best civilian jobs through military training with high percentages of women, consider doing so. Much of the content there applies to these lists as well.

We did not include these groups of lists with the assumption that men should consider civilian jobs with high percentages of men or that women should consider civilian jobs with high percentages of women. Instead, these lists are here because we think they are interesting and perhaps helpful in considering nontraditional civilian career options. For example, some men would do very well in and enjoy some of the jobs with high percentages of women but may not have considered them seriously. In a similar way, some women would very much enjoy and do well in some jobs that traditionally have been held by high percentages of men.

We hope that these lists help you consider options that you simply did not seriously consider because of gender stereotypes.

In the jobs on the following lists, more than 70 percent of the workers are men.

Best Civilian Jobs Through Military Training Employing the Highest Percentage of Men

Job	Percent Men
1. Bus and Truck Mechanics and Diesel Engine Specialists	99.5%
2. Drywall and Ceiling Tile Installers	99.2%
3. Brickmasons and Blockmasons	99.1%
4. Pipe Fitters and Steamfitters	98.8%
5. Plumbers	98.8%
6. Elevator Installers and Repairers	98.6%
7. Heating and Air Conditioning Mechanics and Installers	98.6%
8. Refrigeration Mechanics and Installers	98.6%
9. Control and Valve Installers and Repairers, Except Mechanical Door	98.4%
10. Mobile Heavy Equipment Mechanics, Except Engines	98.4%
11. Structural Iron and Steel Workers	98.4%
12. Cement Masons and Concrete Finishers	98.3%
13. Riggers	98.3%
14. Automotive Master Mechanics	98.2%
15. Automotive Specialty Technicians	98.2%
16. Motorboat Mechanics	98.2%
17. Outdoor Power Equipment and Other Small Engine Mechanics	98.2%
18. Automotive Body and Related Repairers	98.1%
19. Construction Carpenters	98.1%
20. Rough Carpenters	98.1%
21. Roofers	97.6%
22. Electricians	97.4%
23. Industrial Machinery Mechanics	97.4%
24. Pest Control Workers	97.4%
25. Mapping Technicians	97.3%
26. Operating Engineers and Other Construction Equipment Operators	97.3%
27. Surveying Technicians	97.3%
28. Crane and Tower Operators	97.2%
29. First-Line Supervisors/Managers of Construction Trades and Extraction Workers	97.1%
30. Mates—Ship, Boat, and Barge	97.1%
31. Pilots, Ship	97.1%
32. Ship and Boat Captains	97.1%

(continued)

(continued)

Best Civilian Jobs Through Military Training Employing the Highest Percentage of Men

Job	Percent Men
33. Stationary Engineers and Boiler Operators	97.0%
34. Boilermakers	96.8%
35. Municipal Fire Fighters	96.7%
36. Electrical Power-Line Installers and Repairers	96.5%
37. Sheet Metal Workers	96.4%
38. Maintenance and Repair Workers, General	95.9%
39. Locksmiths and Safe Repairers	95.8%
40. Aircraft Mechanics and Service Technicians	95.5%
41. Electrical and Electronics Installers and Repairers, Transportation Equipment	95.5%
42. Electrical and Electronics Repairers, Commercial and Industrial Equipment	95.5%
43. Electrical and Electronics Repairers, Powerhouse, Substation, and Relay	95.5%
44. Truck Drivers, Heavy and Tractor-Trailer	95.5%
45. Truck Drivers, Light or Delivery Services	95.5%
46. Highway Maintenance Workers	95.4%
47. Paving, Surfacing, and Tamping Equipment Operators	95.4%
48. Water and Liquid Waste Treatment Plant and System Operators	95.4%
49. Airline Pilots, Copilots, and Flight Engineers	94.8%
50. Commercial Pilots	94.8%
51. First-Line Supervisors/Managers of Mechanics, Installers, and Repairers	94.3%
52. Solderers and Brazers	94.2%
53. Welders, Cutters, and Welder Fitters	94.2%
54. Telecommunications Line Installers and Repairers	94.0%
55. Machinists	93.2%
56. Nuclear Power Reactor Operators	92.6%
57. Power Plant Operators	92.6%
58. Medical Equipment Repairers	92.3%
59. Construction and Building Inspectors	91.5%
60. Hazardous Materials Removal Workers	90.8%
61. Avionics Technicians	88.8%
62. Storage and Distribution Managers	88.3%
63. First-Line Supervisors/Managers of Police and Detectives	87.5%
64. Municipal Fire Fighting and Prevention Supervisors	87.5%
65. Telecommunications Equipment Installers and Repairers, Except Line Installers	86.5%
66. Audio and Video Equipment Technicians	86.4%
67. Computer, Automated Teller, and Office Machine Repairers	86.3%

Best Civilian Jobs Through Military Training Employing the Highest Percentage of Men

Job	Percent Men
68. Police Patrol Officers	85.7%
69. Sheriffs and Deputy Sheriffs	85.7%
70. Transit and Railroad Police	85.7%
71. Painters, Transportation Equipment	85.0%
72. Gas Plant Operators	84.8%
73. Petroleum Pump System Operators, Refinery Operators, and Gaugers	84.8%
74. Taxi Drivers and Chauffeurs	84.5%
75. Printing Machine Operators	84.4%
76. Laborers and Freight, Stock, and Material Movers, Hand	82.7%
77. First-Line Supervisors/Managers of Transportation and Material-Moving Machine and Vehicle Operators	81.9%
78. Camera Operators, Television, Video, and Motion Picture	81.1%
79. Aerospace Engineering and Operations Technicians	79.8%
80. Civil Engineering Technicians	79.8%
81. Electro-Mechanical Technicians	79.8%
82. Mechanical Engineering Technicians	79.8%
83. Chefs and Head Cooks	79.6%
84. First-Line Supervisors/Managers of Production and Operating Workers	79.1%
85. Architectural Drafters	78.4%
86. Civil Drafters	78.4%
87. Criminal Investigators and Special Agents	76.0%
88. Police Detectives	76.0%
89. Security Guards	75.3%
90. Computer Programmers	74.0%
91. Cargo and Freight Agents	73.1%
92. Chemical Technicians	71.9%
93. Correctional Officers and Jailers	70.9%

The jobs in the following four lists are derived from the preceding list of the jobs employing the highest percentage of men.

Best Civilian Jobs Through Military Training Overall Employing a High Percentage of Men

Job	Percent Men	Annual Earnings	Percent Growth	Annual Openings
1. Pipe Fitters and Steamfitters	98.8%	$42,160	15.7%	61,000
2. Plumbers	98.8%	$42,160	15.7%	61,000
3. Airline Pilots, Copilots, and Flight Engineers	94.8%	$138,170	17.2%	7,000
4. Police Patrol Officers	85.7%	$46,290	15.5%	47,000
5. Sheriffs and Deputy Sheriffs	85.7%	$46,290	15.5%	47,000
6. Criminal Investigators and Special Agents	76.0%	$55,790	16.3%	9,000
7. Police Detectives	76.0%	$55,790	16.3%	9,000
8. First-Line Supervisors/Managers of Construction Trades and Extraction Workers	97.1%	$51,970	10.9%	57,000
9. First-Line Supervisors/Managers of Police and Detectives	87.5%	$65,570	15.5%	9,000
10. First-Line Supervisors/Managers of Mechanics, Installers, and Repairers	94.3%	$51,980	12.4%	33,000
11. Heating and Air Conditioning Mechanics and Installers	98.6%	$37,040	19.0%	33,000
12. Refrigeration Mechanics and Installers	98.6%	$37,040	19.0%	33,000
13. Municipal Fire Fighting and Prevention Supervisors	87.5%	$60,840	21.1%	4,000
14. Storage and Distribution Managers	88.3%	$69,120	12.7%	15,000
15. First-Line Supervisors/Managers of Transportation and Material-Moving Machine and Vehicle Operators	81.9%	$47,530	15.3%	22,000
16. Municipal Fire Fighters	96.7%	$39,090	24.3%	21,000
17. Electricians	97.4%	$42,790	11.8%	68,000
18. Automotive Master Mechanics	98.2%	$33,050	15.7%	93,000
19. Automotive Specialty Technicians	98.2%	$33,050	15.7%	93,000
20. Commercial Pilots	94.8%	$55,810	16.8%	2,000
21. Construction and Building Inspectors	91.5%	$44,720	22.3%	6,000
22. Construction Carpenters	98.1%	$35,580	13.8%	210,000
23. Rough Carpenters	98.1%	$35,580	13.8%	210,000
24. Roofers	97.6%	$31,230	16.8%	38,000
25. Aircraft Mechanics and Service Technicians	95.5%	$47,310	13.4%	11,000

Jobs 1 and 2 share 61,000 openings. Jobs 4 and 5 share 47,000 openings. Jobs 6 and 7 share 9,000 openings. Jobs 11 and 12 share 33,000 openings. Job 13 shares 4,000 openings with another job not included in this list. Job 14 shares 15,000 openings with another job not included in this list. Job 16 shares 21,000 openings with another job not included in this list. Jobs 18 and 19 share 93,000 openings. Jobs 22 and 23 share 210,000 openings.

Best-Paying Civilian Jobs Through Military Training Employing a High Percentage of Men

Job	Percent Men	Annual Earnings
1. Airline Pilots, Copilots, and Flight Engineers	94.8%	$130,170
2. Storage and Distribution Managers	88.3%	$69,120
3. Nuclear Power Reactor Operators	92.6%	$66,230
4. First-Line Supervisors/Managers of Police and Detectives	87.5%	$65,570
5. Computer Programmers	74.0%	$63,420
6. Municipal Fire Fighting and Prevention Supervisors	87.5%	$60,840
7. Elevator Installers and Repairers	98.6%	$59,190
8. Commercial Pilots	94.8%	$55,810
9. Criminal Investigators and Special Agents	76.0%	$55,790
10. Police Detectives	76.0%	$55,790
11. Electrical and Electronics Repairers, Powerhouse, Substation, and Relay	95.5%	$54,970
12. Power Plant Operators	92.6%	$53,170
13. Aerospace Engineering and Operations Technicians	79.8%	$52,450
14. First-Line Supervisors/Managers of Mechanics, Installers, and Repairers	94.3%	$51,980
15. First-Line Supervisors/Managers of Construction Trades and Extraction Workers	97.1%	$51,970
16. Gas Plant Operators	84.8%	$51,920
17. Petroleum Pump System Operators, Refinery Operators, and Gaugers	84.8%	$51,060
18. Mates—Ship, Boat, and Barge	97.1%	$50,940
19. Pilots, Ship	97.1%	$50,940
20. Ship and Boat Captains	97.1%	$50,940
21. Telecommunications Equipment Installers and Repairers, Except Line Installers	86.5%	$50,620
22. Electrical Power-Line Installers and Repairers	96.5%	$50,150
23. Transit and Railroad Police	85.7%	$48,850
24. Boilermakers	96.8%	$48,050
25. First-Line Supervisors/Managers of Transportation and Material-Moving Machine and Vehicle Operators	81.9%	$47,530

Fastest-Growing Civilian Jobs Through Military Training Employing a High Percentage of Men

Job	Percent Men	Percent Growth
1. Hazardous Materials Removal Workers	90.8%	31.2%
2. Taxi Drivers and Chauffeurs	84.5%	24.8%
3. Municipal Fire Fighters	96.7%	24.3%
4. Highway Maintenance Workers	95.4%	23.3%
5. Construction and Building Inspectors	91.5%	22.3%
6. Municipal Fire Fighting and Prevention Supervisors	87.5%	21.1%
7. Heating and Air Conditioning Mechanics and Installers	98.6%	19.0%
8. Refrigeration Mechanics and Installers	98.6%	19.0%
9. Pest Control Workers	97.4%	18.4%
10. Audio and Video Equipment Technicians	86.4%	18.1%
11. Airline Pilots, Copilots, and Flight Engineers	94.8%	17.2%
12. Commercial Pilots	94.8%	16.8%
13. Roofers	97.6%	16.8%
14. Chefs and Head Cooks	79.6%	16.7%
15. Criminal Investigators and Special Agents	76.0%	16.3%
16. Police Detectives	76.0%	16.3%
17. Water and Liquid Waste Treatment Plant and System Operators	95.4%	16.2%
18. Locksmiths and Safe Repairers	95.8%	16.1%
19. Cement Masons and Concrete Finishers	98.3%	15.9%
20. Automotive Master Mechanics	98.2%	15.7%
21. Automotive Specialty Technicians	98.2%	15.7%
22. Pipe Fitters and Steamfitters	98.8%	15.7%
23. Plumbers	98.8%	15.7%
24. Truck Drivers, Light or Delivery Services	95.5%	15.7%
25. Paving, Surfacing, and Tamping Equipment Operators	95.4%	15.6%

Civilian Jobs Through Military Training with the Most Openings Employing a High Percentage of Men

Job	Percent Men	Annual Openings
1. Laborers and Freight, Stock, and Material Movers, Hand	82.7%	671,000
2. Truck Drivers, Heavy and Tractor-Trailer	95.5%	274,000
3. Security Guards	75.3%	230,000
4. Construction Carpenters	98.1%	210,000

Civilian Jobs Through Military Training with the Most Openings Employing a High Percentage of Men

Job	Percent Men	Annual Openings
5. Rough Carpenters	98.1%	210,000
6. Truck Drivers, Light or Delivery Services	95.5%	169,000
7. Maintenance and Repair Workers, General	95.9%	154,000
8. Automotive Master Mechanics	98.2%	93,000
9. Automotive Specialty Technicians	98.2%	93,000
10. First-Line Supervisors/Managers of Production and Operating Workers	79.1%	89,000
11. Electricians	97.4%	68,000
12. Pipe Fitters and Steamfitters	98.8%	61,000
13. Plumbers	98.8%	61,000
14. First-Line Supervisors/Managers of Construction Trades and Extraction Workers	97.1%	57,000
15. Correctional Officers and Jailers	70.9%	54,000
16. Solderers and Brazers	94.2%	52,000
17. Welders, Cutters, and Welder Fitters	94.2%	52,000
18. Sheet Metal Workers	96.4%	50,000
19. Police Patrol Officers	85.7%	47,000
20. Sheriffs and Deputy Sheriffs	85.7%	47,000
21. Taxi Drivers and Chauffeurs	84.5%	43,000
22. Roofers	97.6%	38,000
23. Operating Engineers and Other Construction Equipment Operators	97.3%	37,000
24. First-Line Supervisors/Managers of Mechanics, Installers, and Repairers	94.3%	33,000
25. Machinists	93.2%	33,000

Jobs 4 and 5 share 210,000 openings. Jobs 8 and 9 share 93,000 openings. Jobs 12 and 13 share 61,000 openings. Jobs 16 and 17 share 52,000 openings. Jobs 19 and 20 share 47,000 openings.

Best Civilian Jobs Lists Through Military Training Based on Interests

This group of lists organizes the 150 best jobs through military training into 15 interest areas. You can use these lists to quickly identify civilian jobs based on your interests.

Find the interest area or areas that are most appealing to you. Then review the civilian jobs in those areas to identify jobs you want to explore in more detail and look up their descriptions in Part IV. You can also review interest areas where you have had past experience, education, or training to see whether other civilian jobs in those areas would meet your current requirements.

Within each interest area, jobs are listed in order of their combined scores based on earnings, growth, and number of openings.

Note: The interest areas used in these lists are 15 of the 16 used in the *New Guide for Occupational Exploration,* Fourth Edition, published by JIST. The original GOE was developed by the U.S. Department of Labor as an intuitive way to assist in career exploration. The 16 interest areas used in the *New GOE* are based on the 16 career clusters that were developed by the U.S. Department of Education's Office of Vocational and Adult Education around 1999 and that presently are being used by many states to organize their career-oriented programs and career information.

Descriptions for the 16 Interest Areas

Brief descriptions for the 16 GOE interest areas follow. Some of them refer to jobs (as examples) that aren't included in this book.

Also note that we put each of the 150 best jobs into only one interest area list, the one it fit into best. However, many jobs could be included in more than one list, so consider reviewing a variety of these interest areas to find civilian jobs that you might otherwise overlook.

One interest area defined in the following list, Education and Training, accounts for *none* of the 150 jobs that met the criteria for this book and therefore is not represented by a list. The civilian jobs belonging in this interest area either require a bachelor's degree or higher (e.g., secondary school teachers) or cannot be trained for through military experience (e.g., preschool teachers).

- Agriculture and Natural Resources: *An interest in working with plants, animals, forests, or mineral resources for agriculture, horticulture, conservation, extraction, and other purposes.* You can satisfy this interest by working in farming, landscaping, forestry, fishing, mining, and related fields. You may like doing physical work outdoors, such as on a farm or ranch, in a forest, or on a drilling rig. If you have scientific curiosity, you could study plants and animals or analyze biological or rock samples in a lab. If you have management ability, you could own, operate, or manage a fish hatchery, a landscaping business, or a greenhouse.
- Architecture and Construction: *An interest in designing, assembling, and maintaining components of buildings and other structures.* You may want to be part of the team of architects, drafters, and others who design buildings and render the plans. If construction interests you, you can find fulfillment in the many building projects that are being undertaken at all times. If you like to organize and plan, you can find careers in managing these projects. Or you can play a more direct role in putting up and finishing buildings by doing jobs such as plumbing, carpentry, masonry, painting, or roofing, either as a skilled craftsworker or as a helper. You can prepare the building site by operating heavy equipment or install, maintain, and repair vital building equipment and systems such as electricity and heating.
- Arts and Communication: *An interest in creatively expressing feelings or ideas, in communicating news or information, or in performing.* You can satisfy this interest in creative,

verbal, or performing activities. For example, if you enjoy literature, perhaps writing or editing would appeal to you. Journalism and public relations are other fields for people who like to use their writing or speaking skills. Do you prefer to work in the performing arts? If so, you could direct or perform in drama, music, or dance. If you especially enjoy the visual arts, you could create paintings, sculpture, or ceramics or design products or visual displays. A flair for technology might lead you to specialize in photography, broadcast production, or dispatching.

- Business and Administration: *An interest in making a business organization or function run smoothly.* You can satisfy this interest by working in a position of leadership or by specializing in a function that contributes to the overall effort in a business, a nonprofit organization, or a government agency. If you especially enjoy working with people, you may find fulfillment from working in human resources. An interest in numbers may lead you to consider accounting, finance, budgeting, billing, or financial record-keeping. A job as an administrative assistant may interest you if you like a variety of work in a busy environment. If you are good with details and word processing, you may enjoy a job as a secretary or data entry keyer. Or perhaps you would do well as the manager of a business.
- Education and Training: *An interest in helping people learn.* You can satisfy this interest by teaching students, who may be preschoolers, retirees, or any age in between. You may specialize in a particular academic field or work with learners of a particular age, with a particular interest, or with a particular learning problem. Working in a library or museum may give you an opportunity to expand people's understanding of the world.
- Finance and Insurance: *An interest in helping businesses and people be assured of a financially secure future.* You can satisfy this interest by working in a financial or insurance business in a leadership or support role. If you like gathering and analyzing information, you may find fulfillment as an insurance adjuster or financial analyst. Or you may deal with information at the clerical level as a banking or insurance clerk or in person-to-person situations providing customer service. Another way to interact with people is to sell financial or insurance services that will meet their needs.
- Government and Public Administration: *An interest in helping a government agency serve the needs of the public.* You can satisfy this interest by working in a position of leadership or by specializing in a function that contributes to the role of government. You may help protect the public by working as an inspector or examiner to enforce standards. If you enjoy using clerical skills, you may work as a clerk in a law court or government office. Or perhaps you prefer the top-down perspective of a government executive or urban planner.
- Health Science: *An interest in helping people and animals be healthy.* You can satisfy this interest by working in a health-care team as a doctor, therapist, or nurse. You might specialize in one of the many different parts of the body (such as the teeth or eyes) or in one of the many different types of care. Or you may want to be a generalist who deals with the whole patient. If you like technology, you might find satisfaction working with X rays or new methods of diagnosis. You might work with healthy people, helping them eat right. If you enjoy working with animals, you might care for them and keep them healthy.

- Hospitality, Tourism, and Recreation: *An interest in catering to the personal wishes and needs of others so that they may enjoy a clean environment, good food and drink, comfortable lodging away from home, and recreation.* You can satisfy this interest by providing services for the convenience, care, and pampering of others in hotels, restaurants, airplanes, beauty parlors, and so on. You may want to use your love of cooking as a chef. If you like working with people, you may want to provide personal services by being a travel guide, a flight attendant, a concierge, a hairdresser, or a waiter. You may want to work in cleaning and building services if you like a clean environment. If you enjoy sports or games, you may work for an athletic team or casino.
- Human Service: *An interest in improving people's social, mental, emotional, or spiritual well-being.* You can satisfy this interest as a counselor, social worker, or religious worker who helps people sort out their complicated lives or solve personal problems. You may work as a caretaker for very young people or the elderly. Or you may interview people to help identify the social services they need.
- Information Technology: *An interest in designing, developing, managing, and supporting information systems.* You can satisfy this interest by working with hardware, software, multimedia, or integrated systems. If you like to use your organizational skills, you might work as an administrator of a system or database. Or you can solve complex problems as a software engineer or systems analyst. If you enjoy getting your hands on the hardware, you might find work servicing computers, peripherals, and information-intense machines such as cash registers and ATMs.
- Law and Public Safety: *An interest in upholding people's rights or in protecting people and property by using authority, inspecting, or investigating.* You can satisfy this interest by working in law, law enforcement, fire fighting, the military, and related fields. For example, if you enjoy mental challenge and intrigue, you could investigate crimes or fires for a living. If you enjoy working with verbal skills and research skills, you may want to defend citizens in court or research deeds, wills, and other legal documents. If you want to help people in critical situations, you may want to fight fires, work as a police officer, or become a paramedic. Or, if you want more routine work in public safety, perhaps a job in guarding, patrolling, or inspecting would appeal to you. If you have management ability, you could seek a leadership position in law enforcement and the protective services. Work in the military gives you a chance to use technical and leadership skills while serving your country.
- Manufacturing: *An interest in processing materials into intermediate or final products or maintaining and repairing products by using machines or hand tools.* You can satisfy this interest by working in one of many industries that mass-produce goods or by working for a utility that distributes electric power or other resources. You may enjoy manual work, using your hands or hand tools in highly skilled jobs such as assembling engines or electronic equipment. If you enjoy making machines run efficiently or fixing them when they break down, you could seek a job installing or repairing such devices as copiers, aircraft engines, cars, or watches. Perhaps you prefer to set up or operate machines that are used to manufacture products made of food, glass, or paper. You may enjoy cutting and grinding metal and plastic parts to desired shapes and measurements. Or you may wish to operate equipment in systems that provide water and process

wastewater. You may like inspecting, sorting, counting, or weighing products. Another option is to work with your hands and machinery to move boxes and freight in a warehouse. If leadership appeals to you, you could manage people engaged in production and repair.

- Retail and Wholesale Sales and Service: *An interest in bringing others to a particular point of view by personal persuasion and by sales and promotional techniques.* You can satisfy this interest in a variety of jobs that involve persuasion and selling. If you like using knowledge of science, you may enjoy selling pharmaceutical, medical, or electronic products or services. Real estate offers several kinds of sales jobs as well. If you like speaking on the phone, you could work as a telemarketer. Or you may enjoy selling apparel and other merchandise in a retail setting. If you prefer to help people, you may want a job in customer service.
- Scientific Research, Engineering, and Mathematics: *An interest in discovering, collecting, and analyzing information about the natural world; in applying scientific research findings to problems in medicine, the life sciences, human behavior, and the natural sciences; in imagining and manipulating quantitative data; and in applying technology to manufacturing, transportation, and other economic activities.* You can satisfy this interest by working with the knowledge and processes of the sciences. You may enjoy researching and developing new knowledge in mathematics, or perhaps solving problems in the physical, life, or social sciences would appeal to you. You may wish to study engineering and help create new machines, processes, and structures. If you want to work with scientific equipment and procedures, you could seek a job in a research or testing laboratory.
- Transportation, Distribution, and Logistics: *An interest in operations that move people or materials.* You can satisfy this interest by managing a transportation service, by helping vehicles keep on their assigned schedules and routes, or by driving or piloting a vehicle. If you enjoy taking responsibility, perhaps managing a rail line would appeal to you. Or would you rather get out on the highway, on the water, or up in the air? If so, then you could drive a truck from state to state, be employed on a ship, or fly a crop duster over a cornfield. If you prefer to stay closer to home, you could drive a delivery van, taxi, or school bus. You can use your physical strength to load freight and arrange it so it gets to its destination in one piece.

Best Civilian Jobs Through Military Training for People Interested in Agriculture and Natural Resources

Job	Annual Earnings	Percent Growth	Annual Openings
1. First-Line Supervisors/Managers of Construction Trades and Extraction Workers	$51,970	10.9%	57,000
2. Pest Control Workers	$27,170	18.4%	4,000

Best Civilian Jobs Through Military Training for People Interested in Architecture and Construction

Job	Annual Earnings	Percent Growth	Annual Openings
1. Pipe Fitters and Steamfitters	$42,160	15.7%	61,000
2. Plumbers	$42,160	15.7%	61,000
3. Electricians	$42,790	11.8%	68,000
4. Heating and Air Conditioning Mechanics and Installers	$37,040	19.0%	33,000
5. Refrigeration Mechanics and Installers	$37,040	19.0%	33,000
6. Construction Carpenters	$35,580	13.8%	210,000
7. Rough Carpenters	$35,580	13.8%	210,000
8. Elevator Installers and Repairers	$59,190	14.8%	3,000
9. Roofers	$31,230	16.8%	38,000
10. Maintenance and Repair Workers, General	$31,210	15.2%	154,000
11. Structural Iron and Steel Workers	$40,580	15.0%	13,000
12. Sheet Metal Workers	$36,390	12.2%	50,000
13. Telecommunications Line Installers and Repairers	$42,410	10.8%	23,000
14. Cement Masons and Concrete Finishers	$32,030	15.9%	32,000
15. Brickmasons and Blockmasons	$41,860	12.0%	17,000
16. Hazardous Materials Removal Workers	$33,690	31.2%	11,000
17. Highway Maintenance Workers	$30,250	23.3%	27,000
18. Telecommunications Equipment Installers and Repairers, Except Line Installers	$50,620	–4.9%	21,000
19. Operating Engineers and Other Construction Equipment Operators	$35,830	11.6%	37,000
20. Electrical Power-Line Installers and Repairers	$50,150	2.5%	11,000
21. Boilermakers	$48,050	8.7%	2,000
22. Electrical and Electronics Repairers, Powerhouse, Substation, and Relay	$54,970	–0.4%	2,000
23. Riggers	$37,010	13.9%	2,000
24. Architectural Drafters	$40,390	4.6%	9,000
25. Civil Drafters	$40,390	4.6%	9,000
26. Drywall and Ceiling Tile Installers	$34,740	9.0%	17,000
27. Paving, Surfacing, and Tamping Equipment Operators	$30,320	15.6%	7,000
28. Crane and Tower Operators	$38,870	8.2%	4,000

Jobs 1 and 2 share 61,000 openings. Jobs 4 and 5 share 33,000 openings. Jobs 6 and 7 share 210,000 openings.

Best Civilian Jobs Through Military Training for People Interested in Arts and Communication

Job	Annual Earnings	Percent Growth	Annual Openings
1. Technical Directors/Managers	$53,860	10.0%	11,000
2. Graphic Designers	$38,390	15.2%	35,000
3. Interpreters and Translators	$34,800	19.9%	4,000
4. Audio and Video Equipment Technicians	$32,940	18.1%	5,000
5. Camera Operators, Television, Video, and Motion Picture	$41,610	14.2%	4,000
6. Music Composers and Arrangers	$34,810	10.4%	11,000
7. Photographers	$26,100	12.3%	23,000

Job 1 shares 11,000 openings with four other jobs not included in this list. Job 6 shares 11,000 openings with another job not included in this list.

Best Civilian Jobs Through Military Training for People Interested in Business and Administration

Job	Annual Earnings	Percent Growth	Annual Openings
1. Legal Secretaries	$37,750	17.4%	41,000
2. Executive Secretaries and Administrative Assistants	$35,960	12.4%	218,000
3. First-Line Supervisors/Managers of Office and Administrative Support Workers	$42,400	8.1%	167,000
4. Payroll and Timekeeping Clerks	$31,360	17.3%	36,000
5. Human Resources Assistants, Except Payroll and Timekeeping	$32,730	16.7%	28,000
6. Office Clerks, General	$23,070	8.4%	695,000
7. Bookkeeping, Accounting, and Auditing Clerks	$29,490	5.9%	291,000
8. First-Line Supervisors/Managers of Housekeeping and Janitorial Workers	$30,330	19.0%	21,000
9. Production, Planning, and Expediting Clerks	$37,590	7.7%	24,000
10. Postal Service Clerks	$48,310	0.0%	4,000
11. Secretaries, Except Legal, Medical, and Executive	$26,670	–2.5%	231,000
12. Shipping, Receiving, and Traffic Clerks	$25,180	3.7%	121,000

Best Civilian Jobs Through Military Training for People Interested in Finance and Insurance

Job	Annual Earnings	Percent Growth	Annual Openings
1. Tellers	$21,300	6.8%	108,000

Best Civilian Jobs Through Military Training for People Interested in Government and Public Administration

Job	Annual Earnings	Percent Growth	Annual Openings
1. Construction and Building Inspectors	$44,720	22.3%	6,000
2. Court Reporters	$41,640	14.8%	3,000

Best Civilian Jobs Through Military Training for People Interested in Health Science

Job	Annual Earnings	Percent Growth	Annual Openings
1. Dental Hygienists	$60,890	43.3%	17,000
2. Medical Assistants	$25,350	52.1%	93,000
3. Dental Assistants	$29,520	42.7%	45,000
4. Radiologic Technicians	$45,950	23.2%	17,000
5. Radiologic Technologists	$45,950	23.2%	17,000
6. Physical Therapist Assistants	$39,490	44.2%	7,000
7. Cardiovascular Technologists and Technicians	$40,420	32.6%	5,000
8. Occupational Therapist Assistants	$39,750	34.1%	2,000
9. Surgical Technologists	$34,830	29.5%	12,000
10. Licensed Practical and Licensed Vocational Nurses	$35,230	17.1%	84,000
11. Medical and Clinical Laboratory Technicians	$31,700	25.0%	14,000
12. Medical Records and Health Information Technicians	$26,690	28.9%	14,000
13. Pharmacy Technicians	$24,390	28.6%	35,000
14. Nursing Aides, Orderlies, and Attendants	$21,440	22.3%	307,000
15. Orthotists and Prosthetists	$53,760	18.0%	fewer than 500
16. Biological Technicians	$34,270	17.2%	8,000
17. Medical Equipment Preparers	$24,880	20.0%	8,000

Jobs 4 and 5 share 17,000 openings.

Best Civilian Jobs Through Military Training for People Interested in Hospitality, Tourism, and Recreation

Job	Annual Earnings	Percent Growth	Annual Openings
1. Food Preparation Workers	$17,040	19.7%	294,000
2. Combined Food Preparation and Serving Workers, Including Fast Food	$14,790	17.1%	751,000
3. Cooks, Restaurant	$19,840	16.6%	207,000
4. First-Line Supervisors/Managers of Food Preparation and Serving Workers	$26,050	16.6%	187,000
5. Hotel, Motel, and Resort Desk Clerks	$17,810	17.2%	62,000
6. Chefs and Head Cooks	$32,330	16.7%	11,000
7. Cooks, Short Order	$17,230	11.8%	58,000

Best Civilian Jobs Through Military Training for People Interested in Human Service

Job	Annual Earnings	Percent Growth	Annual Openings
1. Social and Human Service Assistants	$25,030	29.7%	61,000
2. Directors, Religious Activities and Education	$32,540	18.5%	10,000

Best Civilian Jobs Through Military Training for People Interested in Information Technology

Job	Annual Earnings	Percent Growth	Annual Openings
1. Computer Support Specialists	$40,610	23.0%	87,000
2. Computer Programmers	$63,420	2.0%	28,000
3. Computer, Automated Teller, and Office Machine Repairers	$36,060	3.8%	31,000

Best Civilian Jobs Through Military Training for People Interested in Law and Public Safety

Job	Annual Earnings	Percent Growth	Annual Openings
1. Paralegals and Legal Assistants	$41,170	29.7%	28,000
2. Criminal Investigators and Special Agents	$55,790	16.3%	9,000
3. Police Detectives	$55,790	16.3%	9,000
4. First-Line Supervisors/Managers of Police and Detectives	$65,570	15.5%	9,000
5. Municipal Fire Fighting and Prevention Supervisors	$60,840	21.1%	4,000
6. Police Patrol Officers	$46,290	15.5%	47,000
7. Sheriffs and Deputy Sheriffs	$46,290	15.5%	47,000
8. Municipal Fire Fighters	$39,090	24.3%	21,000
9. Emergency Medical Technicians and Paramedics	$26,080	27.3%	21,000
10. Lifeguards, Ski Patrol, and Other Recreational Protective Service Workers	$16,910	20.4%	49,000
11. Security Guards	$20,760	12.6%	230,000
12. Correctional Officers and Jailers	$34,090	6.7%	54,000
13. Transit and Railroad Police	$48,850	9.2%	fewer than 500

Jobs 2 and 3 share 9,000 openings. Jobs 6 and 7 share 47,000 openings. Job 8 shares 21,000 openings with another job not included in this list.

Best Civilian Jobs Through Military Training for People Interested in Manufacturing

Job	Annual Earnings	Percent Growth	Annual Openings
1. First-Line Supervisors/Managers of Mechanics, Installers, and Repairers	$51,980	12.4%	33,000
2. Automotive Master Mechanics	$33,050	15.7%	93,000
3. Automotive Specialty Technicians	$33,050	15.7%	93,000
4. Aircraft Mechanics and Service Technicians	$47,310	13.4%	11,000
5. Bus and Truck Mechanics and Diesel Engine Specialists	$36,620	14.4%	32,000
6. First-Line Supervisors/Managers of Production and Operating Workers	$46,140	2.7%	89,000
7. Water and Liquid Waste Treatment Plant and System Operators	$34,930	16.2%	6,000
8. Desktop Publishers	$32,800	23.2%	8,000
9. Electrical and Electronics Repairers, Commercial and Industrial Equipment	$44,120	9.7%	8,000
10. Painters, Transportation Equipment	$34,840	14.1%	10,000

Best Civilian Jobs Through Military Training for People Interested in Manufacturing

Job	Annual Earnings	Percent Growth	Annual Openings
11. Automotive Body and Related Repairers	$34,810	10.3%	18,000
12. Mobile Heavy Equipment Mechanics, Except Engines	$39,410	8.8%	14,000
13. Packers and Packagers, Hand	$17,390	10.1%	194,000
14. Medical Equipment Repairers	$39,570	14.8%	4,000
15. Motorboat Mechanics	$32,780	15.1%	7,000
16. Avionics Technicians	$46,630	9.1%	2,000
17. Gas Plant Operators	$51,920	7.7%	2,000
18. Machinists	$34,350	4.3%	33,000
19. Solderers and Brazers	$30,990	5.0%	52,000
20. Welders, Cutters, and Welder Fitters	$30,990	5.0%	52,000
21. Locksmiths and Safe Repairers	$30,880	16.1%	5,000
22. Power Plant Operators	$53,170	–0.4%	5,000
23. Aircraft Structure, Surfaces, Rigging, and Systems Assemblers	$43,990	7.8%	4,000
24. Industrial Machinery Mechanics	$39,740	–0.2%	13,000
25. Outdoor Power Equipment and Other Small Engine Mechanics	$25,810	14.0%	10,000
26. Stationary Engineers and Boiler Operators	$44,600	3.4%	5,000
27. Petroleum Pump System Operators, Refinery Operators, and Gaugers	$51,060	–8.6%	6,000
28. Control and Valve Installers and Repairers, Except Mechanical Door	$44,120	4.9%	4,000
29. Electrical and Electronics Installers and Repairers, Transportation Equipment	$41,490	6.6%	2,000
30. Nuclear Power Reactor Operators	$66,230	–0.5%	1,000
31. Inspectors, Testers, Sorters, Samplers, and Weighers	$29,200	–2.6%	85,000
32. Printing Machine Operators	$30,730	2.9%	26,000

Jobs 2 and 3 share 93,000 openings. Jobs 19 and 20 share 52,000 openings.

Best Civilian Jobs Through Military Training for People Interested in Retail and Wholesale Sales and Service

Job	Annual Earnings	Percent Growth	Annual Openings
1. Retail Salespersons	$19,140	17.3%	1,350,000
2. Purchasing Agents, Except Wholesale, Retail, and Farm Products	$49,030	8.1%	19,000
3. First-Line Supervisors/Managers of Retail Sales Workers	$32,840	3.8%	229,000

Best Civilian Jobs Through Military Training for People Interested in Scientific Research, Engineering, and Mathematics

Job	Annual Earnings	Percent Growth	Annual Openings
1. Civil Engineering Technicians	$39,210	14.1%	10,000
2. Nuclear Equipment Operation Technicians	$61,120	13.7%	1,000
3. Mechanical Engineering Technicians	$44,830	12.3%	5,000
4. Electro-Mechanical Technicians	$43,880	9.7%	2,000
5. Mapping Technicians	$31,290	9.6%	9,000
6. Surveying Technicians	$31,290	9.6%	9,000
7. Aerospace Engineering and Operations Technicians	$52,450	8.5%	1,000
8. Chemical Technicians	$38,500	4.4%	7,000

Job 2 shares 1,000 openings with another job not on this list. Jobs 5 and 6 share 9,000 openings.

Best Civilian Jobs Through Military Training for People Interested in Transportation, Distribution, and Logistics

Job	Annual Earnings	Percent Growth	Annual Openings
1. Airline Pilots, Copilots, and Flight Engineers	$138,170	17.2%	7,000
2. Bus Drivers, Transit and Intercity	$31,010	21.7%	34,000
3. Commercial Pilots	$55,810	16.8%	2,000
4. Storage and Distribution Managers	$69,120	12.7%	15,000
5. Taxi Drivers and Chauffeurs	$19,980	24.8%	43,000
6. Truck Drivers, Heavy and Tractor-Trailer	$34,280	12.9%	274,000
7. First-Line Supervisors/Managers of Transportation and Material-Moving Machine and Vehicle Operators	$47,530	15.3%	22,000

Best Civilian Jobs Through Military Training for People Interested in Transportation, Distribution, and Logistics

Job	Annual Earnings	Percent Growth	Annual Openings
8. Truck Drivers, Light or Delivery Services	$24,790	15.7%	169,000
9. Laborers and Freight, Stock, and Material Movers, Hand	$20,610	10.2%	671,000
10. Mates—Ship, Boat, and Barge	$50,940	4.8%	2,000
11. Pilots, Ship	$50,940	4.8%	2,000
12. Ship and Boat Captains	$50,940	4.8%	2,000
13. Cargo and Freight Agents	$35,860	–5.6%	12,000

Job 4 shares 15,000 openings with another job not included in this list. Jobs 10, 11, and 12 share 2,000 openings.

Best Civilian Jobs Through Military Training Based on Personality Types

These lists organize the 150 best jobs into groups matching six personality types. The personality types are Realistic, Investigative, Artistic, Social, Enterprising, and Conventional. This system was developed by John L. Holland and is used in the *Self-Directed Search (SDS)* and other career assessment inventories and information systems.

If you have used one of these career inventories or systems, the lists will help you identify civilian jobs that most closely match these personality types. Even if you have not used one of these systems, the concept of personality types and the jobs that are related to them can help you identify civilian jobs that most closely match the type of person you are.

We've ranked the jobs within each personality type based on their combined scores for earnings, growth, and annual job openings. As in the job lists for interest areas, only one list for each personality type is given in this section. Note that each job is listed in the one personality type it most closely matches, even though it might also fit into others. Consider reviewing the jobs for more than one personality type so you don't overlook possible civilian jobs that would interest you.

For brief descriptions of the six personality types used in the lists, see page 25 in Part I. Select the two or three descriptions that most closely resemble you and then use the lists to identify jobs that best fit these personality types.

Best Civilian Jobs Through Military Training for People with a Realistic Personality Type

Job	Annual Earnings	Percent Growth	Annual Openings
1. Radiologic Technicians	$45,950	23.2%	17,000
2. Radiologic Technologists	$45,950	23.2%	17,000
3. Pipe Fitters and Steamfitters	$42,160	15.7%	61,000
4. Plumbers	$42,160	15.7%	61,000
5. Technical Directors/Managers	$53,860	16.6%	11,000
6. Airline Pilots, Copilots, and Flight Engineers	$138,170	17.2%	7,000
7. Municipal Fire Fighters	$39,090	24.3%	21,000
8. Heating and Air Conditioning Mechanics and Installers	$37,040	19.0%	33,000
9. Refrigeration Mechanics and Installers	$37,040	19.0%	33,000
10. Municipal Fire Fighting and Prevention Supervisors	$60,840	21.1%	4,000
11. Electricians	$42,790	11.8%	68,000
12. Construction Carpenters	$35,580	13.8%	210,000
13. Rough Carpenters	$35,580	13.8%	210,000
14. Automotive Master Mechanics	$33,050	15.7%	93,000
15. Automotive Specialty Technicians	$33,050	15.7%	93,000
16. Surgical Technologists	$34,830	29.5%	12,000
17. Food Preparation Workers	$17,040	19.7%	294,000
18. Commercial Pilots	$55,810	16.8%	2,000
19. Bus Drivers, Transit and Intercity	$31,010	21.7%	34,000
20. Truck Drivers, Heavy and Tractor-Trailer	$34,280	12.9%	274,000
21. Hazardous Materials Removal Workers	$33,690	31.2%	11,000
22. Combined Food Preparation and Serving Workers, Including Fast Food	$14,790	17.1%	751,000
23. Taxi Drivers and Chauffeurs	$19,980	24.8%	43,000
24. Medical and Clinical Laboratory Technicians	$31,700	25.0%	14,000
25. Maintenance and Repair Workers, General	$31,210	15.2%	154,000
26. Roofers	$31,230	16.8%	38,000
27. Structural Iron and Steel Workers	$40,580	15.0%	13,000
28. Bus and Truck Mechanics and Diesel Engine Specialists	$36,620	14.4%	32,000
29. Cooks, Restaurant	$19,840	16.6%	207,000
30. Highway Maintenance Workers	$30,250	23.3%	27,000
31. Sheet Metal Workers	$36,390	12.2%	50,000
32. Telecommunications Line Installers and Repairers	$42,410	10.8%	23,000
33. Truck Drivers, Light or Delivery Services	$24,790	15.7%	169,000
34. Brickmasons and Blockmasons	$41,860	12.0%	17,000

Best Civilian Jobs Through Military Training for People with a Realistic Personality Type

Job	Annual Earnings	Percent Growth	Annual Openings
35. Elevator Installers and Repairers	$59,190	14.8%	3,000
36. Cement Masons and Concrete Finishers	$32,030	15.9%	32,000
37. Lifeguards, Ski Patrol, and Other Recreational Protective Service Workers	$16,910	20.4%	49,000
38. Operating Engineers and Other Construction Equipment Operators	$35,830	11.6%	37,000
39. Desktop Publishers	$32,800	23.2%	8,000
40. Civil Engineering Technicians	$39,210	14.1%	10,000
41. Biological Technicians	$34,270	17.2%	8,000
42. Mechanical Engineering Technicians	$44,830	12.3%	5,000
43. Electrical and Electronics Repairers, Commercial and Industrial Equipment	$44,120	9.7%	8,000
44. Nuclear Equipment Operation Technicians	$61,120	13.7%	1,000
45. Telecommunications Equipment Installers and Repairers, Except Line Installers	$50,620	–4.9%	21,000
46. Laborers and Freight, Stock, and Material Movers, Hand	$20,610	10.2%	671,000
47. Water and Liquid Waste Treatment Plant and System Operators	$34,930	16.2%	6,000
48. Mobile Heavy Equipment Mechanics, Except Engines	$39,410	8.8%	14,000
49. Painters, Transportation Equipment	$34,840	14.1%	10,000
50. Medical Equipment Repairers	$39,570	14.8%	4,000
51. Correctional Officers and Jailers	$34,090	6.7%	54,000
52. Electrical Power-Line Installers and Repairers	$50,150	2.5%	11,000
53. Automotive Body and Related Repairers	$34,810	10.3%	18,000
54. Medical Equipment Preparers	$24,880	20.0%	8,000
55. Packers and Packagers, Hand	$17,390	10.1%	194,000
56. Cooks, Short Order	$17,230	11.8%	58,000
57. Gas Plant Operators	$51,920	7.7%	2,000
58. Avionics Technicians	$46,630	9.1%	2,000
59. Drywall and Ceiling Tile Installers	$34,740	9.0%	17,000
60. Boilermakers	$48,050	8.7%	2,000
61. Computer, Automated Teller, and Office Machine Repairers	$36,060	3.8%	31,000
62. Motorboat Mechanics	$32,780	15.1%	7,000
63. Power Plant Operators	$53,170	–0.4%	5,000
64. Solderers and Brazers	$30,990	5.0%	52,000
65. Welders, Cutters, and Welder Fitters	$30,990	5.0%	52,000

(continued)

(continued)

Best Civilian Jobs Through Military Training for People with a Realistic Personality Type

Job	Annual Earnings	Percent Growth	Annual Openings
66. Aircraft Structure, Surfaces, Rigging, and Systems Assemblers	$43,990	7.8%	4,000
67. Electro-Mechanical Technicians	$43,880	9.7%	2,000
68. Machinists	$34,350	4.3%	33,000
69. Architectural Drafters	$40,390	4.6%	9,000
70. Civil Drafters	$40,390	4.6%	9,000
71. Industrial Machinery Mechanics	$39,740	–0.2%	13,000
72. Mates—Ship, Boat, and Barge	$50,940	4.8%	2,000
73. Pilots, Ship	$50,940	4.8%	2,000
74. Control and Valve Installers and Repairers, Except Mechanical Door	$44,120	4.9%	4,000
75. Petroleum Pump System Operators, Refinery Operators, and Gaugers	$51,060	–8.6%	6,000
76. Riggers	$37,010	13.9%	2,000
77. Locksmiths and Safe Repairers	$30,880	16.1%	5,000
78. Pest Control Workers	$27,170	18.4%	4,000
79. Stationary Engineers and Boiler Operators	$44,600	3.4%	5,000
80. Electrical and Electronics Repairers, Powerhouse, Substation, and Relay	$54,970	–0.4%	2,000
81. Paving, Surfacing, and Tamping Equipment Operators	$30,320	15.6%	7,000
82. Outdoor Power Equipment and Other Small Engine Mechanics	$25,810	14.0%	10,000
83. Crane and Tower Operators	$38,870	8.2%	4,000
84. Nuclear Power Reactor Operators	$66,230	–0.5%	1,000
85. Inspectors, Testers, Sorters, Samplers, and Weighers	$29,200	–2.6%	85,000
86. Electrical and Electronics Installers and Repairers, Transportation Equipment	$41,490	6.6%	2,000
87. Chemical Technicians	$38,500	4.4%	7,000
88. Surveying Technicians	$31,290	9.6%	9,000
89. Printing Machine Operators	$30,730	2.9%	26,000

Jobs 1 and 2 share 17,000 openings. Jobs 3 and 4 share 61,000 openings. Job 5 shares 11,000 openings with four other jobs not included in this list. Job 7 shares 21,000 openings with another job not included in this list. Jobs 8 and 9 share 33,000 openings. Job 10 shares 4,000 openings with another job not included in this list. Jobs 12 and 13 share 210,000 openings. Jobs 14 and 15 share 93,000 openings. Job 44 shares 1,000 openings with another job not included in this list. Jobs 64 and 65 share 52,000 openings. Jobs 69 and 70 share 9,000 openings. Jobs 72 and 73 share 2,000 openings. Job 88 shares 9,000 openings with another job not included in this list.

Best Civilian Jobs Through Military Training for People with an Investigative Personality Type

Job	Annual Earnings	Percent Growth	Annual Openings
1. Computer Support Specialists	$40,610	23.0%	87,000
2. Computer Programmers	$63,420	2.0%	28,000
3. Aircraft Mechanics and Service Technicians	$47,310	13.4%	11,000
4. Cardiovascular Technologists and Technicians	$40,420	32.6%	5,000
5. Aerospace Engineering and Operations Technicians	$52,450	8.5%	1,000

Best Civilian Jobs Through Military Training for People with an Artistic Personality Type

Job	Annual Earnings	Percent Growth	Annual Openings
1. Graphic Designers	$38,390	15.2%	35,000
2. Camera Operators, Television, Video, and Motion Picture	$41,610	14.2%	4,000
3. Court Reporters	$41,640	14.8%	3,000
4. Interpreters and Translators	$34,800	19.9%	4,000
5. Music Composers and Arrangers	$34,810	10.4%	11,000
6. Photographers	$26,100	12.3%	23,000

Job 5 shares 11,000 openings with another job not included in this list.

Best Civilian Jobs Through Military Training for People with a Social Personality Type

Job	Annual Earnings	Percent Growth	Annual Openings
1. Dental Hygienists	$60,890	43.3%	17,000
2. Medical Assistants	$25,350	52.1%	93,000
3. Physical Therapist Assistants	$39,490	44.2%	7,000
4. Dental Assistants	$29,520	42.7%	45,000
5. Police Patrol Officers	$46,290	15.5%	47,000
6. Sheriffs and Deputy Sheriffs	$46,290	15.5%	47,000
7. Licensed Practical and Licensed Vocational Nurses	$35,230	17.1%	84,000
8. Nursing Aides, Orderlies, and Attendants	$21,440	22.3%	307,000
9. Occupational Therapist Assistants	$39,750	34.1%	2,000

(continued)

(continued)

Best Civilian Jobs Through Military Training for People with a Social Personality Type

Job	Annual Earnings	Percent Growth	Annual Openings
10. Social and Human Service Assistants	$25,030	29.7%	61,000
11. Emergency Medical Technicians and Paramedics	$26,080	27.3%	21,000
12. Orthotists and Prosthetists	$53,760	18.0%	fewer than 500
13. Directors, Religious Activities and Education	$32,540	18.5%	10,000
14. Security Guards	$20,760	12.6%	230,000

Jobs 5 and 6 share 47,000 openings.

Best Civilian Jobs Through Military Training for People with an Enterprising Personality Type

Job	Annual Earnings	Percent Growth	Annual Openings
1. Paralegals and Legal Assistants	$41,170	29.7%	28,000
2. Retail Salespersons	$19,140	17.3%	1,350,000
3. Criminal Investigators and Special Agents	$55,790	16.3%	9,000
4. Police Detectives	$55,790	16.3%	9,000
5. First-Line Supervisors/Managers of Mechanics, Installers, and Repairers	$51,980	12.4%	33,000
6. Storage and Distribution Managers	$69,120	12.7%	15,000
7. First-Line Supervisors/Managers of Construction Trades and Extraction Workers	$51,970	10.9%	57,000
8. First-Line Supervisors/Managers of Police and Detectives	$65,570	15.5%	9,000
9. First-Line Supervisors/Managers of Food Preparation and Serving Workers	$26,050	16.6%	187,000
10. First-Line Supervisors/Managers of Housekeeping and Janitorial Workers	$30,330	19.0%	21,000
11. First-Line Supervisors/Managers of Transportation and Material-Moving Machine and Vehicle Operators	$47,530	15.3%	22,000
12. First-Line Supervisors/Managers of Office and Administrative Support Workers	$42,400	8.1%	167,000
13. Chefs and Head Cooks	$32,330	16.7%	11,000
14. First-Line Supervisors/Managers of Retail Sales Workers	$32,840	3.8%	229,000
15. Purchasing Agents, Except Wholesale, Retail, and Farm Products	$49,030	8.1%	19,000

Best Civilian Jobs Through Military Training for People with an Enterprising Personality Type

Job	Annual Earnings	Percent Growth	Annual Openings
16. First-Line Supervisors/Managers of Production and Operating Workers	$46,140	2.7%	89,000
17. Ship and Boat Captains	$50,940	4.8%	2,000
18. Transit and Railroad Police	$48,850	9.2%	fewer than 500

Jobs 3 and 4 share 9,000 openings. Job 6 shares 15,000 openings with another job not included in this list. Job 17 shares 2,000 openings with two other jobs not included in this list.

Best Civilian Jobs Through Military Training for People with a Conventional Personality Type

Job	Annual Earnings	Percent Growth	Annual Openings
1. Legal Secretaries	$37,750	17.4%	41,000
2. Executive Secretaries and Administrative Assistants	$35,960	12.4%	218,000
3. Construction and Building Inspectors	$44,720	22.3%	6,000
4. Payroll and Timekeeping Clerks	$31,360	17.3%	36,000
5. Medical Records and Health Information Technicians	$26,690	28.9%	14,000
6. Bookkeeping, Accounting, and Auditing Clerks	$29,490	5.9%	291,000
7. Human Resources Assistants, Except Payroll and Timekeeping	$32,730	16.7%	28,000
8. Pharmacy Technicians	$24,390	28.6%	35,000
9. Audio and Video Equipment Technicians	$32,940	18.1%	5,000
10. Office Clerks, General	$23,070	8.4%	695,000
11. Production, Planning, and Expediting Clerks	$37,590	7.7%	24,000
12. Hotel, Motel, and Resort Desk Clerks	$17,810	17.2%	62,000
13. Secretaries, Except Legal, Medical, and Executive	$26,670	–2.5%	231,000
14. Shipping, Receiving, and Traffic Clerks	$25,180	3.7%	121,000
15. Mapping Technicians	$31,290	9.6%	9,000
16. Postal Service Clerks	$48,310	0.0%	4,000
17. Tellers	$21,300	6.8%	108,000
18. Cargo and Freight Agents	$35,860	–5.6%	12,000

Job 15 shares 9,000 openings with another job not included in this list.

Bonus Lists: Civilian Work Experiences of Veterans

In this book we focus on civilian jobs that are linked to military training and that have good economic rewards. But maybe you're wondering about what kinds of jobs are *actually held* by veterans of military service. That's what these two bonus lists are about.

Jobs Held by Veterans

We analyzed the data gathered by the Census Bureau as part of their August 2005 Current Population Survey, which included questions about both prior military service and current employment. From this data we were able to assemble the following list of the civilian jobs most commonly held by veterans. Note that the numbers indicate how many veterans were identified in these jobs *in this survey sample.* They are not national totals, but because the sample is meant to represent the nation, they give a good idea of the *relative* numbers of workers nationwide.

It is an extremely diverse set of jobs and includes several that are not among the best 150 and therefore are not described in Part IV of this book. However, the appendix lists several resources where you can read up on any of these jobs.

Top 20 Civilian Jobs Held by Veterans

Job	Number of Veterans Working
1. Driver/Sales Workers (includes Truck Drivers, Heavy and Tractor-Trailer; and Truck Drivers, Light or Delivery Services)	333
2. Managers, All Other	191
3. First-Line Supervisors/Managers of Retail Sales Workers	169
4. Farmers and Ranchers	126
5. Retail Salespersons	119
6. Carpenters (includes Construction Carpenters and Rough Carpenters)	118
7. Chief Executives	116
8. Security Guards and Gaming Surveillance Officers (includes Gaming Surveillance Officers and Gaming Investigators; and Security Guards)	110
9. Occupational Therapist Assistants	109
10. Building Cleaning Workers, All Other	109
11. Sales Representatives, Wholesale and Manufacturing	85
12. First-Line Supervisors/Managers of Non-Retail Sales Workers	80
13. First-Line Supervisors/Managers of Construction Trades and Extraction Workers	76
14. Electricians	76

Top 20 Civilian Jobs Held by Veterans

Job	Number of Veterans Working
15. Police and Sheriff's Patrol Officers (includes Police Patrol Officers; and Sheriffs and Deputy Sheriffs)	73
16. Construction Managers	72
17. Lawyers	70
18. General and Operations Managers	65
19. Laborers and Freight, Stock, and Material Movers, Hand	62
20. Real Estate Brokers and Sales Agents	59

Fields Where Veterans Are Working

We also analyzed the survey data to see what civilian fields (or industries) veterans are working in. Some fields are growing much faster than others; for example, health care is much hotter than manufacturing. Therefore, when you are planning your civilian career goal, your choice of a field can be just as important as your choice of an occupation. For more details on this subject you may want to read *40 Best Fields for Your Career* (JIST).

Here are the top 20 civilian fields where veterans were working. As before, the numbers reflect only the number of responses to this survey, but by comparing them you can get an idea of the national distribution of veterans in various industries.

Top 20 Fields Where Veterans Are Working

Field	Number of Veterans Working
1. Retail Trade	639
2. Construction	633
3. Manufacturing—Durable Goods	582
4. Transportation and Warehousing	561
5. Public Administration	530
6. Professional and Technical Services	404
7. Health Care and Social Services	394
8. Educational Services	290
9. Other Services, Except Private Households	271
10. Management, Administrative and Waste Management Services	268
11. Wholesale Trade	255
12. Manufacturing—Nondurable Goods	251
13. Agriculture, Forestry, Fishing, and Hunting	213

(continued)

(continued)

Top 20 Fields Where Veterans Are Working

Field	Number of Veterans Working
14. Finance and Insurance	198
15. Accommodation and Food Services	190
16. Real Estate and Rental and Leasing	162
17. Information	153
18. Arts, Entertainment, and Recreation	115
19. Utilities	102
20. Mining	48

PART IV

Descriptions of the Best Civilian Jobs Through Military Training

This part provides descriptions for all the civilian jobs included in one or more of the lists in Part III. The introduction gives more details on how to use and interpret the civilian job descriptions, but here is some additional information:

- Job descriptions are arranged in alphabetical order by job title. This approach allows you to find a description quickly if you know its correct title from one of the lists in Part IV.
- If you are using this section to browse for interesting options, we suggest you begin with the Table of Contents. Part III features many interesting lists that will help you identify job titles to explore in more detail. If you have not browsed the lists in Part III, consider spending some time there. The lists are interesting and will help you identify civilian job titles you can find described in the material that follows. The job titles in Part IV are also listed in the Table of Contents.
- The descriptions here give you only an overview of the jobs. You need more information before you can make a final choice. For suggestions for further exploration, see the appendix.
- Note that every civilian job description here includes the name of at least one military job that can provide training. You can find descriptions of all of these military jobs in Part II.

Aerospace Engineering and Operations Technicians

- Annual Earnings: $52,450
- Growth: 8.5%
- Annual Job Openings: 1,000
- Self-Employed: 0.5%
- Part-Time: 6.7%
- Civilian Training Route: Associate degree

Operate, install, calibrate, and maintain integrated computer/communications systems consoles; simulators; and other data acquisition, test, and measurement instruments and equipment to launch, track, position, and evaluate air and space vehicles. May record and interpret test data. Inspect, diagnose, maintain, and operate test setups and equipment to detect malfunctions. Record and interpret test data on parts, assemblies, and mechanisms. Confer with engineering personnel regarding details and implications of test procedures and results. Adjust, repair, or replace faulty components of test setups and equipment. Identify required data, data acquisition plans, and test parameters, setting up equipment to conform to these specifications. Construct and maintain test facilities for aircraft parts and systems according to specifications. Operate and calibrate computer systems and devices to comply with test requirements and to perform data acquisition and analysis. Test aircraft systems under simulated operational conditions, performing systems readiness tests and pre- and post-operational checkouts, to establish design or fabrication parameters. Fabricate and install parts and systems to be tested in test equipment, using hand tools, power tools, and test instruments. Finish vehicle instrumentation and deinstrumentation. Exchange cooling system components in various vehicles.

Military Job That Provides Training for It (see the description in Part II): Non-Destructive Testers

Personality Type: Investigative. Investigative occupations frequently involve working with ideas and require an extensive amount of thinking. These occupations can involve searching for facts and figuring out problems mentally.

GOE—Interest Area: 15. Scientific Research, Engineering, and Mathematics. **Work Group:** 15.09. Engineering Technology. **Other Civilian Jobs in This Work Group:** Cartographers and Photogrammetrists; Civil Engineering Technicians; Electrical and Electronic Engineering Technicians; Electrical and Electronics Drafters; Electrical Drafters; Electrical Engineering Technicians; Electro-Mechanical Technicians; Electronic Drafters; Electronics Engineering Technicians; Environmental Engineering Technicians; Mapping Technicians; Mechanical Drafters; Mechanical Engineering Technicians; Surveying and Mapping Technicians; Surveying Technicians.

Skills—Installation: Installing equipment, machines, wiring, or programs to meet specifications. **Technology Design:** Generating or adapting equipment and technology to serve user needs. **Operation Monitoring:** Watching gauges, dials, or other indicators to make sure a machine is working properly. **Troubleshooting:** Determining causes of operating errors and deciding what to do about them. **Repairing:** Repairing machines or systems, using the needed tools. **Science:** Using scientific rules and methods to solve problems. **Operation and Control:** Controlling operations of equipment or systems. **Operations Analysis:** Analyzing needs and product requirements to create a design.

Work Environment: Indoors; noisy; sitting; using hands on objects, tools, or controls; repetitive motions.

Aircraft Mechanics and Service Technicians

- Annual Earnings: $47,310
- Growth: 13.4%
- Annual Job Openings: 11,000
- Self-Employed: 3.0%
- Part-Time: 1.8%
- Civilian Training Route: Postsecondary vocational training

Diagnose, adjust, repair, or overhaul aircraft engines and assemblies, such as hydraulic and pneumatic systems. Read and interpret maintenance manuals, service bulletins, and other specifications to determine the feasibility and method of repairing or replacing malfunctioning or damaged components. Inspect completed work to certify that maintenance meets standards and that aircraft are ready for operation. Maintain repair logs, documenting all preventive and corrective aircraft maintenance. Conduct routine and special inspections as required by regulations. Examine and inspect aircraft components, including landing gear, hydraulic systems, and de-icers, to locate cracks, breaks, leaks, or other problem. Inspect airframes for wear or other defects. Maintain, repair, and rebuild aircraft structures; functional components; and parts such as wings and fuselage, rigging, hydraulic units, oxygen systems, fuel systems, electrical systems, gaskets, and seals. Measure the tension of control cables. Replace or repair worn, defective, or damaged components, using hand tools, gauges, and testing equipment. Measure parts for wear, using precision instruments. Assemble and install electrical, plumbing, mechanical, hydraulic, and structural components and accessories, using hand tools and power tools. Test operation of engines and other systems, using test equipment such as ignition analyzers, compression checkers, distributor timers, and ammeters. Obtain fuel and oil samples and check them for contamination. Reassemble engines following repair or inspection and re-install engines in aircraft. Read and interpret pilots' descriptions of problems to diagnose causes. Modify aircraft structures, space vehicles, systems, or components, following drawings, schematics, charts, engineering orders, and technical publications. Install and align repaired or replacement parts for subsequent riveting or welding, using clamps and wrenches. Locate and mark dimensions and reference lines on defective or replacement parts, using templates, scribes, compasses, and steel rules. Clean, strip, prime, and sand structural surfaces and materials to prepare them for bonding. Service and maintain aircraft and related apparatus by performing activities such as flushing crankcases, cleaning screens, and lubricating moving parts.

Military Jobs That Provide Training for It (see the descriptions in Part II): Aircraft Mechanics; Electronic Instrument and Equipment Repairers; Non-Destructive Testers

Personality Type: Realistic. Realistic occupations frequently involve work activities that include practical, hands-on problems and solutions. They often deal with plants, animals, and real-world materials like wood, tools, and machinery. Many of the occupations require working outside and do not involve a lot of paperwork or working closely with others.

GOE—**Interest Area:** 13. Manufacturing. **Work Group:** 13.14. Vehicle and Facility Mechanical Work. **Other Civilian Jobs in This Work Group:** Aircraft Structure, Surfaces, Rigging, and Systems Assemblers; Automotive Body and Related Repairers; Automotive Glass Installers and Repairers; Automotive Master Mechanics; Automotive Service Technicians and Mechanics; Automotive Specialty Technicians; Bus and Truck Mechanics and Diesel Engine Specialists; Farm Equipment Mechanics; Fiberglass Laminators and Fabricators; Mobile Heavy Equipment Mechanics, Except Engines; Motorboat Mechanics; Motorcycle Mechanics; Outdoor Power Equipment and Other Small Engine Mechanics; Rail Car Repairers; Recreational Vehicle Service Technicians; Tire Repairers and Changers.

Skills—Repairing: Repairing machines or systems, using the needed tools. **Equipment Maintenance:** Performing routine maintenance on equipment and determining when and what kind of maintenance is needed. **Operation Monitoring:** Watching gauges, dials, or other indicators to make sure a machine is working properly. **Installation:** Installing equipment, machines, wiring, or programs to meet specifications. **Troubleshooting:** Determining causes of operating errors and deciding what to do about them. **Operation and Control:** Controlling operations of equipment or systems. **Quality Control Analysis:** Conducting tests and inspections of products, services, or processes to evaluate quality or performance. **Complex Problem Solving:** Identifying complex problems and reviewing related information to develop and evaluate options and implement solutions.

Work Environment: Noisy; contaminants; cramped work space, awkward positions; standing; using hands on objects, tools, or controls; bending or twisting the body.

Aircraft Structure, Surfaces, Rigging, and Systems Assemblers

- Annual Earnings: $43,990
- Growth: 7.8%
- Annual Job Openings: 4,000
- Self-Employed: 0.0%
- Part-Time: 1.7%
- Civilian Training Route: Long-term on-the-job training

Assemble, fit, fasten, and install parts of airplanes, space vehicles, or missiles, such as tails, wings, fuselage, bulkheads, stabilizers, landing gear, rigging and control equipment, or heating and ventilating systems. Form loops or splices in cables, using clamps and fittings, or reweave cable strands. Align and fit structural assemblies manually or signal crane operators to position assemblies for joining. Align, fit, assemble, connect, and install system components, using jigs, fixtures, measuring instruments, hand tools, and power tools. Assemble and fit prefabricated parts to form subassemblies. Assemble, install, and connect parts, fittings, and assemblies on aircraft, using layout tools; hand tools; power tools; and fasteners such as bolts, screws, rivets, and clamps. Attach brackets, hinges, or clips to secure or support components and subassemblies, using bolts, screws, rivets, chemical bonding, or welding. Select and install accessories in swaging machines, using hand tools. Fit and fasten sheet metal coverings to surface areas and other sections of aircraft prior to welding or riveting. Lay out and mark reference points and locations for installation of parts and components, using jigs, templates, and measuring and marking instruments. Inspect and test installed units, parts, systems, and assemblies for fit, alignment, performance, defects, and compliance with standards, using measuring instruments and test equipment. Install mechanical linkages and actuators and verify tension of cables, using tensiometers. Join structural assemblies such as wings, tails, and fuselage. Measure and cut cables and tubing, using master templates, measuring instruments, and cable cutters or saws. Read and interpret blueprints, illustrations, and specifications to determine layouts, sequences of operations, or identities and relationships of parts. Prepare and load live ammunition, missiles, and bombs onto aircraft according to established procedures. Adjust, repair, rework, or replace parts and assemblies to eliminate malfunctions and to ensure proper operation. Cut, trim, file, bend, and smooth parts and verify sizes and fitting tolerances to ensure proper fit and clearance of parts. Install and connect control cables to electronically controlled units, using hand tools, ring locks, cotter keys, threaded connectors, turnbuckles, and related devices.

Military Job That Provides Training for It (see the description in Part II): Aircraft Mechanics

Personality Type: Realistic. Realistic occupations frequently involve work activities that include practical, hands-on problems and solutions. They often deal with plants, animals, and real-world materials like wood, tools, and machinery. Many of the occupations require working outside and do not involve a lot of paperwork or working closely with others.

GOE—Interest Area: 13. Manufacturing. **Work Group:** 13.14. Vehicle and Facility Mechanical Work. **Other Civilian Jobs in This Work Group:** Aircraft Mechanics and Service Technicians; Automotive Body and Related Repairers; Automotive Glass Installers and Repairers; Automotive Master Mechanics; Automotive Service Technicians and Mechanics; Automotive Specialty Technicians; Bus and Truck Mechanics and Diesel Engine Specialists; Farm Equipment Mechanics; Fiberglass Laminators and Fabricators; Mobile Heavy Equipment Mechanics, Except Engines; Motorboat Mechanics; Motorcycle Mechanics; Outdoor Power Equipment and Other Small Engine Mechanics; Rail Car Repairers; Recreational Vehicle Service Technicians; Tire Repairers and Changers.

Skills—No data available.

Work Environment: More often indoors than outdoors; hazardous equipment; standing; using hands on objects, tools, or controls; repetitive motions.

Airline Pilots, Copilots, and Flight Engineers

- Annual Earnings: $138,170
- Growth: 17.2%
- Annual Job Openings: 7,000
- Self-Employed: 2.4%
- Part-Time: 14.8%
- Civilian Training Route: Bachelor's degree

Pilot and navigate the flight of multi-engine aircraft in regularly scheduled service for the transport of passengers and cargo. Requires Federal Air Transport rating and certification in specific aircraft type used. Use instrumentation to guide flights when visibility is poor. Respond to and report in-flight emergencies and malfunctions. Work as part of a flight team with other crew members, especially during takeoffs and landings. Contact control towers for takeoff clearances, arrival instructions, and other information, using radio equipment. Steer aircraft along planned routes with the assistance of autopilot and flight management computers. Monitor gauges, warning devices, and control panels to verify aircraft performance and to regulate engine speed. Start engines, operate controls, and pilot airplanes to transport passengers, mail, or freight while adhering to flight plans, regulations, and procedures. Inspect aircraft for defects and malfunctions according to pre-flight checklists. Check passenger and cargo distributions and fuel amounts to ensure that weight and balance specifications are met. Monitor engine operation, fuel consumption, and functioning of aircraft systems during flights. Confer with flight dispatchers and weather forecasters to keep abreast of flight conditions. Coordinate flight activities with ground crews and air-traffic control and inform crew members of flight and test procedures. Order changes in fuel supplies, loads, routes, or schedules to ensure safety of flights. Choose routes, altitudes, and speeds that will provide the fastest, safest, and smoothest flights. Direct activities of aircraft crews during flights. Brief crews about flight details such as destinations, duties, and responsibilities. Record in logbooks information such as flight times, distances flown, and fuel consumption. Make announcements regarding flights, using public address systems. File instrument flight plans with air traffic control to ensure that flights are coordinated with other air traffic. Perform minor maintenance work or arrange for major maintenance. Instruct other pilots and student pilots in aircraft operations and the principles of flight. Conduct in-flight tests and evaluations at specified altitudes and in all types of weather to determine the receptivity and other characteristics of equipment and systems.

Military Jobs That Provide Training for It (see the descriptions in Part II): Airplane Navigators; Airplane Pilots; Flight Engineers; Helicopter Pilots

Personality Type: Realistic. Realistic occupations frequently involve work activities that include practical, hands-on problems and solutions. They often deal with plants, animals, and real-world materials like wood, tools, and machinery. Many of the occupations require working outside and do not involve a lot of paperwork or working closely with others.

GOE—Interest Area: 16. Transportation, Distribution, and Logistics. **Work Group:** 16.02. Air Vehicle Operation. **Other Civilian Jobs in This Work Group:** Commercial Pilots.

Skills—Operation Monitoring: Watching gauges, dials, or other indicators to make sure a machine is working properly. **Operation and Control:** Controlling operations of equipment or systems. **Systems Analysis:** Determining how a system should work and how changes in conditions, operations, and the environment will affect outcomes. **Judgment and Decision Making:** Considering the relative costs and benefits of potential actions to choose the most appropriate one. **Troubleshooting:** Determining causes of operating errors and deciding what to do about them. **Systems Evaluation:** Identifying measures or indicators of system performance and the actions needed to improve or correct performance relative to the goals of the system. **Science:** Using scientific rules and methods to solve problems. **Monitoring:** Monitoring/assessing your performance or that of other individuals or organizations to make improvements or take corrective action.

Work Environment: Indoors; noisy; contaminants; radiation; sitting; using hands on objects, tools, or controls.

Architectural Drafters

- Annual Earnings: $40,390
- Growth: 4.6%
- Annual Job Openings: 9,000
- Self-Employed: 6.1%
- Part-Time: 8.4%
- Civilian Training Route: Postsecondary vocational training

The job openings listed here are shared with Civil Drafters.

Prepare detailed drawings of architectural designs and plans for buildings and structures according to specifications provided by architect. Analyze building codes, by-laws, space and site requirements, and other technical documents and reports to determine their effect on architectural designs. Operate computer-aided drafting (CAD) equipment or conventional drafting station to produce designs, working drawings, charts, forms, and records. Coordinate structural, electrical, and mechanical designs and determine a method of presentation to graphically represent building plans. Obtain and assemble data to complete architectural designs, visiting job sites to compile measurements as necessary. Lay out and plan interior room arrangements for commercial buildings, using computer-assisted drafting (CAD) equipment and software. Draw rough and detailed scale plans for foundations, buildings, and structures based on preliminary concepts, sketches, engineering calculations, specification sheets, and other data. Supervise, coordinate, and inspect the work of draftspersons, technicians, and technologists on construction projects. Represent architect on construction site, ensuring builder compliance with design specifications and advising on design corrections under architect's supervision. Check dimensions of materials to be used and assign numbers to lists of materials. Determine procedures and instructions to be followed according to design specifications and quantity of required materials. Analyze technical implications of architect's design concept, calculating weights, volumes, and stress factors. Create freehand drawings and lettering to accompany drawings. Prepare colored drawings of landscape and interior designs for presentation to client. Reproduce drawings on copy machines or trace copies of plans and drawings, using transparent paper or cloth, ink, pencil, and standard drafting instruments. Prepare cost estimates, contracts, bidding documents, and technical reports for specific projects under an architect's supervision. Calculate heat loss and gain of buildings and structures to determine required equipment specifications, following standard procedures. Build landscape, architectural, and display models.

Military Job That Provides Training for It (see the description in Part II): Surveying, Mapping, and Drafting Technicians

Personality Type: Realistic. Realistic occupations frequently involve work activities that include practical, hands-on problems and solutions. They often deal with plants, animals, and real-world materials like wood, tools, and machinery. Many of the occupations require working outside and do not involve a lot of paperwork or working closely with others.

GOE—Interest Area: 02. Architecture and Construction. **Work Group:** 02.03. Architecture/Construction Engineering Technologies. **Other Civilian Jobs in This Work Group:** Architectural and Civil Drafters; Civil Drafters; Surveyors.

Skills—Operations Analysis: Analyzing needs and product requirements to create a design.

Coordination: Adjusting actions in relation to others' actions. **Active Learning:** Understanding the implications of new information for both current and future problem-solving and decision-making. **Technology Design:** Generating or adapting equipment and technology to serve user needs. **Mathematics:** Using mathematics to solve problems. **Complex Problem Solving:** Identifying complex problems and reviewing related information to develop and evaluate options and implement solutions. **Persuasion:** Persuading others to change their minds or behavior. **Monitoring:** Monitoring/assessing your performance or that of other individuals or organizations to make improvements or take corrective action.

Work Environment: Indoors; noisy; sitting; using hands on objects, tools, or controls; repetitive motions.

Audio and Video Equipment Technicians

- Annual Earnings: $32,940
- Growth: 18.1%
- Annual Job Openings: 5,000
- Self-Employed: 5.9%
- Part-Time: 18.3%
- Civilian Training Route: Long-term on-the-job training

Set up or set up and operate audio and video equipment, including microphones, sound speakers, video screens, projectors, video monitors, recording equipment, connecting wires and cables, sound and mixing boards, and related electronic equipment for concerts, sports events, meetings and conventions, presentations, and news conferences. May also set up and operate associated spotlights and other custom lighting systems. Notify supervisors when major equipment repairs are needed. Monitor incoming and outgoing pictures and sound feeds to ensure quality; notify directors of any possible problems. Mix and regulate sound inputs and feeds or coordinate audio feeds with television pictures. Install, adjust, and operate electronic equipment used to record, edit, and transmit radio and television programs, cable programs, and motion pictures. Design layouts of audio and video equipment and perform upgrades and maintenance. Perform minor repairs and routine cleaning of audio and video equipment. Diagnose and resolve media system problems in classrooms. Switch sources of video input from one camera or studio to another, from film to live programming, or from network to local programming. Meet with directors and senior members of camera crews to discuss assignments and determine filming sequences, camera movements, and picture composition. Construct and position properties, sets, lighting equipment, and other equipment. Compress, digitize, duplicate, and store audio and video data. Obtain, set up, and load videotapes for scheduled productions or broadcasts. Edit videotapes by erasing and removing portions of programs and adding video or sound as required. Direct and coordinate activities of assistants and other personnel during production. Plan and develop pre-production ideas into outlines, scripts, storyboards, and graphics, using own ideas or specifications of assignments. Maintain inventories of audiotapes and videotapes and related supplies. Determine formats, approaches, content, levels, and media to effectively meet objectives within budgetary constraints, utilizing research, knowledge, and training. Record and edit audio material such as movie soundtracks, using audio recording and editing equipment. Inform users of audiotaping and videotaping service policies and procedures. Obtain and preview musical performance programs prior to events to become familiar with the order and approximate times of pieces. Produce rough and finished graphics and graphic designs. Locate and secure settings, properties, effects, and other production necessities.

Military Job That Provides Training for It (see the description in Part II): Audiovisual and Broadcast Technicians

Personality Type: Conventional. Conventional occupations frequently involve following set procedures and routines. These occupations can include working with data and details more than with ideas. Usually there is a clear line of authority to follow.

GOE—Interest Area: 03. Arts and Communication. **Work Group:** 03.09. Media Technology. **Other Civilian Jobs in This Work Group:** Broadcast Technicians; Camera Operators, Television, Video, and Motion Picture; Film and Video Editors; Multi-Media Artists and Animators; Photographers; Radio Operators; Sound Engineering Technicians.

Skills—Installation: Installing equipment, machines, wiring, or programs to meet specifications. **Operation and Control:** Controlling operations of equipment or systems. **Equipment Maintenance:** Performing routine maintenance on equipment and determining when and what kind of maintenance is needed. **Troubleshooting:** Determining causes of operating errors and deciding what to do about them. **Operation Monitoring:** Watching gauges, dials, or other indicators to make sure a machine is working properly. **Repairing:** Repairing machines or systems, using the needed tools. **Systems Analysis:** Determining how a system should work and how changes in conditions, operations, and the environment will affect outcomes. **Technology Design:** Generating or adapting equipment and technology to serve user needs.

Work Environment: Indoors; standing; using hands on objects, tools, or controls.

Automotive Body and Related Repairers

- Annual Earnings: $34,810
- Growth: 10.3%
- Annual Job Openings: 18,000
- Self-Employed: 17.6%
- Part-Time: 6.7%
- Civilian Training Route: Long-term on-the-job training

Repair and refinish automotive vehicle bodies and straighten vehicle frames. File, grind, sand, and smooth filled or repaired surfaces, using power tools and hand tools. Sand body areas to be painted and cover bumpers, windows, and trim with masking tape or paper to protect them from the paint. Follow supervisors' instructions as to which parts to restore or replace and how much time the job should take. Remove damaged sections of vehicles, using metal-cutting guns, air grinders, and wrenches, and install replacement parts, using wrenches or welding equipment. Cut and tape plastic separating film to outside repair areas to avoid damaging surrounding surfaces during repair procedure and remove tape and wash surfaces after repairs are complete. Prime and paint repaired surfaces, using paint spray guns and motorized sanders. Inspect repaired vehicles for dimensional accuracy and test drive them to ensure proper alignment and handling. Mix polyester resins and hardeners to be used in restoring damaged areas. Chain or clamp frames and sections to alignment machines that use hydraulic pressure to align damaged components. Fill small dents that cannot be worked out with plastic or solder. Fit and weld replacement parts into place, using wrenches and welding equipment, and grind down welds to smooth them, using power grinders and other tools. Position dolly blocks against surfaces of dented areas and beat opposite surfaces to remove dents, using hammers. Remove damaged panels and identify the family and properties of the plastic used on a vehicle. Review damage reports, prepare or review repair cost estimates, and plan work to be performed. Remove small pits and dimples in body metal, using pick hammers and punches. Remove upholstery, accessories, electrical window-and-seat-operating equipment, and trim to gain access to vehicle bodies and fenders. Clean work areas, using air hoses, to remove damaged material and discarded fiberglass strips used in repair procedures. Adjust or align headlights, wheels, and brake systems. Apply heat to plastic panels, using hot-air welding guns or immersion in hot water, and press the softened panels back into shape by hand. Soak fiberglass matting in resin mixtures and apply layers of matting over repair areas to specified thicknesses.

Military Job That Provides Training for It (see the description in Part II): Automotive and Heavy Equipment Mechanics

Personality Type: Realistic. Realistic occupations frequently involve work activities that include practical, hands-on problems and solutions. They often deal with plants, animals, and real-world materials like wood, tools, and machinery. Many of the occupations require working outside and do not involve a lot of paperwork or working closely with others.

GOE—Interest Area: 13. Manufacturing. **Work Group:** 13.14. Vehicle and Facility Mechanical Work. **Other Civilian Jobs in This Work Group:** Aircraft Mechanics and Service Technicians; Aircraft Structure, Surfaces, Rigging, and Systems Assemblers; Automotive Glass Installers and Repairers; Automotive Master Mechanics; Automotive Service Technicians and Mechanics; Automotive Specialty Technicians; Bus and Truck Mechanics and Diesel Engine Specialists; Farm Equipment Mechanics; Fiberglass Laminators and Fabricators; Mobile Heavy Equipment Mechanics, Except Engines; Motorboat Mechanics; Motorcycle Mechanics; Outdoor Power Equipment and Other Small Engine Mechanics; Rail Car Repairers; Recreational Vehicle Service Technicians; Tire Repairers and Changers.

Skills—No data available.

Work Environment: Noisy; contaminants; hazardous equipment; standing; using hands on objects, tools, or controls; repetitive motions.

Automotive Master Mechanics

- Annual Earnings: $33,050
- Growth: 15.7%
- Annual Job Openings: 93,000
- Self-Employed: 14.8%
- Part-Time: 7.0%
- Civilian Training Route: Postsecondary vocational training

The job openings listed here are shared with Automotive Specialty Technicians.

Repair automobiles, trucks, buses, and other vehicles. Master mechanics repair virtually any part on the vehicle or specialize in the transmission system. Examine vehicles to determine extent of damage or malfunctions. Test drive vehicles and test components and systems, using equipment such as infrared engine analyzers, compression gauges, and computerized diagnostic devices. Repair, reline, replace, and adjust brakes. Review work orders and discuss work with supervisors. Follow checklists to ensure all important parts are examined, including belts, hoses, steering systems, spark plugs, brake and fuel systems, wheel bearings, and other potentially troublesome areas. Plan work procedures, using charts, technical manuals, and experience. Test and adjust repaired systems to meet manufacturers' performance specifications. Confer with customers to obtain descriptions of vehicle problems and to discuss work to be performed and future repair requirements. Perform routine and scheduled maintenance services such as oil changes, lubrications, and tune-ups. Disassemble units and inspect parts for wear, using micrometers, calipers, and gauges. Overhaul or replace carburetors, blowers, generators, distributors, starters, and pumps. Repair and service air conditioning, heating, engine-cooling, and electrical systems. Repair or replace parts such as pistons, rods, gears, valves, and bearings. Tear down, repair, and rebuild faulty assemblies such as power systems, steering systems, and linkages. Rewire ignition systems, lights, and instrument panels. Repair radiator leaks. Install and repair accessories such as radios, heaters, mirrors, and windshield wipers. Repair manual and automatic transmissions. Repair or replace shock absorbers. Align vehicles' front ends. Rebuild parts such as crankshafts and cylinder blocks. Repair damaged automobile bodies. Replace and adjust headlights.

Military Job That Provides Training for It (see the description in Part II): Automotive and Heavy Equipment Mechanics

Personality Type: Realistic. Realistic occupations frequently involve work activities that include practical, hands-on problems and solutions. They often deal with plants, animals, and real-world materials like wood, tools, and machinery. Many of the occupations require working outside and do not involve a lot of paperwork or working closely with others.

GOE—Interest Area: 13. Manufacturing. **Work Group:** 13.14. Vehicle and Facility Mechanical Work. **Other Civilian Jobs in This Work Group:** Aircraft Mechanics and Service Technicians; Aircraft Structure, Surfaces, Rigging, and Systems Assemblers; Automotive Body and Related Repairers; Automotive Glass Installers and Repairers; Automotive Service Technicians and Mechanics; Automotive Specialty Technicians; Bus and Truck Mechanics and Diesel Engine Specialists; Farm Equipment Mechanics; Fiberglass Laminators and Fabricators; Mobile Heavy Equipment Mechanics, Except Engines; Motorboat Mechanics; Motorcycle Mechanics; Outdoor Power Equipment and Other Small Engine Mechanics; Rail Car Repairers; Recreational Vehicle Service Technicians; Tire Repairers and Changers.

Skills—Repairing: Repairing machines or systems, using the needed tools. **Troubleshooting:** Determining causes of operating errors and deciding what to do about them. **Installation:** Installing equipment, machines, wiring, or programs to meet specifications. **Equipment Maintenance:** Performing routine maintenance on equipment and determining when and what kind of maintenance is needed. **Operation Monitoring:** Watching gauges, dials, or other indicators to make sure a machine is working properly. **Complex Problem Solving:** Identifying complex problems and reviewing related information to develop and evaluate options and implement solutions. **Active Learning:** Understanding the implications of new information for both current and future problem-solving and decision-making. **Equipment Selection:** Determining the kinds of tools and equipment needed to do a job.

Work Environment: Noisy; contaminants; hazardous equipment; minor burns, cuts, bites, or stings; standing; using hands on objects, tools, or controls.

Automotive Specialty Technicians

- Annual Earnings: $33,050
- Growth: 15.7%
- Annual Job Openings: 93,000
- Self-Employed: 14.8%
- Part-Time: 7.0%
- Civilian Training Route: Postsecondary vocational training

The job openings listed here are shared with Automotive Master Mechanics.

Repair only one system or component on a vehicle, such as brakes, suspension, or radiator. Examine vehicles, compile estimates of repair costs, and secure customers' approval to perform repairs. Repair, overhaul, and adjust automobile brake systems. Use electronic test equipment to locate and correct malfunctions in fuel, ignition, and emissions control systems. Repair and replace defective ball joint suspensions, brake shoes, and wheel bearings. Inspect and test new vehicles for damage; then record findings so that necessary repairs can be made. Test electronic computer components in automobiles to ensure that they are working properly. Tune automobile engines to ensure proper and efficient functioning. Install and repair air conditioners and service components such as compressors, condensers, and controls. Repair, replace, and adjust defective carburetor parts and gasoline filters. Remove and replace defective mufflers and tailpipes. Repair and replace automobile leaf springs. Rebuild, repair, and test automotive fuel injection units. Align and repair wheels, axles, frames, torsion bars, and steering mechanisms of automobiles, using special alignment equipment and wheel-balancing machines. Repair, install, and adjust hydraulic and electromagnetic automatic lift mechanisms used to raise and lower automobile windows, seats, and tops. Repair and rebuild clutch systems. Convert vehicle fuel systems from gasoline to butane gas operations and repair and service operating butane fuel units.

Military Job That Provides Training for It (see the description in Part II): Automotive and Heavy Equipment Mechanics

Personality Type: Realistic. Realistic occupations frequently involve work activities that include practical, hands-on problems and solutions. They often deal with plants, animals, and real-world materials like wood, tools, and machinery. Many of the occupations require working outside and do not involve a lot of paperwork or working closely with others.

GOE—Interest Area: 13. Manufacturing. **Work Group:** 13.14. Vehicle and Facility Mechanical Work. **Other Civilian Jobs in This Work Group:** Aircraft Mechanics and Service Technicians; Aircraft Structure, Surfaces, Rigging, and Systems Assemblers; Automotive

Body and Related Repairers; Automotive Glass Installers and Repairers; Automotive Master Mechanics; Automotive Service Technicians and Mechanics; Bus and Truck Mechanics and Diesel Engine Specialists; Farm Equipment Mechanics; Fiberglass Laminators and Fabricators; Mobile Heavy Equipment Mechanics, Except Engines; Motorboat Mechanics; Motorcycle Mechanics; Outdoor Power Equipment and Other Small Engine Mechanics; Rail Car Repairers; Recreational Vehicle Service Technicians; Tire Repairers and Changers.

Skills—Repairing: Repairing machines or systems, using the needed tools. **Troubleshooting:** Determining causes of operating errors and deciding what to do about them. **Operation Monitoring:** Watching gauges, dials, or other indicators to make sure a machine is working properly. **Equipment Maintenance:** Performing routine maintenance on equipment and determining when and what kind of maintenance is needed. **Installation:** Installing equipment, machines, wiring, or programs to meet specifications. **Equipment Selection:** Determining the kinds of tools and equipment needed to do a job. **Active Learning:** Understanding the implications of new information for both current and future problem-solving and decision-making. **Monitoring:** Monitoring/assessing your performance or that of other individuals or organizations to make improvements or take corrective action.

Work Environment: Contaminants; cramped work space, awkward positions; minor burns, cuts, bites, or stings; standing; using hands on objects, tools, or controls; bending or twisting the body.

Avionics Technicians

- Annual Earnings: $46,630
- Growth: 9.1%
- Annual Job Openings: 2,000
- Self-Employed: 0.0%
- Part-Time: 4.9%
- Civilian Training Route: Postsecondary vocational training

Install, inspect, test, adjust, or repair avionics equipment, such as radar, radio, navigation, and missile control systems in aircraft or space vehicles. Set up and operate ground support and test equipment to perform functional flight tests of electrical and electronic systems. Test and troubleshoot instruments, components, and assemblies, using circuit testers, oscilloscopes, and voltmeters. Keep records of maintenance and repair work. Coordinate work with that of engineers, technicians, and other aircraft maintenance personnel. Interpret flight test data to diagnose malfunctions and systemic performance problems. Install electrical and electronic components, assemblies, and systems in aircraft, using hand tools, power tools, and soldering irons. Adjust, repair, or replace malfunctioning components or assemblies, using hand tools and soldering irons. Connect components to assemblies such as radio systems, instruments, magnetos, inverters, and in-flight refueling systems, using hand tools and soldering irons. Assemble components such as switches, electrical controls, and junction boxes, using hand tools and soldering irons. Fabricate parts and test aids as required. Lay out installation of aircraft assemblies and systems, following documentation such as blueprints, manuals, and wiring diagrams. Assemble prototypes or models of circuits, instruments, and systems so that they can be used for testing. Operate computer-aided drafting and design applications to design avionics system modifications.

Military Jobs That Provide Training for It (see the descriptions in Part II): Aircraft Mechanics; Avionics Technicians; Electronic Instrument and Equipment Repairers; Weapons Maintenance Technicians

Personality Type: Realistic. Realistic occupations frequently involve work activities that include practical, hands-on problems and solutions. They often deal with plants, animals, and real-world materials like wood, tools, and machinery. Many of the occupations require working outside and do not involve a lot of paperwork or working closely with others.

GOE—Interest Area: 13. Manufacturing. **Work Group:** 13.12. Electrical and Electronic Repair. **Other Civilian Jobs in This Work Group:** Electric Motor, Power Tool, and Related Repairers; Electrical and Electronics Installers and Repairers, Transportation Equipment; Electrical and Electronics Repairers, Commercial and Industrial Equipment; Electronic Equipment Installers and Repairers, Motor Vehicles; Electronic Home Entertainment Equipment Installers and Repairers; Radio Mechanics.

Skills—Installation: Installing equipment, machines, wiring, or programs to meet specifications. **Repairing:** Repairing machines or systems, using the needed tools. **Equipment Mainte-nance:** Performing routine maintenance on equipment and determining when and what kind of maintenance is needed. **Trouble-shooting:** Determining causes of operating errors and deciding what to do about them. **Operation Monitoring:** Watching gauges, dials, or other indicators to make sure a machine is working properly. **Operation and Control:** Controlling operations of equipment or systems. **Quality Control Analysis:** Conducting tests and inspections of products, services, or processes to evaluate quality or performance. **Systems Evaluation:** Identifying measures or indicators of system performance and the actions needed to improve or correct performance relative to the goals of the system.

Work Environment: Indoors; noisy; contaminants; hazardous conditions; sitting; using hands on objects, tools, or controls.

B

Biological Technicians

- Annual Earnings: $34,270
- Growth: 17.2%
- Annual Job Openings: 8,000
- Self-Employed: 0.0%
- Part-Time: 9.5%
- Civilian Training Route: Associate degree

Assist biological and medical scientists in laboratories. Set up, operate, and maintain laboratory instruments and equipment; monitor experiments; make observations; and calculate and record results. May analyze organic substances, such as blood, food, and drugs. Keep detailed logs of all work-related activities. Monitor laboratory work to ensure compliance with set standards. Isolate, identify, and prepare specimens for examination. Use computers, computer-interfaced equipment, robotics, or high-technology industrial applications to perform work duties. Conduct research or assist in the conduct of research, including the collection of information and samples such as blood, water, soil, plants, and animals. Set up, adjust, calibrate, clean, maintain, and troubleshoot laboratory and field equipment. Provide technical support and services for scientists and engineers working in fields such as agriculture, environmental science, resource management, biology, and health sciences. Clean, maintain, and prepare supplies and work areas. Participate in the research, development, or manufacturing of medicinal and pharmaceutical preparations. Conduct standardized biological, microbiological, or biochemical tests and laboratory analyses to evaluate the quantity or quality of physical or chemical substances in food or other products. Analyze experimental data and interpret results to write reports and summaries of findings. Measure or weigh compounds and solutions for use in testing or animal feed. Monitor and observe experiments, recording production and test data for evaluation by research personnel. Examine animals and specimens to detect the presence of disease or other problems. Conduct or supervise operational programs such as fish hatcheries, greenhouses, and livestock production programs. Feed livestock or laboratory animals.

Military Job That Provides Training for It (see the description in Part II): Medical Laboratory Technicians

Personality Type: Realistic. Realistic occupations frequently involve work activities that include practical, hands-on problems and solutions. They often deal with plants, animals, and real-world materials like wood, tools, and machinery. Many of the occupations require working outside and do not involve a lot of paperwork or working closely with others.

GOE—Interest Area: 08. Health Science. **Work Group:** 08.06. Medical Technology. **Other Civilian Jobs in This Work Group:** Cardiovascular Technologists and Technicians; Diagnostic Medical Sonographers; Medical and Clinical Laboratory Technicians; Medical and Clinical Laboratory Technologists; Medical Equipment Preparers; Medical Records and Health Information Technicians; Nuclear Medicine Technologists; Opticians, Dispensing; Orthotists and Prosthetists; Radiologic Technicians; Radiologic Technologists; Radiologic Technologists and Technicians.

Skills—Science: Using scientific rules and methods to solve problems. **Equipment Maintenance:** Performing routine maintenance on equipment and determining when and what kind of maintenance is needed. **Active Learning:** Understanding the implications of new information for both current and future problem-solving and decision-making. **Quality Control Analysis:** Conducting tests and inspections of products, services, or processes to evaluate quality or performance. **Troubleshooting:** Determining causes of operating errors and deciding what to do about them. **Mathematics:** Using mathematics to solve problems. **Learning Strategies:** Selecting and using training/instructional methods and procedures appropriate for the situation when learning or teaching new things. **Technology Design:** Generating or adapting equipment and technology to serve user needs.

Work Environment: Indoors; standing; using hands on objects, tools, or controls; repetitive motions.

Boilermakers

- Annual Earnings: $48,050
- Growth: 8.7%
- Annual Job Openings: 2,000
- Self-Employed: 0.0%
- Part-Time: No data available
- Civilian Training Route: Long-term on-the-job training

Construct, assemble, maintain, and repair stationary steam boilers and boiler house auxiliaries. Align structures or plate sections to assemble boiler frame tanks or vats, following blueprints. Work involves use of hand and power tools, plumb bobs, levels, wedges, dogs, or turnbuckles. Assist in testing assembled vessels. Direct cleaning of boilers and boiler furnaces. Inspect and repair boiler fittings, such as safety valves, regulators, automatic-control mechanisms, water columns, and auxiliary machines. Bolt or arc-weld pressure vessel structures and parts together, using wrenches and welding equipment. Examine boilers, pressure vessels, tanks, and vats to locate defects such as leaks, weak spots, and defective sections so that they can be repaired. Repair or replace defective pressure vessel parts, such as safety valves and regulators, using torches, jacks, caulking hammers, power saws, threading dies, welding equipment, and metalworking machinery. Inspect assembled vessels and individual components, such as tubes, fittings, valves, controls, and auxiliary mechanisms, to locate any defects. Attach rigging and signal crane or hoist operators to lift heavy frame and plate sections and other parts into place. Bell, bead with power hammers, or weld pressure vessel tube ends to ensure leakproof joints. Lay out plate, sheet steel, or other heavy metal and locate and mark bending and cutting lines, using protractors, compasses, and drawing instruments or templates. Install manholes, handholes, taps, tubes, valves, gauges, and feedwater connections in drums of water tube boilers, using hand tools. Study blueprints to determine locations, relationships, and dimensions of parts. Straighten or reshape bent pressure vessel plates and structure parts, using hammers, jacks, and torches. Shape seams, joints, and irregular edges of pressure vessel sections and structural parts to attain specified fit of parts, using cutting torches, hammers, files, and metalworking machines. Position, align, and secure structural parts and related assemblies to boiler frames, tanks, or vats of pressure vessels, following blueprints. Locate and mark reference points for columns or plates on boiler foundations, following blueprints and using straightedges, squares, transits, and measuring instruments. Shape and fabricate parts, such as stacks, uptakes, and chutes, to adapt pressure vessels, heat exchangers, and piping to premises, using heavy-metalworking machines such as brakes, rolls, and drill presses. Clean pressure vessel equipment, using scrapers, wire brushes, and cleaning solvents.

Military Job That Provides Training for It (see the description in Part II): Plumbers and Pipe Fitters

Personality Type: Realistic. Realistic occupations frequently involve work activities that include practical, hands-on problems and solutions. They often deal with plants, animals, and real-world materials like wood, tools, and machinery. Many of the occupations require working outside and do not involve a lot of paperwork or working closely with others.

GOE—Interest Area: 02. Architecture and Construction. **Work Group:** 02.04. Construction Crafts. **Other Civilian Jobs in This Work Group:** Brickmasons and Blockmasons; Carpet Installers; Cement Masons and Concrete Finishers; Commercial Divers; Construction Carpenters; Crane and Tower Operators; Drywall and Ceiling Tile Installers; Electricians; Fence Erectors; Floor Layers, Except Carpet, Wood, and Hard Tiles; Floor Sanders and Finishers; Glaziers; Hazardous Materials Removal Workers; Insulation Workers, Floor, Ceiling, and Wall; Insulation Workers, Mechanical; Manufactured Building and Mobile Home Installers; Operating Engineers and

B

Other Construction Equipment Operators; Painters, Construction and Maintenance; Paperhangers; Paving, Surfacing, and Tamping Equipment Operators; Pile-Driver Operators; Pipe Fitters and Steamfitters; Pipelayers; Plasterers and Stucco Masons; Plumbers; Plumbers, Pipefitters, and Steamfitters; Rail-Track Laying and Maintenance Equipment Operators; Refractory Materials Repairers, Except Brickmasons; Reinforcing Iron and Rebar Workers; Riggers; Roofers; Rough Carpenters; Security and Fire Alarm Systems Installers; Segmental Pavers; Sheet Metal Workers; Stone Cutters and Carvers, Manufacturing; Stonemasons; Structural Iron and Steel Workers; Tapers; Terrazzo Workers and Finishers; Tile and Marble Setters.

Skills—Repairing: Repairing machines or systems, using the needed tools. **Installation:** Installing equipment, machines, wiring, or programs to meet specifications. **Equipment Maintenance:** Performing routine maintenance on equipment and determining when and what kind of maintenance is needed. **Operation Monitoring:** Watching gauges, dials, or other indicators to make sure a machine is working properly. **Troubleshooting:** Determining causes of operating errors and deciding what to do about them. **Mathematics:** Using mathematics to solve problems. **Operation and Control:** Controlling operations of equipment or systems. **Equipment Selection:** Determining the kinds of tools and equipment needed to do a job.

Work Environment: Noisy; very hot or cold; contaminants; minor burns, cuts, bites, or stings; standing; using hands on objects, tools, or controls.

Bookkeeping, Accounting, and Auditing Clerks

- Annual Earnings: $29,490
- Growth: 5.9%
- Annual Job Openings: 291,000
- Self-Employed: 7.0%
- Part-Time: 29.5%
- Civilian Training Route: Moderate-term on-the-job training

Compute, classify, and record numerical data to keep financial records complete. Perform any combination of routine calculating, posting, and verifying duties to obtain primary financial data for use in maintaining accounting records. May also check the accuracy of figures, calculations, and postings pertaining to business transactions recorded by other workers. Operate computers programmed with accounting software to record, store, and analyze information. Check figures, postings, and documents for correct entry, mathematical accuracy, and proper codes. Comply with federal, state, and company policies, procedures, and regulations. Debit, credit, and total accounts on computer spreadsheets and databases, using specialized accounting software. Classify, record, and summarize numerical and financial data to compile and keep financial records, using journals and ledgers or computers. Calculate, prepare, and issue bills, invoices, account statements, and other financial statements according to established procedures. Code documents according to company procedures. Compile statistical, financial, accounting, or auditing reports and tables pertaining to such matters as cash receipts, expenditures, accounts payable and receivable, and profits and losses. Operate 10-key calculators, typewriters, and copy machines to perform calculations and produce documents. Access computerized financial information to answer general questions as well as those related to specific accounts. Reconcile or note and report discrepancies found in records. Perform financial calculations such as amounts due, interest charges, balances, discounts, equity, and principal. Perform general office duties such as filing, answering telephones, and handling routine correspondence. Prepare bank deposits by compiling data from cashiers; verifying and balancing receipts; and sending cash, checks, or other forms of payment to banks. Receive, record, and bank cash, checks, and vouchers. Calculate and prepare checks for utilities, taxes, and other payments. Compare computer printouts to manually maintained journals to determine if they match. Reconcile records of bank transactions. Prepare trial balances of books. Monitor status of loans and accounts to ensure that payments are up to date. Transfer details from separate journals to general ledgers or data-processing sheets. Compile budget data and documents based on estimated revenues and expenses and previous budgets. Calculate costs of materials, overhead, and other expenses, based on estimates, quotations, and price lists.

Military Jobs That Provide Training for It (see the descriptions in Part II): Finance and Accounting Specialists; Warehousing and Distribution Specialists

Personality Type: Conventional. Conventional occupations frequently involve following set procedures and routines. These occupations can include working with data and details more than with ideas. Usually there is a clear line of authority to follow.

GOE—Interest Area: 04. Business and Administration. **Work Group:** 04.06. Mathematical Clerical Support. **Other Civilian Jobs in This Work Group:** Billing and Posting Clerks and Machine Operators; Billing, Cost, and Rate Clerks; Brokerage Clerks; Payroll and Timekeeping Clerks; Statement Clerks; Tax Preparers.

Skills—No data available.

Work Environment: Indoors; sitting; repetitive motions.

B

Brickmasons and Blockmasons

- Annual Earnings: $41,860
- Growth: 12.0%
- Annual Job Openings: 17,000
- Self-Employed: 28.6%
- Part-Time: No data available
- Civilian Training Route: Long-term on-the-job training

Lay and bind building materials, such as brick, structural tile, concrete block, cinderblock, glass block, and terra-cotta block, with mortar and other substances to construct or repair walls, partitions, arches, sewers, and other structures. Construct corners by fastening in plumb position a corner pole or building a corner pyramid of bricks and filling in between the corners, using a line from corner to corner to guide each course, or layer, of brick. Measure distance from reference points and mark guidelines to lay out work, using plumb bobs and levels. Fasten or fuse brick or other building material to structure with wire clamps, anchor holes, torch, or cement. Calculate angles and courses and determine vertical and horizontal alignment of courses. Break or cut bricks, tiles, or blocks to size, using trowel edge, hammer, or power saw. Remove excess mortar with trowels and hand tools and finish mortar joints with jointing tools for a sealed, uniform appearance. Interpret blueprints and drawings to determine specifications and to calculate the materials required. Apply and smooth mortar or other mixture over work surface. Mix specified amounts of sand, clay, dirt, or mortar powder with water to form refractory mixtures. Examine brickwork or structure to determine need for repair. Clean working surface to remove scale, dust, soot, or chips of brick and mortar, using broom, wire brush, or scraper. Lay and align bricks, blocks, or tiles to build or repair structures or high-temperature equipment, such as cupola, kilns, ovens, or furnaces. Remove burned or damaged brick or mortar, using sledgehammer, crowbar, chipping gun, or chisel. Spray or spread refractory material over brickwork to protect against deterioration.

Military Job That Provides Training for It (see the description in Part II): Construction Specialists

Personality Type: Realistic. Realistic occupations frequently involve work activities that include practical, hands-on problems and solutions. They often deal with plants, animals, and real-world materials like wood, tools, and machinery. Many of the occupations require working outside and do not involve a lot of paperwork or working closely with others.

GOE—Interest Area: 02. Architecture and Construction. **Work Group:** 02.04. Construction Crafts. **Other Civilian Jobs in This Work Group:** Boilermakers; Carpet Installers; Cement Masons and Concrete Finishers; Commercial Divers; Construction Carpenters; Crane and Tower Operators; Drywall and Ceiling Tile Installers; Electricians; Fence Erectors; Floor Layers, Except Carpet, Wood, and Hard Tiles; Floor Sanders and Finishers; Glaziers; Hazardous Materials Removal Workers; Insulation Workers, Floor, Ceiling, and Wall; Insulation Workers, Mechanical; Manufactured Building and Mobile Home Installers; Operating Engineers and Other Construction Equipment Operators; Painters, Construction and Maintenance; Paperhangers; Paving, Surfacing, and Tamping Equipment Operators; Pile-Driver Operators; Pipe Fitters and Steamfitters; Pipelayers; Plasterers and Stucco Masons; Plumbers; Plumbers, Pipefitters, and Steamfitters; Rail-Track Laying and Maintenance Equipment Operators; Refractory Materials Repairers, Except Brickmasons; Reinforcing Iron and Rebar Workers; Riggers; Roofers; Rough Carpenters; Security and Fire Alarm Systems Installers; Segmental Pavers; Sheet Metal Workers; Stone Cutters and Carvers, Manufacturing; Stonemasons; Structural Iron and Steel Workers; Tapers; Terrazzo Workers and Finishers; Tile and Marble Setters.

Skills—No data available.

Work Environment: Outdoors; very hot or cold; hazardous equipment; standing; using hands on objects, tools, or controls; bending or twisting the body.

Bus and Truck Mechanics and Diesel Engine Specialists

- Annual Earnings: $36,620
- Growth: 14.4%
- Annual Job Openings: 32,000
- Self-Employed: 5.3%
- Part-Time: 2.8%
- Civilian Training Route: Postsecondary vocational training

Diagnose, adjust, repair, or overhaul trucks, buses, and all types of diesel engines. Includes mechanics working primarily with automobile diesel engines. Use hand tools such as screwdrivers, pliers, wrenches, pressure gauges, and precision instruments, as well as power tools such as pneumatic wrenches, lathes, welding equipment, and jacks and hoists. Inspect brake systems, steering mechanisms, wheel bearings, and other important parts to ensure that they are in proper operating condition. Perform routine maintenance such as changing oil, checking batteries, and lubricating equipment and machinery. Adjust and reline brakes, align wheels, tighten bolts and screws, and reassemble equipment. Raise trucks, buses, and heavy parts or equipment, using hydraulic jacks or hoists. Test drive trucks and buses to diagnose malfunctions or to ensure that they are working properly. Inspect, test, and listen to defective equipment to diagnose malfunctions, using test instruments such as handheld computers, motor analyzers, chassis charts, and pressure gauges. Examine and adjust protective guards, loose bolts, and specified safety devices. Inspect and verify dimensions and clearances of parts to ensure conformance to factory specifications. Specialize in repairing and maintaining parts of the engine, such as fuel injection systems. Attach test instruments to equipment and read dials and gauges to diagnose malfunctions. Rewire ignition systems, lights, and instrument panels. Recondition and replace parts, pistons, bearings, gears, and valves. Repair and adjust seats, doors, and windows and install and repair accessories. Inspect, repair, and maintain automotive and mechanical equipment and machinery such as pumps and compressors. Disassemble and overhaul internal combustion engines, pumps, generators, transmissions, clutches, and differential units. Rebuild gas or diesel engines. Align front ends and suspension systems. Operate valve-grinding machines to grind and reset valves.

Military Job That Provides Training for It (see the description in Part II): Automotive and Heavy Equipment Mechanics

Personality Type: Realistic. Realistic occupations frequently involve work activities that include practical, hands-on problems and solutions. They often deal with plants, animals, and real-world materials like wood, tools, and machinery. Many of the occupations require working outside and do not involve a lot of paperwork or working closely with others.

GOE—Interest Area: 13. Manufacturing. **Work Group:** 13.14. Vehicle and Facility Mechanical Work. **Other Civilian Jobs in This Work Group:** Aircraft Mechanics and Service Technicians; Aircraft Structure, Surfaces, Rigging, and Systems Assemblers; Automotive Body and Related Repairers; Automotive Glass Installers and Repairers; Automotive Master Mechanics; Automotive Service Technicians and Mechanics; Automotive Specialty Technicians; Farm Equipment Mechanics; Fiberglass Laminators and Fabricators; Mobile Heavy Equipment Mechanics, Except Engines;

Motorboat Mechanics; Motorcycle Mechanics; Outdoor Power Equipment and Other Small Engine Mechanics; Rail Car Repairers; Recreational Vehicle Service Technicians; Tire Repairers and Changers.

Skills—No data available.

Work Environment: Noisy; very bright or dim lighting; contaminants; hazardous equipment; standing; using hands on objects, tools, or controls.

Bus Drivers, Transit and Intercity

- Annual Earnings: $31,010
- Growth: 21.7%
- Annual Job Openings: 34,000
- Self-Employed: 0.5%
- Part-Time: 38.4%
- Civilian Training Route: Moderate-term on-the-job training

Drive bus or motor coach, including regular route operations, charters, and private carriage. May assist passengers with baggage. May collect fares or tickets. Inspect vehicles and check gas, oil, and water levels prior to departure. Drive vehicles over specified routes or to specified destinations according to time schedules to transport passengers, complying with traffic regulations. Park vehicles at loading areas so that passengers can board. Assist passengers with baggage and collect tickets or cash fares. Report delays or accidents. Advise passengers to be seated and orderly while on vehicles. Regulate heating, lighting, and ventilating systems for passenger comfort. Load and unload baggage in baggage compartments. Record cash receipts and ticket fares. Make minor repairs to vehicle and change tires.

Military Job That Provides Training for It (see the description in Part II): Vehicle Drivers

Personality Type: Realistic. Realistic occupations frequently involve work activities that include practical, hands-on problems and solutions. They often deal with plants, animals, and real-world materials like wood, tools, and machinery. Many of the occupations require working outside and do not involve a lot of paperwork or working closely with others.

GOE—Interest Area: 16. Transportation, Distribution, and Logistics. **Work Group:** 16.06. Other Services Requiring Driving. **Other Civilian Jobs in This Work Group:** Ambulance Drivers and Attendants, Except Emergency Medical Technicians; Bus Drivers, School; Couriers and Messengers; Driver/Sales Workers; Parking Lot Attendants; Postal Service Mail Carriers; Taxi Drivers and Chauffeurs.

Skills—No data available.

Work Environment: Outdoors; noisy; contaminants; sitting; using hands on objects, tools, or controls; repetitive motions.

Camera Operators, Television, Video, and Motion Picture

- Annual Earnings: $41,610
- Growth: 14.2%
- Annual Job Openings: 4,000
- Self-Employed: 21.1%
- Part-Time: 27.6%
- Civilian Training Route: Moderate-term on-the-job training

Operate television, video, or motion picture camera to photograph images or scenes for various purposes, such as TV broadcasts, advertising, video production, or motion pictures. Operate television or motion picture cameras to record scenes for television broadcasts, advertising, or motion pictures. Compose and frame each shot, applying the technical aspects of light, lenses, film, filters, and camera settings to achieve the effects sought by directors. Operate zoom lenses, changing images according to specifications and rehearsal instructions. Use cameras in any of several different camera mounts, such as stationary, track-mounted, or crane-mounted. Test, clean, and maintain equipment to ensure proper working condition. Adjust positions and controls of cameras, printers, and related equipment to change focus, exposure, and lighting. Gather and edit raw footage on location to send to television affiliates for broadcast, using electronic news-gathering or film-production equipment. Confer with directors, sound and lighting technicians, electricians, and other crew members to discuss assignments and determine filming sequences, desired effects, camera movements, and lighting requirements. Observe sets or locations for potential problems and to determine filming and lighting requirements. Instruct camera operators regarding camera setups, angles, distances, movement, and variables and cues for starting and stopping filming. Select and assemble cameras, accessories, equipment, and film stock to be used during filming, using knowledge of filming techniques, requirements, and computations. Label and record contents of exposed film and note details on report forms. Read charts and compute ratios to determine variables such as lighting, shutter angles, filter factors, and camera distances. Set up cameras, optical printers, and related equipment to produce photographs and special effects. View films to resolve problems of exposure control, subject and camera movement, changes in subject distance, and related variables. Reload camera magazines with fresh raw film stock. Read and analyze work orders and specifications to determine locations of subject material, work procedures, sequences of operations, and machine setups. Receive raw film stock and maintain film inventories.

Military Jobs That Provide Training for It (see the descriptions in Part II): Audiovisual and Broadcast Technicians; Communications Equipment Operators; Photographic Specialists

Personality Type: Artistic. Artistic occupations frequently involve working with forms, designs, and patterns. They often require self-expression, and the work can be done without following a clear set of rules.

GOE—Interest Area: 03. Arts and Communication. **Work Group:** 03.09. Media Technology. **Other Civilian Jobs in This Work Group:** Audio and Video Equipment Technicians; Broadcast Technicians; Film and Video Editors; Multi-Media Artists and Animators; Photographers; Radio Operators; Sound Engineering Technicians.

C

Skills—Operation Monitoring: Watching gauges, dials, or other indicators to make sure a machine is working properly. **Equipment Maintenance:** Performing routine maintenance on equipment and determining when and what kind of maintenance is needed. **Operation and Control:** Controlling operations of equipment or systems. **Troubleshooting:** Determining causes of operating errors and deciding what to do about them. **Equipment Selection:** Determining the kinds of tools and equipment needed to do a job. **Active Listening:** Giving full attention to what other people are saying, taking time to understand the points being made, asking questions as appropriate, and not interrupting at inappropriate times. **Coordination:** Adjusting actions in relation to others' actions. **Operations Analysis:** Analyzing needs and product requirements to create a design.

Work Environment: More often indoors than outdoors; very bright or dim lighting; standing; using hands on objects, tools, or controls.

Cardiovascular Technologists and Technicians

- Annual Earnings: $40,420
- Growth: 32.6%
- Annual Job Openings: 5,000
- Self-Employed: 0.4%
- Part-Time: 17.2%
- Civilian Training Route: Associate degree

Conduct tests on pulmonary or cardiovascular systems of patients for diagnostic purposes. May conduct or assist in electrocardiograms, cardiac catheterizations, pulmonary-functions, lung capacity, and similar tests. Monitor patients' blood pressure and heart rate, using electrocardiogram (EKG) equipment, during diagnostic and therapeutic procedures to notify the physician if something appears wrong. Monitor patients' comfort and safety during tests, alerting physicians to abnormalities or changes in patient responses. Explain testing procedures to patient to obtain cooperation and reduce anxiety. Prepare reports of diagnostic procedures for interpretation by physician. Observe gauges, recorder, and video screens of data analysis system during imaging of cardiovascular system. Conduct electrocardiogram (EKG), phonocardiogram, echocardiogram, stress testing, or other cardiovascular tests to record patients' cardiac activity, using specialized electronic test equipment, recording devices, and laboratory instruments. Obtain and record patient identification, medical history, or test results. Prepare and position patients for testing. Attach electrodes to the patients' chests, arms, and legs; connect electrodes to leads from the electrocardiogram (EKG) machine; and operate the EKG machine to obtain a reading. Adjust equipment and controls according to physicians' orders or established protocol. Check, test, and maintain cardiology equipment, making minor repairs when necessary, to ensure proper operation. Supervise and train other cardiology technologists and students. Assist physicians in diagnosis and treatment of cardiac and peripheral vascular treatments, for example, assisting with balloon angioplasties to treat blood vessel blockages. Operate diagnostic imaging equipment to produce contrast-enhanced radiographs of heart and cardiovascular system. Inject contrast medium into patients' blood vessels. Observe ultrasound display screen and listen to signals to record vascular information such as blood pressure, limb volume changes, oxygen saturation, and cerebral circulation. Assess cardiac physiology and calculate valve areas from blood flow velocity measurements. Compare measurements of heart wall thickness and chamber sizes to standard norms to identify abnormalities. Activate fluoroscope and camera to produce images used to guide catheter through cardiovascular system.

Military Job That Provides Training for It (see the description in Part II): Cardiopulmonary and EEG Technicians

Personality Type: Investigative. Investigative occupations frequently involve working with ideas and require an extensive amount of thinking. These occupations can involve searching for facts and figuring out problems mentally.

GOE—Interest Area: 08. Health Science. **Work Group:** 08.06. Medical Technology. **Other Civilian Jobs in This Work Group:** Biological Technicians; Diagnostic Medical Sonographers; Medical and Clinical Laboratory Technicians; Medical and Clinical Laboratory Technologists; Medical Equipment Preparers; Medical Records and Health Information Technicians; Nuclear Medicine Technologists; Opticians, Dispensing; Orthotists and Prosthetists; Radiologic Technicians; Radiologic Technologists; Radiologic Technologists and Technicians.

Skills—Operation Monitoring: Watching gauges, dials, or other indicators to make sure a machine is working properly. **Science:** Using scientific rules and methods to solve problems. **Equipment Maintenance:** Performing routine maintenance on equipment and determining when and what kind of maintenance is needed. **Instructing:** Teaching others how to do something. **Service Orientation:** Actively looking for ways to help people. **Operation and Control:** Controlling operations of equipment or systems. **Management of Material Resources:** Obtaining and seeing to the appropriate use of equipment, facilities, and materials needed to do certain work. **Equipment Selection:** Determining the kinds of tools and equipment needed to do a job.

Work Environment: Indoors; radiation; disease or infections; standing; walking and running; using hands on objects, tools, or controls.

Cargo and Freight Agents

- Annual Earnings: $35,860
- Growth: –5.6%
- Annual Job Openings: 12,000
- Self-Employed: 0.0%
- Part-Time: 13.0%
- Civilian Training Route: Moderate-term on-the-job training

Expedite and route movement of incoming and outgoing cargo and freight shipments in airline, train, and trucking terminals and shipping docks. Take orders from customers and arrange pickup of freight and cargo for delivery to loading platform. Prepare and examine bills of lading to determine shipping charges and tariffs. Negotiate and arrange transport of goods with shipping or freight companies. Notify consignees, passengers, or customers of the arrival of freight or baggage and arrange for delivery. Advise clients on transportation and payment methods. Prepare manifests showing baggage, mail, and freight weights and number of passengers on airplanes and transmit data to destinations. Determine method of shipment and prepare bills of lading, invoices, and other shipping documents. Check import/export documentation to determine cargo contents and classify goods into different fee or tariff groups, using a tariff coding system. Estimate freight or postal rates and record shipment costs and weights. Enter shipping information into a computer by hand or by using a hand-held scanner that reads bar codes on goods. Retrieve stored items and trace lost shipments as necessary. Pack goods for shipping, using tools such as staplers, strapping machines, and hammers. Direct delivery trucks to shipping doors or designated marshalling areas and help load and unload goods safely. Inspect and count items received and check them against invoices or other documents, recording shortages and rejecting damaged goods. Install straps, braces, and padding to loads to prevent shifting or damage during shipment. Keep records of all goods shipped, received, and stored. Coordinate and supervise activities of workers engaged in packing and shipping merchandise. Arrange insurance coverage for goods. Direct or participate in cargo loading to ensure completeness of load and even distribution of weight. Open cargo containers and unwrap contents, using steel cutters, crowbars, or other hand tools. Attach address labels, identification codes, and shipping instructions to containers. Contact vendors or claims adjustment departments to resolve problems with shipments or contact service depots to arrange for repairs. Route received goods to first available flight or to appropriate storage areas or departments, using forklifts, handtrucks, or other equipment. Maintain a supply of packing materials.

Military Jobs That Provide Training for It (see the descriptions in Part II): Cargo Specialists; Transportation Specialists

Personality Type: Conventional. Conventional occupations frequently involve following set procedures and routines. These occupations can include working with data and details more than with ideas. Usually there is a clear line of authority to follow.

GOE—Interest Area: 16. Transportation, Distribution, and Logistics. **Work Group:** 16.07. Transportation Support Work. **Other Civilian Jobs in This Work Group:** Bridge and Lock Tenders; Cleaners of Vehicles and Equipment; Laborers and Freight, Stock, and Material Movers, Hand; Railroad Brake, Signal, and Switch Operators; Traffic Technicians.

Skills—No data available.

Work Environment: Indoors; sitting; repetitive motions.

Cement Masons and Concrete Finishers

- Annual Earnings: $32,030
- Growth: 15.9%
- Annual Job Openings: 32,000
- Self-Employed: 3.1%
- Part-Time: 8.5%
- Civilian Training Route: Moderate-term on-the-job training

Smooth and finish surfaces of poured concrete, such as floors, walks, sidewalks, roads, or curbs, using a variety of hand and power tools. Align forms for sidewalks, curbs, or gutters; patch voids; and use saws to cut expansion joints. Check the forms that hold the concrete to see that they are properly constructed. Set the forms that hold concrete to the desired pitch and depth and align them. Spread, level, and smooth concrete, using rake, shovel, hand or power trowel, hand or power screed, and float. Mold expansion joints and edges, using edging tools, jointers, and straightedge. Monitor how the wind, heat, or cold affect the curing of the concrete throughout the entire process. Signal truck driver to position truck to facilitate pouring concrete and move chute to direct concrete on forms. Produce rough concrete surface, using broom. Operate power vibrator to compact concrete. Direct the casting of the concrete and supervise laborers who use shovels or special tools to spread it. Mix cement, sand, and water to produce concrete, grout, or slurry, using hoe, trowel, tamper, scraper, or concrete-mixing machine. Cut out damaged areas, drill holes for reinforcing rods, and position reinforcing rods to repair concrete, using power saw and drill. Wet surface to prepare for bonding, fill holes and cracks with grout or slurry, and smooth, using trowel. Wet concrete surface and rub with stone to smooth surface and obtain specified finish. Clean chipped area, using wire brush, and feel and observe surface to determine if it is rough or uneven. Apply hardening and sealing compounds to cure surface of concrete and waterproof or restore surface. Chip, scrape, and grind high spots, ridges, and rough projections to finish concrete, using pneumatic chisels, power grinders, or hand tools. Spread roofing paper on surface of foundation and spread concrete onto roofing paper with trowel to form terrazzo base. Build wooden molds and clamp molds around area to be repaired, using hand tools. Sprinkle colored marble or stone chips, powdered steel, or coloring powder over surface to produce prescribed finish. Cut metal division strips and press them into terrazzo base so that top edges form desired design or pattern. Fabricate concrete beams, columns, and panels. Waterproof or restore concrete surfaces, using appropriate compounds.

Military Job That Provides Training for It (see the description in Part II): Construction Specialists

Personality Type: Realistic. Realistic occupations frequently involve work activities that include practical, hands-on problems and solutions. They often deal with plants, animals, and real-world materials like wood, tools, and machinery. Many of the occupations require working outside and do not involve a lot of paperwork or working closely with others.

GOE—Interest Area: 02. Architecture and Construction. **Work Group:** 02.04. Construction Crafts. **Other Civilian Jobs in This Work Group:** Boilermakers; Brickmasons and Blockmasons; Carpet Installers; Commercial Divers; Construction Carpenters; Crane and Tower Operators; Drywall and Ceiling Tile Installers; Electricians; Fence Erectors; Floor Layers, Except Carpet, Wood, and Hard Tiles; Floor Sanders and Finishers; Glaziers; Hazardous Materials Removal Workers; Insulation Workers, Floor, Ceiling, and Wall; Insulation Workers, Mechanical; Manufactured Building and Mobile Home Installers; Operating Engineers and Other Construction Equipment Operators; Painters, Construction and Maintenance; Paperhangers; Paving, Surfacing, and Tamping Equipment Operators; Pile-Driver Operators; Pipe Fitters and Steamfitters; Pipelayers; Plasterers and Stucco Masons; Plumbers; Plumbers, Pipefitters, and Steamfitters; Rail-Track Laying and Maintenance Equipment Operators; Refractory Materials Repairers, Except Brickmasons; Reinforcing Iron and Rebar Workers; Riggers; Roofers; Rough Carpenters; Security and Fire Alarm Systems Installers; Segmental Pavers; Sheet Metal Workers; Stone Cutters and Carvers, Manufacturing; Stonemasons; Structural Iron and Steel Workers; Tapers; Terrazzo Workers and Finishers; Tile and Marble Setters.

Skills—No data available.

C

Work Environment: Outdoors; noisy; hazardous equipment; standing; using hands on objects, tools, or controls; bending or twisting the body.

Chefs and Head Cooks

- Annual Earnings: $32,330
- Growth: 16.7%
- Annual Job Openings: 11,000
- Self-Employed: 4.4%
- Part-Time: 8.7%
- Civilian Training Route: Work experience in a related occupation

Direct the preparation, seasoning, and cooking of salads, soups, fish, meats, vegetables, desserts, or other foods. May plan and price menu items, order supplies, and keep records and accounts. May participate in cooking. Check the quality of raw and cooked food products to ensure that standards are met. Monitor sanitation practices to ensure that employees follow standards and regulations. Check the quantity and quality of received products. Order or requisition food and other supplies needed to ensure efficient operation. Supervise and coordinate activities of cooks and workers engaged in food preparation. Inspect supplies, equipment, and work areas to ensure conformance to established standards. Determine how food should be presented and create decorative food displays. Instruct cooks and other workers in the preparation, cooking, garnishing, and presentation of food. Estimate amounts and costs of required supplies, such as food and ingredients. Collaborate with other personnel to plan and develop recipes and menus, taking into account such factors as seasonal availability of ingredients and the likely number of customers. Analyze recipes to assign prices to menu items based on food, labor, and overhead costs. Prepare and cook foods of all types, either on a regular basis or for special guests or functions. Determine production schedules and staff requirements necessary to ensure timely delivery of services. Recruit and hire staff, including cooks and other kitchen workers. Meet with customers to discuss menus for special occasions such as weddings, parties, and banquets. Demonstrate new cooking techniques and equipment to staff. Meet with sales representatives to negotiate prices and order supplies. Arrange for equipment purchases and repairs. Record production and operational data on specified forms. Plan, direct, and supervise the food preparation and cooking activities of multiple kitchens or restaurants in an establishment such as a restaurant chain, hospital, or hotel. Coordinate planning, budgeting, and purchasing for all the food operations within establishments such as clubs, hotels, or restaurant chains.

Military Job That Provides Training for It (see the description in Part II): Food Service Specialists

Personality Type: Enterprising. Enterprising occupations frequently involve starting up and carrying out projects. These occupations can involve leading people and making many decisions. They sometimes require risk taking and often deal with business.

GOE—Interest Area: 09. Hospitality, Tourism, and Recreation. **Work Group:** 09.04. Food and Beverage Preparation. **Other Civilian Jobs in This Work Group:** Butchers and Meat Cutters; Cooks, Fast Food; Cooks, Institution and Cafeteria; Cooks, Private Household; Cooks, Restaurant; Cooks, Short Order; Dishwashers; Food Preparation Workers.

Skills—Management of Financial Resources: Determining how money will be spent to get the work done and accounting for these expenditures. **Equipment Maintenance:** Performing routine maintenance on equipment and determining when and what kind of maintenance is needed. **Repairing:** Repairing machines or systems, using the needed tools. **Management of Personnel Resources:** Motivating, developing, and directing people as they work; identifying the best people for the job. **Service Orientation:** Actively looking for ways to help people. **Negotiation:** Bringing others together and trying to reconcile differences. **Systems Analysis:** Determining how a system should work and how changes in conditions, operations, and the environment will affect outcomes. **Quality Control Analysis:** Conducting tests and inspections of products, services, or processes to evaluate quality or performance.

Work Environment: Minor burns, cuts, bites, or stings; standing; walking and running; using hands on objects, tools, or controls; bending or twisting the body; repetitive motions.

Chemical Technicians

- Annual Earnings: $38,500
- Growth: 4.4%
- Annual Job Openings: 7,000
- Self-Employed: 0.0%
- Part-Time: 5.6%
- Civilian Training Route: Associate degree

Conduct chemical and physical laboratory tests to assist scientists in making qualitative and quantitative analyses of solids, liquids, and gaseous materials for purposes such as research and development of new products or processes; quality control; maintenance of environmental standards; and other work involving experimental, theoretical, or practical application of chemistry and related sciences. Monitor product quality to ensure compliance to standards and specifications. Set up and conduct chemical experiments, tests, and analyses using techniques such as chromatography, spectroscopy, physical and chemical separation techniques, and microscopy. Conduct chemical and physical laboratory tests to assist scientists in making qualitative and quantitative analyses of solids, liquids, and gaseous materials. Compile and interpret results of tests and analyses. Provide technical support and assistance to chemists and engineers. Prepare chemical solutions for products and processes following standardized formulas or create experimental formulas. Maintain, clean, and sterilize laboratory instruments and equipment. Write technical reports or prepare graphs and charts to document experimental results. Order and inventory materials to maintain supplies. Develop and conduct programs of sampling and analysis to maintain quality standards of raw materials, chemical intermediates, and products. Direct or monitor other workers producing chemical products. Operate experimental pilot plants, assisting with experimental design. Develop new chemical engineering processes or production techniques. Design and fabricate experimental apparatus to develop new products and processes.

Military Jobs That Provide Training for It (see the descriptions in Part II): Medical Laboratory Technicians; Non-Destructive Testers

Personality Type: Realistic. Realistic occupations frequently involve work activities that include practical, hands-on problems and solutions. They often deal with plants, animals, and real-world materials like wood, tools, and machinery. Many of the occupations require working outside and do not involve a lot of paperwork or working closely with others.

GOE—Interest Area: 15. Scientific Research, Engineering, and Mathematics. **Work Group:** 15.05. Physical Science Laboratory Technology. **Other Civilian Jobs in This Work Group:** Nuclear Equipment Operation Technicians; Nuclear Technicians.

Skills—Operation Monitoring: Watching gauges, dials, or other indicators to make sure a machine is working properly. **Science:** Using scientific rules and methods to solve problems. **Quality Control Analysis:** Conducting tests and inspections of products, services, or processes to evaluate quality or performance. **Equipment Maintenance:** Performing routine maintenance on equipment and determining when and what kind of maintenance is needed. **Operation and Control:** Controlling operations of equipment or systems. **Repairing:** Repairing machines or systems, using the needed tools. **Mathematics:** Using mathematics to solve problems. **Troubleshooting:** Determining causes of operating errors and deciding what to do about them.

Work Environment: Indoors; noisy; contaminants; hazardous conditions; standing.

Civil Drafters

- Annual Earnings: $40,390
- Growth: 4.6%
- Annual Job Openings: 9,000
- Self-Employed: 6.1%
- Part-Time: 8.4%
- Civilian Training Route: Postsecondary vocational training

The job openings listed here are shared with Architectural Drafters.

Prepare drawings and topographical and relief maps used in civil engineering projects, such as highways, bridges, pipelines, flood control projects, and water and sewerage control systems. Produce drawings, using computer-assisted drafting systems (CAD) or drafting machines or by hand, using compasses, dividers, protractors, triangles, and other drafting devices. Draft plans and detailed drawings for structures, installations, and construction projects such as highways, sewage disposal systems, and dikes, working from sketches or notes. Draw maps, diagrams, and profiles, using cross-sections and surveys, to represent elevations, topographical contours, subsurface formations, and structures. Correlate, interpret, and modify data obtained from topographical surveys, well logs, and geophysical prospecting reports. Finish and duplicate drawings and documentation packages according to required mediums and specifications for reproduction, using blueprinting, photography, or other duplicating methods. Review rough sketches, drawings, specifications, and other engineering data received from civil engineers to ensure that they conform to design concepts. Supervise and train other technologists, technicians, and drafters. Supervise or conduct field surveys, inspections, or technical investigations to obtain data required to revise construction drawings. Determine the order of work and method of presentation, such as orthographic or isometric drawing. Calculate excavation tonnage and prepare graphs and fill-hauling diagrams for use in earth-moving operations. Explain drawings to production or construction teams and provide adjustments as necessary. Locate and identify symbols located on topographical surveys to denote geological and geophysical formations or oilfield installations. Calculate weights, volumes, and stress factors and their implications for technical aspects of designs. Determine quality, cost, strength, and quantity of required materials and enter figures on materials lists. Plot characteristics of boreholes for oil and gas wells from photographic subsurface survey recordings and other data, representing depth, degree, and direction of inclination.

Military Job That Provides Training for It (see the description in Part II): Surveying, Mapping, and Drafting Technicians

Personality Type: Realistic. Realistic occupations frequently involve work activities that include practical, hands-on problems and solutions. They often deal with plants, animals, and real-world materials like wood, tools, and machinery. Many of the occupations require working outside and do not involve a lot of paperwork or working closely with others.

GOE—Interest Area: 02. Architecture and Construction. **Work Group:** 02.03. Architecture/Construction Engineering Technologies. **Other Civilian Jobs in This Work Group:** Architectural and Civil Drafters; Architectural Drafters; Surveyors.

Skills—No data available.

Work Environment: Indoors; sitting; repetitive motions.

Civil Engineering Technicians

- Annual Earnings: $39,210
- Growth: 14.1%
- Annual Job Openings: 10,000
- Self-Employed: 0.3%
- Part-Time: 6.7%
- Civilian Training Route: Associate degree

Apply theory and principles of civil engineering in planning, designing, and overseeing construction and maintenance of structures and facilities under the direction of engineering staff or physical scientists. Calculate dimensions, square footage, profile and component specifications, and material quantities, using calculator or computer. Draft detailed dimensional drawings and design layouts for projects and to ensure conformance to specifications. Analyze proposed site factors and design maps, graphs, tracings, and diagrams to illustrate findings. Read and review project blueprints and structural specifications to determine dimensions of structure or system and material requirements. Prepare reports and document project activities and data. Confer with supervisor to determine project details such as plan preparation, acceptance testing, and evaluation of field conditions. Inspect project site and evaluate contractor work to detect design malfunctions and ensure conformance to design specifications and applicable codes. Plan and conduct field surveys to locate new sites and analyze details of project sites. Develop plans and estimate costs for installation of systems, utilization of facilities, or construction of structures. Report maintenance problems occurring at project site to supervisor and negotiate changes to resolve system conflicts. Conduct materials test and analysis, using tools and equipment and applying engineering knowledge. Respond to public suggestions and complaints. Evaluate facility to determine suitability for occupancy and square footage availability.

Military Jobs That Provide Training for It (see the descriptions in Part II): Construction Specialists; Surveying, Mapping, and Drafting Technicians

Personality Type: Realistic. Realistic occupations frequently involve work activities that

C

include practical, hands-on problems and solutions. They often deal with plants, animals, and real-world materials like wood, tools, and machinery. Many of the occupations require working outside and do not involve a lot of paperwork or working closely with others.

GOE—Interest Area: 15. Scientific Research, Engineering, and Mathematics. **Work Group:** 15.09. Engineering Technology. **Other Civilian Jobs in This Work Group:** Aerospace Engineering and Operations Technicians; Cartographers and Photogrammetrists; Electrical and Electronic Engineering Technicians; Electrical and Electronics Drafters; Electrical Drafters; Electrical Engineering Technicians; Electro-Mechanical Technicians; Electronic Drafters; Electronics Engineering Technicians; Environmental Engineering Technicians; Mapping Technicians; Mechanical Drafters; Mechanical Engineering Technicians; Surveying and Mapping Technicians; Surveying Technicians.

Skills—Mathematics: Using mathematics to solve problems. **Science:** Using scientific rules and methods to solve problems. **Operations Analysis:** Analyzing needs and product requirements to create a design. **Complex Problem Solving:** Identifying complex problems and reviewing related information to develop and evaluate options and implement solutions. **Writing:** Communicating effectively in writing as appropriate for the needs of the audience. **Active Learning:** Understanding the implications of new information for both current and future problem-solving and decision-making. **Reading Comprehension:** Understanding written sentences and paragraphs in work-related documents. **Technology Design:** Generating or adapting equipment and technology to serve user needs.

Work Environment: More often indoors than outdoors; sitting.

Combined Food Preparation and Serving Workers, Including Fast Food

- Annual Earnings: $14,790
- Growth: 17.1%
- Annual Job Openings: 751,000
- Self-Employed: 0.1%
- Part-Time: 54.3%
- Civilian Training Route: Short-term on-the-job training

Perform duties that combine food preparation and food service. Accept payment from customers and make change as necessary. Request and record customer orders and compute bills, using cash registers, multicounting machines, or pencil and paper. Clean and organize eating and service areas. Serve customers in eating places that specialize in fast service and inexpensive carry-out food. Prepare and serve cold drinks or frozen milk drinks or desserts, using drink-dispensing, milkshake, or frozen custard machines. Select food items from serving or storage areas and place them in dishes, on serving trays, or in takeout bags. Prepare simple foods and beverages such as sandwiches, salads, and coffee. Notify kitchen personnel of shortages or special orders. Cook or reheat food items such as french fries. Wash dishes, glassware, and silverware after meals. Collect and return dirty dishes to the kitchen for washing. Relay food orders to cooks. Distribute food to servers. Serve food and beverages to guests at banquets or other social functions. Provide caterers with assistance in food preparation or service. Pack food, dishes, utensils, tablecloths, and accessories for transportation from catering or food preparation establishments to locations designated by customers. Arrange tables and decorations according to instructions.

Military Job That Provides Training for It (see the description in Part II): Food Service Specialists

Personality Type: Realistic. Realistic occupations frequently involve work activities that include practical, hands-on problems and solutions. They often deal with plants, animals, and real-world materials like wood, tools, and machinery. Many of the occupations require working outside and do not involve a lot of paperwork or working closely with others.

GOE—Interest Area: 09. Hospitality, Tourism, and Recreation. **Work Group:** 09.05. Food and Beverage Service. **Other Civilian Jobs in This Work Group:** Bartenders; Counter Attendants, Cafeteria, Food Concession, and Coffee Shop; Dining Room and Cafeteria Attendants and Bartender Helpers; Food Servers, Nonrestaurant; Hosts and Hostesses, Restaurant, Lounge, and Coffee Shop; Waiters and Waitresses.

Skills—No data available.

Work Environment: Indoors; minor burns, cuts, bites, or stings; standing; walking and running; using hands on objects, tools, or controls; repetitive motions.

Commercial Pilots

- Annual Earnings: $55,810
- Growth: 16.8%
- Annual Job Openings: 2,000
- Self-Employed: 2.5%
- Part-Time: 14.8%
- Civilian Training Route: Postsecondary vocational training

Pilot and navigate the flight of small fixed or rotary winged aircraft primarily for the transport of cargo and passengers. Requires Commercial Rating. Check aircraft prior to flights to ensure that the engines, controls, instruments, and other systems are functioning properly. Start engines, operate controls, and pilot airplanes to transport passengers, mail, or freight while adhering to flight plans, regulations, and procedures. Contact control towers for takeoff clearances, arrival instructions, and other information, using radio equipment. Monitor engine operation, fuel consumption, and functioning of aircraft systems during flights. Consider airport altitudes, outside temperatures, plane weights, and wind speeds and directions to calculate the speed needed to become airborne. Order changes in fuel supplies, loads, routes, or schedules to ensure safety of flights. Obtain and review data such as load weights, fuel supplies, weather conditions, and flight schedules to determine flight plans and to see if changes might be necessary. Plan flights, following government and company regulations, using aeronautical charts and navigation instruments. Use instrumentation to pilot aircraft when visibility is poor. Check baggage or cargo to ensure that it has been loaded correctly. Request changes in altitudes or routes as circumstances dictate. Choose routes, altitudes, and speeds that will provide the fastest, safest, and smoothest flights. Coordinate flight activities with ground crews and air-traffic control and inform crew members of flight and test procedures. Write specified information in flight records, such as flight times, altitudes flown, and fuel consumption. Teach company regulations and procedures to other pilots. Instruct other pilots and student pilots in aircraft operations. Co-pilot aircraft or perform captain's duties if required. File instrument flight plans with air traffic control so that flights can be coordinated with other air traffic. Conduct in-flight tests and evaluations at specified altitudes and in all types of weather to determine the receptivity and other characteristics of equipment and systems. Rescue and evacuate injured persons. Supervise other crew members. Perform minor aircraft maintenance and repair work or arrange for major maintenance.

Military Jobs That Provide Training for It (see the descriptions in Part II): Airplane Navigators; Airplane Pilots; Flight Engineers; Helicopter Pilots

Personality Type: Realistic. Realistic occupations frequently involve work activities that include practical, hands-on problems and solutions. They often deal with plants, animals, and real-world materials like wood, tools, and machinery. Many of the occupations require working outside and do not involve a lot of paperwork or working closely with others.

GOE—Interest Area: 16. Transportation, Distribution, and Logistics. **Work Group:** 16.02. Air Vehicle Operation. **Other Civilian Jobs in This Work Group:** Airline Pilots, Copilots, and Flight Engineers.

Skills—Operation Monitoring: Watching gauges, dials, or other indicators to make sure a machine is working properly. **Operation and Control:** Controlling operations of equipment or systems. **Troubleshooting:** Determining causes of operating errors and deciding what to do about them. **Judgment and Decision Making:** Considering the relative costs and benefits of potential actions to choose the most appropriate one. **Systems Evaluation:** Identifying measures or indicators of system performance and the actions needed to improve or correct performance relative to the goals of the system. **Critical Thinking:** Using logic and reasoning to identify the strengths and weaknesses of alternative solutions, conclusions, or approaches to problems. **Systems Analysis:** Determining how a system should work and how changes in conditions, operations, and the environment will affect outcomes. **Active Listening:** Giving full attention to what other people are saying, taking time to understand the points being made, asking questions as appropriate, and not interrupting at inappropriate times.

Work Environment: Outdoors; noisy; very hot or cold; contaminants; sitting; using hands on objects, tools, or controls.

Computer Programmers

- Annual Earnings: $63,420
- Growth: 2.0%
- Annual Job Openings: 28,000
- Self-Employed: 4.5%
- Part-Time: 6.0%
- Civilian Training Route: Bachelor's degree

Convert project specifications and statements of problems and procedures to detailed logical flow charts for coding into computer language. Develop and write computer programs to store, locate, and retrieve specific documents, data,

and information. May program Web sites. Correct errors by making appropriate changes and rechecking the program to ensure that the desired results are produced. Conduct trial runs of programs and software applications to be sure that they will produce the desired information and that the instructions are correct. Compile and write documentation of program development and subsequent revisions, inserting comments in the coded instructions so others can understand the program. Write, update, and maintain computer programs or software packages to handle specific jobs such as tracking inventory, storing or retrieving data, or controlling other equipment. Consult with managerial, engineering, and technical personnel to clarify program intent, identify problems, and suggest changes. Perform or direct revision, repair, or expansion of existing programs to increase operating efficiency or adapt to new requirements. Write, analyze, review, and rewrite programs, using workflow chart and diagram and applying knowledge of computer capabilities, subject matter, and symbolic logic. Write or contribute to instructions or manuals to guide end users. Investigate whether networks, workstations, the central processing unit of the system, or peripheral equipment are responding to a program's instructions. Prepare detailed workflow charts and diagrams that describe input, output, and logical operation and convert them into a series of instructions coded in a computer language. Perform systems analysis and programming tasks to maintain and control the use of computer systems software as a systems programmer. Consult with and assist computer operators or system analysts to define and resolve problems in running computer programs. Assign, coordinate, and review work and activities of programming personnel. Collaborate with computer manufacturers and other users to develop new programming methods. Train subordinates in programming and program coding.

Military Job That Provides Training for It (see the description in Part II): Computer Systems Specialists

Personality Type: Investigative. Investigative occupations frequently involve working with ideas and require an extensive amount of thinking. These occupations can involve searching for facts and figuring out problems mentally.

GOE—Interest Area: 11. Information Technology. **Work Group:** 11.02. Information Technology Specialties. **Other Civilian Jobs in This Work Group:** Computer and Information Scientists, Research; Computer Operators; Computer Security Specialists; Computer Software Engineers, Applications; Computer Software Engineers, Systems Software; Computer Support Specialists; Computer Systems Analysts; Computer Systems Engineers/Architects; Database Administrators; Network Designers; Network Systems and Data Communications Analysts; Software Quality Assurance Engineers and Testers; Web Administrators; Web Developers.

Skills—Programming: Writing computer programs for various purposes. **Operations Analysis:** Analyzing needs and product requirements to create a design. **Technology Design:** Generating or adapting equipment and technology to serve user needs. **Systems Analysis:** Determining how a system should work and how changes in conditions, operations, and the environment will affect outcomes. **Troubleshooting:** Determining causes of operating errors and deciding what to do about them. **Installation:** Installing equipment, machines, wiring, or programs to meet specifications. **Complex Problem Solving:** Identifying complex problems and reviewing related information to develop and evaluate options and implement solutions. **Critical Thinking:** Using logic and reasoning to identify the strengths and weaknesses of alternative solutions, conclusions, or approaches to problems.

Work Environment: Indoors; sitting; using hands on objects, tools, or controls; repetitive motions.

Computer Support Specialists

- Annual Earnings: $40,610
- Growth: 23.0%
- Annual Job Openings: 87,000
- Self-Employed: 0.9%
- Part-Time: 8.3%
- Civilian Training Route: Associate degree

Provide technical assistance to computer system users. Answer questions or resolve computer problems for clients in person, via telephone, or from remote location. May provide assistance concerning the use of computer hardware and software, including printing, installation, word processing, electronic mail, and operating systems. Answer user inquiries regarding computer software or hardware operation to resolve problems. Enter commands and observe system functioning to verify correct operations and detect errors. Install and perform minor repairs to hardware, software, or peripheral equipment, following design or installation specifications. Oversee the daily performance of computer systems. Set up equipment for employee use, performing or ensuring proper installation of cables, operating systems, or appropriate software. Maintain records of daily data communication transactions, problems and remedial actions taken, or installation activities. Read technical manuals, confer with users, or conduct computer diagnostics to investigate and resolve problems or to provide technical assistance and support. Confer with staff, users, and management to establish requirements for new systems or modifications. Develop training materials and procedures or train users in the proper use of hardware or software. Refer major hardware or software problems or defective products to vendors or technicians for service. Prepare evaluations of software or hardware and recommend improvements or upgrades. Read trade magazines and technical manuals or attend conferences and seminars to maintain knowledge of hardware and software. Supervise and coordinate workers engaged in problem-solving, monitoring, and installing data communication equipment and software. Inspect equipment and read order sheets to prepare for delivery to users. Modify and customize commercial programs for internal needs. Conduct office automation feasibility studies, including workflow analysis, space design, or cost comparison analysis.

Military Job That Provides Training for It (see the description in Part II): Computer Systems Specialists

Personality Type: Investigative. Investigative occupations frequently involve working with ideas and require an extensive amount of thinking. These occupations can involve searching for facts and figuring out problems mentally.

GOE—Interest Area: 11. Information Technology. **Work Group:** 11.02. Information Technology Specialties. **Other Civilian Jobs in This Work Group:** Computer and Information Scientists, Research; Computer Operators; Computer Programmers; Computer Security

Specialists; Computer Software Engineers, Applications; Computer Software Engineers, Systems Software; Computer Systems Analysts; Computer Systems Engineers/Architects; Database Administrators; Network Designers; Network Systems and Data Communications Analysts; Software Quality Assurance Engineers and Testers; Web Administrators; Web Developers.

Skills—Repairing: Repairing machines or systems, using the needed tools. **Troubleshooting:** Determining causes of operating errors and deciding what to do about them. **Installation:** Installing equipment, machines, wiring, or programs to meet specifications. **Equipment Maintenance:** Performing routine maintenance on equipment and determining when and what kind of maintenance is needed. **Writing:** Communicating effectively in writing as appropriate for the needs of the audience. **Persuasion:** Persuading others to change their minds or behavior. **Systems Evaluation:** Identifying measures or indicators of system performance and the actions needed to improve or correct performance relative to the goals of the system. **Social Perceptiveness:** Being aware of others' reactions and understanding why they react as they do.

Work Environment: Indoors; noisy; sitting; repetitive motions.

Computer, Automated Teller, and Office Machine Repairers

- Annual Earnings: $36,060
- Growth: 3.8%
- Annual Job Openings: 31,000
- Self-Employed: 13.7%
- Part-Time: 9.9%
- Civilian Training Route: Postsecondary vocational training

Repair, maintain, or install computers; word-processing systems; automated teller machines; and electronic office machines, such as duplicating and fax machines. Converse with customers to determine details of equipment problems. Reassemble machines after making repairs or replacing parts. Travel to customers' stores or offices to service machines or to provide emergency repair service. Reinstall software programs or adjust settings on existing software to fix machine malfunctions. Advise customers concerning equipment operation, maintenance, and programming. Assemble machines according to specifications, using hand tools, power tools, and measuring devices. Test new systems to ensure that they are in working order. Operate machines to test functioning of parts and mechanisms. Maintain records of equipment maintenance work and repairs. Install and configure new equipment, including operating software and peripheral equipment. Maintain parts inventories and order any additional parts needed for repairs. Update existing equipment, performing tasks such as installing updated circuit boards or additional memory. Test components and circuits of faulty equipment to locate defects, using oscilloscopes, signal generators,

C

ammeters, voltmeters, or special diagnostic software programs. Align, adjust, and calibrate equipment according to specifications. Repair, adjust, or replace electrical and mechanical components and parts, using hand tools, power tools, and soldering or welding equipment. Complete repair bills, shop records, time cards, and expense reports. Disassemble machine to examine parts such as wires, gears, and bearings for wear and defects, using hand tools, power tools, and measuring devices. Clean, oil, and adjust mechanical parts to maintain machines' operating efficiency and to prevent breakdowns. Enter information into computers to copy programs from one electronic component to another or to draw, modify, or store schematics. Read specifications such as blueprints, charts, and schematics to determine machine settings and adjustments. Lay cable and hook up electrical connections between machines, power sources, and phone lines. Analyze equipment performance records to assess equipment functioning.

Military Jobs That Provide Training for It (see the descriptions in Part II): Avionics Technicians; Computer Systems Specialists; Electronic Instrument and Equipment Repairers; Precision Instrument and Equipment Repairers

Personality Type: Realistic. Realistic occupations frequently involve work activities that include practical, hands-on problems and solutions. They often deal with plants, animals, and real-world materials like wood, tools, and machinery. Many of the occupations require working outside and do not involve a lot of paperwork or working closely with others.

GOE—Interest Area: 11. Information Technology. **Work Group:** 11.03. Digital Equipment Repair. **Other Civilian Jobs in This Work Group:** Coin, Vending, and Amusement Machine Servicers and Repairers.

Skills—Installation: Installing equipment, machines, wiring, or programs to meet specifications. **Repairing:** Repairing machines or systems, using the needed tools. **Troubleshooting:** Determining causes of operating errors and deciding what to do about them. **Equipment Maintenance:** Performing routine maintenance on equipment and determining when and what kind of maintenance is needed. **Management of Material Resources:** Obtaining and seeing to the appropriate use of equipment, facilities, and materials needed to do certain work. **Programming:** Writing computer programs for various purposes. **Systems Evaluation:** Identifying measures or indicators of system performance and the actions needed to improve or correct performance relative to the goals of the system. **Technology Design:** Generating or adapting equipment and technology to serve user needs.

Work Environment: Indoors; sitting; using hands on objects, tools, or controls; repetitive motions.

Construction and Building Inspectors

- Annual Earnings: $44,720
- Growth: 22.3%
- Annual Job Openings: 6,000
- Self-Employed: 10.2%
- Part-Time: 7.8%
- Civilian Training Route: Work experience in a related occupation

Inspect structures, using engineering skills to determine structural soundness and compliance with specifications, building codes, and other regulations. Inspections may be general in nature or may be limited to a specific area, such as electrical systems or plumbing. Use survey instruments; metering devices; tape measures; and test equipment, such as concrete strength measurers, to perform inspections. Inspect bridges, dams, highways, buildings, wiring, plumbing, electrical circuits, sewers, heating systems, and foundations during and after construction for structural quality, general safety, and conformance to specifications and codes. Maintain daily logs and supplement inspection records with photographs. Review and interpret plans, blueprints, site layouts, specifications, and construction methods to ensure compliance to legal requirements and safety regulations. Inspect and monitor construction sites to ensure adherence to safety standards, building codes, and specifications. Measure dimensions and verify level, alignment, and elevation of structures and fixtures to ensure compliance to building plans and codes. Issue violation notices and stop-work orders, conferring with owners, violators, and authorities to explain regulations and recommend rectifications. Issue permits for construction, relocation, demolition, and occupancy. Approve and sign plans that meet required specifications. Compute estimates of work completed or of needed renovations or upgrades and approve payment for contractors. Monitor installation of plumbing, wiring, equipment, and appliances to ensure that installation is performed properly and is in compliance with applicable regulations. Examine lifting and conveying devices, such as elevators, escalators, moving sidewalks, lifts and hoists, inclined railways, ski lifts, and amusement rides, to ensure safety and proper functioning. Train, direct, and supervise other construction inspectors. Evaluate premises for cleanliness, including proper garbage disposal and lack of vermin infestation.

Military Job That Provides Training for It (see the description in Part II): Construction Specialists

Personality Type: Conventional. Conventional occupations frequently involve following set procedures and routines. These occupations can include working with data and details more than with ideas. Usually there is a clear line of authority to follow.

GOE—Interest Area: 07. Government and Public Administration. **Work Group:** 07.03. Regulations Enforcement. **Other Civilian Jobs in This Work Group:** Agricultural Inspectors; Aviation Inspectors; Compliance Officers, Except Agriculture, Construction, Health and Safety, and Transportation; Environmental Compliance Inspectors; Equal Opportunity Representatives and Officers; Financial Examiners; Fire Inspectors; Fish and Game Wardens; Forest Fire Inspectors and Prevention Specialists; Freight and Cargo Inspectors; Government Property Inspectors and Investigators; Immigration and Customs Inspectors; Licensing Examiners and Inspectors; Nuclear Monitoring Technicians; Occupational Health and Safety Specialists; Occupational Health and Safety Technicians; Tax Examiners, Collectors, and Revenue Agents; Transportation Vehicle, Equipment, and Systems Inspectors, Except Aviation.

Skills—Mathematics: Using mathematics to solve problems. **Persuasion:** Persuading others to change their minds or behavior. **Quality**

Control Analysis: Conducting tests and inspections of products, services, or processes to evaluate quality or performance. **Reading Comprehension:** Understanding written sentences and paragraphs in work-related documents. **Science:** Using scientific rules and methods to solve problems. **Time Management:** Managing one's own time and the time of others. **Installation:** Installing equipment, machines, wiring, or programs to meet specifications. **Active Learning:** Understanding the implications of new information for both current and future problem-solving and decision-making.

Work Environment: More often outdoors than indoors; noisy; contaminants; hazardous equipment; standing.

Construction Carpenters

- Annual Earnings: $35,580
- Growth: 13.8%
- Annual Job Openings: 210,000
- Self-Employed: 32.4%
- Part-Time: 8.2%
- Civilian Training Route: Long-term on-the-job training

The job openings listed here are shared with Rough Carpenters.

Construct, erect, install, and repair structures and fixtures of wood, plywood, and wallboard, using carpenter's hand tools and power tools. Measure and mark cutting lines on materials, using ruler, pencil, chalk, and marking gauge. Follow established safety rules and regulations and maintain a safe and clean environment. Verify trueness of structure, using plumb bob and level. Shape or cut materials to specified measurements, using hand tools, machines, or power saw. Study specifications in blueprints, sketches, or building plans to prepare project layout and determine dimensions and materials required. Assemble and fasten materials to make framework or props, using hand tools and wood screws, nails, dowel pins, or glue. Build or repair cabinets, doors, frameworks, floors, and other wooden fixtures used in buildings, using woodworking machines, carpenter's hand tools, and power tools. Erect scaffolding and ladders for assembling structures above ground level. Remove damaged or defective parts or sections of structures and repair or replace, using hand tools. Install structures and fixtures, such as windows, frames, floorings, and trim, or hardware, using carpenter's hand and power tools. Select and order lumber and other required materials. Maintain records, document actions, and present written progress reports. Finish surfaces of woodwork or wallboard in houses and buildings, using paint, hand tools, and paneling. Prepare cost estimates for clients or employers. Arrange for subcontractors to deal with special areas such as heating and electrical wiring work. Inspect ceiling or floor tile, wall coverings, siding, glass, or woodwork to detect broken or damaged structures. Work with or remove hazardous material. Construct forms and chutes for pouring concrete. Cover subfloors with building paper to keep out moisture and lay hardwood, parquet, and wood-strip-block floors by nailing floors to subfloor or cementing them to mastic or asphalt base. Fill cracks and other defects in plaster or plasterboard and sand patch, using patching plaster, trowel, and sanding tool. Perform minor plumbing, welding, or concrete mixing work. Apply shock-absorbing, sound-deadening, and decorative paneling to ceilings and walls.

Military Job That Provides Training for It (see the description in Part II): Construction Specialists

Personality Type: Realistic. Realistic occupations frequently involve work activities that include practical, hands-on problems and solutions. They often deal with plants, animals, and real-world materials like wood, tools, and machinery. Many of the occupations require working outside and do not involve a lot of paperwork or working closely with others.

GOE—Interest Area: 02. Architecture and Construction. **Work Group:** 02.04. Construction Crafts. **Other Civilian Jobs in This Work Group:** Boilermakers; Brickmasons and Blockmasons; Carpet Installers; Cement Masons and Concrete Finishers; Commercial Divers; Crane and Tower Operators; Drywall and Ceiling Tile Installers; Electricians; Fence Erectors; Floor Layers, Except Carpet, Wood, and Hard Tiles; Floor Sanders and Finishers; Glaziers; Hazardous Materials Removal Workers; Insulation Workers, Floor, Ceiling, and Wall; Insulation Workers, Mechanical; Manufactured Building and Mobile Home Installers; Operating Engineers and Other Construction Equipment Operators; Painters, Construction and Maintenance; Paperhangers; Paving, Surfacing, and Tamping Equipment Operators; Pile-Driver Operators; Pipe Fitters and Steamfitters; Pipelayers; Plasterers and Stucco Masons; Plumbers; Plumbers, Pipefitters, and Steamfitters; Rail-Track Laying and Maintenance Equipment Operators; Refractory Materials Repairers, Except Brickmasons; Reinforcing Iron and Rebar Workers; Riggers; Roofers; Rough Carpenters; Security and Fire Alarm Systems Installers; Segmental Pavers; Sheet Metal Workers; Stone Cutters and Carvers, Manufacturing; Stonemasons; Structural Iron and Steel Workers; Tapers; Terrazzo Workers and Finishers; Tile and Marble Setters.

Skills—Management of Personnel Resources: Motivating, developing, and directing people as they work; identifying the best people for the job. **Management of Material Resources:** Obtaining and seeing to the appropriate use of equipment, facilities, and materials needed to do certain work. **Management of Financial Resources:** Determining how money will be spent to get the work done and accounting for these expenditures. **Repairing:** Repairing machines or systems, using the needed tools. **Equipment Maintenance:** Performing routine maintenance on equipment and determining when and what kind of maintenance is needed. **Quality Control Analysis:** Conducting tests and inspections of products, services, or processes to evaluate quality or performance. **Installation:** Installing equipment, machines, wiring, or programs to meet specifications. **Mathematics:** Using mathematics to solve problems.

Work Environment: Outdoors; noisy; hazardous equipment; standing; walking and running; using hands on objects, tools, or controls.

Control and Valve Installers and Repairers, Except Mechanical Door

- Annual Earnings: $44,120
- Growth: 4.9%
- Annual Job Openings: 4,000
- Self-Employed: 0.0%
- Part-Time: No data available
- Civilian Training Route: Moderate-term on-the-job training

Install, repair, and maintain mechanical regulating and controlling devices, such as electric meters, gas regulators, thermostats, safety and flow valves, and other mechanical governors. Turn meters on or off to establish or close service. Turn valves to allow measured amounts of air or gas to pass through meters at specified flow rates. Report hazardous field situations and damaged or missing meters. Record meter readings and installation data on meter cards, work orders, or field service orders or enter data into hand-held computers. Connect regulators to test stands and turn screw adjustments until gauges indicate that inlet and outlet pressures meet specifications. Disassemble and repair mechanical control devices or valves, such as regulators, thermostats, or hydrants, using power tools, hand tools, and cutting torches. Record maintenance information, including test results, material usage, and repairs made. Disconnect and/or remove defective or unauthorized meters, using hand tools. Lubricate wearing surfaces of mechanical parts, using oils or other lubricants. Test valves and regulators for leaks and accurate temperature and pressure settings, using precision testing equipment. Install regulators and related equipment such as gas meters, odorization units, and gas pressure telemetering equipment. Shut off service and notify repair crews when major repairs are required, such as the replacement of underground pipes or wiring. Examine valves or mechanical control device parts for defects, dents, or loose attachments and mark malfunctioning areas of defective units. Attach air hoses to meter inlets; then plug outlets and observe gauges for pressure losses to test internal seams for leaks. Dismantle meters and replace or adjust defective parts such as cases, shafts, gears, disks, and recording mechanisms, using soldering irons and hand tools. Advise customers on proper installation of valves or regulators and related equipment. Connect hoses from provers to meter inlets and outlets and raise prover bells until prover gauges register zero. Make adjustments to meter components, such as setscrews or timing mechanisms, so that they conform to specifications. Replace defective parts, such as bellows, range springs, and toggle switches, and reassemble units according to blueprints, using cam presses and hand tools.

Military Jobs That Provide Training for It (see the descriptions in Part II): Power Plant Electricians; Powerhouse Mechanics

Personality Type: Realistic. Realistic occupations frequently involve work activities that include practical, hands-on problems and solutions. They often deal with plants, animals, and real-world materials like wood, tools, and machinery. Many of the occupations require working outside and do not involve a lot of paperwork or working closely with others.

GOE—Interest Area: 13. Manufacturing. **Work Group:** 13.13. Machinery Repair. **Other Civilian Jobs in This Work Group:** Bicycle Repairers; Home Appliance Repairers; Industrial

Machinery Mechanics; Locksmiths and Safe Repairers; Maintenance Workers, Machinery; Mechanical Door Repairers; Millwrights; Signal and Track Switch Repairers.

Skills—Installation: Installing equipment, machines, wiring, or programs to meet specifications. **Repairing:** Repairing machines or systems, using the needed tools. **Equipment Maintenance:** Performing routine maintenance on equipment and determining when and what kind of maintenance is needed. **Operation Monitoring:** Watching gauges, dials, or other indicators to make sure a machine is working properly. **Troubleshooting:** Determining causes of operating errors and deciding what to do about them. **Quality Control Analysis:** Conducting tests and inspections of products, services, or processes to evaluate quality or performance. **Science:** Using scientific rules and methods to solve problems. **Operation and Control:** Controlling operations of equipment or systems.

Work Environment: Outdoors; very hot or cold; very bright or dim lighting; contaminants; cramped work space, awkward positions; hazardous conditions.

Cooks, Restaurant

- Annual Earnings: $19,840
- Growth: 16.6%
- Annual Job Openings: 207,000
- Self-Employed: 0.8%
- Part-Time: 8.7%
- Civilian Training Route: Long-term on-the-job training

Prepare, season, and cook soups, meats, vegetables, desserts, or other foodstuffs in restaurants. May order supplies, keep records and accounts, price items on menu, or plan menu. Inspect food preparation and serving areas to ensure observance of safe, sanitary food-handling practices. Turn or stir foods to ensure even cooking. Season and cook food according to recipes or personal judgment and experience. Observe and test foods to determine if they have been cooked sufficiently, using methods such as tasting them, smelling them, or piercing them with utensils. Weigh, measure, and mix ingredients according to recipes or personal judgment, using various kitchen utensils and equipment. Portion, arrange, and garnish food and serve food to waiters or patrons. Regulate temperature of ovens, broilers, grills, and roasters. Substitute for or assist other cooks during emergencies or rush periods. Bake, roast, broil, and steam meats, fish, vegetables, and other foods. Wash, peel, cut, and seed fruits and vegetables to prepare them for consumption. Estimate expected food consumption, requisition or purchase supplies, or procure food from storage. Carve and trim meats such as beef, veal, ham, pork, and lamb for hot or cold service or for sandwiches. Coordinate and supervise work of kitchen staff. Consult with supervisory staff to plan menus, taking into consideration factors such as costs and special event needs. Butcher and dress animals, fowl, or shellfish or cut and bone meat prior to cooking. Prepare relishes and hors d'oeuvres. Bake breads, rolls, cakes, and pastries. Keep records and accounts. Plan and price menu items.

Military Job That Provides Training for It (see the description in Part II): Food Service Specialists

Personality Type: Realistic. Realistic occupations frequently involve work activities that include practical, hands-on problems and solutions. They often deal with plants, animals, and

C

real-world materials like wood, tools, and machinery. Many of the occupations require working outside and do not involve a lot of paperwork or working closely with others.

GOE—Interest Area: 09. Hospitality, Tourism, and Recreation. **Work Group:** 09.04. Food and Beverage Preparation. **Other Civilian Jobs in This Work Group:** Butchers and Meat Cutters; Chefs and Head Cooks; Cooks, Fast Food; Cooks, Institution and Cafeteria; Cooks, Private Household; Cooks, Short Order; Dishwashers; Food Preparation Workers.

Skills—No data available.

Work Environment: Indoors; very hot or cold; minor burns, cuts, bites, or stings; standing; using hands on objects, tools, or controls; repetitive motions.

Cooks, Short Order

- Annual Earnings: $17,230
- Growth: 11.8%
- Annual Job Openings: 58,000
- Self-Employed: 0.9%
- Part-Time: 8.7%
- Civilian Training Route: Short-term on-the-job training

Prepare and cook to order a variety of foods that require only a short preparation time. May take orders from customers and serve patrons at counters or tables. Clean food preparation equipment, work areas, and counters or tables. Plan work on orders so that items served together are finished at the same time. Grill, cook, and fry foods such as french fries, eggs, and pancakes. Take orders from customers and cook foods requiring short preparation times according to customer requirements. Grill and garnish hamburgers or other meats such as steaks and chops. Complete orders from steam tables, placing food on plates and serving customers at tables or counters. Perform simple food preparation tasks such as making sandwiches, carving meats, and brewing coffee. Order supplies and stock them on shelves. Accept payments and make change or write charge slips as necessary.

Military Job That Provides Training for It (see the description in Part II): Food Service Specialists

Personality Type: Realistic. Realistic occupations frequently involve work activities that include practical, hands-on problems and solutions. They often deal with plants, animals, and real-world materials like wood, tools, and machinery. Many of the occupations require working outside and do not involve a lot of paperwork or working closely with others.

GOE—Interest Area: 09. Hospitality, Tourism, and Recreation. **Work Group:** 09.04. Food and Beverage Preparation. **Other Civilian Jobs in This Work Group:** Butchers and Meat Cutters; Chefs and Head Cooks; Cooks, Fast Food; Cooks, Institution and Cafeteria; Cooks, Private Household; Cooks, Restaurant; Dishwashers; Food Preparation Workers.

Skills—Troubleshooting: Determining causes of operating errors and deciding what to do about them. **Management of Personnel Resources:** Motivating, developing, and directing people as they work; identifying the best people for the job. **Time Management:** Managing one's own time and the time of others. **Judgment and Decision Making:** Considering the relative costs and benefits of potential actions to choose the most appropriate one. **Operation and Control:** Controlling operations of equipment or systems. **Instructing:** Teaching others how to do something. **Service Orientation:** Actively looking for ways to help people. **Systems Evaluation:** Identifying measures or indicators of system performance and the actions needed to improve or correct performance relative to the goals of the system.

Work Environment: Indoors; very hot or cold; minor burns, cuts, bites, or stings; standing; using hands on objects, tools, or controls; repetitive motions.

Correctional Officers and Jailers

- Annual Earnings: $34,090
- Growth: 6.7%
- Annual Job Openings: 54,000
- Self-Employed: 0.0%
- Part-Time: 2.1%
- Civilian Training Route: Moderate-term on-the-job training

Guard inmates in penal or rehabilitative institution in accordance with established regulations and procedures. May guard prisoners in transit between jail, courtroom, prison, or other point. Includes deputy sheriffs and police who spend the majority of their time guarding prisoners in correctional institutions. Monitor conduct of prisoners according to established policies, regulations, and procedures to prevent escape or violence. Inspect conditions of locks, window bars, grills, doors, and gates at correctional facilities to ensure that they will prevent escapes. Search prisoners, cells, and vehicles for weapons, valuables, or drugs. Guard facility entrances to screen visitors. Search for and recapture escapees. Inspect mail for the presence of contraband. Take prisoners into custody and escort to locations within and outside of facility, such as visiting room, courtroom, or airport. Record information such as prisoner identification, charges, and incidences of inmate disturbance. Use weapons, handcuffs, and physical force to maintain discipline and order among prisoners. Conduct fire, safety, and sanitation inspections. Provide to supervisors oral and written reports of the quality and quantity of work performed by inmates, inmate disturbances and rule violations, and unusual occurrences. Settle disputes between inmates. Drive passenger vehicles and trucks used to transport inmates to other institutions, courtrooms, hospitals, and work sites. Arrange daily schedules for prisoners, including library visits, work assignments, family visits, and counseling appointments. Assign duties to inmates, providing instructions as needed. Issue clothing, tools, and other authorized items to inmates. Serve meals and distribute commissary items to prisoners. Investigate crimes that have occurred within an institution or assist police in their investigations of crimes and inmates. Maintain records of prisoners' identification and charges. Supervise and coordinate work of other correctional service officers. Sponsor inmate recreational activities such as newspapers and self-help groups.

Military Job That Provides Training for It (see the description in Part II): Law Enforcement and Security Specialists

Personality Type: Realistic. Realistic occupations frequently involve work activities that include practical, hands-on problems and solutions. They often deal with plants, animals, and real-world materials like wood, tools, and machinery. Many of the occupations require working outside and do not involve a lot of paperwork or working closely with others.

C

GOE—Interest Area: 12. Law and Public Safety. **Work Group:** 12.04. Law Enforcement and Public Safety. **Other Civilian Jobs in This Work Group:** Bailiffs; Criminal Investigators and Special Agents; Detectives and Criminal Investigators; Fire Investigators; Forensic Science Technicians; Parking Enforcement Workers; Police and Sheriff's Patrol Officers; Police Detectives; Police Identification and Records Officers; Police Patrol Officers; Sheriffs and Deputy Sheriffs; Transit and Railroad Police.

Skills—Social Perceptiveness: Being aware of others' reactions and understanding why they react as they do. **Persuasion:** Persuading others to change their minds or behavior. **Negotiation:** Bringing others together and trying to reconcile differences. **Writing:** Communicating effectively in writing as appropriate for the needs of the audience. **Speaking:** Talking to others to convey information effectively. **Monitoring:** Monitoring/assessing your performance or that of other individuals or organizations to make improvements or take corrective action. **Active Listening:** Giving full attention to what other people are saying, taking time to understand the points being made, asking questions as appropriate, and not interrupting at inappropriate times. **Critical Thinking:** Using logic and reasoning to identify the strengths and weaknesses of alternative solutions, conclusions, or approaches to problems.

Work Environment: More often indoors than outdoors; noisy; contaminants; disease or infections; standing.

Court Reporters

- Annual Earnings: $41,640
- Growth: 14.8%
- Annual Job Openings: 3,000
- Self-Employed: 10.9%
- Part-Time: 12.0%
- Civilian Training Route: Postsecondary vocational training

Use verbatim methods and equipment to capture, store, retrieve, and transcribe pretrial and trial proceedings or other information. Includes stenocaptioners who operate computerized stenographic captioning equipment to provide captions of live or prerecorded broadcasts for hearing-impaired viewers. Take notes in shorthand or use a stenotype or shorthand machine that prints letters on a paper tape. Provide transcripts of proceedings upon request of judges, lawyers, or the public. Record verbatim proceedings of courts, legislative assemblies, committee meetings, and other proceedings, using computerized recording equipment, electronic stenograph machines, or stenomasks. Transcribe recorded proceedings in accordance with established formats. Ask speakers to clarify inaudible statements. File a legible transcript of records of a court case with the court clerk's office. File and store shorthand notes of court session. Respond to requests during court sessions to read portions of the proceedings already recorded. Record depositions and other proceedings for attorneys. Verify accuracy of transcripts by checking copies against original records of proceedings and accuracy of rulings by checking with judges. Record symbols on computer disks or CD-ROM; then translate and display them as text in computer-aided transcription process.

Military Job That Provides Training for It (see the description in Part II): Legal Specialists and Court Reporters

Personality Type: Artistic. Artistic occupations frequently involve working with forms, designs, and patterns. They often require self-expression, and the work can be done without following a clear set of rules.

GOE—Interest Area: 07. Government and Public Administration. **Work Group:** 07.04. Public Administration Clerical Support. **Other Civilian Jobs in This Work Group:** Court Clerks; Court, Municipal, and License Clerks; License Clerks; Municipal Clerks.

Skills—Reading Comprehension: Understanding written sentences and paragraphs in work-related documents. **Active Listening:** Giving full attention to what other people are saying, taking time to understand the points being made, asking questions as appropriate, and not interrupting at inappropriate times. **Equipment Selection:** Determining the kinds of tools and equipment needed to do a job. **Operation and Control:** Controlling operations of equipment or systems. **Equipment Maintenance:** Performing routine maintenance on equipment and determining when and what kind of maintenance is needed. **Operation Monitoring:** Watching gauges, dials, or other indicators to make sure a machine is working properly. **Time Management:** Managing one's own time and the time of others. **Operations Analysis:** Analyzing needs and product requirements to create a design.

Work Environment: Indoors; noisy; sitting; using hands on objects, tools, or controls; repetitive motions.

Crane and Tower Operators

- Annual Earnings: $38,870
- Growth: 8.2%
- Annual Job Openings: 4,000
- Self-Employed: 0.0%
- Part-Time: 2.3%
- Civilian Training Route: Long-term on-the-job training

Operate mechanical boom and cable or tower and cable equipment to lift and move materials, machines, or products in many directions. Determine load weights and check them against lifting capacities to prevent overload. Move levers, depress foot pedals, and turn dials to operate cranes, cherry pickers, electromagnets, or other moving equipment for lifting, moving, and placing loads. Inspect cables and grappling devices for wear and install or replace cables as needed. Clean, lubricate, and maintain mechanisms such as cables, pulleys, and grappling devices, making repairs as necessary. Inspect and adjust crane mechanisms and lifting accessories to prevent malfunctions and damage. Direct helpers engaged in placing blocking and outrigging under cranes. Load and unload bundles from trucks and move containers to storage bins, using moving equipment. Weigh bundles, using floor scales, and record weights for company records. Review daily work and delivery schedules to determine orders, sequences of deliveries, and special loading instructions. Direct truck drivers backing vehicles into loading bays and cover, uncover, and secure loads for delivery. Inspect bundle packaging for conformance to regulations and customer requirements and remove and batch packaging tickets.

C

Military Job That Provides Training for It (see the description in Part II): Construction Equipment Operators

Personality Type: Realistic. Realistic occupations frequently involve work activities that include practical, hands-on problems and solutions. They often deal with plants, animals, and real-world materials like wood, tools, and machinery. Many of the occupations require working outside and do not involve a lot of paperwork or working closely with others.

GOE—Interest Area: 02. Architecture and Construction. **Work Group:** 02.04. Construction Crafts. **Other Civilian Jobs in This Work Group:** Boilermakers; Brickmasons and Blockmasons; Carpet Installers; Cement Masons and Concrete Finishers; Commercial Divers; Construction Carpenters; Drywall and Ceiling Tile Installers; Electricians; Fence Erectors; Floor Layers, Except Carpet, Wood, and Hard Tiles; Floor Sanders and Finishers; Glaziers; Hazardous Materials Removal Workers; Insulation Workers, Floor, Ceiling, and Wall; Insulation Workers, Mechanical; Manufactured Building and Mobile Home Installers; Operating Engineers and Other Construction Equipment Operators; Painters, Construction and Maintenance; Paperhangers; Paving, Surfacing, and Tamping Equipment Operators; Pile-Driver Operators; Pipe Fitters and Steamfitters; Pipelayers; Plasterers and Stucco Masons; Plumbers; Plumbers, Pipefitters, and Steamfitters; Rail-Track Laying and Maintenance Equipment Operators; Refractory Materials Repairers, Except Brickmasons; Reinforcing Iron and Rebar Workers; Riggers; Roofers; Rough Carpenters; Security and Fire Alarm Systems Installers; Segmental Pavers; Sheet Metal Workers; Stone Cutters and Carvers, Manufacturing; Stonemasons; Structural Iron and Steel Workers; Tapers; Terrazzo Workers and Finishers; Tile and Marble Setters.

Skills—Equipment Maintenance: Performing routine maintenance on equipment and determining when and what kind of maintenance is needed. **Operation Monitoring:** Watching gauges, dials, or other indicators to make sure a machine is working properly. **Operation and Control:** Controlling operations of equipment or systems. **Repairing:** Repairing machines or systems, using the needed tools. **Equipment Selection:** Determining the kinds of tools and equipment needed to do a job. **Installation:** Installing equipment, machines, wiring, or programs to meet specifications. **Technology Design:** Generating or adapting equipment and technology to serve user needs. **Management of Personnel Resources:** Motivating, developing, and directing people as they work; identifying the best people for the job.

Work Environment: Noisy; very bright or dim lighting; contaminants; high places; using hands on objects, tools, or controls; repetitive motions.

Criminal Investigators and Special Agents

- Annual Earnings: $55,790
- Growth: 16.3%
- Annual Job Openings: 9,000
- Self-Employed: 0.0%
- Part-Time: 2.5%
- Civilian Training Route: Work experience in a related occupation

The job openings listed here are shared with Immigration and Customs Inspectors; Police Detectives; and Police Identification and Records Officers.

Investigate alleged or suspected criminal violations of federal, state, or local laws to determine if evidence is sufficient to recommend prosecution. Record evidence and documents, using equipment such as cameras and photocopy machines. Obtain and verify evidence by interviewing and observing suspects and witnesses or by analyzing records. Examine records to locate links in chains of evidence or information. Prepare reports that detail investigation findings. Determine scope, timing, and direction of investigations. Collaborate with other offices and agencies to exchange information and coordinate activities. Testify before grand juries concerning criminal activity investigations. Analyze evidence in laboratories or in the field. Investigate organized crime, public corruption, financial crime, copyright infringement, civil rights violations, bank robbery, extortion, kidnapping, and other violations of federal or state statutes. Identify case issues and evidence needed, based on analysis of charges, complaints, or allegations of law violations. Obtain and use search and arrest warrants. Serve subpoenas or other official papers. Collaborate with other authorities on activities such as surveillance, transcription, and research. Develop relationships with informants to obtain information related to cases. Search for and collect evidence such as fingerprints, using investigative equipment. Collect and record physical information about arrested suspects, including fingerprints, height and weight measurements, and photographs. Compare crime scene fingerprints with those from suspects or fingerprint files to identify perpetrators, using computers. Administer counter-terrorism and counter-narcotics reward programs. Provide protection for individuals such as government leaders, political candidates, and visiting foreign dignitaries. Perform undercover assignments and maintain surveillance, including monitoring authorized wiretaps. Manage security programs designed to protect personnel, facilities, and information. Issue security clearances.

Military Job That Provides Training for It (see the description in Part II): Law Enforcement and Security Specialists

Personality Type: Enterprising. Enterprising occupations frequently involve starting up and carrying out projects. These occupations can involve leading people and making many decisions. They sometimes require risk taking and often deal with business.

GOE—Interest Area: 12. Law and Public Safety. **Work Group:** 12.04. Law Enforcement and Public Safety. **Other Civilian Jobs in This Work Group:** Bailiffs; Correctional Officers and Jailers; Detectives and Criminal Investigators; Fire Investigators; Forensic Science Technicians; Parking Enforcement Workers; Police and Sheriff's Patrol Officers; Police Detectives; Police Identification and Records Officers; Police Patrol Officers; Sheriffs and Deputy Sheriffs; Transit and Railroad Police.

Skills—Negotiation: Bringing others together and trying to reconcile differences. **Programming:** Writing computer programs for various purposes. **Judgment and Decision Making:** Considering the relative costs and benefits of potential actions to choose the most appropriate one. **Operations Analysis:** Analyzing needs and product requirements to create a design. **Service Orientation:** Actively looking for ways to help people. **Persuasion:** Persuading others to change their minds or behavior. **Complex Problem Solving:** Identifying complex problems and reviewing related information to develop and evaluate options and implement solutions. **Equipment Selection:** Determining the kinds of tools and equipment needed to do a job.

Work Environment: More often outdoors than indoors; noisy; very hot or cold; standing.

Dental Assistants

- Annual Earnings: $29,520
- Growth: 42.7%
- Annual Job Openings: 45,000
- Self-Employed: 0.0%
- Part-Time: 38.9%
- Civilian Training Route: Moderate-term on-the-job training

Assist dentist, set up patient and equipment, and keep records. Prepare patient, sterilize and disinfect instruments, set up instrument trays, prepare materials, and assist dentist during dental procedures. Expose dental diagnostic X rays. Record treatment information in patient records. Take and record medical and dental histories and vital signs of patients. Provide postoperative instructions prescribed by dentist. Assist dentist in management of medical and dental emergencies. Pour, trim, and polish study casts. Instruct patients in oral hygiene and plaque control programs. Make preliminary impressions for study casts and occlusal registrations for mounting study casts. Clean and polish removable appliances. Clean teeth, using dental instruments. Apply protective coating of fluoride to teeth. Fabricate temporary restorations and custom impressions from preliminary impressions. Schedule appointments, prepare bills, and receive payment for dental services; complete insurance forms; and maintain records, manually or using computer.

Military Job That Provides Training for It (see the description in Part II): Dental Specialists

Personality Type: Social. Social occupations frequently involve working with, communicating with, and teaching people. These occupations often involve helping or providing service to others.

GOE—Interest Area: 08. Health Science. **Work Group:** 08.03. Dentistry. **Other Civilian Jobs in This Work Group:** Dental Hygienists; Dentists, General; Oral and Maxillofacial Surgeons; Orthodontists; Prosthodontists.

Skills—Equipment Maintenance: Performing routine maintenance on equipment and determining when and what kind of maintenance is needed. **Social Perceptiveness:** Being aware of others' reactions and understanding why they react as they do. **Operation and Control:** Controlling operations of equipment or systems. **Management of Material Resources:** Obtaining and seeing to the appropriate use of equipment, facilities, and materials needed to do certain work. **Operation Monitoring:** Watching gauges, dials, or other indicators to make sure a machine is working properly. **Equipment Selection:** Determining the kinds of tools and equipment needed to do a job. **Installation:** Installing equipment, machines, wiring, or programs to meet specifications. **Troubleshooting:** Determining causes of operating errors and deciding what to do about them.

Work Environment: Indoors; contaminants; disease or infections; using hands on objects, tools, or controls; bending or twisting the body; repetitive motions.

Dental Hygienists

- Annual Earnings: $60,890
- Growth: 43.3%
- Annual Job Openings: 17,000
- Self-Employed: 0.3%
- Part-Time: 56.0%
- Civilian Training Route: Associate degree

Clean teeth and examine oral areas, head, and neck for signs of oral disease. May educate patients on oral hygiene, take and develop X rays, or apply fluoride or sealants. Clean calcareous deposits, accretions, and stains from teeth and beneath margins of gums, using dental instruments. Feel and visually examine gums for sores and signs of disease. Chart conditions of decay and disease for diagnosis and treatment by dentist. Feel lymph nodes under patient's chin to detect swelling or tenderness that could indicate presence of oral cancer. Apply fluorides and other cavity-preventing agents to arrest dental decay. Examine gums, using probes, to locate periodontal recessed gums and signs of gum disease. Expose and develop X-ray film. Provide clinical services and health education to improve and maintain oral health of schoolchildren. Remove excess cement from coronal surfaces of teeth. Make impressions for study casts. Place, carve, and finish amalgam restorations. Administer local anesthetic agents. Conduct dental health clinics for community groups to augment services of dentist. Remove sutures and dressings. Place and remove rubber dams, matrices, and temporary restorations.

Military Job That Provides Training for It (see the description in Part II): Dental Specialists

Personality Type: Social. Social occupations frequently involve working with, communicating with, and teaching people. These occupations often involve helping or providing service to others.

GOE—Interest Area: 08. Health Science. **Work Group:** 08.03. Dentistry. **Other Civilian Jobs in This Work Group:** Dental Assistants; Dentists, General; Oral and Maxillofacial Surgeons; Orthodontists; Prosthodontists.

Skills—Active Learning: Understanding the implications of new information for both current and future problem-solving and decision-making. **Time Management:** Managing one's own time and the time of others. **Persuasion:** Persuading others to change their minds or behavior. **Reading Comprehension:** Understanding written sentences and paragraphs in work-related documents. **Science:** Using scientific rules and methods to solve problems. **Social Perceptiveness:** Being aware of others' reactions and understanding why they react as they do. **Writing:** Communicating effectively in writing as appropriate for the needs of the audience. **Equipment Selection:** Determining the kinds of tools and equipment needed to do a job.

Work Environment: Indoors; radiation; disease or infections; sitting; using hands on objects, tools, or controls; repetitive motions.

Desktop Publishers

- Annual Earnings: $32,800
- Growth: 23.2%
- Annual Job Openings: 8,000
- Self-Employed: 1.1%
- Part-Time: 4.7%
- Civilian Training Route: Postsecondary vocational training

Format typescript and graphic elements, using computer software to produce publication-ready material. Check preliminary and final proofs for errors and make necessary corrections. Operate desktop publishing software and equipment to design, lay out, and produce camera-ready copy. View monitors for visual representation of work in progress and for instructions and feedback throughout process, making modifications as necessary. Enter text into computer keyboard and select the size and style of type, column width, and appropriate spacing for printed materials. Store copies of publications on paper, magnetic tape, film, or diskette. Position text and art elements from a variety of databases in a visually appealing way to design print or Web pages, using knowledge of type styles and size and layout patterns. Enter digitized data into electronic prepress system computer memory, using scanner, camera, keyboard, or mouse. Edit graphics and photos, using pixel or bitmap editing, airbrushing, masking, or image retouching. Import text and art elements such as electronic clip art or electronic files from photographs that have been scanned or produced with a digital camera, using computer software. Prepare sample layouts for approval, using computer software. Study layout or other design instructions to determine work to be done and sequence of operations. Load floppy disks or tapes containing information into system. Convert various types of files for printing or for the Internet, using computer software. Enter data, such as coordinates of images and color specifications, into system to retouch and make color corrections. Select number of colors and determine color separations. Transmit, deliver, or mail publication master to printer for production into film and plates. Collaborate with graphic artists, editors, and writers to produce master copies according to design specifications. Create special effects such as vignettes, mosaics, and image combining and add elements such as sound and animation to electronic publications.

Military Job That Provides Training for It (see the description in Part II): Administrative Support Specialists

Personality Type: Realistic. Realistic occupations frequently involve work activities that include practical, hands-on problems and solutions. They often deal with plants, animals, and real-world materials like wood, tools, and machinery. Many of the occupations require working outside and do not involve a lot of paperwork or working closely with others.

GOE—Interest Area: 13. Manufacturing. **Work Group:** 13.08. Graphic Arts Production. **Other Civilian Jobs in This Work Group:** Bindery Workers; Etchers and Engravers; Job Printers; Photographic Process Workers; Photographic Processing Machine Operators; Prepress Technicians and Workers; Printing Machine Operators.

Skills—Operation and Control: Controlling operations of equipment or systems. **Operations Analysis:** Analyzing needs and product requirements to create a design. **Time Management:** Managing one's own time and the time of others. **Service Orientation:** Actively looking for ways to help people. **Active Listening:** Giving full attention to what other people are saying, taking time to understand the points being made, asking questions as appropriate, and not interrupting at inappropriate times. **Writing:** Communicating effectively in writing as appropriate for the needs of the audience. **Reading Comprehension:** Understanding written sentences and paragraphs in work-related documents. **Complex Problem Solving:** Identifying complex problems and reviewing related information to develop and evaluate options and implement solutions.

Work Environment: Indoors; sitting; repetitive motions.

Directors, Religious Activities and Education

- Annual Earnings: $32,540
- Growth: 18.5%
- Annual Job Openings: 10,000
- Self-Employed: 0.0%
- Part-Time: 27.9%
- Civilian Training Route: Bachelor's degree

Direct and coordinate activities of a denominational group to meet religious needs of students. Plan, direct, or coordinate church school programs designed to promote religious education among church membership. May provide counseling and guidance relative to marital, health, financial, and religious problems. Select appropriate curricula and class structures for educational programs. Attend workshops, seminars, and conferences to obtain program ideas, information, and resources. Train and supervise religious education instructional staff. Analyze revenue and program cost data to determine budget priorities. Counsel individuals regarding interpersonal, health, financial, and religious problems. Participate in denominational activities aimed at goals such as promoting interfaith understanding or providing aid to new or small congregations. Plan and conduct conferences dealing with the interpretation of religious ideas and convictions. Visit congregation members' homes, or arrange for pastoral visits, to provide information and resources regarding religious education programs. Locate and distribute resources such as periodicals and curricula to enhance the effectiveness of educational programs. Schedule special events such as camps, conferences, meetings, seminars, and retreats. Interpret religious education activities to the public through speaking, leading discussions, and writing articles for local and national publications. Publicize programs through sources such as newsletters, bulletins, and mailings. Implement program plans by ordering needed materials, scheduling speakers, reserving space, and handling other administrative details. Identify and recruit potential volunteer workers. Develop and direct study courses and religious education programs within congregations. Confer with clergy members, congregation officials, and congregation organizations to encourage support of and participation in religious education activities. Collaborate with other ministry members to establish goals and objectives for religious education programs and to develop ways to encourage program participation. Analyze member participation and changes in congregation emphasis to determine needs for religious education.

Military Job That Provides Training for It (see the description in Part II): Religious Program Specialists

Personality Type: Social. Social occupations frequently involve working with, communicating with, and teaching people. These occupations often involve helping or providing service to others.

GOE—Interest Area: 10. Human Service. **Work Group:** 10.02. Religious Work. **Other Civilian Jobs in This Work Group:** Clergy.

Skills—Management of Financial Resources: Determining how money will be spent to get the work done and accounting for these expenditures. **Management of Personnel Resources:** Motivating, developing, and directing people as they work; identifying the best people for the

D

job. **Social Perceptiveness:** Being aware of others' reactions and understanding why they react as they do. **Systems Analysis:** Determining how a system should work and how changes in conditions, operations, and the environment will affect outcomes. **Management of Material Resources:** Obtaining and seeing to the appropriate use of equipment, facilities, and materials needed to do certain work. **Service Orientation:** Actively looking for ways to help people. **Systems Evaluation:** Identifying measures or indicators of system performance and the actions needed to improve or correct performance relative to the goals of the system. **Writing:** Communicating effectively in writing as appropriate for the needs of the audience.

Work Environment: Indoors; sitting.

Drywall and Ceiling Tile Installers

- Annual Earnings: $34,740
- Growth: 9.0%
- Annual Job Openings: 17,000
- Self-Employed: 23.4%
- Part-Time: 8.0%
- Civilian Training Route: Moderate-term on-the-job training

Apply plasterboard or other wallboard to ceilings or interior walls of buildings. Apply or mount acoustical tiles or blocks, strips, or sheets of shock-absorbing materials to ceilings and walls of buildings to reduce or reflect sound. Materials may be of decorative quality. Includes lathers who fasten wooden, metal, or rockboard lath to walls, ceilings, or partitions of buildings to provide support base for plaster, fireproofing, or acoustical material. Fasten metal or rockboard lath to the structural framework of walls, ceilings, and partitions of buildings, using nails, screws, staples, or wire-ties. Apply cement to backs of tiles and press tiles into place, aligning them with layout marks or joints of previously laid tile. Apply or mount acoustical tile or blocks, strips, or sheets of shock-absorbing materials to ceilings and walls of buildings to reduce reflection of sound or to decorate rooms. Assemble and install metal framing and decorative trim for windows, doorways, and vents. Cut and screw together metal channels to make floor and ceiling frames according to plans for the location of rooms and hallways. Cut metal or wood framing and trim to size, using cutting tools. Measure and cut openings in panels or tiles for electrical outlets, windows, vents, and plumbing and other fixtures, using keyhole saws or other cutting tools. Fit and fasten wallboard or drywall into position on wood or metal frameworks, using glue, nails, or screws. Hang dry lines (stretched string) to wall moldings in order to guide positioning of main runners. Hang drywall panels on metal frameworks of walls and ceilings in offices, schools, and other large buildings, using lifts or hoists to adjust panel heights when necessary. Inspect furrings, mechanical mountings, and masonry surface for plumbness and level, using spirit or water levels. Install horizontal and vertical metal or wooden studs to frames so that wallboard can be attached to interior walls. Measure and mark surfaces to lay out work according to blueprints and drawings, using tape measures, straightedges or squares, and marking devices. Nail channels or wood furring strips to surfaces to provide mounting for tile. Read blueprints and other specifications to determine methods of installation, work procedures, and material and tool requirements. Scribe and cut edges of tile to fit walls where wall molding is not specified. Seal joints between ceiling tiles and walls. Cut fixture and border tiles to size, using keyhole saws, and insert them into surrounding frameworks. Suspend angle iron grids and channel irons from ceilings, using wire.

Military Job That Provides Training for It (see the description in Part II): Construction Specialists

Personality Type: Realistic. Realistic occupations frequently involve work activities that include practical, hands-on problems and solutions. They often deal with plants, animals, and real-world materials like wood, tools, and machinery. Many of the occupations require working outside and do not involve a lot of paperwork or working closely with others.

GOE—Interest Area: 02. Architecture and Construction. **Work Group:** 02.04. Construction Crafts. **Other Civilian Jobs in This Work Group:** Boilermakers; Brickmasons and Blockmasons; Carpet Installers; Cement Masons and Concrete Finishers; Commercial Divers; Construction Carpenters; Crane and Tower Operators; Electricians; Fence Erectors; Floor Layers, Except Carpet, Wood, and Hard Tiles; Floor Sanders and Finishers; Glaziers; Hazardous Materials Removal Workers; Insulation Workers, Floor, Ceiling, and Wall; Insulation Workers, Mechanical; Manufactured Building and Mobile Home Installers; Operating Engineers and Other Construction Equipment Operators; Painters, Construction and Maintenance; Paperhangers; Paving, Surfacing, and Tamping Equipment Operators; Pile-Driver Operators; Pipe Fitters and Steamfitters; Pipelayers; Plasterers and Stucco Masons; Plumbers; Plumbers, Pipefitters, and Steamfitters; Rail-Track Laying and Maintenance Equipment Operators; Refractory Materials Repairers, Except Brickmasons; Reinforcing Iron and Rebar Workers; Riggers; Roofers; Rough Carpenters; Security and Fire Alarm Systems Installers; Segmental Pavers; Sheet Metal Workers; Stone Cutters and Carvers, Manufacturing; Stonemasons; Structural Iron and Steel Workers; Tapers; Terrazzo Workers and Finishers; Tile and Marble Setters.

Skills—No data available.

Work Environment: Indoors; contaminants; hazardous equipment; minor burns, cuts, bites, or stings; standing; using hands on objects, tools, or controls.

Electrical and Electronics Installers and Repairers, Transportation Equipment

- Annual Earnings: $41,490
- Growth: 6.6%
- Annual Job Openings: 2,000
- Self-Employed: 0.0%
- Part-Time: 5.5%
- Civilian Training Route: Postsecondary vocational training

Install, adjust, or maintain mobile electronics communication equipment, including sound, sonar, security, navigation, and surveillance systems on trains, watercraft, or other mobile equipment. Inspect and test electrical systems and equipment to locate and diagnose malfunctions, using visual inspections, testing devices, and computer software. Reassemble and test equipment after repairs. Splice wires with knives or cutting pliers and solder connections

E

to fixtures, outlets, and equipment. Install new fuses, electrical cables, or power sources as required. Locate and remove or repair circuit defects such as blown fuses or malfunctioning transistors. Adjust, repair, or replace defective wiring and relays in ignition, lighting, air-conditioning, and safety control systems, using electrician's tools. Refer to schematics and manufacturers' specifications that show connections and provide instructions on how to locate problems. Maintain equipment service records. Cut openings and drill holes for fixtures, outlet boxes, and fuse holders, using electric drills and routers. Measure, cut, and install frameworks and conduit to support and connect wiring, control panels, and junction boxes, using hand tools. Install electrical equipment such as air-conditioning, heating, or ignition systems and components such as generator brushes and commutators, using hand tools. Install fixtures, outlets, terminal boards, switches, and wall boxes, using hand tools. Repair or rebuild equipment such as starters, generators, distributors, or door controls, using electrician's tools. Confer with customers to determine the nature of malfunctions. Estimate costs of repairs based on parts and labor requirements.

Military Jobs That Provide Training for It (see the descriptions in Part II): Automotive and Heavy Equipment Mechanics; Electronic Instrument and Equipment Repairers; Ship Electricians

Personality Type: Realistic. Realistic occupations frequently involve work activities that include practical, hands-on problems and solutions. They often deal with plants, animals, and real-world materials like wood, tools, and machinery. Many of the occupations require working outside and do not involve a lot of paperwork or working closely with others.

GOE—Interest Area: 13. Manufacturing. **Work Group:** 13.12. Electrical and Electronic Repair. **Other Civilian Jobs in This Work Group:** Avionics Technicians; Electric Motor, Power Tool, and Related Repairers; Electrical and Electronics Repairers, Commercial and Industrial Equipment; Electronic Equipment Installers and Repairers, Motor Vehicles; Electronic Home Entertainment Equipment Installers and Repairers; Radio Mechanics.

Skills—Installation: Installing equipment, machines, wiring, or programs to meet specifications. **Repairing:** Repairing machines or systems, using the needed tools. **Troubleshooting:** Determining causes of operating errors and deciding what to do about them. **Complex Problem Solving:** Identifying complex problems and reviewing related information to develop and evaluate options and implement solutions. **Operation Monitoring:** Watching gauges, dials, or other indicators to make sure a machine is working properly. **Equipment Selection:** Determining the kinds of tools and equipment needed to do a job. **Equipment Maintenance:** Performing routine maintenance on equipment and determining when and what kind of maintenance is needed. **Operation and Control:** Controlling operations of equipment or systems.

Work Environment: Outdoors; contaminants; hazardous conditions; standing; using hands on objects, tools, or controls; repetitive motions.

Electrical and Electronics Repairers, Commercial and Industrial Equipment

- Annual Earnings: $44,120
- Growth: 9.7%
- Annual Job Openings: 8,000
- Self-Employed: 0.0%
- Part-Time: 5.5%
- Civilian Training Route: Postsecondary vocational training

Repair, test, adjust, or install electronic equipment, such as industrial controls, transmitters, and antennas. Perform scheduled preventive maintenance tasks, such as checking, cleaning, and repairing equipment, to detect and prevent problems. Examine work orders and converse with equipment operators to detect equipment problems and to ascertain whether mechanical or human errors contributed to the problems. Operate equipment to demonstrate proper use and to analyze malfunctions. Set up and test industrial equipment to ensure that it functions properly. Test faulty equipment to diagnose malfunctions, using test equipment and software and applying knowledge of the functional operation of electronic units and systems. Repair and adjust equipment, machines, and defective components, replacing worn parts such as gaskets and seals in watertight electrical equipment. Calibrate testing instruments and installed or repaired equipment to prescribed specifications. Advise management regarding customer satisfaction, product performance, and suggestions for product improvements. Study blueprints, schematics, manuals, and other specifications to determine installation procedures. Inspect components of industrial equipment for accurate assembly and installation and for defects such as loose connections and frayed wires. Maintain equipment logs that record performance problems, repairs, calibrations, and tests. Coordinate efforts with other workers involved in installing and maintaining equipment or components. Maintain inventory of spare parts. Consult with customers, supervisors, and engineers to plan layout of equipment and to resolve problems in system operation and maintenance. Install repaired equipment in various settings, such as industrial or military establishments. Send defective units to the manufacturer or to a specialized repair shop for repair. Determine feasibility of using standardized equipment and develop specifications for equipment required to perform additional functions. Enter information into computer to copy program or to draw, modify, or store schematics, applying knowledge of software package used. Sign overhaul documents for equipment replaced or repaired. Develop or modify industrial electronic devices, circuits, and equipment according to available specifications.

Military Jobs That Provide Training for It (see the descriptions in Part II): Aircraft Mechanics; Avionics Technicians; Communications Equipment Operators; Computer Systems Specialists; Electrical Products Repairers; Electronic Instrument and Equipment Repairers; Non-Destructive Testers; Power Plant Electricians; Precision Instrument and Equipment Repairers; Radar and Sonar Operators; Ship Electricians; Weapons Maintenance Technicians

Personality Type: Realistic. Realistic occupations frequently involve work activities that include practical, hands-on problems and solutions. They often deal with plants, animals, and real-world materials like wood, tools, and

E

machinery. Many of the occupations require working outside and do not involve a lot of paperwork or working closely with others.

GOE—Interest Area: 13. Manufacturing. **Work Group:** 13.12. Electrical and Electronic Repair. **Other Civilian Jobs in This Work Group:** Avionics Technicians; Electric Motor, Power Tool, and Related Repairers; Electrical and Electronics Installers and Repairers, Transportation Equipment; Electronic Equipment Installers and Repairers, Motor Vehicles; Electronic Home Entertainment Equipment Installers and Repairers; Radio Mechanics.

Skills—Installation: Installing equipment, machines, wiring, or programs to meet specifications. **Repairing:** Repairing machines or systems, using the needed tools. **Operation Monitoring:** Watching gauges, dials, or other indicators to make sure a machine is working properly. **Troubleshooting:** Determining causes of operating errors and deciding what to do about them. **Equipment Maintenance:** Performing routine maintenance on equipment and determining when and what kind of maintenance is needed. **Operation and Control:** Controlling operations of equipment or systems. **Systems Analysis:** Determining how a system should work and how changes in conditions, operations, and the environment will affect outcomes. **Science:** Using scientific rules and methods to solve problems.

Work Environment: Indoors; noisy; cramped work space, awkward positions; hazardous conditions; standing; using hands on objects, tools, or controls.

Electrical and Electronics Repairers, Powerhouse, Substation, and Relay

- Annual Earnings: $54,970
- Growth: –0.4%
- Annual Job Openings: 2,000
- Self-Employed: 0.0%
- Part-Time: 5.5%
- Civilian Training Route: Postsecondary vocational training

Inspect, test, repair, or maintain electrical equipment in generating stations, substations, and in-service relays. Construct, test, maintain, and repair substation relay and control systems. Inspect and test equipment and circuits to identify malfunctions or defects, using wiring diagrams and testing devices such as ohmmeters, voltmeters, or ammeters. Consult manuals, schematics, wiring diagrams, and engineering personnel to troubleshoot and solve equipment problems and to determine optimum equipment functioning. Notify facility personnel of equipment shutdowns. Open and close switches to isolate defective relays; then perform adjustments or repairs. Prepare and maintain records detailing tests, repairs, and maintenance. Analyze test data to diagnose malfunctions, to determine performance characteristics of systems, and to evaluate effects of system modifications. Test insulators and bushings of equipment by inducing voltage across insulation, testing current, and calculating insulation loss. Repair, replace, and clean equipment and components such as circuit breakers, brushes, and commutators. Disconnect voltage regulators, bolts, and screws and connect replacement regulators to high-voltage lines. Schedule and supervise the construction and testing of special devices and the implementation of unique monitoring or control systems. Run signal quality and connectivity tests for individual cables and record results. Schedule and supervise splicing or termination of cables in color-code order. Test oil in circuit breakers and transformers for dielectric strength, refilling oil periodically. Maintain inventories of spare parts for all equipment, requisitioning parts as necessary. Set forms and pour concrete footings for installation of heavy equipment.

Military Jobs That Provide Training for It (see the descriptions in Part II): Power Plant Electricians; Power Plant Operators; Powerhouse Mechanics; Ship Electricians

Personality Type: Realistic. Realistic occupations frequently involve work activities that include practical, hands-on problems and solutions. They often deal with plants, animals, and real-world materials like wood, tools, and machinery. Many of the occupations require working outside and do not involve a lot of paperwork or working closely with others.

GOE—Interest Area: 02. Architecture and Construction. **Work Group:** 02.05. Systems and Equipment Installation, Maintenance, and Repair. **Other Civilian Jobs in This Work Group:** Electrical Power-Line Installers and Repairers; Elevator Installers and Repairers; Heating and Air Conditioning Mechanics and Installers; Maintenance and Repair Workers, General; Refrigeration Mechanics and Installers; Telecommunications Equipment Installers and Repairers, Except Line Installers; Telecommunications Line Installers and Repairers.

Skills—Installation: Installing equipment, machines, wiring, or programs to meet specifications. **Repairing:** Repairing machines or systems, using the needed tools. **Equipment Maintenance:** Performing routine maintenance on equipment and determining when and what kind of maintenance is needed. **Troubleshooting:** Determining causes of operating errors and deciding what to do about them. **Operation Monitoring:** Watching gauges, dials, or other indicators to make sure a machine is working properly. **Operation and Control:** Controlling operations of equipment or systems. **Science:** Using scientific rules and methods to solve problems. **Programming:** Writing computer programs for various purposes.

Work Environment: Outdoors; noisy; very bright or dim lighting; hazardous conditions; standing; using hands on objects, tools, or controls.

Electrical Power-Line Installers and Repairers

- Annual Earnings: $50,150
- Growth: 2.5%
- Annual Job Openings: 11,000
- Self-Employed: 2.3%
- Part-Time: 0.9%
- Civilian Training Route: Long-term on-the-job training

Install or repair cables or wires used in electrical power or distribution systems. May erect poles and light- or heavy-duty transmission towers. Adhere to safety practices and procedures, such as checking equipment regularly and erecting barriers around work areas. Open switches or attach grounding devices to remove electrical hazards from disturbed or fallen lines or to facilitate repairs. Climb poles or use truck-mounted buckets to access equipment. Place insulating or fireproofing materials over conductors and joints. Install, maintain, and repair electrical distribution and transmission systems, including conduits; cables; wires; and related equipment such as transformers, circuit breakers, and switches. Identify defective sectionalizing devices, circuit breakers, fuses, voltage regulators, transformers, switches, relays, or wiring, using wiring diagrams and electrical-testing instruments. Drive vehicles equipped with tools and materials to job sites. Coordinate work assignment preparation and completion with other workers. String wire conductors and cables between poles, towers, trenches, pylons, and buildings, setting lines in place and using winches to adjust tension. Inspect and test power lines and auxiliary equipment to locate and identify problems, using reading and testing instruments. Test conductors according to electrical diagrams and specifications to identify corresponding conductors and to prevent incorrect connections. Replace damaged poles with new poles and straighten the poles. Install watt-hour meters and connect service drops between power lines and consumers' facilities. Attach crossarms, insulators, and auxiliary equipment to poles prior to installing them. Travel in trucks, helicopters, and airplanes to inspect lines for freedom from obstruction and adequacy of insulation. Dig holes, using augers, and set poles, using cranes and power equipment. Trim trees that could be hazardous to the functioning of cables or wires. Splice or solder cables together or to overhead transmission lines, customer service lines, or street light lines, using hand tools, epoxies, or specialized equipment. Cut and peel lead sheathing and insulation from defective or newly installed cables and conduits prior to splicing.

Military Job That Provides Training for It (see the description in Part II): Power Plant Electricians

Personality Type: Realistic. Realistic occupations frequently involve work activities that include practical, hands-on problems and solutions. They often deal with plants, animals, and real-world materials like wood, tools, and machinery. Many of the occupations require working outside and do not involve a lot of paperwork or working closely with others.

GOE—Interest Area: 02. Architecture and Construction. **Work Group:** 02.05. Systems and Equipment Installation, Maintenance, and Repair. **Other Civilian Jobs in This Work Group:** Electrical and Electronics Repairers, Powerhouse, Substation, and Relay; Elevator Installers and Repairers; Heating and Air Conditioning Mechanics and Installers; Maintenance and Repair Workers, General; Refrigeration Mechanics and Installers; Telecommunications Equipment Installers and Repairers, Except Line Installers; Telecommunications Line Installers and Repairers.

Skills—Repairing: Repairing machines or systems, using the needed tools. **Installation:** Installing equipment, machines, wiring, or programs to meet specifications. **Equipment Maintenance:** Performing routine maintenance on equipment and determining when and what kind of maintenance is needed. **Operation Monitoring:** Watching gauges, dials, or other indicators to make sure a machine is working properly. **Troubleshooting:** Determining causes of operating errors and deciding what to do about them. **Operation and Control:** Controlling operations of equipment or systems. **Equipment Selection:** Determining the kinds of tools and equipment needed to do a job. **Systems Analysis:** Determining how a system should work and how changes in conditions, operations, and the environment will affect outcomes.

Work Environment: Outdoors; very hot or cold; high places; hazardous conditions; hazardous equipment; using hands on objects, tools, or controls.

Electricians

- Annual Earnings: $42,790
- Growth: 11.8%
- Annual Job Openings: 68,000
- Self-Employed: 9.5%
- Part-Time: 3.3%
- Civilian Training Route: Long-term on-the-job training

Install, maintain, and repair electrical wiring, equipment, and fixtures. Ensure that work is in accordance with relevant codes. May install or service street lights, intercom systems, or electrical control systems. Assemble, install, test, and maintain electrical or electronic wiring, equipment, appliances, apparatus, and fixtures, using hand tools and power tools. Diagnose malfunctioning systems, apparatus, and components, using test equipment and hand tools, to locate the cause of a breakdown and correct the problem. Connect wires to circuit breakers, transformers, or other components. Inspect electrical systems, equipment, and components to identify hazards, defects, and the need for adjustment or repair and to ensure compliance with codes. Advise management on whether continued operation of equipment could be hazardous. Test electrical systems and continuity of circuits in electrical wiring, equipment, and fixtures, using testing devices such as ohmmeters, voltmeters, and oscilloscopes, to ensure compatibility and safety of system. Maintain current electrician's license or identification card to meet governmental regulations. Plan layout and installation of electrical wiring, equipment, and fixtures based on job specifications and local codes. Direct and train workers to install, maintain, or repair electrical wiring, equipment, and fixtures. Prepare sketches or follow blueprints to determine the location of wiring and equipment and to ensure conformance to building and safety codes. Use a variety of tools and equipment, such as power construction equipment; measuring devices; power tools; and testing equipment, including oscilloscopes, ammeters, and test lamps. Install ground leads and connect power cables to equipment such as motors. Perform business management duties such as maintaining records and files, preparing reports, and ordering supplies and equipment. Repair or replace wiring, equipment, and fixtures, using hand tools and power tools. Work from ladders, scaffolds, and roofs to install, maintain, or repair electrical wiring, equipment, and fixtures. Place conduit, pipes, or tubing inside designated partitions, walls, or other concealed areas and pull insulated wires or cables through the conduit to complete circuits between boxes. Construct and fabricate parts, using hand tools and specifications.

Military Jobs That Provide Training for It (see the descriptions in Part II): Building Electricians; Power Plant Electricians; Ship Electricians

Personality Type: Realistic. Realistic occupations frequently involve work activities that include practical, hands-on problems and solutions. They often deal with plants, animals, and real-world materials like wood, tools, and machinery. Many of the occupations require working outside and do not involve a lot of paperwork or working closely with others.

GOE—Interest Area: 02. Architecture and Construction. **Work Group:** 02.04. Construction Crafts. **Other Civilian Jobs in This Work Group:** Boilermakers; Brickmasons and Blockmasons; Carpet Installers; Cement Masons and Concrete Finishers; Commercial Divers; Construction Carpenters; Crane and Tower Operators; Drywall and Ceiling Tile Installers; Fence Erectors; Floor Layers, Except Carpet, Wood, and Hard Tiles; Floor Sanders and Finishers; Glaziers; Hazardous Materials Removal Workers; Insulation Workers, Floor, Ceiling, and Wall; Insulation Workers, Mechanical; Manufactured Building and Mobile Home Installers; Operating Engineers and Other Construction Equipment Operators; Painters, Construction and Maintenance; Paperhangers; Paving, Surfacing, and Tamping Equipment Operators; Pile-Driver Operators; Pipe Fitters and Steamfitters; Pipelayers; Plasterers and Stucco Masons; Plumbers; Plumbers, Pipefitters, and Steamfitters; Rail-Track Laying and Maintenance Equipment Operators; Refractory Materials Repairers, Except Brickmasons; Reinforcing Iron and Rebar Workers; Riggers; Roofers; Rough Carpenters; Security and Fire Alarm Systems Installers; Segmental Pavers; Sheet Metal Workers; Stone Cutters and Carvers, Manufacturing; Stonemasons; Structural Iron and Steel Workers; Tapers; Terrazzo Workers and Finishers; Tile and Marble Setters.

Skills—Installation: Installing equipment, machines, wiring, or programs to meet specifications. **Repairing:** Repairing machines or systems, using the needed tools. **Equipment Maintenance:** Performing routine maintenance on equipment and determining when and what kind of maintenance is needed. **Troubleshooting:** Determining causes of operating errors and deciding what to do about them. **Technology Design:** Generating or adapting equipment and technology to serve user needs. **Operation and Control:** Controlling operations of equipment or systems. **Operation Monitoring:** Watching gauges, dials, or other indicators to make sure a machine is working properly. **Equipment Selection:** Determining the kinds of tools and equipment needed to do a job.

Work Environment: Outdoors; noisy; minor burns, cuts, bites, or stings; standing; walking and running; using hands on objects, tools, or controls.

Electro-Mechanical Technicians

- Annual Earnings: $43,880
- Growth: 9.7%
- Annual Job Openings: 2,000
- Self-Employed: 0.5%
- Part-Time: 6.7%
- Civilian Training Route: Associate degree

Operate, test, and maintain unmanned, automated, servo-mechanical, or electromechanical equipment. May operate unmanned submarines, aircraft, or other equipment at worksites, such as oil rigs, deep ocean exploration, or hazardous waste removal. May assist engineers in testing and designing robotics equipment. Test performance of electromechanical assemblies, using test instruments such as oscilloscopes, electronic voltmeters, and bridges. Read blueprints, schematics, diagrams, and technical orders to determine methods and sequences of assembly. Install electrical and electronic parts and hardware in housings or assemblies, using soldering equipment and hand tools. Align, fit, and assemble component parts, using hand tools, power tools, fixtures, templates, and microscopes. Inspect parts for surface defects. Analyze and record test results and prepare written testing documentation. Verify dimensions and clearances of parts to ensure conformance to specifications, using precision measuring instruments. Operate metalworking machines to fabricate housings, jigs, fittings, and fixtures. Repair, rework, and calibrate hydraulic and pneumatic assemblies and systems to meet operational specifications and tolerances. Train others to install, use, and maintain robots. Develop, test, and program new robots.

Military Job That Provides Training for It (see the description in Part II): Unmanned Vehicle (UV) Operations Specialists

Personality Type: Realistic. Realistic occupations frequently involve work activities that include practical, hands-on problems and solutions. They often deal with plants, animals, and real-world materials like wood, tools, and machinery. Many of the occupations require working outside and do not involve a lot of paperwork or working closely with others.

GOE—Interest Area: 15. Scientific Research, Engineering, and Mathematics. **Work Group:** 15.09. Engineering Technology. **Other Civilian Jobs in This Work Group:** Aerospace Engineering and Operations Technicians; Cartographers and Photogrammetrists; Civil Engineering Technicians; Electrical and Electronic Engineering Technicians; Electrical and Electronics Drafters; Electrical Drafters; Electrical Engineering Technicians; Electronic Drafters; Electronics Engineering Technicians; Environmental Engineering Technicians; Mapping Technicians; Mechanical Drafters; Mechanical Engineering Technicians; Surveying and Mapping Technicians; Surveying Technicians.

Skills—Equipment Maintenance: Performing routine maintenance on equipment and determining when and what kind of maintenance is needed. **Operation Monitoring:** Watching gauges, dials, or other indicators to make sure a machine is working properly. **Installation:** Installing equipment, machines, wiring, or programs to meet specifications. **Quality Control Analysis:** Conducting tests and inspections of products, services, or processes to evaluate quality or performance. **Operation and Control:** Controlling operations of equipment or systems. **Troubleshooting:** Determining causes of operating errors and deciding what to do about them. **Repairing:** Repairing machines or systems, using the needed tools. **Mathematics:** Using mathematics to solve problems.

Work Environment: Indoors; noisy; contaminants; hazardous equipment; standing; using hands on objects, tools, or controls.

Elevator Installers and Repairers

- Annual Earnings: $59,190
- Growth: 14.8%
- Annual Job Openings: 3,000
- Self-Employed: 0.4%
- Part-Time: No data available
- Civilian Training Route: Long-term on-the-job training

Assemble, install, repair, or maintain electric or hydraulic freight or passenger elevators, escalators, or dumbwaiters. Assemble, install, repair, and maintain elevators, escalators, moving sidewalks, and dumbwaiters, using hand and power tools and testing devices such as test lamps, ammeters, and voltmeters. Test newly installed equipment to ensure that it meets specifications, such as stopping at floors for set amounts of time. Locate malfunctions in brakes, motors, switches, and signal and control systems, using test equipment. Check that safety regulations and building codes are met and complete service reports verifying conformance to standards. Connect electrical wiring to control panels and electric motors. Read and interpret blueprints to determine the layout of system components, frameworks, and foundations and to select installation equipment. Adjust safety controls; counterweights; door mechanisms; and components such as valves, ratchets, seals, and brake linings. Inspect wiring connections, control panel hookups, door installations, and alignments and clearances of cars and hoistways to ensure that equipment will operate properly. Disassemble defective units and repair or replace parts such as locks, gears, cables, and electric wiring. Maintain logbooks that detail all repairs and checks performed. Participate in additional training to keep skills up to date. Attach guide shoes and rollers to minimize the lateral motion of cars as they travel through shafts. Connect car frames to counterweights, using steel cables. Bolt or weld steel rails to the walls of shafts to guide elevators, working from scaffolding or platforms. Assemble elevator cars, installing each car's platform, walls, and doors. Install outer doors and door frames at elevator entrances on each floor of a structure. Install electrical wires and controls by attaching conduit along shaft walls from floor to floor and then pulling plastic-covered wires through the conduit. Cut prefabricated sections of framework, rails, and other components to specified dimensions. Operate elevators to determine power demands and test power consumption to detect overload factors. Assemble electrically powered stairs, steel frameworks, and tracks and install associated motors and electrical wiring.

Military Jobs That Provide Training for It (see the descriptions in Part II): Construction Specialists; Ship Electricians

Personality Type: Realistic. Realistic occupations frequently involve work activities that include practical, hands-on problems and solutions. They often deal with plants, animals, and real-world materials like wood, tools, and machinery. Many of the occupations require working outside and do not involve a lot of paperwork or working closely with others.

GOE—Interest Area: 02. Architecture and Construction. **Work Group:** 02.05. Systems and Equipment Installation, Maintenance, and Repair. **Other Civilian Jobs in This Work Group:** Electrical and Electronics Repairers, Powerhouse, Substation, and Relay; Electrical Power-Line Installers and Repairers; Heating and Air Conditioning Mechanics and Installers; Maintenance and Repair Workers, General; Refrigeration Mechanics and Installers; Telecommunications Equipment Installers and Repairers, Except Line Installers; Telecommunications Line Installers and Repairers.

Skills—Installation: Installing equipment, machines, wiring, or programs to meet specifications. **Repairing:** Repairing machines or systems, using the needed tools. **Troubleshooting:** Determining causes of operating errors and deciding what to do about them. **Equipment Maintenance:** Performing routine maintenance on equipment and determining when and what kind of maintenance is needed. **Quality Control Analysis:** Conducting tests and inspections of products, services, or processes to evaluate quality or performance. **Technology Design:** Generating or adapting equipment and technology to serve user needs. **Equipment Selection:** Determining the kinds of tools and equipment needed to do a job. **Operation Monitoring:** Watching gauges, dials, or other indicators to make sure a machine is working properly.

Work Environment: Contaminants; high places; hazardous conditions; hazardous equipment; standing; using hands on objects, tools, or controls.

Emergency Medical Technicians and Paramedics

- Annual Earnings: $26,080
- Growth: 27.3%
- Annual Job Openings: 21,000
- Self-Employed: 0.1%
- Part-Time: 10.6%
- Civilian Training Route: Postsecondary vocational training

Assess injuries, administer emergency medical care, and extricate trapped individuals. Transport injured or sick persons to medical facilities. Administer first-aid treatment and life-support care to sick or injured persons in pre-hospital setting. Operate equipment such as electrocardiograms (EKGs), external defibrillators, and bag-valve mask resuscitators in advanced life-support environments. Assess nature and extent of illness or injury to establish and prioritize medical procedures. Maintain vehicles and medical and communication equipment and replenish first-aid equipment and supplies. Observe, record, and report to physician the patient's condition or injury, the treatment provided, and reactions to drugs and treatment. Perform emergency diagnostic and treatment procedures, such as stomach suction, airway management, or heart monitoring, during ambulance ride. Administer drugs, orally or by injection, and perform intravenous procedures under a physician's direction. Comfort and reassure patients. Coordinate work with other emergency medical team members and police and fire department personnel. Communicate with dispatchers and treatment center personnel to provide information about situation, to arrange reception of victims, and to receive instructions for further treatment. Immobilize patient for placement on stretcher and ambulance transport, using backboard or other spinal immobilization device. Decontaminate ambulance interior following treatment of patient with infectious disease and report case to proper authorities. Drive mobile intensive care unit to specified location, following instructions from emergency medical dispatcher. Coordinate with treatment center personnel to obtain patients' vital statistics and medical history, to determine the circumstances of the emergency, and to administer emergency treatment.

Military Job That Provides Training for It (see the description in Part II): Medical Service Technicians

Personality Type: Social. Social occupations frequently involve working with, communicating with, and teaching people. These occupations often involve helping or providing service to others.

GOE—Interest Area: 12. Law and Public Safety. **Work Group:** 12.06. Emergency Responding. **Other Civilian Jobs in This Work Group:** Fire Fighters; Forest Fire Fighters; Municipal Fire Fighters.

Skills—Equipment Maintenance: Performing routine maintenance on equipment and determining when and what kind of maintenance is needed. **Operation Monitoring:** Watching gauges, dials, or other indicators to make sure a machine is working properly. **Service Orientation:** Actively looking for ways to help people. **Social Perceptiveness:** Being aware of others' reactions and understanding why they react as they do. **Operation and Control:** Controlling operations of equipment or systems. **Coordination:** Adjusting actions in relation to others' actions. **Equipment Selection:** Determining the kinds of tools and equipment needed to do a job. **Speaking:** Talking to others to convey information effectively.

Work Environment: Outdoors; noisy; very bright or dim lighting; contaminants; cramped work space, awkward positions; disease or infections.

Executive Secretaries and Administrative Assistants

- Annual Earnings: $35,960
- Growth: 12.4%
- Annual Job Openings: 218,000
- Self-Employed: 1.2%
- Part-Time: 20.3%
- Civilian Training Route: Moderate-term on-the-job training

Provide high-level administrative support by conducting research; preparing statistical reports; handling information requests; and performing clerical functions such as preparing correspondence, receiving visitors, arranging conference calls, and scheduling meetings. May also train and supervise lower-level clerical staff. Manage and maintain executives' schedules. Prepare invoices, reports, memos, letters, financial statements, and other documents, using word-processing, spreadsheet, database, or presentation software. Open, sort, and distribute incoming correspondence, including faxes and e-mail. Read and analyze incoming memos, submissions, and reports to determine their significance and plan their distribution. File and retrieve corporate documents, records, and reports. Greet visitors and determine whether they should be given access to specific individuals. Prepare responses to correspondence containing routine inquiries. Perform general office duties such as ordering supplies, maintaining records management systems, and performing basic bookkeeping work. Prepare agendas and make arrangements for committee, board, and other meetings. Make travel arrangements for executives. Conduct research, compile data, and prepare papers for consideration and presentation by executives, committees, and boards of directors. Compile, transcribe, and distribute minutes of meetings. Attend meetings to record minutes. Coordinate and direct office services, such as records and budget preparation, personnel, and housekeeping, to aid executives. Meet with individuals, special-interest groups, and others on behalf of executives, committees, and boards of directors. Set up and oversee administrative policies and procedures for offices or organizations. Supervise and train other clerical staff. Review operating practices and procedures to determine whether improvements can be made in areas such as workflow, reporting procedures, or expenditures. Interpret administrative and operating policies and procedures for employees.

Military Job That Provides Training for It (see the description in Part II): Administrative Support Specialists

Personality Type: Conventional. Conventional occupations frequently involve following set procedures and routines. These occupations can include working with data and details more than with ideas. Usually there is a clear line of authority to follow.

GOE—Interest Area: 04. Business and Administration. **Work Group:** 04.04. Secretarial Support. **Other Civilian Jobs in This Work Group:** Legal Secretaries; Medical Secretaries; Secretaries, Except Legal, Medical, and Executive.

Skills—No data available.

Work Environment: Indoors; sitting; repetitive motions.

First-Line Supervisors/ Managers of Construction Trades and Extraction Workers

- Annual Earnings: $51,970
- Growth: 10.9%
- Annual Job Openings: 57,000
- Self-Employed: 24.7%
- Part-Time: 3.8%
- Civilian Training Route: Work experience in a related occupation

Directly supervise and coordinate activities of construction or extraction workers. Examine and inspect work progress, equipment, and construction sites to verify safety and to ensure that specifications are met. Read specifications such as blueprints to determine construction requirements and to plan procedures. Estimate material and worker requirements to complete jobs. Supervise, coordinate, and schedule the activities of construction or extractive workers. Confer with managerial and technical personnel, other departments, and contractors to resolve problems and to coordinate activities. Coordinate work activities with other construction project activities. Locate, measure, and mark site locations and placement of structures and equipment, using measuring and marking equipment. Order or requisition materials and supplies. Record information such as personnel, production, and operational data on specified forms and reports. Assign work to employees based on material and worker requirements of specific jobs. Provide assistance to workers engaged in construction or extraction activities, using hand tools and equipment. Train workers in construction methods, operation of equipment, safety procedures, and company policies. Analyze worker and production problems and recommend solutions, such as improving production methods or implementing motivational plans. Arrange for repairs of equipment and machinery. Suggest or initiate personnel actions such as promotions, transfers, and hires.

Military Jobs That Provide Training for It (see the descriptions in Part II): Building Electricians; Construction Equipment Operators; Construction Specialists

Personality Type: Enterprising. Enterprising occupations frequently involve starting up and carrying out projects. These occupations can involve leading people and making many decisions. They sometimes require risk taking and often deal with business.

GOE—Interest Area: 01. Agriculture and Natural Resources. **Work Group:** 01.01. Managerial Work in Agriculture and Natural Resources. **Other Civilian Jobs in This Work Group:** Aquacultural Managers; Crop and Livestock Managers; Farm Labor Contractors; Farm, Ranch, and Other Agricultural Managers; Farmers and Ranchers; First-Line Supervisors/Managers of Agricultural Crop and Horticultural Workers; First-Line Supervisors/Managers of Animal Husbandry and Animal Care Workers; First-Line Supervisors/Managers of Aquacultural Workers; First-Line Supervisors/Managers of Farming, Fishing, and Forestry Workers; First-Line Supervisors/Managers of Landscaping, Lawn Service, and Groundskeeping Workers; First-Line Supervisors/Managers of Logging Workers; Nursery and Greenhouse Managers; Park Naturalists; Purchasing Agents and Buyers, Farm Products.

Skills—Management of Material Resources: Obtaining and seeing to the appropriate use of equipment, facilities, and materials needed to do certain work. **Installation:** Installing equipment, machines, wiring, or programs to meet specifications. **Equipment Maintenance:** Performing routine maintenance on equipment and determining when and what kind of maintenance is needed. **Coordination:** Adjusting actions in relation to others' actions. **Repairing:** Repairing machines or systems, using the needed tools. **Management of Personnel Resources:** Motivating, developing, and directing people as they work; identifying the best people for the job. **Equipment Selection:** Determining the kinds of tools and equipment needed to do a job. **Negotiation:** Bringing others together and trying to reconcile differences.

Work Environment: Outdoors; noisy; very hot or cold; contaminants; hazardous equipment; standing.

First-Line Supervisors/Managers of Food Preparation and Serving Workers

- Annual Earnings: $26,050
- Growth: 16.6%
- Annual Job Openings: 187,000
- Self-Employed: 3.7%
- Part-Time: 15.5%
- Civilian Training Route: Work experience in a related occupation

Supervise workers engaged in preparing and serving food. Compile and balance cash receipts at the end of the day or shift. Resolve customer complaints regarding food service. Inspect supplies, equipment, and work areas to ensure efficient service and conformance to standards. Train workers in food preparation and in service, sanitation, and safety procedures. Control inventories of food, equipment, smallware, and liquor and report shortages to designated personnel. Observe and evaluate workers and work procedures to ensure quality standards and service. Assign duties, responsibilities, and workstations to employees in accordance with work requirements. Estimate ingredients and supplies required to prepare a recipe. Perform personnel actions such as hiring and firing staff, consulting with other managers as necessary. Analyze operational problems, such as theft and wastage, and establish procedures to alleviate these problems.

Specify food portions and courses, production and time sequences, and workstation and equipment arrangements. Recommend measures for improving work procedures and worker performance to increase service quality and enhance job safety. Greet and seat guests and present menus and wine lists. Present bills and accept payments. Forecast staff, equipment, and supply requirements based on a master menu. Record production and operational data on specified forms. Perform serving duties such as carving meat, preparing flambé dishes, or serving wine and liquor. Purchase or requisition supplies and equipment needed to ensure quality and timely delivery of services. Collaborate with other personnel to plan menus, serving arrangements, and related details. Supervise and check the assembly of regular and special diet trays and the delivery of food trolleys to hospital patients. Schedule parties and take reservations. Develop departmental objectives, budgets, policies, procedures, and strategies. Develop equipment maintenance schedules and arrange for repairs. Evaluate new products for usefulness and suitability.

Military Job That Provides Training for It (see the description in Part II): Food Service Specialists

Personality Type: Enterprising. Enterprising occupations frequently involve starting up and carrying out projects. These occupations can involve leading people and making many decisions. They sometimes require risk taking and often deal with business.

GOE—Interest Area: 09. Hospitality, Tourism, and Recreation. **Work Group:** 09.01. Managerial Work in Hospitality and Tourism. **Other Civilian Jobs in This Work Group:** First-Line Supervisors/Managers of Personal Service Workers; Food Service Managers; Gaming Managers; Gaming Supervisors; Lodging Managers.

Skills—No data available.

Work Environment: Indoors; minor burns, cuts, bites, or stings; standing; walking and running; using hands on objects, tools, or controls; repetitive motions.

First-Line Supervisors/ Managers of Housekeeping and Janitorial Workers

- Annual Earnings: $30,330
- Growth: 19.0%
- Annual Job Openings: 21,000
- Self-Employed: 8.9%
- Part-Time: 14.9%
- Civilian Training Route: Work experience in a related occupation

Supervise work activities of cleaning personnel in hotels, hospitals, offices, and other establishments. Direct activities for stopping the spread of infections in facilities such as hospitals. Inspect work performed to ensure that it meets specifications and established standards. Plan and prepare employee work schedules. Perform or assist with cleaning duties as necessary. Investigate complaints about service and equipment and take corrective action. Coordinate activities with other departments to ensure that services are provided in an efficient and timely manner. Check equipment to ensure that it is in working order. Inspect and evaluate the physical condition of facilities to determine the type of work required. Select the most suitable cleaning materials for different types of linens, furniture, flooring, and surfaces. Instruct staff in work policies and procedures and the use and maintenance of equipment. Issue supplies and equipment to workers. Forecast necessary levels of staffing and stock at different times to facilitate effective scheduling and ordering. Inventory stock to ensure that supplies and equipment are available in adequate amounts. Evaluate employee performance and recommend personnel actions such as promotions, transfers, and dismissals. Confer with staff to resolve performance and personnel problems and to discuss company policies. Establish and implement operational standards and procedures for the departments they supervise. Recommend or arrange for additional services such as painting, repair work, renovations, and the replacement of furnishings and equipment. Select and order or purchase new equipment, supplies, and furnishings. Recommend changes that could improve service and increase operational efficiency. Maintain required records of work hours, budgets, payrolls, and other information. Screen job applicants and hire new employees. Supervise in-house services such as laundries, maintenance and repair, dry cleaning, and valet services. Advise managers, desk clerks, or admitting personnel of rooms ready for occupancy. Perform financial tasks such as estimating costs and preparing and managing budgets. Prepare activity and personnel reports and reports containing information such as occupancy, hours worked, facility usage, work performed, and departmental expenses.

Military Job That Provides Training for It (see the description in Part II): Administrative Support Specialists

Personality Type: Enterprising. Enterprising occupations frequently involve starting up and carrying out projects. These occupations can involve leading people and making many decisions. They sometimes require risk taking and often deal with business.

GOE—Interest Area: 04. Business and Administration. **Work Group:** 04.02. Managerial Work in Business Detail. **Other Civilian Jobs in This Work Group:** Administrative Services Managers; First-Line Supervisors/Managers of Office and Administrative Support Workers; Meeting and Convention Planners.

Skills—Management of Personnel Resources: Motivating, developing, and directing people as they work; identifying the best people for the job. **Monitoring:** Monitoring/assessing your performance or that of other individuals or organizations to make improvements or take corrective action. **Service Orientation:** Actively looking for ways to help people. **Equipment Maintenance:** Performing routine maintenance on equipment and determining when and what kind of maintenance is needed. **Systems Evaluation:** Identifying measures or indicators of system performance and the actions needed to improve or correct performance relative to the goals of the system. **Writing:** Communicating effectively in writing as appropriate for the needs of the audience. **Equipment Selection:** Determining the kinds of tools and equipment needed to do a job. **Persuasion:** Persuading others to change their minds or behavior.

Work Environment: Indoors; contaminants; disease or infections; standing; walking and running.

F

First-Line Supervisors/ Managers of Mechanics, Installers, and Repairers

- Annual Earnings: $51,980
- Growth: 12.4%
- Annual Job Openings: 33,000
- Self-Employed: 0.3%
- Part-Time: 1.0%
- Civilian Training Route: Work experience in a related occupation

Supervise and coordinate the activities of mechanics, installers, and repairers. Determine schedules, sequences, and assignments for work activities based on work priority, quantity of equipment, and skill of personnel. Patrol and monitor work areas and examine tools and equipment to detect unsafe conditions or violations of procedures or safety rules. Monitor employees' work levels and review work performance. Examine objects, systems, or facilities and analyze information to determine needed installations, services, or repairs. Participate in budget preparation and administration, coordinating purchasing and documentation and monitoring departmental expenditures. Counsel employees about work-related issues and assist employees in correcting job-skill deficiencies. Requisition materials and supplies, such as tools, equipment, and replacement parts. Compute estimates and actual costs of factors such as materials, labor, and outside contractors. Conduct or arrange for worker training in safety, repair, and maintenance techniques; operational procedures; or equipment use. Interpret specifications, blueprints, and job orders to construct templates and lay out reference points for workers. Investigate accidents and injuries and prepare reports of findings. Confer with personnel, such as management, engineering, quality control, customer, and union workers' representatives, to coordinate work activities, resolve employee grievances, and identify and review resource needs. Recommend or initiate personnel actions, such as hires, promotions, transfers, discharges, and disciplinary measures. Perform skilled repair and maintenance operations, using equipment such as hand and power tools, hydraulic presses and shears, and welding equipment. Compile operational and personnel records, such as time and production records, inventory data, repair and maintenance statistics, and test results. Develop, implement, and evaluate maintenance policies and procedures. Monitor tool inventories and the condition and maintenance of shops to ensure adequate working conditions. Inspect, test, and measure completed work, using devices such as hand tools and gauges to verify conformance to standards and repair requirements.

Military Jobs That Provide Training for It (see the descriptions in Part II): Aircraft Mechanics; Automotive and Heavy Equipment Mechanics; Avionics Technicians; Building Electricians; Communications Equipment Operators; Electrical Products Repairers; Electronic Instrument and Equipment Repairers; Heating and Cooling Mechanics; Power Plant Operators; Powerhouse Mechanics; Precision Instrument and Equipment Repairers; Survival Equipment Specialists; Water and Sewage Treatment Plant Operators; Weapons Maintenance Technicians; Welders and Metal Workers

Personality Type: Enterprising. Enterprising occupations frequently involve starting up and carrying out projects. These occupations can involve leading people and making many decisions. They sometimes require risk taking and often deal with business.

GOE—Interest Area: 13. Manufacturing. **Work Group:** 13.01. Managerial Work in Manufacturing. **Other Civilian Jobs in This Work Group:** First-Line Supervisors/Managers of Helpers, Laborers, and Material Movers, Hand; First-Line Supervisors/Managers of Production and Operating Workers; Industrial Production Managers.

Skills—Installation: Installing equipment, machines, wiring, or programs to meet specifications. **Repairing:** Repairing machines or systems, using the needed tools. **Management of Personnel Resources:** Motivating, developing, and directing people as they work; identifying the best people for the job. **Management of Material Resources:** Obtaining and seeing to the appropriate use of equipment, facilities, and materials needed to do certain work. **Management of Financial Resources:** Determining how money will be spent to get the work done and accounting for these expenditures. **Equipment Maintenance:** Performing routine maintenance on equipment and determining when and what kind of maintenance is needed. **Troubleshooting:** Determining causes of operating errors and deciding what to do about them. **Negotiation:** Bringing others together and trying to reconcile differences.

Work Environment: More often indoors than outdoors; noisy; very hot or cold; contaminants; standing.

First-Line Supervisors/ Managers of Office and Administrative Support Workers

- Annual Earnings: $42,400
- Growth: 8.1%
- Annual Job Openings: 167,000
- Self-Employed: 1.5%
- Part-Time: 8.3%
- Civilian Training Route: Work experience in a related occupation

Supervise and coordinate the activities of clerical and administrative support workers. Resolve customer complaints and answer customers' questions regarding policies and procedures. Supervise the work of office, administrative, or customer service employees to ensure adherence to quality standards, deadlines, and proper procedures, correcting errors or problems. Provide employees with guidance in handling difficult or complex problems and in resolving escalated complaints or disputes. Implement corporate and departmental policies, procedures, and service standards in conjunction with management. Discuss job performance problems with employees to identify causes and issues and to work on resolving problems. Train and instruct employees in job duties and company policies or arrange for training to be provided. Evaluate employees' job performance and conformance to regulations and recommend appropriate personnel action. Recruit, interview, and select employees. Review records and reports pertaining to activities such as production, payroll, and shipping to verify details, monitor work activities, and evaluate performance. Interpret and communicate work procedures and company policies to staff. Prepare and issue work schedules, deadlines, and duty assignments of office or administrative staff. Maintain records pertaining to inventory, personnel, orders, supplies, and machine maintenance. Compute figures such as balances, totals, and commissions. Research, compile, and prepare reports, manuals, correspondence, and other information required by management or governmental agencies. Coordinate activities with other supervisory personnel and with other work units or departments. Analyze financial activities of establishments or departments and provide input into budget planning and preparation processes. Develop or update procedures, policies, and standards. Make recommendations to management concerning such issues as staffing decisions and procedural changes. Consult with managers and other personnel to resolve problems in areas such as equipment performance, output quality, and work schedules. Participate in the work of subordinates to facilitate productivity or to overcome difficult aspects of work.

Military Jobs That Provide Training for It (see the descriptions in Part II): Administrative Support Specialists; Computer Systems Specialists; Electronic Instrument and Equipment Repairers; Finance and Accounting Specialists; Medical Record Technicians; Personnel Specialists; Preventive Maintenance Analysts; Warehousing and Distribution Specialists

Personality Type: Enterprising. Enterprising occupations frequently involve starting up and carrying out projects. These occupations can involve leading people and making many decisions. They sometimes require risk taking and often deal with business.

GOE—Interest Area: 04. Business and Administration. **Work Group:** 04.02. Managerial Work in Business Detail. **Other Civilian Jobs in This Work Group:** Administrative Services Managers; First-Line Supervisors/Managers of Housekeeping and Janitorial Workers; Meeting and Convention Planners.

Skills—Management of Personnel Resources: Motivating, developing, and directing people as they work; identifying the best people for the job. **Management of Financial Resources:** Determining how money will be spent to get the work done and accounting for these expenditures. **Negotiation:** Bringing others together and trying to reconcile differences. **Management of Material Resources:** Obtaining and seeing to the appropriate use of equipment, facilities, and materials needed to do certain work. **Persuasion:** Persuading others to change their minds or behavior. **Monitoring:** Monitoring/assessing your performance or that of other individuals or organizations to make improvements or take corrective action. **Service Orientation:** Actively looking for ways to help people. **Systems Analysis:** Determining how a system should work and how changes in conditions, operations, and the environment will affect outcomes.

Work Environment: Indoors; noisy; sitting.

First-Line Supervisors/ Managers of Police and Detectives

- Annual Earnings: $65,570
- Growth: 15.5%
- Annual Job Openings: 9,000
- Self-Employed: 0.0%
- Part-Time: 0.9%
- Civilian Training Route: Work experience in a related occupation

Supervise and coordinate activities of members of police force. Explain police operations to subordinates to assist them in performing their job duties. Inform personnel of changes in regulations and policies, implications of new or amended laws, and new techniques of police work. Supervise and coordinate the investigation of criminal cases, offering guidance and expertise to investigators and ensuring that procedures are conducted in accordance with laws and regulations. Investigate and resolve personnel problems within organization and charges of misconduct against staff. Train staff in proper police work procedures. Maintain logs; prepare reports; and direct the preparation, handling, and maintenance of departmental records. Monitor and evaluate the job performance of subordinates and authorize promotions and transfers. Direct collection, preparation, and handling of evidence and personal property of prisoners. Develop, implement, and revise departmental policies and procedures. Conduct raids and order detention of witnesses and suspects for questioning. Prepare work schedules and assign duties to subordinates. Discipline staff for violation of department rules and regulations. Cooperate with court personnel and officials from other law enforcement agencies and testify in court as necessary. Review contents of written orders to ensure adherence to legal requirements. Inspect facilities, supplies, vehicles, and equipment to ensure conformance to standards. Prepare news releases and respond to police correspondence. Requisition and issue equipment and supplies. Meet with civic, educational, and community groups to develop community programs and events and to discuss law enforcement subjects. Direct release or transfer of prisoners. Prepare budgets and manage expenditures of department funds.

Military Job That Provides Training for It (see the description in Part II): Law Enforcement and Security Specialists

Personality Type: Enterprising. Enterprising occupations frequently involve starting up and carrying out projects. These occupations can involve leading people and making many decisions. They sometimes require risk taking and often deal with business.

GOE—Interest Area: 12. Law and Public Safety. **Work Group:** 12.01. Managerial Work in Law and Public Safety. **Other Civilian Jobs in This Work Group:** Emergency Management Specialists; First-Line Supervisors/Managers of Correctional Officers; First-Line Supervisors/ Managers of Fire Fighting and Prevention Workers; Forest Fire Fighting and Prevention Supervisors; Municipal Fire Fighting and Prevention Supervisors.

Skills—Management of Personnel Resources: Motivating, developing, and directing people as they work; identifying the best people for the job. **Persuasion:** Persuading others to change their minds or behavior. **Negotiation:** Bringing others together and trying to reconcile differences. **Social Perceptiveness:** Being aware of others' reactions and understanding why they react as they do. **Service Orientation:** Actively looking for ways to help people. **Monitoring:** Monitoring/assessing your performance or that of other individuals or organizations to make improvements or take corrective action. **Judgment and Decision Making:** Considering the relative costs and benefits of potential actions to choose the most appropriate one. **Management of Material Resources:** Obtaining and seeing to the appropriate use of equipment, facilities, and materials needed to do certain work.

Work Environment: More often outdoors than indoors; very hot or cold; very bright or dim lighting; hazardous equipment; sitting.

First-Line Supervisors/ Managers of Production and Operating Workers

- Annual Earnings: $46,140
- Growth: 2.7%
- Annual Job Openings: 89,000
- Self-Employed: 3.9%
- Part-Time: 2.3%
- Civilian Training Route: Work experience in a related occupation

Supervise and coordinate the activities of production and operating workers, such as inspectors, precision workers, machine setters and operators, assemblers, fabricators, and plant and system operators. Enforce safety and sanitation regulations. Direct and coordinate the activities of employees engaged in the production or processing of goods, such as inspectors, machine setters, and fabricators. Read and analyze charts, work orders, production schedules, and other records and reports to determine production requirements and to evaluate current production estimates and outputs. Confer with other supervisors to coordinate operations and activities within or between departments. Plan and establish work schedules, assignments, and production sequences to meet production goals. Inspect materials, products, or equipment to detect defects or malfunctions. Demonstrate equipment operations and work and safety procedures to new employees or assign employees to experienced workers for training. Observe work and monitor gauges, dials, and other indicators to ensure that operators conform to production or processing standards. Interpret specifications, blueprints, job orders, and company policies and procedures for workers. Confer with management or subordinates to resolve worker problems, complaints, or grievances. Maintain operations data such as time, production, and cost records and prepare management reports of production results. Recommend or implement measures to motivate employees and to improve production methods, equipment performance, product quality, or efficiency. Determine standards, budgets, production goals, and rates based on company policies, equipment and labor availability, and workloads. Requisition materials, supplies, equipment parts, or repair services. Recommend personnel actions such as hirings and promotions. Set up and adjust machines and equipment. Calculate labor and equipment requirements and production specifications, using standard formulas. Plan and develop new products and production processes.

Military Jobs That Provide Training for It (see the descriptions in Part II): Petroleum Supply Specialists; Power Plant Operators; Precision Instrument and Equipment Repairers; Water and Sewage Treatment Plant Operators; Welders and Metal Workers

Personality Type: Enterprising. Enterprising occupations frequently involve starting up and carrying out projects. These occupations can involve leading people and making many decisions. They sometimes require risk taking and often deal with business.

GOE—Interest Area: 13. Manufacturing. **Work Group:** 13.01. Managerial Work in Manufacturing. **Other Civilian Jobs in This Work Group:** First-Line Supervisors/Managers of Helpers, Laborers, and Material Movers, Hand; First-Line Supervisors/Managers of Mechanics, Installers, and Repairers; Industrial Production Managers.

Skills—Management of Personnel Resources: Motivating, developing, and directing people as they work; identifying the best people for the job. **Operation Monitoring:** Watching gauges, dials, or other indicators to make sure a machine is working properly. **Operation and Control:** Controlling operations of equipment or systems. **Quality Control Analysis:** Conducting tests and inspections of products, services, or processes to evaluate quality or performance. **Systems Analysis:** Determining how a system should work and how changes in conditions, operations, and the environment will affect outcomes. **Operations Analysis:** Analyzing needs and product requirements to create a design. **Monitoring:** Monitoring/assessing your performance or that of other individuals or organizations to make improvements or take corrective action. **Systems Evaluation:** Identifying measures or indicators of system performance and the actions needed to improve or correct performance relative to the goals of the system.

Work Environment: Indoors; noisy; contaminants; hazardous equipment; standing; walking and running.

First-Line Supervisors/ Managers of Retail Sales Workers

- Annual Earnings: $32,840
- Growth: 3.8%
- Annual Job Openings: 229,000
- Self-Employed: 31.9%
- Part-Time: 9.4%
- Civilian Training Route: Work experience in a related occupation

Directly supervise sales workers in a retail establishment or department. Duties may include management functions, such as purchasing, budgeting, accounting, and personnel work, in addition to supervisory duties. Provide customer service by greeting and assisting customers and responding to customer inquiries and complaints. Assign employees to specific duties. Monitor sales activities to ensure that customers receive satisfactory service and quality goods. Direct and supervise employees engaged in sales, inventory-taking, reconciling cash receipts, or performing services for customers. Inventory stock and reorder when inventory drops to a specified level. Keep records of purchases, sales, and requisitions. Enforce safety, health, and security rules. Examine products purchased for resale or received for storage to assess the condition of each product or item. Hire, train, and evaluate personnel in sales or marketing establishments, promoting or firing workers when appropriate. Perform work activities of subordinates, such as cleaning and organizing shelves and displays and selling merchandise. Establish and implement policies, goals, objectives, and procedures for their department. Instruct staff on how to handle difficult and complicated sales. Formulate pricing policies for merchandise according to profitability requirements. Estimate consumer demand and determine the types and amounts of goods to be sold. Examine merchandise to ensure that it is correctly priced and displayed and that it functions as advertised. Plan and prepare work schedules and keep records of employees' work schedules and time cards. Review inventory and sales records to prepare reports for management and budget departments. Plan and coordinate advertising campaigns and sales promotions and prepare merchandise displays and advertising copy. Confer with company officials to develop methods and procedures to increase sales, expand markets, and promote business. Establish credit policies and operating procedures. Plan budgets and authorize payments and merchandise returns.

Military Job That Provides Training for It (see the description in Part II): Sales and Stock Specialists

Personality Type: Enterprising. Enterprising occupations frequently involve starting up and carrying out projects. These occupations can involve leading people and making many decisions. They sometimes require risk taking and often deal with business.

GOE—Interest Area: 14. Retail and Wholesale Sales and Service. **Work Group:** 14.01. Managerial Work in Retail/Wholesale Sales and Service. **Other Civilian Jobs in This Work Group:** Advertising and Promotions Managers; First-Line Supervisors/Managers of Non-Retail Sales Workers; Funeral Directors; Marketing Managers; Property, Real Estate, and Community Association Managers; Purchasing Managers; Sales Managers.

Skills—Management of Personnel Resources: Motivating, developing, and directing people as they work; identifying the best people for the job. **Management of Financial Resources:** Determining how money will be spent to get the work done and accounting for these expenditures. **Persuasion:** Persuading others to change their minds or behavior. **Repairing:** Repairing machines or systems, using the needed tools. **Equipment Maintenance:** Performing routine maintenance on equipment and determining when and what kind of maintenance is needed. **Monitoring:** Monitoring/assessing your performance or that of other individuals or organizations to make improvements or take corrective action. **Instructing:** Teaching others how to do something. **Social Perceptiveness:** Being aware of others' reactions and understanding why they react as they do.

Work Environment: Indoors; hazardous equipment; standing; walking and running; using hands on objects, tools, or controls.

First-Line Supervisors/ Managers of Transportation and Material-Moving Machine and Vehicle Operators

- Annual Earnings: $47,530
- Growth: 15.3%
- Annual Job Openings: 22,000
- Self-Employed: 1.3%
- Part-Time: 4.9%
- Civilian Training Route: Work experience in a related occupation

Directly supervise and coordinate activities of transportation and material-moving machine and vehicle operators and helpers. Enforce safety rules and regulations. Plan work assignments and equipment allocations to meet transportation, operations, or production goals. Confer with customers, supervisors, contractors, and other personnel to exchange information and to resolve problems. Direct workers in transportation or related services, such as pumping, moving, storing, and loading and unloading of materials or people. Resolve worker problems or collaborate with employees to assist in problem resolution. Review orders, production schedules, blueprints, and shipping and receiving notices to determine work sequences and material shipping dates, types, volumes, and destinations. Monitor fieldwork to ensure that it is being performed properly and that materials are being used as they should be. Recommend and implement measures to improve worker motivation, equipment performance, work methods, and customer services. Maintain or verify records of time, materials, expenditures, and crew activities. Interpret transportation and tariff regulations, shipping orders, safety regulations, and company policies and procedures for workers. Explain and demonstrate work tasks to new workers or assign workers to more experienced workers for further training. Prepare, compile, and submit reports on work activities, operations, production, and work-related accidents. Recommend or implement personnel actions such as employee selection, evaluation, and rewards or disciplinary actions. Requisition needed personnel, supplies, equipment, parts, or repair services. Inspect or test materials, stock, vehicles, equipment, and facilities to ensure that they are safe, are free of defects, and meet specifications. Plan and establish transportation routes. Compute and estimate cash, payroll, transportation, personnel, and storage requirements. Dispatch personnel and vehicles in response to telephone or radio reports of emergencies. Perform or schedule repairs and preventive maintenance of vehicles and other equipment. Examine, measure, and weigh cargo or materials to determine specific handling requirements. Provide workers with assistance in performing tasks such as coupling railroad cars or loading vehicles.

Military Jobs That Provide Training for It (see the descriptions in Part II): Flight Operations Specialists; Transportation Specialists; Vehicle Drivers

Personality Type: Enterprising. Enterprising occupations frequently involve starting up and carrying out projects. These occupations can involve leading people and making many decisions. They sometimes require risk taking and often deal with business.

GOE—Interest Area: 16. Transportation, Distribution, and Logistics. **Work Group:** 16.01. Managerial Work in Transportation. **Other Civilian Jobs in This Work Group:** Aircraft Cargo Handling Supervisors; Postmasters and Mail Superintendents; Railroad Conductors and Yardmasters; Storage and Distribution Managers; Transportation Managers; Transportation, Storage, and Distribution Managers.

Skills—Management of Personnel Resources: Motivating, developing, and directing people as they work; identifying the best people for the job. **Management of Financial Resources:** Determining how money will be spent to get the work done and accounting for these expenditures. **Management of Material Resources:** Obtaining and seeing to the appropriate use of equipment, facilities, and materials needed to do certain work. **Social Perceptiveness:** Being aware of others' reactions and understanding why they react as they do. **Systems Evaluation:** Identifying measures or indicators of system performance and the actions needed to improve or correct performance relative to the goals of the system. **Monitoring:** Monitoring/assessing your performance or that of other individuals or organizations to make improvements or take corrective action. **Operations Analysis:** Analyzing needs and product requirements to create a design. **Persuasion:** Persuading others to change their minds or behavior.

Work Environment: Indoors; noisy; contaminants; sitting.

Food Preparation Workers

- Annual Earnings: $17,040
- Growth: 19.7%
- Annual Job Openings: 294,000
- Self-Employed: 0.7%
- Part-Time: 53.7%
- Civilian Training Route: Short-term on-the-job training

Perform a variety of food preparation duties other than cooking, such as preparing cold foods and shellfish, slicing meat, and brewing coffee or tea. Clean work areas, equipment, utensils, dishes, and silverware. Store food in designated containers and storage areas to prevent spoilage. Prepare a variety of foods according to customers' orders or supervisors' instructions, following approved procedures. Package take-out foods or serve food to customers. Portion and wrap the food or place it directly on plates for service to patrons. Place food trays over food warmers for immediate service or store them in refrigerated storage cabinets. Inform supervisors when supplies are getting low or equipment is not working properly. Weigh or measure ingredients. Assist cooks and kitchen staff with various tasks as needed and provide cooks with needed items. Wash, peel, and cut various foods to prepare for cooking or serving. Receive and store food supplies, equipment, and utensils in refrigerators, cupboards, and other storage areas. Stock cupboards and refrigerators and tend salad bars and buffet meals. Remove trash and clean kitchen garbage containers. Prepare and serve a variety of beverages such as coffee, tea, and soft drinks. Carry food supplies, equipment, and utensils to and from storage and work areas. Make special dressings and sauces as condiments for sandwiches. Scrape leftovers from dishes into garbage containers. Use manual or electric appliances to clean, peel, slice, and trim foods. Stir and strain soups and sauces. Distribute food to waiters and waitresses to serve to customers. Keep records of the quantities of food used. Load dishes, glasses, and tableware into dishwashing machines. Butcher and clean fowl, fish, poultry, and shellfish to prepare for cooking or serving. Cut, slice, or grind meat, poultry, and seafood to prepare for cooking. Work on assembly lines adding cutlery, napkins, food, and other items to trays in hospitals, cafeterias, airline kitchens, and similar establishments. Mix ingredients for green salads, molded fruit salads, vegetable salads, and pasta salads. Distribute menus to hospital patients, collect diet sheets, and deliver food trays and snacks to nursing units or directly to patients.

Military Job That Provides Training for It (see the description in Part II): Food Service Specialists

Personality Type: Realistic. Realistic occupations frequently involve work activities that include practical, hands-on problems and solutions. They often deal with plants, animals, and real-world materials like wood, tools, and machinery. Many of the occupations require working outside and do not involve a lot of paperwork or working closely with others.

GOE—Interest Area: 09. Hospitality, Tourism, and Recreation. **Work Group:** 09.04. Food and Beverage Preparation. **Other Civilian Jobs in This Work Group:** Butchers and Meat Cutters; Chefs and Head Cooks; Cooks, Fast Food; Cooks, Institution and Cafeteria; Cooks, Private Household; Cooks, Restaurant; Cooks, Short Order; Dishwashers.

Skills—No data available.

Work Environment: Indoors; minor burns, cuts, bites, or stings; standing; walking and running; using hands on objects, tools, or controls; repetitive motions.

Gas Plant Operators

- Annual Earnings: $51,920
- Growth: 7.7%
- Annual Job Openings: 2,000
- Self-Employed: 0.1%
- Part-Time: 0.8%
- Civilian Training Route: Long-term on-the-job training

Distribute or process gas for utility companies and others by controlling compressors to maintain specified pressures on main pipelines. Determine causes of abnormal pressure variances and make corrective recommendations such as installation of pipes to relieve overloading. Distribute or process gas for utility companies or industrial plants, using panel boards, control boards, and semi-automatic equipment. Start and shut down plant equipment. Test gas, chemicals, and air during processing to assess factors such as purity and moisture content and to detect quality problems or gas or chemical leaks. Adjust temperature, pressure, vacuum, level, flow rate, and transfer of gas to maintain processes at required levels or to correct problems. Change charts in recording meters. Calculate gas ratios to detect deviations from specifications, using testing apparatus. Clean, maintain, and repair equipment, using hand tools, or request that repair and maintenance work be performed. Collaborate with other operators to solve unit problems. Monitor equipment functioning; observe temperature, level, and flow gauges; and perform regular unit checks to ensure that all equipment is operating as it should. Control fractioning columns, compressors, purifying towers, heat exchangers, and related equipment to extract nitrogen and oxygen from air. Control equipment to regulate flow and pressure of gas to feedlines of boilers, furnaces, and related steam-generating or heating equipment. Operate construction equipment to install and maintain gas distribution systems. Signal or direct workers who tend auxiliary equipment. Record, review, and compile operations records; test results; and gauge readings such as temperatures, pressures, concentrations, and flows. Read logsheets to determine product demand and disposition or to detect malfunctions. Monitor transportation and storage of flammable and other potentially dangerous products to ensure that safety guidelines are followed. Contact maintenance crews when necessary. Control operation of compressors, scrubbers, evaporators, and refrigeration equipment to liquefy, compress, or regasify natural gas.

Military Job That Provides Training for It (see the description in Part II): Power Plant Operators

Personality Type: Realistic. Realistic occupations frequently involve work activities that include practical, hands-on problems and solutions. They often deal with plants, animals, and real-world materials like wood, tools, and machinery. Many of the occupations require working outside and do not involve a lot of paperwork or working closely with others.

GOE—Interest Area: 13. Manufacturing. **Work Group:** 13.16. Utility Operation and Energy Distribution. **Other Civilian Jobs in This Work Group:** Chemical Plant and System Operators; Gas Compressor and Gas Pumping Station Operators; Nuclear Power Reactor Operators; Petroleum Pump System Operators, Refinery Operators, and Gaugers; Power Distributors and Dispatchers; Power Plant Operators; Ship Engineers; Stationary Engineers and Boiler Operators; Water and Liquid Waste Treatment Plant and System Operators.

Skills—No data available.

Work Environment: Indoors; contaminants; hazardous conditions; standing; using hands on objects, tools, or controls.

Graphic Designers

- Annual Earnings: $38,390
- Growth: 15.2%
- Annual Job Openings: 35,000
- Self-Employed: 25.6%
- Part-Time: 21.3%
- Civilian Training Route: Bachelor's degree

Design or create graphics to meet specific commercial or promotional needs, such as packaging, displays, or logos. May use a variety of media to achieve artistic or decorative effects. Create designs, concepts, and sample layouts based on knowledge of layout principles and esthetic design concepts. Determine size and arrangement of illustrative material and copy and select style and size of type. Use computer software to generate new images. Mark up, paste, and assemble final layouts to prepare layouts for printer. Draw and print charts, graphs, illustrations, and other artwork, using computer. Review final layouts and suggest improvements as needed. Confer with clients to discuss and determine layout design. Develop graphics and layouts for product illustrations, company logos, and Internet Web sites. Key information into computer equipment to create layouts for client or supervisor. Prepare illustrations or rough sketches of material, discussing them with clients or supervisors and making necessary changes. Study illustrations and photographs to plan presentation of materials, products, or services. Prepare notes and instructions for workers who assemble and prepare final layouts for printing. Develop negatives and prints to produce layout photographs, using negative and print developing equipment and tools. Photograph layouts, using camera, to make layout prints for supervisors or clients. Produce still and animated graphics for on-air and taped portions of television news broadcasts, using electronic video equipment.

Military Job That Provides Training for It (see the description in Part II): Graphic Designers and Illustrators

Personality Type: Artistic. Artistic occupations frequently involve working with forms, designs, and patterns. They often require self-expression, and the work can be done without following a clear set of rules.

GOE—Interest Area: 03. Arts and Communication. **Work Group:** 03.05. Design. **Other Civilian Jobs in This Work Group:** Commercial and Industrial Designers; Fashion Designers; Floral Designers; Interior Designers; Merchandise Displayers and Window Trimmers; Set and Exhibit Designers.

Skills—Persuasion: Persuading others to change their minds or behavior. **Operations Analysis:** Analyzing needs and product requirements to create a design. **Troubleshooting:** Determining causes of operating errors and deciding what to do about them. **Time Management:** Managing one's own time and the time of others. **Complex Problem Solving:** Identifying complex problems and reviewing related information to develop and evaluate options and implement solutions. **Quality Control Analysis:** Conducting tests and inspections of products, services, or processes to evaluate quality or performance. **Writing:** Communicating effectively in writing as appropriate for the needs of the audience. **Operation and Control:** Controlling operations of equipment or systems.

Work Environment: Indoors; sitting; using hands on objects, tools, or controls; repetitive motions.

Hazardous Materials Removal Workers

- Annual Earnings: $33,690
- Growth: 31.2%
- Annual Job Openings: 11,000
- Self-Employed: 0.0%
- Part-Time: 5.0%
- Civilian Training Route: Moderate-term on-the-job training

Identify, remove, pack, transport, or dispose of hazardous materials, including asbestos, lead-based paint, waste oil, fuel, transmission fluid, radioactive materials, contaminated soil, and so on. Specialized training and certification in hazardous materials handling or a confined entry permit are generally required. May operate earth-moving equipment or trucks. Follow prescribed safety procedures and comply with federal laws regulating waste disposal methods. Record numbers of containers stored at disposal sites and specify amounts and types of equipment and waste disposed. Drive trucks or other heavy equipment to convey contaminated waste to designated sea or ground locations. Operate machines and equipment to remove, package, store, or transport loads of waste materials. Load and unload materials into containers and onto trucks, using hoists or forklifts. Clean contaminated equipment or areas for re-use, using detergents and solvents, sandblasters, filter pumps, and steam cleaners. Construct scaffolding or build containment areas prior to beginning abatement or decontamination work. Remove asbestos or lead from surfaces, using hand and power tools such as scrapers, vacuums, and high-pressure sprayers. Unload baskets of irradiated elements onto packaging machines that automatically insert fuel elements into canisters and secure lids. Apply chemical compounds to lead-based paint, allow compounds to dry; then scrape the hazardous material into containers for removal or storage. Identify asbestos, lead, or other hazardous materials that need to be removed, using monitoring devices. Pull tram cars along underwater tracks and position cars to receive irradiated fuel elements; then pull loaded cars to mechanisms that automatically unload elements onto underwater tables. Package, store, and move irradiated fuel elements in the underwater storage basin of a nuclear reactor plant, using machines and equipment. Organize and track the locations of hazardous items in landfills. Operate cranes to move and load baskets, casks, and canisters. Manipulate handgrips of mechanical arms to place irradiated fuel elements into baskets. Mix and pour concrete into forms to encase waste material for disposal.

Military Job That Provides Training for It (see the description in Part II): Environmental Health and Safety Specialists

Personality Type: Realistic. Realistic occupations frequently involve work activities that include practical, hands-on problems and solutions. They often deal with plants, animals, and real-world materials like wood, tools, and machinery. Many of the occupations require working outside and do not involve a lot of paperwork or working closely with others.

GOE—Interest Area: 02. Architecture and Con-struction. **Work Group:** 02.04. Construction Crafts. **Other Civilian Jobs in This Work Group:** Boilermakers; Brickmasons and Blockmasons; Carpet Installers; Cement Masons and Concrete Finishers; Commercial Divers; Construction Carpenters; Crane and Tower Operators; Drywall and Ceiling Tile Installers; Electricians; Fence Erectors; Floor Layers, Except Carpet, Wood, and Hard Tiles; Floor Sanders and Finishers; Glaziers; Insulation Workers, Floor, Ceiling, and Wall; Insulation Workers, Mechanical; Manufactured Building and Mobile Home Installers; Operating Engineers and Other Construction Equipment Operators; Painters, Construction and Maintenance; Paperhangers; Paving, Surfacing, and Tamping Equipment Operators; Pile-Driver Operators; Pipe Fitters and Steamfitters; Pipelayers; Plasterers and Stucco Masons; Plumbers; Plumbers, Pipefitters, and Steamfitters; Rail-Track Laying and Maintenance Equipment Operators; Refractory Materials Repairers, Except Brickmasons; Reinforcing Iron and Rebar Workers; Riggers; Roofers; Rough Carpenters; Security and Fire Alarm Systems Installers; Segmental Pavers; Sheet Metal Workers; Stone Cutters and Carvers, Manufacturing; Stonemasons; Structural Iron and Steel Workers; Tapers; Terrazzo Workers and Finishers; Tile and Marble Setters.

Skills—Operation Monitoring: Watching gauges, dials, or other indicators to make sure a machine is working properly. **Equipment Maintenance:** Performing routine maintenance on equipment and determining when and what kind of maintenance is needed.

Repairing: Repairing machines or systems, using the needed tools. **Operation and Control:** Controlling operations of equipment or systems. **Troubleshooting:** Determining causes of operating errors and deciding what to do about them. **Science:** Using scientific rules and methods to solve problems. **Systems Analysis:** Determining how a system should work and how changes in conditions, operations, and the environment will affect outcomes. **Quality Control Analysis:** Conducting tests and inspections of products, services, or processes to evaluate quality or performance.

Work Environment: Outdoors; very hot or cold; contaminants; hazardous conditions; using hands on objects, tools, or controls; repetitive motions.

Heating and Air Conditioning Mechanics and Installers

- Annual Earnings: $37,040
- Growth: 19.0%
- Annual Job Openings: 33,000
- Self-Employed: 13.1%
- Part-Time: 3.6%
- Civilian Training Route: Long-term on-the-job training

The job openings listed here are shared with Refrigeration Mechanics and Installers.

Install, service, and repair heating and air conditioning systems in residences and commercial establishments. Obtain and maintain required certifications. Comply with all applicable standards, policies, and procedures, including safety procedures and the maintenance of a clean work area. Repair or replace defective equipment, components, or wiring. Test electrical circuits and components for continuity, using electrical test equipment. Reassemble and test equipment following repairs. Inspect and test system to verify system compliance with plans and specifications and to detect and locate malfunctions. Discuss heating-cooling system malfunctions with users to isolate problems or to verify that malfunctions have been corrected. Test pipe or tubing joints and connections for leaks, using pressure gauge or soap-and-water solution. Record and report all faults, deficiencies, and other unusual occurrences, as well as the time and materials expended on work orders. Adjust system controls to setting recommended by manufacturer to balance system, using hand tools. Recommend, develop, and perform preventive and general maintenance procedures such as cleaning, power-washing, and vacuuming equipment; oiling parts; and changing filters. Lay out and connect electrical wiring between controls and equipment according to wiring diagram, using electrician's hand tools. Install auxiliary components to heating-cooling equipment, such as expansion and discharge valves, air ducts, pipes, blowers, dampers, flues, and stokers, following blueprints. Assist with other work in coordination with repair and maintenance teams. Install, connect, and adjust thermostats, humidistats, and timers, using hand tools. Generate work orders that address deficiencies in need of correction. Join pipes or tubing to equipment and to fuel, water, or refrigerant source to form complete circuit. Assemble, position, and mount heating or cooling equipment, following blueprints. Study blueprints, design specifications, and manufacturers' recommendations to ascertain the configuration of heating or cooling equipment components and to ensure the proper installation of components. Cut and drill holes in floors, walls, and roof to install equipment, using power saws and drills.

Military Job That Provides Training for It (see the description in Part II): Heating and Cooling Mechanics

Personality Type: Realistic. Realistic occupations frequently involve work activities that include practical, hands-on problems and solutions. They often deal with plants, animals, and real-world materials like wood, tools, and machinery. Many of the occupations require working outside and do not involve a lot of paperwork or working closely with others.

GOE—Interest Area: 02. Architecture and Construction. **Work Group:** 02.05. Systems and Equipment Installation, Maintenance, and Repair. **Other Civilian Jobs in This Work Group:** Electrical and Electronics Repairers, Powerhouse, Substation, and Relay; Electrical Power-Line Installers and Repairers; Elevator Installers and Repairers; Maintenance and Repair Workers, General; Refrigeration Mechanics and Installers; Telecommunications Equipment Installers and Repairers, Except Line Installers; Telecommunications Line Installers and Repairers.

Skills—Repairing: Repairing machines or systems, using the needed tools. **Installation:** Installing equipment, machines, wiring, or programs to meet specifications. **Equipment Maintenance:** Performing routine maintenance on equipment and determining when and what kind of maintenance is needed. **Troubleshooting:** Determining causes of operating errors and deciding what to do about them. **Systems Evaluation:** Identifying measures or indicators of system performance and the actions needed to improve or correct performance relative to the goals of the system. **Systems Analysis:** Determining how a system should work and how changes in conditions, operations, and the environment will affect outcomes. **Coordination:** Adjusting actions in relation to others' actions. **Science:** Using scientific rules and methods to solve problems.

Work Environment: Outdoors; very hot or cold; contaminants; hazardous conditions; minor burns, cuts, bites, or stings; using hands on objects, tools, or controls.

Highway Maintenance Workers

- Annual Earnings: $30,250
- Growth: 23.3%
- Annual Job Openings: 27,000
- Self-Employed: 1.2%
- Part-Time: 6.3%
- Civilian Training Route: Moderate-term on-the-job training

Maintain highways, municipal and rural roads, airport runways, and rights-of-way. Duties include patching broken or eroded pavement and repairing guardrails, highway markers, and snow fences. May also mow or clear brush from along road or plow snow from roadway. Flag motorists to warn them of obstacles or repair work ahead. Set out signs and cones around work areas to divert traffic. Drive trucks or tractors with adjustable attachments to sweep debris from paved surfaces, mow grass and weeds, and remove snow and ice. Dump, spread, and tamp asphalt, using pneumatic tampers, to repair joints and patch broken pavement. Drive trucks to transport crews and equipment to worksites. Inspect, clean, and repair drainage systems, bridges, tunnels, and other structures. Haul and spread sand, gravel, and clay to fill washouts and repair road shoulders. Erect, install, or repair guardrails, road shoulders, berms, highway markers, warning signals, and highway lighting, using hand tools and power tools. Remove litter and debris from roadways, including debris from rock slides and mudslides. Clean and clear debris from culverts, catch basins, drop inlets, ditches, and other drain structures. Perform roadside landscaping work, such as clearing weeds and brush and planting and trimming trees. Paint traffic control lines and place pavement traffic messages by hand or using machines. Inspect markers to verify accurate installation. Apply poisons along roadsides and in animal burrows to eliminate unwanted roadside vegetation and rodents. Measure and mark locations for installation of markers, using tape, string, or chalk. Apply oil to road surfaces, using sprayers. Blend compounds to form adhesive mixtures used for marker installation. Place and remove snow fences used to prevent the accumulation of drifting snow on highways.

Military Job That Provides Training for It (see the description in Part II): Construction Equipment Operators

Personality Type: Realistic. Realistic occupations frequently involve work activities that include practical, hands-on problems and solutions. They often deal with plants, animals, and real-world materials like wood, tools, and machinery. Many of the occupations require working outside and do not involve a lot of paperwork or working closely with others.

GOE—Interest Area: 02. Architecture and Construction. **Work Group:** 02.06. Construction Support/Labor. **Other Civilian Jobs in This Work Group:** Construction Laborers; Helpers—Brickmasons, Blockmasons, Stonemasons, and Tile and Marble Setters; Helpers—Carpenters; Helpers—Electricians; Helpers—Installation, Maintenance, and Repair Workers; Helpers—Painters, Paperhangers, Plasterers, and Stucco Masons; Helpers—Pipelayers, Plumbers, Pipefitters, and Steamfitters; Helpers—Roofers; Septic Tank Servicers and Sewer Pipe Cleaners.

Skills—Equipment Maintenance: Performing routine maintenance on equipment and determining when and what kind of maintenance is needed. **Repairing:** Repairing machines or systems, using the needed tools. **Installation:** Installing equipment, machines, wiring, or programs to meet specifications. **Operation and Control:** Controlling operations of equipment or systems. **Management of Material Resources:** Obtaining and seeing to the appropriate use of equipment, facilities, and materials needed to do certain work. **Troubleshooting:** Determining causes of operating errors and deciding what to do about them. **Equipment Selection:** Determining the kinds of tools and equipment needed to do a job. **Systems Analysis:** Determining how a system should work and how changes in conditions, operations, and the environment will affect outcomes.

Work Environment: Outdoors; noisy; very hot or cold; contaminants; hazardous equipment; using hands on objects, tools, or controls.

Hotel, Motel, and Resort Desk Clerks

- Annual Earnings: $17,810
- Growth: 17.2%
- Annual Job Openings: 62,000
- Self-Employed: 0.4%
- Part-Time: 24.6%
- Civilian Training Route: Short-term on-the-job training

Accommodate hotel, motel, and resort patrons by registering and assigning rooms to guests, issuing room keys, transmitting and receiving messages, keeping records of occupied rooms and guests' accounts, making and confirming reservations, and presenting statements to and collecting payments from departing guests. Greet, register, and assign rooms to guests of hotels or motels. Verify customers' credit and establish how the customer will pay for the accommodation. Keep records of room availability and guests' accounts manually or using computers. Compute bills, collect payments, and make change for guests. Perform simple bookkeeping activities, such as balancing cash accounts. Issue room keys and escort instructions to bellhops. Review accounts and charges with guests during the checkout process. Post charges, such as those for rooms, food, liquor, or telephone calls, to ledgers manually or by using computers. Transmit and receive messages, using telephones or telephone switchboards. Contact housekeeping or maintenance staff when guests report problems. Make and confirm reservations. Answer inquiries pertaining to hotel services; registration of guests; and shopping, dining, entertainment, and travel directions. Record guest comments or complaints, referring customers to managers as necessary. Advise housekeeping staff when rooms have been vacated and are ready for cleaning. Arrange tours, taxis, or restaurant reservations for customers. Deposit guests' valuables in hotel safes or safe-deposit boxes. Date-stamp, sort, and rack incoming mail and messages.

Military Job That Provides Training for It (see the description in Part II): Recreation, Welfare, and Morale Specialists

Personality Type: Conventional. Conventional occupations frequently involve following set procedures and routines. These occupations can include working with data and details more than with ideas. Usually there is a clear line of authority to follow.

GOE—Interest Area: 09. Hospitality, Tourism, and Recreation. **Work Group:** 09.03. Hospitality and Travel Services. **Other Civilian Jobs in This Work Group:** Baggage Porters and Bellhops; Concierges; Flight Attendants; Janitors and Cleaners, Except Maids and Housekeeping Cleaners; Maids and Housekeeping Cleaners; Reservation and Transportation Ticket Agents and Travel Clerks; Tour Guides and Escorts; Transportation Attendants, Except Flight Attendants and Baggage Porters; Travel Agents; Travel Guides.

Skills—No data available.

Work Environment: Indoors; standing; using hands on objects, tools, or controls; repetitive motions.

H

Human Resources Assistants, Except Payroll and Timekeeping

- Annual Earnings: $32,730
- Growth: 16.7%
- Annual Job Openings: 28,000
- Self-Employed: 0.1%
- Part-Time: 6.1%
- Civilian Training Route: Short-term on-the-job training

Compile and keep personnel records. Record data for each employee, such as address, weekly earnings, absences, amount of sales or pro-

duction, supervisory reports on ability, and date of and reason for termination. Compile and type reports from employment records. File employment records. Search employee files and furnish information to authorized persons. Explain company personnel policies, benefits, and procedures to employees or job applicants. Process, verify, and maintain documentation relating to personnel activities such as staffing, recruitment, training, grievances, performance evaluations, and classifications. Record data for each employee, including such information as addresses, weekly earnings, absences, amount of sales or production, supervisory reports on performance, and dates of and reasons for terminations. Process and review employment applications to evaluate qualifications or eligibility of applicants. Answer questions regarding examinations, eligibility, salaries, benefits, and other pertinent information. Examine employee files to answer inquiries and provide information for personnel actions. Gather personnel records from other departments or employees. Search employee files to obtain information for authorized persons and organizations such as credit bureaus and finance companies. Interview job applicants to obtain and verify information used to screen and evaluate them. Request information from law enforcement officials, previous employers, and other references to determine applicants' employment acceptability. Compile and prepare reports and documents pertaining to personnel activities. Inform job applicants of their acceptance or rejection of employment. Select applicants meeting specified job requirements and refer them to hiring personnel. Arrange for in-house and external training activities. Arrange for advertising or posting of job vacancies and notify eligible workers of position availability. Provide assistance in administering employee benefit programs and worker's compensation plans. Prepare badges, passes, and identification cards and perform other security-related duties. Administer and score applicant and employee aptitude, personality, and interest assessment instruments.

Military Jobs That Provide Training for It (see the descriptions in Part II): Personnel Specialists; Recruiting Specialists

Personality Type: Conventional. Conventional occupations frequently involve following set procedures and routines. These occupations can include working with data and details more than with ideas. Usually there is a clear line of authority to follow.

GOE—Interest Area: 04. Business and Administration. **Work Group:** 04.07. Records and Materials Processing. **Other Civilian Jobs in This Work Group:** Correspondence Clerks; File Clerks; Marking Clerks; Meter Readers, Utilities; Office Clerks, General; Order Fillers, Wholesale and Retail Sales; Postal Service Clerks; Postal Service Mail Sorters, Processors, and Processing Machine Operators; Procurement Clerks; Production, Planning, and Expediting Clerks; Shipping, Receiving, and Traffic Clerks; Stock Clerks and Order Fillers; Stock Clerks, Sales Floor; Stock Clerks—Stockroom, Warehouse, or Storage Yard; Weighers, Measurers, Checkers, and Samplers, Recordkeeping.

Skills—No data available.

Work Environment: Indoors; noisy; sitting.

Industrial Machinery Mechanics

- Annual Earnings: $39,740
- Growth: –0.2%
- Annual Job Openings: 13,000
- Self-Employed: 2.3%
- Part-Time: 1.5%
- Civilian Training Route: Long-term on-the-job training

Repair, install, adjust, or maintain industrial production and processing machinery or refinery and pipeline distribution systems. Disassemble machinery and equipment to remove parts and make repairs. Repair and replace broken or malfunctioning components of machinery and equipment. Examine parts for defects such as breakage and excessive wear. Repair and maintain the operating condition of industrial production and processing machinery and equipment. Reassemble equipment after completion of inspections, testing, or repairs. Observe and test the operation of machinery and equipment to diagnose malfunctions, using voltmeters and other testing devices. Operate newly repaired machinery and equipment to verify the adequacy of repairs. Clean, lubricate, and adjust parts, equipment, and machinery. Analyze test results, machine error messages, and information obtained from operators to diagnose equipment problems. Record repairs and maintenance performed. Study blueprints and manufacturers' manuals to determine correct installation and operation of machinery. Record parts and materials used and order or requisition new parts and materials as necessary. Cut and weld metal to repair broken metal parts, fabricate new parts, and assemble new equipment. Demonstrate equipment functions and features to machine operators. Enter codes and instructions to program computer-controlled machinery.

Military Jobs That Provide Training for It (see the descriptions in Part II): Machinists; Power Plant Electricians; Power Plant Operators; Powerhouse Mechanics; Precision Instrument and Equipment Repairers

Personality Type: Realistic. Realistic occupations frequently involve work activities that include practical, hands-on problems and solutions. They often deal with plants, animals, and real-world materials like wood, tools, and machinery. Many of the occupations require working outside and do not involve a lot of paperwork or working closely with others.

GOE—Interest Area: 13. Manufacturing. **Work Group:** 13.13. Machinery Repair. **Other Civilian Jobs in This Work Group:** Bicycle Repairers; Control and Valve Installers and Repairers, Except Mechanical Door; Home Appliance Repairers; Locksmiths and Safe Repairers; Maintenance Workers, Machinery; Mechanical Door Repairers; Millwrights; Signal and Track Switch Repairers.

Skills—Repairing: Repairing machines or systems, using the needed tools. **Installation:** Installing equipment, machines, wiring, or programs to meet specifications. **Equipment Maintenance:** Performing routine maintenance on equipment and determining when and what kind of maintenance is needed. **Operation Monitoring:** Watching gauges, dials, or other indicators to make sure a machine is working properly. **Troubleshooting:** Determining causes of operating errors and deciding what to do about them. **Technology Design:** Generating or adapting equipment and technology to serve user needs. **Operation and Control:** Controlling operations of equipment or systems. **Equipment Selection:** Determining the kinds of tools and equipment needed to do a job.

Work Environment: Noisy; contaminants; hazardous conditions; hazardous equipment; standing; using hands on objects, tools, or controls.

Inspectors, Testers, Sorters, Samplers, and Weighers

- Annual Earnings: $29,200
- Growth: –2.6%
- Annual Job Openings: 85,000
- Self-Employed: 1.9%
- Part-Time: 6.7%
- Civilian Training Route: Moderate-term on-the-job training

Inspect, test, sort, sample, or weigh nonagricultural raw materials or processed, machined, fabricated, or assembled parts or products for defects, wear, and deviations from specifications. May use precision measuring instruments and complex test equipment. Discard or reject products, materials, and equipment not meeting specifications. Analyze and interpret blueprints, data, manuals, and other materials to determine specifications, inspection and testing procedures, adjustment and certification methods, formulas, and measuring instruments required. Inspect, test, or measure materials, products, installations, and work for conformance to specifications. Notify supervisors and other personnel of production problems and assist in identifying and correcting these problems. Discuss inspection results with those responsible for products and recommend necessary corrective actions. Record inspection or test data, such as weights, temperatures, grades, or moisture content and quantities inspected or graded. Mark items with details such as grade and acceptance or rejection status. Observe and monitor production operations and equipment to ensure conformance to specifications and make or order necessary process or assembly adjustments. Measure dimensions of products to verify conformance to specifications, using measuring instruments such as rulers, calipers, gauges, or micrometers. Analyze test data and make computations as necessary to determine test results. Collect or select samples for testing or for use as models. Check arriving materials to ensure that they match purchase orders and submit discrepancy reports when problems are found. Compare colors, shapes, textures, or grades of products or materials with color charts, templates, or samples to verify conformance to standards. Write test and inspection reports describing results, recommendations, and needed repairs. Read dials and meters to verify that equipment is functioning at specified levels. Remove defects, such as chips and burrs, and lap corroded or pitted surfaces. Clean, maintain, repair, and calibrate measuring instruments and test equipment such as dial indicators, fixed gauges, and height gauges. Adjust, clean, or repair products or processing equipment to correct defects found during inspections. Stack and arrange tested products for further processing, shipping, or packaging and transport products to other workstations as necessary.

Military Jobs That Provide Training for It (see the descriptions in Part II): Non-Destructive Testers; Petroleum Supply Specialists; Precision Instrument and Equipment Repairers; Survival Equipment Specialists

Personality Type: Realistic. Realistic occupations frequently involve work activities that include practical, hands-on problems and solutions. They often deal with plants, animals, and real-world materials like wood, tools, and machinery. Many of the occupations require working outside and do not involve a lot of paperwork or working closely with others.

GOE—Interest Area: 13. Manufacturing. **Work Group:** 13.07. Production Quality Control. **Other Civilian Jobs in This Work Group:** Graders and Sorters, Agricultural Products.

Skills—No data available.

Work Environment: Noisy; standing; using hands on objects, tools, or controls; repetitive motions.

Interpreters and Translators

- Annual Earnings: $34,800
- Growth: 19.9%
- Annual Job Openings: 4,000
- Self-Employed: 13.5%
- Part-Time: No data available
- Civilian Training Route: Long-term on-the-job training

Translate or interpret written, oral, or sign language text into another language for others. Follow ethical codes that protect the confidentiality of information. Identify and resolve conflicts related to the meanings of words, concepts, practices, or behaviors. Proofread, edit, and revise translated materials. Translate messages simultaneously or consecutively into specified languages orally or by using hand signs, maintaining message content, context, and style as much as possible. Check translations of technical terms and terminology to ensure that they are accurate and remain consistent throughout translation revisions. Read written materials such as legal documents, scientific works, or news reports and rewrite material into specified languages. Refer to reference materials such as dictionaries, lexicons, encyclopedias, and computerized terminology banks as needed to ensure translation accuracy. Compile terminology and information to be used in translations, including technical terms such as those for legal or medical material. Adapt translations to students' cognitive and grade levels, collaborating with educational team members as necessary. Listen to speakers' statements to determine meanings and to prepare translations, using electronic listening systems as necessary. Check original texts or confer with authors to ensure that translations retain the content, meaning, and feeling of the original material. Compile information about the content and context of information to be translated, as well as details of the groups for whom translation or interpretation is being performed. Discuss translation requirements with clients and determine any fees to be charged for services provided. Adapt software and accompanying technical documents to another language and culture. Educate students, parents, staff, and teachers about the roles and functions of educational interpreters. Train and supervise other translators/interpreters. Travel with or guide tourists who speak another language.

Military Jobs That Provide Training for It (see the descriptions in Part II): Intelligence Specialists; Interpreters and Translators

Personality Type: Artistic. Artistic occupations frequently involve working with forms, designs, and patterns. They often require self-expression, and the work can be done without following a clear set of rules.

GOE—Interest Area: 03. Arts and Communication. **Work Group:** 03.03. News, Broadcasting, and Public Relations. **Other Civilian Jobs in This Work Group:** Broadcast News Analysts; Public Relations Specialists; Reporters and Correspondents.

Skills—No data available.

Work Environment: Indoors; sitting; repetitive motions.

Laborers and Freight, Stock, and Material Movers, Hand

- Annual Earnings: $20,610
- Growth: 10.2%
- Annual Job Openings: 671,000
- Self-Employed: 0.6%
- Part-Time: 25.1%
- Civilian Training Route: Short-term on-the-job training

Manually move freight, stock, or other materials or perform other unskilled general labor. Includes all unskilled manual laborers not elsewhere classified. Attach identifying tags to containers or mark them with identifying information. Read work orders or receive oral instructions to determine work assignments and material and equipment needs. Record numbers of units handled and moved, using daily production sheets or work tickets. Move freight, stock, and other materials to and from storage and production areas, loading docks, delivery vehicles, ships, and containers by hand or using trucks, tractors, and other equipment. Sort cargo before loading and unloading. Assemble product containers and crates, using hand tools and precut lumber. Load and unload ship cargo, using winches and other hoisting devices. Connect hoses and operate equipment to move liquid materials into and out of storage tanks on vessels. Pack containers and re-pack damaged containers. Carry needed tools and supplies from storage or trucks and return them after use. Install protective devices, such as bracing, padding, or strapping, to prevent shifting or damage to items being transported. Maintain equipment storage areas to ensure that inventory is protected. Attach slings, hooks, and other devices to lift cargo and guide loads. Carry out general yard duties such as performing shunting on railway lines. Adjust controls to guide, position, and move equipment such as cranes, booms, and cameras. Guide loads being lifted to prevent swinging. Adjust or replace equipment parts such as rollers, belts, plugs, and caps, using hand tools. Stack cargo in locations such as transit sheds or in holds of ships as directed, using pallets or cargo boards. Connect electrical equipment to power sources so that it can be tested before use. Set up the equipment needed to produce special lighting and sound effects during performances. Bundle and band material such as fodder and tobacco leaves, using banding machines. Rig and dismantle props and equipment such as frames, scaffolding, platforms, or backdrops, using hand tools. Check out, rent, or requisition all equipment needed for productions or for set construction. Direct spouts and position receptacles such as bins, carts, and containers so they can be loaded.

Military Job That Provides Training for It (see the description in Part II): Warehousing and Distribution Specialists

Personality Type: Realistic. Realistic occupations frequently involve work activities that include practical, hands-on problems and solutions. They often deal with plants, animals, and real-world materials like wood, tools, and machinery. Many of the occupations require working outside and do not involve a lot of paperwork or working closely with others.

GOE—Interest Area: 16. Transportation, Distribution, and Logistics. **Work Group:** 16.07. Transportation Support Work. **Other Civilian Jobs in This Work Group:** Bridge and Lock Tenders; Cargo and Freight Agents; Cleaners of Vehicles and Equipment; Railroad Brake, Signal, and Switch Operators; Traffic Technicians.

Skills—No data available.

Work Environment: Outdoors; noisy; very hot or cold; contaminants; standing; using hands on objects, tools, or controls.

Legal Secretaries

- Annual Earnings: $37,750
- Growth: 17.4%
- Annual Job Openings: 41,000
- Self-Employed: 1.2%
- Part-Time: 20.3%
- Civilian Training Route: Postsecondary vocational training

Perform secretarial duties, utilizing legal terminology, procedures, and documents. Prepare legal papers and correspondence, such as summonses, complaints, motions, and subpoenas. May also assist with legal research. Prepare and process legal documents and papers, such as summonses, subpoenas, complaints, appeals, motions, and pretrial agreements. Mail, fax, or arrange for delivery of legal correspondence to clients, witnesses, and court officials. Receive and place telephone calls. Schedule and make appointments. Make photocopies of correspondence, documents, and other printed matter. Organize and maintain law libraries, documents, and case files. Assist attorneys in collecting information such as employment, medical, and other records. Attend legal meetings, such as client interviews, hearings, or depositions, and take notes. Draft and type office memos. Review legal publications and perform database searches to identify laws and court decisions relevant to pending cases. Submit articles and information from searches to attorneys for review and approval for use. Complete various forms such as accident reports, trial and courtroom requests, and applications for clients.

Military Job That Provides Training for It (see the description in Part II): Legal Specialists and Court Reporters

Personality Type: Conventional. Conventional occupations frequently involve following set procedures and routines. These occupations can include working with data and details more than with ideas. Usually there is a clear line of authority to follow.

GOE—Interest Area: 04. Business and Administration. **Work Group:** 04.04. Secretarial Support. **Other Civilian Jobs in This Work Group:** Executive Secretaries and Administrative Assistants; Medical Secretaries; Secretaries, Except Legal, Medical, and Executive.

Skills—Writing: Communicating effectively in writing as appropriate for the needs of the audience. **Time Management:** Managing one's own time and the time of others. **Reading Comprehension:** Understanding written sentences and paragraphs in work-related documents. **Social Perceptiveness:** Being aware of others' reactions and understanding why they react as they do. **Judgment and Decision**

Making: Considering the relative costs and benefits of potential actions to choose the most appropriate one. **Active Listening:** Giving full attention to what other people are saying, taking time to understand the points being made, asking questions as appropriate, and not interrupting at inappropriate times. **Speaking:** Talking to others to convey information effectively. **Learning Strategies:** Selecting and using training/instructional methods and procedures appropriate for the situation when learning or teaching new things.

Work Environment: Indoors; sitting; repetitive motions.

Licensed Practical and Licensed Vocational Nurses

- Annual Earnings: $35,230
- Growth: 17.1%
- Annual Job Openings: 84,000
- Self-Employed: 0.6%
- Part-Time: 21.9%
- Civilian Training Route: Postsecondary vocational training

Care for ill, injured, convalescent, or disabled persons in hospitals, nursing homes, clinics, private homes, group homes, and similar institutions. May work under the supervision of a registered nurse. Licensing required. Observe patients, charting and reporting changes in patients' conditions, such as adverse reactions to medication or treatment, and taking any necessary action. Administer prescribed medications or start intravenous fluids and note times and amounts on patients' charts. Answer patients' calls and determine how to assist them. Measure and record patients' vital signs, such as height, weight, temperature, blood pressure, pulse, and respiration. Provide basic patient care and treatments, such as taking temperatures or blood pressures, dressing wounds, treating bedsores, giving enemas or douches, rubbing with alcohol, massaging, or performing catheterizations. Help patients with bathing, dressing, maintaining personal hygiene, moving in bed, or standing and walking. Supervise nurses' aides and assistants. Work as part of a health-care team to assess patient needs, plan and modify care, and implement interventions. Record food and fluid intake and output. Evaluate nursing intervention outcomes, conferring with other health-care team members as necessary. Assemble and use equipment such as catheters, tracheotomy tubes, and oxygen suppliers. Collect samples such as blood, urine, and sputum from patients and perform routine laboratory tests on samples. Prepare patients for examinations, tests, or treatments and explain procedures. Prepare food trays and examine them for conformance to prescribed diet. Apply compresses, ice bags, and hot water bottles. Clean rooms and make beds. Inventory and requisition supplies and instruments. Provide medical treatment and personal care to patients in private home settings, such as cooking, keeping rooms orderly, seeing that patients are comfortable and in good spirits, and instructing family members in simple nursing tasks. Sterilize equipment and supplies, using germicides, sterilizer, or autoclave. Assist in delivery, care, and feeding of infants. Wash and dress bodies of deceased persons. Make appointments, keep records, and perform other clerical duties in doctors' offices and clinics. Set up equipment and prepare medical treatment rooms.

Military Job That Provides Training for It (see the description in Part II): Medical Care Technicians

Personality Type: Social. Social occupations frequently involve working with, communicating with, and teaching people. These occupations often involve helping or providing service to others.

GOE—Interest Area: 08. Health Science. **Work Group:** 08.08. Patient Care and Assistance. **Other Civilian Jobs in This Work Group:** Home Health Aides; Nursing Aides, Orderlies, and Attendants; Psychiatric Aides; Psychiatric Technicians.

Skills—Science: Using scientific rules and methods to solve problems. **Operation Monitoring:** Watching gauges, dials, or other indicators to make sure a machine is working properly. **Service Orientation:** Actively looking for ways to help people. **Judgment and Decision Making:** Considering the relative costs and benefits of potential actions to choose the most appropriate one. **Active Listening:** Giving full attention to what other people are saying, taking time to understand the points being made, asking questions as appropriate, and not interrupting at inappropriate times. **Management of Personnel Resources:** Motivating, developing, and directing people as they work; identifying the best people for the job. **Writing:** Communicating effectively in writing as appropriate for the needs of the audience. **Time Management:** Managing one's own time and the time of others.

Work Environment: Indoors; disease or infections; standing; walking and running.

Lifeguards, Ski Patrol, and Other Recreational Protective Service Workers

- Annual Earnings: $16,910
- Growth: 20.4%
- Annual Job Openings: 49,000
- Self-Employed: 0.2%
- Part-Time: 63.8%
- Civilian Training Route: Short-term on-the-job training

Monitor recreational areas, such as pools, beaches, or ski slopes, to provide assistance and protection to participants. Rescue distressed persons, using rescue techniques and equipment. Contact emergency medical personnel in case of serious injury. Patrol or monitor recreational areas such as trails, slopes, and swimming areas on foot, in vehicles, or from towers. Examine injured persons and administer first aid or cardiopulmonary resuscitation if necessary, utilizing training and medical supplies and equipment. Instruct participants in skiing, swimming, or other recreational activities and provide safety precaution information. Warn recreational participants of inclement weather, unsafe areas, or illegal conduct. Complete and maintain records of weather and beach conditions, emergency medical treatments performed, and other relevant incident information. Inspect recreational equipment, such as rope tows, T-bars, J-bars, and chair lifts, for safety hazards and damage or wear. Provide assistance with staff selection, training, and supervision. Inspect recreational facilities for cleanliness. Observe activities in assigned areas, using binoculars to detect hazards, disturbances, or safety infractions. Provide assistance in the safe use of equipment such as ski lifts. Operate underwater recovery units. Participate in recreational demonstrations to entertain resort guests.

Military Job That Provides Training for It (see the description in Part II): Law Enforcement and Security Specialists

Personality Type: Realistic. Realistic occupations frequently involve work activities that include practical, hands-on problems and solutions. They often deal with plants, animals, and real-world materials like wood, tools, and machinery. Many of the occupations require working outside and do not involve a lot of paperwork or working closely with others.

GOE—Interest Area: 12. Law and Public Safety. **Work Group:** 12.05. Safety and Security. **Other Civilian Jobs in This Work Group:** Animal Control Workers; Crossing Guards; Gaming Surveillance Officers and Gaming Investigators; Private Detectives and Investigators; Security Guards; Transportation Security Screeners.

Skills—No data available.

Work Environment: Indoors; noisy; sitting.

Locksmiths and Safe Repairers

- Annual Earnings: $30,880
- Growth: 16.1%
- Annual Job Openings: 5,000
- Self-Employed: 37.6%
- Part-Time: 18.2%
- Civilian Training Route: Moderate-term on-the-job training

Repair and open locks, make keys, change locks and safe combinations, and install and repair safes. Cut new or duplicate keys, using keycutting machines. Keep records of company locks and keys. Insert new or repaired tumblers into locks to change combinations. Move picklocks in cylinders to open door locks without keys. Disassemble mechanical or electrical locking devices and repair or replace worn tumblers, springs, and other parts, using hand tools. Repair and adjust safes, vault doors, and vault components, using hand tools, lathes, drill presses, and welding and acetylene cutting apparatus. Install safes, vault doors, and deposit boxes according to blueprints, using equipment such as powered drills, taps, dies, truck cranes, and dollies. Open safe locks by drilling. Remove interior and exterior finishes on safes and vaults and spray on new finishes.

Military Job That Provides Training for It (see the description in Part II): Precision Instrument and Equipment Repairers

Personality Type: Realistic. Realistic occupations frequently involve work activities that include practical, hands-on problems and solutions. They often deal with plants, animals, and real-world materials like wood, tools, and machinery. Many of the occupations require working outside and do not involve a lot of paperwork or working closely with others.

GOE—Interest Area: 13. Manufacturing. **Work Group:** 13.13. Machinery Repair. **Other Civilian Jobs in This Work Group:** Bicycle Repairers; Control and Valve Installers and Repairers, Except Mechanical Door; Home Appliance Repairers; Industrial Machinery Mechanics; Maintenance Workers, Machinery; Mechanical Door Repairers; Millwrights; Signal and Track Switch Repairers.

Skills—Installation: Installing equipment, machines, wiring, or programs to meet specifications. **Repairing:** Repairing machines or systems, using the needed tools. **Equipment Maintenance:** Performing routine maintenance on equipment and determining when and what kind of maintenance is needed. **Troubleshooting:** Determining causes of operating errors and deciding what to do about them. **Equipment Selection:** Determining the kinds of tools and equipment needed to do a job. **Service Orientation:** Actively looking for ways to help people. **Management of Material Resources:** Obtaining and seeing to the appropriate use of equipment, facilities, and materials needed to do certain work. **Technology Design:** Generating or adapting equipment and technology to serve user needs.

Work Environment: More often outdoors than indoors; noisy; very bright or dim lighting; standing; using hands on objects, tools, or controls.

Machinists

- Annual Earnings: $34,350
- Growth: 4.3%
- Annual Job Openings: 33,000
- Self-Employed: 1.0%
- Part-Time: 1.8%
- Civilian Training Route: Long-term on-the-job training

Set up and operate a variety of machine tools to produce precision parts and instruments. Includes precision instrument makers who fabricate, modify, or repair mechanical instruments. May also fabricate and modify parts to make or repair machine tools or maintain industrial machines, applying knowledge of mechanics, shop mathematics, metal properties, layout, and machining procedures. Calculate dimensions and tolerances, using knowledge of mathematics and instruments such as micrometers and vernier calipers. Machine parts to specifications, using machine tools such as lathes, milling machines, shapers, or grinders. Measure, examine, and test completed units to detect defects and ensure conformance to specifications, using precision instruments such as micrometers. Set up, adjust, and operate all of the basic machine tools and many specialized or advanced variation tools to perform precision machining operations. Align and secure holding fixtures, cutting tools, attachments, accessories, and materials onto machines. Monitor the feed and speed of machines during the machining process. Study sample parts, blueprints, drawings, and engineering information to determine methods and sequences of operations needed to fabricate products and determine product dimensions and tolerances. Select the appropriate tools, machines, and materials to be used in preparation of machinery work. Lay out, measure, and mark metal stock to display placement of cuts. Observe and listen to operating machines or equipment to diagnose machine malfunctions and to determine need for adjustments or repairs. Check workpieces to ensure that they are properly lubricated and cooled. Maintain industrial machines, applying knowledge of mechanics, shop mathematics, metal properties, layout, and machining procedures. Position and fasten workpieces. Operate equipment to verify operational efficiency. Install repaired parts into equipment or install new equipment. Clean and lubricate machines, tools, and equipment to remove grease, rust, stains, and foreign matter. Advise clients about the materials being used for finished products. Program computers and electronic instruments such as numerically controlled machine tools. Set controls to regulate machining or enter commands to retrieve, input, or edit computerized machine control media. Confer with engineering, supervisory, and manufacturing personnel to exchange technical information. Dismantle machines or equipment, using hand tools and power tools, to examine parts for defects and replace defective parts where needed.

Military Jobs That Provide Training for It (see the descriptions in Part II): Machinists; Welders and Metal Workers

Personality Type: Realistic. Realistic occupations frequently involve work activities that include practical, hands-on problems and solutions. They often deal with plants, animals, and real-world materials like wood, tools, and machinery. Many of the occupations require working outside and do not involve a lot of paperwork or working closely with others.

GOE—Interest Area: 13. Manufacturing. **Work Group:** 13.05. Production Machining Technology. **Other Civilian Jobs in This Work Group:** Computer-Controlled Machine Tool Operators, Metal and Plastic; Foundry Mold and Coremakers; Lay-Out Workers, Metal and Plastic; Model Makers, Metal and Plastic; Numerical Tool and Process Control Programmers; Patternmakers, Metal and Plastic; Tool and Die Makers; Tool Grinders, Filers, and Sharpeners.

Skills—Operation Monitoring: Watching gauges, dials, or other indicators to make sure a machine is working properly. **Operation and Control:** Controlling operations of equipment or systems. **Equipment Maintenance:** Performing routine maintenance on equipment and determining when and what kind of maintenance is needed. **Quality Control Analysis:** Conducting tests and inspections of products, services, or processes to evaluate quality or performance. **Installation:** Installing equipment, machines, wiring, or programs to meet specifications. **Equipment Selection:** Determining the kinds of tools and equipment needed to do a job. **Repairing:** Repairing machines or systems, using the needed tools. **Troubleshooting:** Determining causes of operating errors and deciding what to do about them.

Work Environment: Indoors; noisy; hazardous equipment; standing; using hands on objects, tools, or controls; repetitive motions.

Maintenance and Repair Workers, General

- Annual Earnings: $31,210
- Growth: 15.2%
- Annual Job Openings: 154,000
- Self-Employed: 0.6%
- Part-Time: 6.0%
- Civilian Training Route: Moderate-term on-the-job training

Perform work involving the skills of two or more maintenance or craft occupations to keep machines, mechanical equipment, or the structure of an establishment in repair. Duties may involve pipe fitting; boiler making; insulating; welding; machining; carpentry; repairing electrical or mechanical equipment; installing, aligning, and balancing new equipment; and repairing buildings, floors, or stairs. Repair or replace defective equipment parts, using hand tools and power tools, and reassemble equipment. Perform routine preventive maintenance to ensure that machines continue to run smoothly, building systems operate efficiently, and the physical condition of buildings does not deteriorate. Inspect drives, motors, and belts; check fluid levels; replace filters; and perform other maintenance actions, following checklists. Use tools ranging from common hand and power tools, such as hammers, hoists, saws, drills, and wrenches, to precision measuring instruments and electrical and electronic testing devices. Assemble, install, or repair wiring, electrical and electronic components, pipe systems and plumbing, machinery, and equipment. Diagnose mechanical problems and determine how to correct them, checking blueprints, repair manuals, and parts catalogs as necessary. Inspect, operate, and test machinery and equipment to diagnose machine malfunctions. Record maintenance and repair work performed and the costs of the work. Clean and lubricate shafts, bearings, gears, and other parts of machinery. Dismantle devices to gain access to and remove defective parts, using hoists, cranes, hand tools, and power tools. Plan and lay out repair work, using diagrams, drawings, blueprints, maintenance manuals, and schematic diagrams. Adjust functional parts of devices and control instruments, using hand tools, levels, plumb bobs, and straightedges. Order parts, supplies, and equipment from catalogs and suppliers or obtain them from storerooms. Paint and repair roofs, windows, doors, floors, woodwork, plaster, drywall, and other parts of building structures. Operate cutting torches or welding equipment to cut or join metal parts. Align and balance new equipment after installation. Inspect used parts to determine changes in dimensional requirements, using rules, calipers, micrometers, and other measuring instruments. Set up and operate machine tools to repair or fabricate machine parts, jigs and fixtures, and tools. Maintain and repair specialized equipment and machinery found in cafeterias, laundries, hospitals, stores, offices, and factories.

Military Jobs That Provide Training for It (see the descriptions in Part II): Automotive and Heavy Equipment Mechanics; Marine Engine Mechanics; Powerhouse Mechanics; Preventive Maintenance Analysts; Survival Equipment Specialists; Weapons Maintenance Technicians

Personality Type: Realistic. Realistic occupations frequently involve work activities that include practical, hands-on problems and solutions. They often deal with plants, animals, and real-world materials like wood, tools, and machinery. Many of the occupations require working outside and do not involve a lot of paperwork or working closely with others.

GOE—Interest Area: 02. Architecture and Construction. **Work Group:** 02.05. Systems and Equipment Installation, Maintenance, and Repair. **Other Civilian Jobs in This Work Group:** Electrical and Electronics Repairers, Powerhouse, Substation, and Relay; Electrical Power-Line Installers and Repairers; Elevator Installers and Repairers; Heating and Air Conditioning Mechanics and Installers; Refrigeration Mechanics and Installers; Telecommunications Equipment Installers and Repairers, Except Line Installers; Telecommunications Line Installers and Repairers.

Skills—Equipment Maintenance: Performing routine maintenance on equipment and determining when and what kind of maintenance is needed. **Installation:** Installing equipment, machines, wiring, or programs to meet specifications. **Repairing:** Repairing machines or systems, using the needed tools. **Troubleshooting:** Determining causes of operating errors and deciding what to do about them. **Operation Monitoring:** Watching gauges, dials, or other indicators to make sure a machine is working properly. **Operation and Control:** Controlling operations of equipment or systems. **Equipment Selection:** Determining the kinds of tools and equipment needed to do a job. **Technology Design:** Generating or adapting equipment and technology to serve user needs.

Work Environment: Indoors; noisy; minor burns, cuts, bites, or stings; standing; walking and running; using hands on objects, tools, or controls.

Mapping Technicians

- Annual Earnings: $31,290
- Growth: 9.6%
- Annual Job Openings: 9,000
- Self-Employed: 4.3%
- Part-Time: 4.3%
- Civilian Training Route: Moderate-term on-the-job training

The job openings listed here are shared with Surveying Technicians.

Calculate mapmaking information from field notes and draw and verify accuracy of topographical maps. Check all layers of maps to ensure accuracy, identifying and marking errors and making corrections. Determine scales, line sizes, and colors to be used for hard copies of computerized maps, using plotters. Monitor mapping work and the updating of maps to ensure accuracy, the inclusion of new and/or changed information, and compliance with rules and regulations. Identify and compile database information to create maps in response to requests. Produce and update overlay maps to show information boundaries, water locations, and topographic features on various base maps and at different scales. Trace contours and topographic details to generate maps that denote specific land and property locations and geographic attributes. Lay out and match aerial photographs in sequences in which they were taken and identify any areas missing from photographs. Compare topographical features and contour lines with images from aerial photographs, old maps, and other reference materials to verify the accuracy of their identification. Compute and measure scaled distances between reference points to establish relative positions of adjoining prints and enable the creation of photographic mosaics. Research resources such as survey maps and legal descriptions to verify property lines and to obtain information needed for mapping. Form three-dimensional images of aerial photographs taken from different locations, using mathematical techniques and plotting instruments. Enter GPS data, legal deeds, field notes, and land survey reports into GIS workstations so that information can be transformed into graphic land descriptions such as maps and drawings. Analyze aerial photographs to detect and interpret significant military, industrial, resource, or topographical data. Redraw and correct maps, such as revising parcel maps to reflect tax code area changes, using information from official records and surveys. Train staff members in duties such as tax mapping, the use of computerized mapping equipment, and the interpretation of source documents.

Military Jobs That Provide Training for It (see the descriptions in Part II): Construction Specialists; Intelligence Specialists; Surveying, Mapping, and Drafting Technicians

Personality Type: Conventional. Conventional occupations frequently involve following set procedures and routines. These occupations can include working with data and details more than with ideas. Usually there is a clear line of authority to follow.

GOE—Interest Area: 15. Scientific Research, Engineering, and Mathematics. **Work Group:** 15.09. Engineering Technology. **Other Civilian Jobs in This Work Group:** Aerospace Engineering and Operations Technicians; Cartographers and Photogrammetrists; Civil Engineering Technicians; Electrical and Electronic Engineering Technicians; Electrical and Electronics Drafters; Electrical Drafters; Electrical Engineering Technicians; Electro-Mechanical Technicians; Electronic Drafters; Electronics Engineering Technicians; Environmental Engineering Technicians; Mechanical Drafters; Mechanical Engineering Technicians; Surveying and Mapping Technicians; Surveying Technicians.

Skills—Programming: Writing computer programs for various purposes. **Technology Design:** Generating or adapting equipment and technology to serve user needs. **Quality Control Analysis:** Conducting tests and inspections of products, services, or processes to evaluate quality or performance. **Operations Analysis:** Analyzing needs and product requirements to create a design. **Troubleshooting:** Determining causes of operating errors and deciding what to do about them. **Mathematics:** Using mathematics to solve problems. **Science:** Using scientific rules and methods to solve problems. **Active Learning:** Understanding the implications of new information for both current and future problem-solving and decision-making.

Work Environment: Indoors; sitting; using hands on objects, tools, or controls; repetitive motions.

Mates—Ship, Boat, and Barge

- Annual Earnings: $50,940
- Growth: 4.8%
- Annual Job Openings: 2,000
- Self-Employed: 5.4%
- Part-Time: 8.7%
- Civilian Training Route: Work experience in a related occupation

The job openings listed here are shared with Pilots, Ship and with Ship and Boat Captains.

Supervise and coordinate activities of crew aboard ships, boats, barges, or dredges. Participate in activities related to maintenance of vessel security. Assume command of vessels in the event that ships' masters become incapacitated. Arrange for ships to be stocked, fueled, and repaired. Supervise crews in cleaning and maintaining decks, superstructures, and bridges. Determine geographical positions of ships, using lorans, azimuths of celestial bodies, or computers, and use this information to determine the course and speed of a ship. Inspect equipment such as cargo-handling gear; lifesaving equipment; visual-signaling equipment; and fishing, towing, or dredging gear to detect problems. Observe loading and unloading of cargo and equipment to ensure that handling and storage are performed according to specifications. Observe water from ships' mastheads to advise on navigational direction. Steer vessels, utilizing navigational devices such as compasses and sextons and navigational aids such as lighthouses and buoys. Supervise crew members in the repair or replacement of defective gear and equipment. Stand watches on vessels during specified periods while vessels are under way.

Military Jobs That Provide Training for It (see the descriptions in Part II): Quartermasters and Boat Operators; Seamen

Personality Type: Realistic. Realistic occupations frequently involve work activities that include practical, hands-on problems and solutions. They often deal with plants, animals, and real-world materials like wood, tools, and machinery. Many of the occupations require working outside and do not involve a lot of paperwork or working closely with others.

GOE—Interest Area: 16. Transportation, Distribution, and Logistics. **Work Group:** 16.05. Water Vehicle Operation. **Other Civilian Jobs in This Work Group:** Captains, Mates, and Pilots of Water Vessels; Dredge Operators; Motorboat Operators; Pilots, Ship; Sailors and Marine Oilers; Ship and Boat Captains.

Skills—No data available.

Work Environment: More often outdoors than indoors; very hot or cold; standing; using hands on objects, tools, or controls.

Mechanical Engineering Technicians

- Annual Earnings: $44,830
- Growth: 12.3%
- Annual Job Openings: 5,000
- Self-Employed: 0.4%
- Part-Time: 6.7%
- Civilian Training Route: Associate degree

Apply theory and principles of mechanical engineering to modify, develop, and test machinery and equipment under direction of engineering staff or physical scientists. Prepare parts sketches and write work orders and purchase requests to be furnished by outside contractors. Draft detail drawing or sketch for drafting room completion or to request parts fabrication by machine, sheet, or wood shops. Review project instructions and blueprints to ascertain test specifications, procedures, and objectives and test nature of technical problems such as redesign. Review project instructions and specifications to identify, modify, and plan requirements fabrication, assembly, and testing. Devise, fabricate, and assemble new or modified mechanical components for products such as industrial machinery or equipment and measuring instruments. Discuss changes in design, method of manufacture and assembly, and drafting techniques and procedures with staff and coordinate corrections. Set up and conduct tests of complete units and components under operational conditions to investigate proposals for improving equipment performance. Inspect lines and figures for clarity and return erroneous drawings to designer for correction. Analyze test results in relation to design or rated specifications and test objectives and modify or adjust equipment to meet specifications. Evaluate tool drawing designs by measuring drawing dimensions and comparing with original specifications for form and function, using engineering skills. Confer with technicians and submit reports of test results to engineering department and recommend design or material changes. Calculate required capacities for equipment of proposed system to obtain specified performance and submit data to engineering personnel for approval. Record test procedures and results, numerical and graphical data, and recommendations for changes in product or test methods. Read dials and meters to determine amperage, voltage, and electrical output and input at specific operating temperature to analyze parts performance. Estimate cost factors, including labor and material, for purchased and fabricated parts and costs for assembly, testing, or installing. Set up prototype and test apparatus and operate test-controlling equipment to observe and record prototype test results.

Military Job That Provides Training for It (see the description in Part II): Non-Destructive Testers

Personality Type: Realistic. Realistic occupations frequently involve work activities that include practical, hands-on problems and solutions. They often deal with plants, animals, and real-world materials like wood, tools, and machinery. Many of the occupations require working outside and do not involve a lot of paperwork or working closely with others.

GOE—Interest Area: 15. Scientific Research, Engineering, and Mathematics. **Work Group:** 15.09. Engineering Technology. **Other Civilian Jobs in This Work Group:** Aerospace Engineering and Operations Technicians; Cartographers and Photogrammetrists; Civil Engineering Technicians; Electrical and Electronic Engineering Technicians; Electrical and Electronics Drafters; Electrical Drafters; Electrical Engineering Technicians; Electro-Mechanical Technicians; Electronic Drafters; Electronics Engineering Technicians; Environmental Engineering Technicians; Mapping Technicians; Mechanical Drafters; Surveying and Mapping Technicians; Surveying Technicians.

Skills—Installation: Installing equipment, machines, wiring, or programs to meet specifications. **Troubleshooting:** Determining causes of operating errors and deciding what to do about them. **Technology Design:** Generating or adapting equipment and technology to serve user needs. **Operations Analysis:** Analyzing needs and product requirements to create a design. **Equipment Selection:** Determining the kinds of tools and equipment needed to do a job. **Systems Evaluation:** Identifying measures or indicators of system performance and the actions needed to improve or correct performance relative to the goals of the system. **Operation Monitoring:** Watching gauges, dials, or other indicators to make sure a machine is working properly. **Mathematics:** Using mathematics to solve problems.

Work Environment: Indoors; noisy; contaminants; hazardous equipment; sitting.

Medical and Clinical Laboratory Technicians

- Annual Earnings: $31,700
- Growth: 25.0%
- Annual Job Openings: 14,000
- Self-Employed: 0.1%
- Part-Time: 17.3%
- Civilian Training Route: Associate degree

Perform routine medical laboratory tests for the diagnosis, treatment, and prevention of disease. May work under the supervision of a medical technologist. Conduct chemical analyses of body fluids, such as blood and urine, using microscope or automatic analyzer to detect abnormalities or diseases, and enter findings into computer. Set up, adjust, maintain, and clean medical laboratory equipment. Analyze the results of tests and experiments to ensure conformity to specifications, using special mechanical and electrical devices. Analyze and record test data to issue reports that use charts, graphs and narratives. Conduct blood tests for transfusion purposes and perform blood counts. Perform medical research to further control and cure disease. Obtain specimens, cultivating, isolating, and identifying microorganisms for analysis. Examine cells stained with dye to locate abnormalities. Collect blood or tissue samples from patients, observing principles of asepsis to obtain blood sample. Consult with a pathologist to determine a final diagnosis when abnormal cells are found. Inoculate fertilized eggs, broths, or other bacteriological media with organisms. Cut, stain, and mount tissue samples for examination by pathologists. Supervise and instruct other technicians and laboratory assistants. Prepare standard volumetric solutions and reagents to be combined with samples, following standardized formulas or experimental procedures. Prepare vaccines and serums by standard laboratory methods, testing for virus inactivity and sterility. Test raw materials, processes, and finished products to determine quality and quantity of materials or characteristics of a substance.

Military Job That Provides Training for It (see the description in Part II): Medical Laboratory Technicians

Personality Type: Realistic. Realistic occupations frequently involve work activities that include practical, hands-on problems and solutions. They often deal with plants, animals, and real-world materials like wood, tools, and machinery. Many of the occupations require working outside and do not involve a lot of paperwork or working closely with others.

GOE—Interest Area: 08. Health Science. **Work Group:** 08.06. Medical Technology. **Other Civilian Jobs in This Work Group:** Biological Technicians; Cardiovascular Technologists and Technicians; Diagnostic Medical Sonographers; Medical and Clinical Laboratory Technologists; Medical Equipment Preparers; Medical Records and Health Information Technicians; Nuclear Medicine Technologists; Opticians, Dispensing; Orthotists and Prosthetists; Radiologic Technicians; Radiologic Technologists; Radiologic Technologists and Technicians.

Skills—Science: Using scientific rules and methods to solve problems. **Equipment Maintenance:** Performing routine maintenance on equipment and determining when and what kind of maintenance is needed. **Troubleshooting:** Determining causes of operating errors and deciding what to do about them. **Operation Monitoring:** Watching gauges, dials, or other indicators to make sure a machine is working properly. **Quality Control Analysis:** Conducting tests and inspections of products, services, or processes to evaluate quality or performance. **Operation and Control:** Controlling operations of equipment or systems. **Monitoring:** Monitoring/assessing your performance or that of other individuals or organizations to make improvements or take corrective action. **Instructing:** Teaching others how to do something.

Work Environment: Indoors; disease or infections; standing; walking and running; using hands on objects, tools, or controls.

Medical Assistants

- Annual Earnings: $25,350
- Growth: 52.1%
- Annual Job Openings: 93,000
- Self-Employed: 0.0%
- Part-Time: 27.5%
- Civilian Training Route: Moderate-term on-the-job training

Perform administrative and certain clinical duties under the direction of physician. Administrative duties may include scheduling appointments, maintaining medical records, billing, and coding for insurance purposes. Clinical duties may include taking and recording vital signs and medical histories, preparing patients for examination, drawing blood, and administering medications as directed by physician. Interview patients to obtain medical information and measure their vital signs, weight, and height. Show patients to examination rooms and prepare them for the physician. Record patients' medical history, vital statistics, and information such as test results in medical records. Prepare and administer medications as directed by a physician. Collect blood, tissue, or other laboratory specimens; log the specimens; and prepare them for testing. Explain treatment procedures, medications, diets, and physicians' instructions to patients. Help physicians examine and treat patients, handing them instruments and materials or performing such tasks as giving injections or removing sutures. Authorize drug refills and provide prescription information to pharmacies. Prepare treatment rooms for patient examinations, keeping the rooms neat and clean. Clean and sterilize instruments and dispose of contaminated supplies. Schedule appointments for patients. Change dressings on wounds. Greet and log in patients arriving at office or clinic. Contact medical facilities or departments to schedule patients for tests or admission. Perform general office duties such as answering telephones, taking dictation, or completing insurance forms. Inventory and order medical, lab, or office supplies and equipment. Perform routine laboratory tests and sample analyses. Set up medical laboratory equipment. Keep financial records and perform other bookkeeping duties, such as handling credit and collections and mailing monthly statements to patients. Operate X-ray, electrocardiogram (EKG), and other equipment to administer routine diagnostic tests. Give physiotherapy treatments such as diathermy, galvanics, and hydrotherapy.

Military Jobs That Provide Training for It (see the descriptions in Part II): Cardiopulmonary and EEG Technicians; Medical Care Technicians; Medical Service Technicians

Personality Type: Social. Social occupations frequently involve working with, communicating with, and teaching people. These occupations often involve helping or providing service to others.

GOE—Interest Area: 08. Health Science. **Work Group:** 08.02. Medicine and Surgery. **Other Civilian Jobs in This Work Group:** Anesthesiologists; Family and General Practitioners; Internists, General; Medical Transcriptionists; Obstetricians and Gynecologists; Pediatricians, General; Pharmacists; Pharmacy Aides; Pharmacy Technicians; Physician Assistants; Psychiatrists; Registered Nurses; Surgeons; Surgical Technologists.

Skills—Social Perceptiveness: Being aware of others' reactions and understanding why they react as they do. **Service Orientation:** Actively looking for ways to help people. **Instructing:**

Teaching others how to do something. **Operation Monitoring:** Watching gauges, dials, or other indicators to make sure a machine is working properly. **Active Listening:** Giving full attention to what other people are saying, taking time to understand the points being made, asking questions as appropriate, and not interrupting at inappropriate times. **Operation and Control:** Controlling operations of equipment or systems. **Learning Strategies:** Selecting and using training/instructional methods and procedures appropriate for the situation when learning or teaching new things. **Mathematics:** Using mathematics to solve problems.

Work Environment: Indoors; disease or infections; standing; walking and running; using hands on objects, tools, or controls.

Medical Equipment Preparers

- Annual Earnings: $24,880
- Growth: 20.0%
- Annual Job Openings: 8,000
- Self-Employed: 2.7%
- Part-Time: 27.5%
- Civilian Training Route: Short-term on-the-job training

Prepare, sterilize, install, or clean laboratory or healthcare equipment. May perform routine laboratory tasks and operate or inspect equipment. Organize and assemble routine and specialty surgical instrument trays and other sterilized supplies, filling special requests as needed. Clean instruments to prepare them for sterilization. Operate and maintain steam autoclaves, keeping records of loads completed, items in loads, and maintenance procedures performed. Record sterilizer test results. Disinfect and sterilize equipment such as respirators, hospital beds, and oxygen and dialysis equipment, using sterilizers, aerators, and washers. Start equipment and observe gauges and equipment operation to detect malfunctions and to ensure equipment is operating to prescribed standards. Examine equipment to detect leaks, worn or loose parts, or other indications of disrepair. Report defective equipment to appropriate supervisors or staff. Check sterile supplies to ensure that they are not outdated. Maintain records of inventory and equipment usage. Attend hospital in-service programs related to areas of work specialization. Purge wastes from equipment by connecting equipment to water sources and flushing water through systems. Deliver equipment to specified hospital locations or to patients' residences. Assist hospital staff with patient care duties such as providing transportation or setting up traction. Install and set up medical equipment, using hand tools.

Military Jobs That Provide Training for It (see the descriptions in Part II): Medical Care Technicians; Medical Service Technicians

Personality Type: Realistic. Realistic occupations frequently involve work activities that include practical, hands-on problems and solutions. They often deal with plants, animals, and real-world materials like wood, tools, and machinery. Many of the occupations require working outside and do not involve a lot of paperwork or working closely with others.

GOE—Interest Area: 08. Health Science. **Work Group:** 08.06. Medical Technology. **Other Civilian Jobs in This Work Group:** Biological Technicians; Cardiovascular Technologists and Technicians; Diagnostic Medical Sonographers; Medical and Clinical Laboratory Technicians;

Medical and Clinical Laboratory Technologists; Medical Records and Health Information Technicians; Nuclear Medicine Technologists; Opticians, Dispensing; Orthotists and Prosthetists; Radiologic Technicians; Radiologic Technologists; Radiologic Technologists and Technicians.

Skills—Operation Monitoring: Watching gauges, dials, or other indicators to make sure a machine is working properly. **Management of Material Resources:** Obtaining and seeing to the appropriate use of equipment, facilities, and materials needed to do certain work. **Equipment Maintenance:** Performing routine maintenance on equipment and determining when and what kind of maintenance is needed. **Quality Control Analysis:** Conducting tests and inspections of products, services, or processes to evaluate quality or performance. **Service Orientation:** Actively looking for ways to help people. **Operation and Control:** Controlling operations of equipment or systems. **Management of Personnel Resources:** Motivating, developing, and directing people as they work; identifying the best people for the job. **Monitoring:** Monitoring/assessing your performance or that of other individuals or organizations to make improvements or take corrective action.

Work Environment: Indoors; contaminants; disease or infections; standing; using hands on objects, tools, or controls; repetitive motions.

Medical Equipment Repairers

- Annual Earnings: $39,570
- Growth: 14.8%
- Annual Job Openings: 4,000
- Self-Employed: 16.2%
- Part-Time: 12.1%
- Civilian Training Route: Associate degree

Test, adjust, or repair biomedical or electromedical equipment. Inspect and test malfunctioning medical and related equipment following manufacturers' specifications, using test and analysis instruments. Examine medical equipment and facility's structural environment and check for proper use of equipment to protect patients and staff from electrical or mechanical hazards and to ensure compliance with safety regulations. Disassemble malfunctioning equipment and remove, repair, and replace defective parts such as motors, clutches, or transformers. Keep records of maintenance, repair, and required updates of equipment. Perform preventive maintenance or service such as cleaning, lubricating, and adjusting equipment. Test and calibrate components and equipment, following manufacturers' manuals and troubleshooting techniques and using hand tools, power tools, and measuring devices. Explain and demonstrate correct operation and preventive maintenance of medical equipment to personnel. Study technical manuals and attend training sessions provided by equipment manufacturers to maintain current knowledge. Plan and carry out work assignments, using blueprints, schematic drawings, technical manuals, wiring diagrams, and liquid and air flow sheets, following prescribed regulations, directives, and other instructions as required. Solder loose connections, using soldering iron. Test, evaluate, and classify excess or in-use medical equipment and determine serviceability, condition, and disposition in accordance with regulations. Research catalogs and repair part lists to locate sources for repair parts, requisitioning parts and recording their receipt. Evaluate technical specifications to identify equipment and systems best suited for intended use and possible purchase based on specifications, user needs, and technical requirements. Contribute expertise to develop medical maintenance standard operating procedures. Compute power and space requirements for installing medical, dental, or related equipment and install units to manufacturers' specifications. Supervise and advise subordinate personnel. Repair shop equipment, metal furniture, and hospital equipment, including welding broken parts and replacing missing parts, or bring item into local shop for major repairs.

Military Jobs That Provide Training for It (see the descriptions in Part II): Electrical Products Repairers; Medical Care Technicians; Precision Instrument and Equipment Repairers

Personality Type: Realistic. Realistic occupations frequently involve work activities that include practical, hands-on problems and solutions. They often deal with plants, animals, and real-world materials like wood, tools, and machinery. Many of the occupations require working outside and do not involve a lot of paperwork or working closely with others.

GOE—Interest Area: 13. Manufacturing. **Work Group:** 13.15. Medical and Technical Equipment Repair. **Other Civilian Jobs in This Work Group:** Camera and Photographic Equipment Repairers; Watch Repairers.

Skills—Repairing: Repairing machines or systems, using the needed tools. **Installation:** Installing equipment, machines, wiring, or programs to meet specifications. **Equipment Maintenance:** Performing routine maintenance on equipment and determining when and what kind of maintenance is needed. **Troubleshooting:** Determining causes of operating errors and deciding what to do about them. **Systems Analysis:** Determining how a system should work and how changes in conditions, operations, and the environment will affect outcomes. **Operation Monitoring:** Watching gauges, dials, or other indicators to make sure a machine is working properly. **Quality Control Analysis:** Conducting tests and inspections of products, services, or processes to evaluate quality or performance. **Science:** Using scientific rules and methods to solve problems.

Work Environment: Indoors; contaminants; disease or infections; standing; using hands on objects, tools, or controls.

Medical Records and Health Information Technicians

- Annual Earnings: $26,690
- Growth: 28.9%
- Annual Job Openings: 14,000
- Self-Employed: 0.1%
- Part-Time: 17.6%
- Civilian Training Route: Associate degree

Compile, process, and maintain medical records of hospital and clinic patients in a manner consistent with medical, administrative, ethical, legal, and regulatory requirements of the health care system. Process, maintain,

compile, and report patient information for health requirements and standards. Protect the security of medical records to ensure that confidentiality is maintained. Process patient admission and discharge documents. Review records for completeness, accuracy, and compliance with regulations. Compile and maintain patients' medical records to document condition and treatment and to provide data for research or cost control and care improvement efforts. Enter data such as demographic characteristics, history and extent of disease, diagnostic procedures, and treatment into computer. Release information to persons and agencies according to regulations. Plan, develop, maintain, and operate a variety of health record indexes and storage and retrieval systems to collect, classify, store, and analyze information. Manage the department and supervise clerical workers, directing and controlling activities of personnel in the medical records department. Transcribe medical reports. Identify, compile, abstract, and code patient data, using standard classification systems. Resolve or clarify codes and diagnoses with conflicting, missing, or unclear information by consulting with doctors or others or by participating in the coding team's regular meetings. Train medical records staff. Assign the patient to diagnosis-related groups (DRGs), using appropriate computer software. Post medical insurance billings. Process and prepare business and government forms. Contact discharged patients, their families, and physicians to maintain registry with follow-up information, such as quality of life and length of survival of cancer patients. Prepare statistical reports, narrative reports, and graphic presentations of information such as tumor registry data for use by hospital staff, researchers, or other users. Consult classification manuals to locate information about disease processes. Compile medical care and census data for statistical reports on diseases treated, surgery performed, or use of hospital beds. Develop in-service educational materials.

Military Jobs That Provide Training for It (see the descriptions in Part II): Medical Care Technicians; Medical Record Technicians

Personality Type: Conventional. Conventional occupations frequently involve following set procedures and routines. These occupations can include working with data and details more than with ideas. Usually there is a clear line of authority to follow.

GOE—Interest Area: 08. Health Science. **Work Group:** 08.06. Medical Technology. **Other Civilian Jobs in This Work Group:** Biological Technicians; Cardiovascular Technologists and Technicians; Diagnostic Medical Sonographers; Medical and Clinical Laboratory Technicians; Medical and Clinical Laboratory Technologists; Medical Equipment Preparers; Nuclear Medicine Technologists; Opticians, Dispensing; Orthotists and Prosthetists; Radiologic Technicians; Radiologic Technologists; Radiologic Technologists and Technicians.

Skills—Systems Evaluation: Identifying measures or indicators of system performance and the actions needed to improve or correct performance relative to the goals of the system. **Active Listening:** Giving full attention to what other people are saying, taking time to understand the points being made, asking questions as appropriate, and not interrupting at inappropriate times. **Reading Comprehension:** Understanding written sentences and paragraphs in work-related documents. **Instructing:** Teaching others how to do something. **Critical Thinking:** Using logic and reasoning to identify the strengths and weaknesses of alternative solutions, conclusions, or approaches to problems. **Time Management:**

Managing one's own time and the time of others. **Service Orientation:** Actively looking for ways to help people. **Learning Strategies:** Selecting and using training/instructional methods and procedures appropriate for the situation when learning or teaching new things.

Work Environment: Indoors; noisy; sitting; using hands on objects, tools, or controls; repetitive motions.

Mobile Heavy Equipment Mechanics, Except Engines

- Annual Earnings: $39,410
- Growth: 8.8%
- Annual Job Openings: 14,000
- Self-Employed: 2.9%
- Part-Time: 3.0%
- Civilian Training Route: Postsecondary vocational training

Diagnose, adjust, repair, or overhaul mobile mechanical, hydraulic, and pneumatic equipment, such as cranes, bulldozers, graders, and conveyors, used in construction, logging, and surface mining. Test mechanical products and equipment after repair or assembly to ensure proper performance and compliance with manufacturers' specifications. Repair and replace damaged or worn parts. Diagnose faults or malfunctions to determine required repairs, using engine diagnostic equipment such as computerized test equipment and calibration devices. Operate and inspect machines or heavy equipment to diagnose defects. Dismantle and reassemble heavy equipment, using hoists and hand tools. Clean, lubricate, and perform other routine maintenance work on equipment and vehicles. Examine parts for damage or excessive wear, using micrometers and gauges. Read and understand operating manuals, blueprints, and technical drawings. Schedule maintenance for industrial machines and equipment and keep equipment service records. Overhaul and test machines or equipment to ensure operating efficiency. Assemble gear systems and align frames and gears. Fit bearings to adjust, repair, or overhaul mobile mechanical, hydraulic, and pneumatic equipment. Weld or solder broken parts and structural members, using electric or gas welders and soldering tools. Clean parts by spraying them with grease solvent or immersing them in tanks of solvent. Adjust, maintain, and repair or replace subassemblies, such as transmissions and crawler heads, using hand tools, jacks, and cranes. Adjust and maintain industrial machinery, using control and regulating devices. Fabricate needed parts or items from sheet metal. Direct workers who are assembling or disassembling equipment or cleaning parts.

Military Jobs That Provide Training for It (see the descriptions in Part II): Automotive and Heavy Equipment Mechanics; Marine Engine Mechanics; Powerhouse Mechanics

Personality Type: Realistic. Realistic occupations frequently involve work activities that include practical, hands-on problems and solutions. They often deal with plants, animals, and real-world materials like wood, tools, and machinery. Many of the occupations require working outside and do not involve a lot of paperwork or working closely with others.

GOE—Interest Area: 13. Manufacturing. **Work Group:** 13.14. Vehicle and Facility Mechanical Work. **Other Civilian Jobs in This Work Group:** Aircraft Mechanics and Service

Technicians; Aircraft Structure, Surfaces, Rigging, and Systems Assemblers; Automotive Body and Related Repairers; Automotive Glass Installers and Repairers; Automotive Master Mechanics; Automotive Service Technicians and Mechanics; Automotive Specialty Technicians; Bus and Truck Mechanics and Diesel Engine Specialists; Farm Equipment Mechanics; Fiberglass Laminators and Fabricators; Motorboat Mechanics; Motorcycle Mechanics; Outdoor Power Equipment and Other Small Engine Mechanics; Rail Car Repairers; Recreational Vehicle Service Technicians; Tire Repairers and Changers.

Skills—Installation: Installing equipment, machines, wiring, or programs to meet specifications. **Repairing:** Repairing machines or systems, using the needed tools. **Equipment Maintenance:** Performing routine maintenance on equipment and determining when and what kind of maintenance is needed. **Operation Monitoring:** Watching gauges, dials, or other indicators to make sure a machine is working properly. **Troubleshooting:** Determining causes of operating errors and deciding what to do about them. **Operation and Control:** Controlling operations of equipment or systems. **Equipment Selection:** Determining the kinds of tools and equipment needed to do a job. **Technology Design:** Generating or adapting equipment and technology to serve user needs.

Work Environment: Noisy; contaminants; hazardous equipment; minor burns, cuts, bites, or stings; standing; using hands on objects, tools, or controls.

Motorboat Mechanics

- Annual Earnings: $32,780
- Growth: 15.1%
- Annual Job Openings: 7,000
- Self-Employed: 18.9%
- Part-Time: 13.2%
- Civilian Training Route: Long-term on-the-job training

Repair and adjust electrical and mechanical equipment of gasoline or diesel-powered inboard or inboard-outboard boat engines. Replace parts such as gears, magneto points, piston rings, and spark plugs and reassemble engines. Adjust generators and replace faulty wiring, using hand tools and soldering irons. Mount motors to boats and operate boats at various speeds on waterways to conduct operational tests. Document inspection and test results and work performed or to be performed. Start motors and monitor performance for signs of malfunctioning such as smoke, excessive vibration, and misfiring. Set starter locks and align and repair steering or throttle controls, using gauges, screwdrivers, and wrenches. Repair engine mechanical equipment such as power tilts, bilge pumps, or power take-offs. Inspect and repair or adjust propellers and propeller shafts. Disassemble and inspect motors to locate defective parts, using mechanic's hand tools and gauges. Adjust carburetor mixtures, electrical point settings, and timing while motors are running in water-filled test tanks. Repair or rework parts, using machine tools such as lathes, mills, drills, and grinders. Idle motors and observe thermometers to determine the effectiveness of cooling systems.

Military Job That Provides Training for It (see the description in Part II): Marine Engine Mechanics

Personality Type: Realistic. Realistic occupations frequently involve work activities that include practical, hands-on problems and solutions. They often deal with plants, animals, and real-world materials like wood, tools, and machinery. Many of the occupations require working outside and do not involve a lot of paperwork or working closely with others.

GOE—Interest Area: 13. Manufacturing. **Work Group:** 13.14. Vehicle and Facility Mechanical Work. **Other Civilian Jobs in This Work Group:** Aircraft Mechanics and Service Technicians; Aircraft Structure, Surfaces, Rigging, and Systems Assemblers; Automotive Body and Related Repairers; Automotive Glass Installers and Repairers; Automotive Master Mechanics; Automotive Service Technicians and Mechanics; Automotive Specialty Technicians; Bus and Truck Mechanics and Diesel Engine Specialists; Farm Equipment Mechanics; Fiberglass Laminators and Fabricators; Mobile Heavy Equipment Mechanics, Except Engines; Motorcycle Mechanics; Outdoor Power Equipment and Other Small Engine Mechanics; Rail Car Repairers; Recreational Vehicle Service Technicians; Tire Repairers and Changers.

Skills—No data available.

Work Environment: More often indoors than outdoors; standing; using hands on objects, tools, or controls.

Municipal Fire Fighters

- Annual Earnings: $39,090
- Growth: 24.3%
- Annual Job Openings: 21,000
- Self-Employed: 0.1%
- Part-Time: 1.5%
- Civilian Training Route: Long-term on-the-job training

The job openings listed here are shared with Forest Fire Fighters.

Control and extinguish municipal fires, protect life and property, and conduct rescue efforts. Administer first aid and cardiopulmonary resuscitation to injured persons. Rescue victims from burning buildings and accident sites. Search burning buildings to locate fire victims. Drive and operate fire fighting vehicles and equipment. Move toward the source of a fire, using knowledge of types of fires, construction design, building materials, and physical layout of properties. Dress with equipment such as fire-resistant clothing and breathing apparatus. Position and climb ladders to gain access to upper levels of buildings or to rescue individuals from burning structures. Take action to contain hazardous chemicals that might catch fire, leak, or spill. Assess fires and situations and report conditions to superiors to receive instructions, using two-way radios. Respond to fire alarms and other calls for assistance, such as automobile and industrial accidents. Operate pumps connected to high-pressure hoses. Select and attach hose nozzles, depending on fire type, and direct streams of water or chemicals onto fires. Create openings in buildings for ventilation or entrance, using axes, chisels, crowbars, electric saws, or core cutters. Inspect fire sites after

M

flames have been extinguished to ensure that there is no further danger. Lay hose lines and connect them to water supplies. Protect property from water and smoke, using waterproof salvage covers, smoke ejectors, and deodorants. Participate in physical training activities to maintain a high level of physical fitness. Salvage property by removing broken glass, pumping out water, and ventilating buildings to remove smoke. Participate in fire drills and demonstrations of fire fighting techniques. Clean and maintain fire stations and fire fighting equipment and apparatus. Collaborate with police to respond to accidents, disasters, and arson investigation calls. Establish firelines to prevent unauthorized persons from entering areas near fires. Inform and educate the public on fire prevention. Inspect buildings for fire hazards and compliance with fire prevention ordinances, testing and checking smoke alarms and fire suppression equipment as necessary.

Military Jobs That Provide Training for It (see the descriptions in Part II): Aircraft Launch and Recovery Specialists; Firefighters

Personality Type: Realistic. Realistic occupations frequently involve work activities that include practical, hands-on problems and solutions. They often deal with plants, animals, and real-world materials like wood, tools, and machinery. Many of the occupations require working outside and do not involve a lot of paperwork or working closely with others.

GOE—Interest Area: 12. Law and Public Safety. **Work Group:** 12.06. Emergency Responding. **Other Civilian Jobs in This Work Group:** Emergency Medical Technicians and Paramedics; Fire Fighters; Forest Fire Fighters.

Skills—Equipment Maintenance: Performing routine maintenance on equipment and determining when and what kind of maintenance is needed. **Service Orientation:** Actively looking for ways to help people. **Equipment Selection:** Determining the kinds of tools and equipment needed to do a job. **Operation Monitoring:** Watching gauges, dials, or other indicators to make sure a machine is working properly. **Social Perceptiveness:** Being aware of others' reactions and understanding why they react as they do. **Coordination:** Adjusting actions in relation to others' actions. **Complex Problem Solving:** Identifying complex problems and reviewing related information to develop and evaluate options and implement solutions. **Learning Strategies:** Selecting and using training/instructional methods and procedures appropriate for the situation when learning or teaching new things.

Work Environment: More often outdoors than indoors; noisy; contaminants; disease or infections; hazardous equipment.

Municipal Fire Fighting and Prevention Supervisors

- Annual Earnings: $60,840
- Growth: 21.1%
- Annual Job Openings: 4,000
- Self-Employed: 0.0%
- Part-Time: 0.4%
- Civilian Training Route: Work experience in a related occupation

The job openings listed here are shared with Forest Fire Fighting and Prevention Supervisors.

Supervise fire fighters who control and extinguish municipal fires, protect life and property,

and conduct rescue efforts. Assign firefighters to jobs at strategic locations to facilitate rescue of persons and maximize application of extinguishing agents. Provide emergency medical services as required and perform light to heavy rescue functions at emergencies. Assess nature and extent of fire, condition of building, danger to adjacent buildings, and water supply status to determine crew or company requirements. Instruct and drill fire department personnel in assigned duties, including firefighting, medical care, hazardous materials response, fire prevention, and related subjects. Evaluate the performance of assigned firefighting personnel. Direct the training of firefighters, assigning of instructors to training classes, and providing of supervisors with reports on training progress and status. Prepare activity reports listing fire call locations, actions taken, fire types and probable causes, damage estimates, and situation dispositions. Maintain required maps and records. Attend in-service training classes to remain current in knowledge of codes, laws, ordinances, and regulations. Evaluate fire station procedures to ensure efficiency and enforcement of departmental regulations. Direct firefighters in station maintenance duties and participate in these duties. Compile and maintain equipment and personnel records, including accident reports. Direct investigation of cases of suspected arson, hazards, and false alarms and submit reports outlining findings. Recommend personnel actions related to disciplinary procedures, performance, leaves of absence, and grievances. Supervise and participate in the inspection of properties to ensure that they are in compliance with applicable fire codes, ordinances, laws, regulations, and standards. Write and submit proposals for repair, modification, or replacement of firefighting equipment. Coordinate the distribution of fire prevention promotional materials. Identify corrective actions needed to bring properties into compliance with applicable fire codes and ordinances and conduct follow-up inspections to see if corrective actions have been taken. Participate in creating fire safety guidelines and evacuation schemes for non-residential buildings.

Military Job That Provides Training for It (see the description in Part II): Firefighters

Personality Type: Realistic. Realistic occupations frequently involve work activities that include practical, hands-on problems and solutions. They often deal with plants, animals, and real-world materials like wood, tools, and machinery. Many of the occupations require working outside and do not involve a lot of paperwork or working closely with others.

GOE—Interest Area: 12. Law and Public Safety. **Work Group:** 12.01. Managerial Work in Law and Public Safety. **Other Civilian Jobs in This Work Group:** Emergency Management Specialists; First-Line Supervisors/Managers of Correctional Officers; First-Line Supervisors/Managers of Fire Fighting and Prevention Workers; First-Line Supervisors/Managers of Police and Detectives; Forest Fire Fighting and Prevention Supervisors.

Skills—Equipment Maintenance: Performing routine maintenance on equipment and determining when and what kind of maintenance is needed. **Management of Personnel Resources:** Motivating, developing, and directing people as they work; identifying the best people for the job. **Service Orientation:** Actively looking for ways to help people. **Operation Monitoring:** Watching gauges, dials, or other indicators to make sure a machine is working properly. **Management of Material Resources:** Obtaining and seeing to the appropriate use of equipment, facilities, and materials needed to do certain work. **Coordination:** Adjusting actions in relation to others' actions. **Judgment and Decision Making:** Considering the relative costs and benefits of potential actions to choose the most appropriate one. **Operation and Control:** Controlling operations of equipment or systems.

Work Environment: More often outdoors than indoors; noisy; contaminants; disease or infections; hazardous equipment.

Music Composers and Arrangers

- Annual Earnings: $34,810
- Growth: 10.4%
- Annual Job Openings: 11,000
- Self-Employed: 44.8%
- Part-Time: 46.1%
- Civilian Training Route: Work experience plus degree

The job openings listed here are shared with Music Directors.

Write and transcribe musical scores. Determine voices, instruments, harmonic structures, rhythms, tempos, and tone balances required to achieve the effects desired in a musical composition. Experiment with different sounds and types and pieces of music, using synthesizers and computers as necessary to test and evaluate ideas. Explore and develop musical ideas based on sources such as imagination or sounds in the environment. Fill in details of orchestral sketches, such as adding vocal parts to scores. Rewrite original musical scores in different musical styles by changing rhythms, harmonies, or tempos. Create original musical forms or write within circumscribed musical forms such as sonatas, symphonies, or operas. Use computers and synthesizers to compose, orchestrate, and arrange music. Score compositions so that they are consistent with instrumental and vocal capabilities such as ranges and keys, using knowledge of music theory. Write changes directly into compositions or use computer software to make changes. Transcribe ideas for musical compositions into musical notation, using instruments, pen and paper, or computers. Write music for commercial media, including advertising jingles or film soundtracks. Transpose music from one voice or instrument to another to accommodate particular musicians. Collaborate with other colleagues, such as copyists, to complete final scores. Study films or scripts to determine how musical scores can be used to create desired effects or moods. Accept commissions to create music for special occasions. Write musical scores for orchestras, bands, choral groups, or individual instrumentalists or vocalists, using knowledge of music theory and of instrumental and vocal capabilities. Study original pieces of music to become familiar with them prior to making any changes. Guide musicians during rehearsals, performances, or recording sessions. Copy parts from scores for individual performers. Confer with producers and directors to define the nature and placement of film or television music. Apply elements of music theory to create musical and tonal structures, including harmonies and melodies.

Military Job That Provides Training for It (see the description in Part II): Musicians

Personality Type: Artistic. Artistic occupations frequently involve working with forms, designs, and patterns. They often require self-expression, and the work can be done without following a clear set of rules.

GOE—Interest Area: 03. Arts and Communication. **Work Group:** 03.07. Music. **Other Civilian Jobs in This Work Group:** Music

Directors; Music Directors and Composers; Musicians and Singers; Musicians, Instrumental; Singers; Talent Directors.

Skills—No data available.

Work Environment: Indoors; sitting.

Nuclear Equipment Operation Technicians

- Annual Earnings: $61,120
- Growth: 13.7%
- Annual Job Openings: 1,000
- Self-Employed: 0.0%
- Part-Time: No data available
- Civilian Training Route: Associate degree

The job openings listed here are shared with Nuclear Monitoring Technicians.

Operate equipment used for the release, control, and utilization of nuclear energy to assist scientists in laboratory and production activities. Follow policies and procedures for radiation workers to ensure personnel safety. Modify, devise, and maintain equipment used in operations. Set control panel switches, according to standard procedures, to route electric power from sources and direct particle beams through injector units. Submit computations to supervisors for review. Calculate equipment operating factors, such as radiation times, dosages, temperatures, gamma intensities, and pressures, using standard formulas and conversion tables. Perform testing, maintenance, repair, and upgrading of accelerator systems. Warn maintenance workers of radiation hazards and direct workers to vacate hazardous areas. Monitor instruments, gauges, and recording devices in control rooms during operation of equipment under direction of nuclear experimenters. Write summaries of activities and record experimental data, such as accelerator performance, systems status, particle beam specification, and beam conditions obtained.

Military Jobs That Provide Training for It (see the descriptions in Part II): Non-Destructive Testers; Power Plant Operators

Personality Type: Realistic. Realistic occupations frequently involve work activities that include practical, hands-on problems and solutions. They often deal with plants, animals, and real-world materials like wood, tools, and machinery. Many of the occupations require working outside and do not involve a lot of paperwork or working closely with others.

GOE—Interest Area: 15. Scientific Research, Engineering, and Mathematics. **Work Group:** 15.05. Physical Science Laboratory Technology. **Other Civilian Jobs in This Work Group:** Chemical Technicians; Nuclear Technicians.

Skills—Operation Monitoring: Watching gauges, dials, or other indicators to make sure a machine is working properly. **Operation and Control:** Controlling operations of equipment or systems. **Science:** Using scientific rules and methods to solve problems. **Mathematics:** Using mathematics to solve problems. **Equipment Maintenance:** Performing routine maintenance on equipment and determining when and what kind of maintenance is needed. **Quality Control Analysis:** Conducting tests and inspections of products, services, or processes to evaluate quality or performance. **Troubleshooting:** Determining causes of operating errors and deciding what to do about them. **Reading Comprehension:** Understanding written sentences and paragraphs in work-related documents.

Work Environment: Indoors; noisy; very hot or cold; radiation; hazardous conditions; hazardous equipment.

Nuclear Power Reactor Operators

- Annual Earnings: $66,230
- Growth: –0.5%
- Annual Job Openings: 1,000
- Self-Employed: 0.0%
- Part-Time: 1.5%
- Civilian Training Route: Long-term on-the-job training

Control nuclear reactors. Adjust controls to position rod and to regulate flux level, reactor period, coolant temperature, and rate of power flow, following standard procedures. Respond to system or unit abnormalities, diagnosing the cause and recommending or taking corrective action. Monitor all systems for normal running conditions, performing activities such as checking gauges to assess output or assess the effects of generator loading on other equipment. Implement operational procedures such as those controlling startup and shutdown activities. Note malfunctions of equipment, instruments, or controls and report these conditions to supervisors. Monitor and operate boilers, turbines, wells, and auxiliary power plant equipment. Dispatch orders and instructions to personnel through radiotelephone or intercommunication systems to coordinate auxiliary equipment operation. Record operating data such as the results of surveillance tests. Participate in nuclear fuel element handling activities such as preparation, transfer, loading, and unloading. Conduct inspections and operations outside of control rooms as necessary. Direct reactor operators in emergency situations in accordance with emergency operating procedures. Authorize maintenance activities on units and changes in equipment and system operational status.

Military Job That Provides Training for It (see the description in Part II): Power Plant Operators

Personality Type: Realistic. Realistic occupations frequently involve work activities that include practical, hands-on problems and solutions. They often deal with plants, animals, and real-world materials like wood, tools, and machinery. Many of the occupations require working outside and do not involve a lot of paperwork or working closely with others.

GOE—Interest Area: 13. Manufacturing. **Work Group:** 13.16. Utility Operation and Energy Distribution. **Other Civilian Jobs in This Work Group:** Chemical Plant and System Operators; Gas Compressor and Gas Pumping Station Operators; Gas Plant Operators; Petroleum Pump System Operators, Refinery Operators, and Gaugers; Power Distributors and Dispatchers; Power Plant Operators; Ship Engineers; Stationary Engineers and Boiler Operators; Water and Liquid Waste Treatment Plant and System Operators.

Skills—Operation Monitoring: Watching gauges, dials, or other indicators to make sure a machine is working properly. **Operation and Control:** Controlling operations of equipment or systems. **Science:** Using scientific rules and methods to solve problems. **Systems Analysis:** Determining how a system should work and how changes in conditions, operations, and the environment will affect outcomes. **Troubleshooting:** Determining causes of operating errors and deciding what to do about them. **Equipment Maintenance:** Performing routine

N

maintenance on equipment and determining when and what kind of maintenance is needed. **Quality Control Analysis:** Conducting tests and inspections of products, services, or processes to evaluate quality or performance. **Systems Evaluation:** Identifying measures or indicators of system performance and the actions needed to improve or correct performance relative to the goals of the system.

Work Environment: Indoors; noisy; radiation; hazardous conditions; hazardous equipment; using hands on objects, tools, or controls.

Nursing Aides, Orderlies, and Attendants

- Annual Earnings: $21,440
- Growth: 22.3%
- Annual Job Openings: 307,000
- Self-Employed: 1.9%
- Part-Time: 28.0%
- Civilian Training Route: Postsecondary vocational training

Provide basic patient care under direction of nursing staff. Perform duties such as feeding, bathing, dressing, grooming, or moving patients or changing linens. Turn and reposition bedridden patients, alone or with assistance, to prevent bedsores. Answer patients' call signals. Feed patients who are unable to feed themselves. Observe patients' conditions, measuring and recording food and liquid intake and output and vital signs, and report changes to professional staff. Provide patient care by supplying and emptying bedpans, applying dressings, and supervising exercise routines. Provide patients with help walking, exercising, and moving in and out of bed. Bathe, groom, shave, dress, or drape patients to prepare them for surgery, treatment, or examination. Collect specimens such as urine, feces, or sputum. Prepare, serve, and collect food trays. Clean rooms and change linens. Transport patients to treatment units, using a wheelchair or stretcher. Deliver messages, documents, and specimens. Answer phones and direct visitors. Administer medications and treatments, such as catheterizations, suppositories, irrigations, enemas, massages, and douches, as directed by a physician or nurse. Restrain patients if necessary. Maintain inventory by storing, preparing, sterilizing, and issuing supplies such as dressing packs and treatment trays. Explain medical instructions to patients and family members. Perform clerical duties such as processing documents and scheduling appointments. Work as part of a medical team that examines and treats clinic outpatients. Set up equipment such as oxygen tents, portable X-ray machines, and overhead irrigation bottles.

Military Job That Provides Training for It (see the description in Part II): Medical Care Technicians

Personality Type: Social. Social occupations frequently involve working with, communicating with, and teaching people. These occupations often involve helping or providing service to others.

GOE—Interest Area: 08. Health Science. **Work Group:** 08.08. Patient Care and Assistance. **Other Civilian Jobs in This Work Group:** Home Health Aides; Licensed Practical and Licensed Vocational Nurses; Psychiatric Aides; Psychiatric Technicians.

Skills—Social Perceptiveness: Being aware of others' reactions and understanding why they react as they do. **Operation Monitoring:**

Watching gauges, dials, or other indicators to make sure a machine is working properly. **Time Management:** Managing one's own time and the time of others. **Service Orientation:** Actively looking for ways to help people. **Monitoring:** Monitoring/assessing your performance or that of other individuals or organizations to make improvements or take corrective action. **Instructing:** Teaching others how to do something. **Technology Design:** Generating or adapting equipment and technology to serve user needs. **Systems Evaluation:** Identifying measures or indicators of system performance and the actions needed to improve or correct performance relative to the goals of the system.

Work Environment: Indoors; disease or infections; standing; walking and running; using hands on objects, tools, or controls; bending or twisting the body.

Occupational Therapist Assistants

- Annual Earnings: $39,750
- Growth: 34.1%
- Annual Job Openings: 2,000
- Self-Employed: 0.0%
- Part-Time: 18.6%
- Civilian Training Route: Associate degree

Assist occupational therapists in providing occupational therapy treatments and procedures. May, in accordance with state laws, assist in development of treatment plans, carry out routine functions, direct activity programs, and document the progress of treatments. Generally requires formal training. Observe and record patients' progress, attitudes, and behavior and maintain this information in client records. Maintain and promote a positive attitude toward clients and their treatment programs. Monitor patients' performance in therapy activities, providing encouragement. Select therapy activities to fit patients' needs and capabilities. Instruct, or assist in instructing, patients and families in home programs, basic living skills, and the care and use of adaptive equipment. Evaluate the daily living skills and capacities of physically, developmentally, or emotionally disabled clients. Aid patients in dressing and grooming themselves. Implement, or assist occupational therapists with implementing, treatment plans designed to help clients function independently. Report to supervisors, verbally or in writing, on patients' progress, attitudes, and behavior. Alter treatment programs to obtain better results if treatment is not having the intended effect. Work under the direction of occupational therapists to plan, implement, and administer educational, vocational, and recreational programs that restore and enhance performance in individuals with functional impairments. Design, fabricate, and repair assistive devices and make adaptive changes to equipment and environments. Assemble, clean, and maintain equipment and materials for patient use. Teach patients how to deal constructively with their emotions. Perform clerical duties such as scheduling appointments, collecting data, and documenting health insurance billings. Transport patients to and from the occupational therapy work area. Demonstrate therapy techniques such as manual and creative arts or games. Order any needed educational or treatment supplies. Assist educational specialists or clinical psychologists in administering situational or diagnostic tests to measure client's abilities or progress.

Military Jobs That Provide Training for It (see the descriptions in Part II): Medical Service

O

Technicians; Physical and Occupational Therapy Specialists

Personality Type: Social. Social occupations frequently involve working with, communicating with, and teaching people. These occupations often involve helping or providing service to others.

GOE—Interest Area: 08. Health Science. **Work Group:** 08.07. Medical Therapy. **Other Civilian Jobs in This Work Group:** Audiologists; Massage Therapists; Occupational Therapist Aides; Occupational Therapists; Physical Therapist Aides; Physical Therapist Assistants; Physical Therapists; Radiation Therapists; Recreational Therapists; Respiratory Therapists; Respiratory Therapy Technicians; Speech-Language Pathologists.

Skills—Social Perceptiveness: Being aware of others' reactions and understanding why they react as they do. **Operations Analysis:** Analyzing needs and product requirements to create a design. **Persuasion:** Persuading others to change their minds or behavior. **Service Orientation:** Actively looking for ways to help people. **Writing:** Communicating effectively in writing as appropriate for the needs of the audience. **Time Management:** Managing one's own time and the time of others. **Monitoring:** Monitoring/assessing your performance or that of other individuals or organizations to make improvements or take corrective action. **Learning Strategies:** Selecting and using training/instructional methods and procedures appropriate for the situation when learning or teaching new things.

Work Environment: Indoors; disease or infections; standing; walking and running; using hands on objects, tools, or controls; bending or twisting the body.

Office Clerks, General

- Annual Earnings: $23,070
- Growth: 8.4%
- Annual Job Openings: 695,000
- Self-Employed: 0.4%
- Part-Time: 29.7%
- Civilian Training Route: Short-term on-the-job training

Perform duties too varied and diverse to be classified in any specific office clerical occupation requiring limited knowledge of office management systems and procedures. Clerical duties may be assigned in accordance with the office procedures of individual establishments and may include a combination of answering telephones, bookkeeping, typing or word processing, stenography, office machine operation, and filing. Collect, count, and disburse money; do basic bookkeeping; and complete banking transactions. Communicate with customers, employees, and other individuals to answer questions, disseminate or explain information, take orders, and address complaints. Answer telephones, direct calls, and take messages. Compile, copy, sort, and file records of office activities, business transactions, and other activities. Complete and mail bills, contracts, policies, invoices, or checks. Operate office machines such as photocopiers and scanners, facsimile machines, voice mail systems, and personal computers. Compute, record, and proofread data and other information, such as records or reports. Maintain and update filing, inventory, mailing, and database systems, either manually or using a computer. Open, sort, and route incoming mail; answer correspondence; and prepare outgoing mail. Review files, records, and other documents to obtain information to respond to requests. Deliver messages and run errands. Inventory and order materials, supplies, and services. Complete work schedules, manage calendars, and arrange appointments. Process and prepare documents such as business or government forms and expense reports. Monitor and direct the work of lower-level clerks. Type, format, proofread, and edit correspondence and other documents from notes or dictating machines, using computers or typewriters. Count, weigh, measure, or organize materials. Train other staff members to perform work activities, such as using computer applications. Prepare meeting agendas, attend meetings, and record and transcribe minutes. Troubleshoot problems involving office equipment, such as computer hardware and software. Make travel arrangements for office personnel.

Military Jobs That Provide Training for It (see the descriptions in Part II): Administrative Support Specialists; Personnel Specialists; Religious Program Specialists

Personality Type: Conventional. Conventional occupations frequently involve following set procedures and routines. These occupations can include working with data and details more than with ideas. Usually there is a clear line of authority to follow.

GOE—Interest Area: 04. Business and Administration. **Work Group:** 04.07. Records and Materials Processing. **Other Civilian Jobs in This Work Group:** Correspondence Clerks; File Clerks; Human Resources Assistants, Except Payroll and Timekeeping; Marking Clerks; Meter Readers, Utilities; Order Fillers, Wholesale and Retail Sales; Postal Service Clerks; Postal Service Mail Sorters, Processors, and Processing Machine Operators; Procurement Clerks; Production, Planning, and Expediting Clerks; Shipping, Receiving, and Traffic Clerks; Stock Clerks and Order Fillers; Stock Clerks, Sales Floor; Stock Clerks—Stockroom, Warehouse, or Storage Yard; Weighers, Measurers, Checkers, and Samplers, Recordkeeping.

Skills—No data available.

Work Environment: Indoors; sitting; using hands on objects, tools, or controls.

Operating Engineers and Other Construction Equipment Operators

- Annual Earnings: $35,830
- Growth: 11.6%
- Annual Job Openings: 37,000
- Self-Employed: 5.4%
- Part-Time: 2.9%
- Civilian Training Route: Moderate-term on-the-job training

Operate one or several types of power construction equipment, such as motor graders, bulldozers, scrapers, compressors, pumps, derricks, shovels, tractors, or front-end loaders, to excavate, move, and grade earth; erect structures; or pour concrete or other hard-surface pavement. May repair and maintain equipment in addition to other duties. Learn and follow safety regulations. Take actions to avoid potential hazards and obstructions such as utility lines, other equipment, other workers, and falling objects. Adjust handwheels and depress pedals to control attachments such as blades, buckets, scrapers, and swing booms. Start engines; move throttles, switches, and levers; and depress pedals to operate machines such as bulldozers, trench excavators, road graders, and backhoes. Locate underground services, such as pipes and wires, prior to beginning work. Monitor operations to ensure that health and safety standards are met. Align machines, cutterheads, or depth gauge makers with reference stakes and guidelines or ground or position equipment by following hand signals of other workers. Load and move dirt, rocks, equipment, and materials, using trucks, crawler tractors, power cranes, shovels, graders, and related equipment. Drive and maneuver equipment equipped with blades in successive passes over working areas to remove topsoil, vegetation, and rocks and to distribute and level earth or terrain. Coordinate machine actions with other activities, positioning or moving loads in response to hand or audio signals from crew members. Operate tractors and bulldozers to perform such tasks as clearing land, mixing sludge, trimming backfills, and building roadways and parking lots. Repair and maintain equipment, making emergency adjustments or assisting with major repairs as necessary. Check fuel supplies at sites to ensure adequate availability. Connect hydraulic hoses, belts, mechanical linkages, or power takeoff shafts to tractors. Operate loaders to pull out stumps, rip asphalt or concrete, rough-grade properties, bury refuse, or perform general cleanup. Select and fasten bulldozer blades or other attachments to tractors, using hitches. Test atmosphere for adequate oxygen and explosive conditions when working in confined spaces. Operate compactors, scrapers, and rollers to level, compact, and cover refuse at disposal grounds. Talk to clients and study instructions, plans, and diagrams to establish work requirements.

Military Jobs That Provide Training for It (see the descriptions in Part II): Construction Equipment Operators; Vehicle Drivers

Personality Type: Realistic. Realistic occupations frequently involve work activities that include practical, hands-on problems and solutions. They often deal with plants, animals, and real-world materials like wood, tools, and machinery. Many of the occupations require working outside and do not involve a lot of paperwork or working closely with others.

GOE—Interest Area: 02. Architecture and Construction. **Work Group:** 02.04. Construction Crafts. **Other Civilian Jobs in This Work Group:** Boilermakers; Brickmasons and Blockmasons; Carpet Installers; Cement Masons and Concrete Finishers; Commercial Divers; Construction Carpenters; Crane and Tower Operators; Drywall and Ceiling Tile Installers; Electricians; Fence Erectors; Floor Layers, Except Carpet, Wood, and Hard Tiles; Floor Sanders and Finishers; Glaziers; Hazardous Materials Removal Workers; Insulation Workers, Floor, Ceiling, and Wall; Insulation Workers, Mechanical; Manufactured Building and Mobile Home Installers; Painters, Construction and Maintenance; Paperhangers; Paving, Surfacing, and Tamping Equipment Operators; Pile-Driver Operators; Pipe Fitters and Steamfitters; Pipelayers; Plasterers and Stucco Masons; Plumbers; Plumbers, Pipefitters, and Steamfitters; Rail-Track Laying and Maintenance Equipment Operators; Refractory Materials Repairers, Except Brickmasons; Reinforcing Iron and Rebar Workers; Riggers; Roofers; Rough Carpenters; Security and Fire Alarm Systems Installers; Segmental Pavers; Sheet Metal Workers; Stone Cutters and Carvers, Manufacturing; Stonemasons; Structural Iron and Steel Workers; Tapers; Terrazzo Workers and Finishers; Tile and Marble Setters.

Skills—Equipment Maintenance: Performing routine maintenance on equipment and determining when and what kind of maintenance is needed. **Installation:** Installing equipment, machines, wiring, or programs to meet specifications. **Operation Monitoring:** Watching gauges, dials, or other indicators to make sure a machine is working properly. **Operation and Control:** Controlling operations of equipment or systems. **Repairing:** Repairing machines or systems, using the needed tools. **Management of Financial Resources:** Determining how money will be spent to get the work done and accounting for these expenditures. **Management of Material Resources:** Obtaining and seeing to the appropriate use of equipment, facilities, and materials needed to do certain work. **Equipment Selection:** Determining the kinds of tools and equipment needed to do a job.

Work Environment: Outdoors; noisy; very hot or cold; contaminants; whole-body vibration; using hands on objects, tools, or controls.

Orthotists and Prosthetists

- Annual Earnings: $53,760
- Growth: 18.0%
- Annual Job Openings: Fewer than 500
- Self-Employed: 14.4%
- Part-Time: 18.2%
- Civilian Training Route: Bachelor's degree

Assist patients with disabling conditions of limbs and spine or with partial or total absence of limb by fitting and preparing orthopedic braces or prostheses. Examine, interview, and measure patients in order to determine their appliance needs and to identify factors that could affect appliance fit. Fit, test, and evaluate devices on patients and make adjustments for proper fit, function, and comfort. Instruct patients in the use and care of orthoses and prostheses. Design orthopedic and prosthetic devices based on physicians' prescriptions and examination and measurement of patients. Maintain patients' records. Make and modify plaster casts of areas that will be fitted with prostheses or orthoses for use in the device construction process. Select materials and components to be used, based on device design. Confer with physicians to formulate specifications and prescriptions for orthopedic or prosthetic devices. Repair, rebuild, and modify prosthetic and orthopedic appliances. Construct and fabricate appliances or supervise others who are constructing the appliances. Train and supervise orthopedic and prosthetic assistants and technicians and other support staff. Update skills and knowledge by attending conferences and seminars. Show and explain orthopedic and prosthetic appliances to health-care workers. Research new ways to construct and use orthopedic and prosthetic devices. Publish research findings and present them at conferences and seminars.

Military Jobs That Provide Training for It (see the descriptions in Part II): Medical Care Technicians; Physical and Occupational Therapy Specialists

Personality Type: Social. Social occupations frequently involve working with, communicating with, and teaching people. These occupations often involve helping or providing service to others.

GOE—Interest Area: 08. Health Science. **Work Group:** 08.06. Medical Technology. **Other Civilian Jobs in This Work Group:** Biological

Technicians; Cardiovascular Technologists and Technicians; Diagnostic Medical Sonographers; Medical and Clinical Laboratory Technicians; Medical and Clinical Laboratory Technologists; Medical Equipment Preparers; Medical Records and Health Information Technicians; Nuclear Medicine Technologists; Opticians, Dispensing; Radiologic Technicians; Radiologic Technologists; Radiologic Technologists and Technicians.

Skills—Technology Design: Generating or adapting equipment and technology to serve user needs. **Management of Financial Resources:** Determining how money will be spent to get the work done and accounting for these expenditures. **Management of Material Resources:** Obtaining and seeing to the appropriate use of equipment, facilities, and materials needed to do certain work. **Service Orientation:** Actively looking for ways to help people. **Management of Personnel Resources:** Motivating, developing, and directing people as they work; identifying the best people for the job. **Operations Analysis:** Analyzing needs and product requirements to create a design. **Quality Control Analysis:** Conducting tests and inspections of products, services, or processes to evaluate quality or performance. **Social Perceptiveness:** Being aware of others' reactions and understanding why they react as they do.

Work Environment: Indoors; noisy; contaminants; disease or infections; hazardous equipment; using hands on objects, tools, or controls.

Outdoor Power Equipment and Other Small Engine Mechanics

- Annual Earnings: $25,810
- Growth: 14.0%
- Annual Job Openings: 10,000
- Self-Employed: 19.2%
- Part-Time: 13.2%
- Civilian Training Route: Moderate-term on-the-job training

Diagnose, adjust, repair, or overhaul small engines used to power lawn mowers, chain saws, and related equipment. Sell parts and equipment. Show customers how to maintain equipment. Record repairs made, time spent, and parts used. Grind, ream, rebore, and retap parts to obtain specified clearances, using grinders, lathes, taps, reamers, boring machines, and micrometers. Test and inspect engines to determine malfunctions, to locate missing and broken parts, and to verify repairs, using diagnostic instruments. Replace motors. Repair or replace defective parts such as magnetos, water pumps, gears, pistons, and carburetors, using hand tools. Remove engines from equipment and position and bolt engines to repair stands. Perform routine maintenance such as cleaning and oiling parts, honing cylinders, and tuning ignition systems. Obtain problem descriptions from customers and prepare cost estimates for repairs. Dismantle engines, using hand tools, and examine parts for defects. Adjust points, valves, carburetors, distributors, and spark plug gaps, using feeler gauges. Repair and maintain gasoline engines used to power equipment such as portable saws, lawn mowers, generators, and compressors. Reassemble engines after repair or maintenance work is complete.

Military Job That Provides Training for It (see the description in Part II): Powerhouse Mechanics

Personality Type: Realistic. Realistic occupations frequently involve work activities that include practical, hands-on problems and solutions. They often deal with plants, animals, and real-world materials like wood, tools, and machinery. Many of the occupations require working outside and do not involve a lot of paperwork or working closely with others.

GOE—Interest Area: 13. Manufacturing. **Work Group:** 13.14. Vehicle and Facility Mechanical Work. **Other Civilian Jobs in This Work Group:** Aircraft Mechanics and Service Technicians; Aircraft Structure, Surfaces, Rigging, and Systems Assemblers; Automotive Body and Related Repairers; Automotive Glass Installers and Repairers; Automotive Master Mechanics; Automotive Service Technicians and Mechanics; Automotive Specialty Technicians; Bus and Truck Mechanics and Diesel Engine Specialists; Farm Equipment Mechanics; Fiberglass Laminators and Fabricators; Mobile Heavy Equipment Mechanics, Except Engines; Motorboat Mechanics; Motorcycle Mechanics; Rail Car Repairers; Recreational Vehicle Service Technicians; Tire Repairers and Changers.

Skills—No data available.

Work Environment: Indoors; contaminants; hazardous equipment; standing; kneeling, crouching, stooping, or crawling; using hands on objects, tools, or controls.

Packers and Packagers, Hand

- Annual Earnings: $17,390
- Growth: 10.1%
- Annual Job Openings: 194,000
- Self-Employed: 0.4%
- Part-Time: 17.8%
- Civilian Training Route: Short-term on-the-job training

Pack or package by hand a wide variety of products and materials. Mark and label containers, container tags, or products, using marking tools. Measure, weigh, and count products and materials. Examine and inspect containers, materials, and products to ensure that packing specifications are met. Record product, packaging, and order information on specified forms and records. Remove completed or defective products or materials, placing them on moving equipment such as conveyors or in specified areas such as loading docks. Seal containers or materials, using glues, fasteners, nails, and hand tools. Load materials and products into package-processing equipment. Assemble, line, and pad cartons, crates, and containers, using hand tools. Clean containers, materials, supplies, or work areas, using cleaning solutions and hand tools. Transport packages to customers' vehicles. Place or pour products or materials into containers, using hand tools and equipment, or fill containers from spouts or chutes. Obtain, move, and sort products, materials, containers, and orders, using hand tools.

Military Job That Provides Training for It (see the description in Part II): Cargo Specialists

P

Personality Type: Realistic. Realistic occupations frequently involve work activities that include practical, hands-on problems and solutions. They often deal with plants, animals, and real-world materials like wood, tools, and machinery. Many of the occupations require working outside and do not involve a lot of paperwork or working closely with others.

GOE—Interest Area: 13. Manufacturing. **Work Group:** 13.17. Loading, Moving, Hoisting, and Conveying. **Other Civilian Jobs in This Work Group:** Conveyor Operators and Tenders; Hoist and Winch Operators; Industrial Truck and Tractor Operators; Machine Feeders and Offbearers; Pump Operators, Except Wellhead Pumpers; Refuse and Recyclable Material Collectors; Tank Car, Truck, and Ship Loaders.

Skills—No data available.

Work Environment: Indoors; noisy; standing; walking and running; using hands on objects, tools, or controls; repetitive motions.

Painters, Transportation Equipment

- Annual Earnings: $34,840
- Growth: 14.1%
- Annual Job Openings: 10,000
- Self-Employed: 5.4%
- Part-Time: 5.7%
- Civilian Training Route: Long-term on-the-job training

Operate or tend painting machines to paint surfaces of transportation equipment, such as automobiles, buses, trucks, trains, boats, and airplanes. Dispose of hazardous waste in an appropriate manner. Select paint according to company requirements and match colors of paint following specified color charts. Mix paints to match color specifications or vehicles' original colors; then stir and thin the paints, using spatulas or power mixing equipment. Remove grease, dirt, paint, and rust from vehicle surfaces in preparation for paint application, using abrasives, solvents, brushes, blowtorches, washing tanks, or sandblasters. Pour paint into spray guns and adjust nozzles and paint mixes to get the proper paint flow and coating thickness. Monitor painting operations to identify flaws such as blisters and streaks so that their causes can be corrected. Sand vehicle surfaces between coats of paint or primer to remove flaws and enhance adhesion for subsequent coats. Disassemble, clean, and reassemble sprayers and power equipment, using solvents, wire brushes, and cloths for cleaning duties. Remove accessories from vehicles, such as chrome or mirrors, and mask other surfaces with tape or paper to protect them from paint. Spray prepared surfaces with specified amounts of primers and decorative or finish coatings. Allow the sprayed product to dry and then touch up any spots that may have been missed. Apply rust-resistant undercoats and caulk and seal seams. Select the correct spray gun system for the material being applied. Apply primer over any repairs made to vehicle surfaces. Adjust controls on infrared ovens, heat lamps, portable ventilators, and exhaust units to speed the drying of vehicles between coats. Fill small dents and scratches with body fillers and smooth surfaces to prepare vehicles for painting. Apply designs, lettering, or other identifying or decorative items to finished products, using paint brushes or paint sprayers. Paint by hand areas that cannot be reached with a spray gun or those that need retouching, using brushes. Sand the final finish and apply sealer once a vehicle has dried properly. Buff and wax the finished paintwork. Lay out logos, symbols, or designs on painted surfaces according to blueprint specifications, using measuring instruments, stencils, and patterns.

Military Job That Provides Training for It (see the description in Part II): Aircraft Mechanics

Personality Type: Realistic. Realistic occupations frequently involve work activities that include practical, hands-on problems and solutions. They often deal with plants, animals, and real-world materials like wood, tools, and machinery. Many of the occupations require working outside and do not involve a lot of paperwork or working closely with others.

GOE—Interest Area: 13. Manufacturing. **Work Group:** 13.09. Hands-On Work, Assorted Materials. **Other Civilian Jobs in This Work Group:** Coil Winders, Tapers, and Finishers; Cutters and Trimmers, Hand; Fabric and Apparel Patternmakers; Glass Blowers, Molders, Benders, and Finishers; Grinding and Polishing Workers, Hand; Molding and Casting Workers; Painting, Coating, and Decorating Workers; Sewers, Hand.

Skills—Repairing: Repairing machines or systems, using the needed tools. **Equipment Maintenance:** Performing routine maintenance on equipment and determining when and what kind of maintenance is needed. **Monitoring:** Monitoring/assessing your performance or that of other individuals or organizations to make improvements or take corrective action. **Technology Design:** Generating or adapting equipment and technology to serve user needs. **Operation and Control:** Controlling operations of equipment or systems. **Coordination:** Adjusting actions in relation to others' actions. **Equipment Selection:** Determining the kinds of tools and equipment needed to do a job. **Science:** Using scientific rules and methods to solve problems.

Work Environment: Noisy; contaminants; hazardous conditions; standing; using hands on objects, tools, or controls; repetitive motions.

Paralegals and Legal Assistants

- Annual Earnings: $41,170
- Growth: 29.7%
- Annual Job Openings: 28,000
- Self-Employed: 4.2%
- Part-Time: 11.1%
- Civilian Training Route: Associate degree

Assist lawyers by researching legal precedent, investigating facts, or preparing legal documents. Conduct research to support a legal proceeding, to formulate a defense, or to initiate legal action. Prepare legal documents, including briefs, pleadings, appeals, wills, contracts, and real estate closing statements. Prepare affidavits or other documents, maintain document file, and file pleadings with court clerk. Gather and analyze research data, such as statutes; decisions; and legal articles, codes, and documents. Investigate facts and law of cases to determine causes of action and to prepare cases. Call upon witnesses to testify at hearing. Direct and coordinate law office activity, including delivery of subpoenas. Arbitrate disputes between parties and assist in real estate closing process. Keep and monitor legal volumes to ensure that law library is up to date. Appraise and inventory real and personal property for estate planning.

Military Job That Provides Training for It (see the description in Part II): Legal Specialists and Court Reporters

P

Personality Type: Enterprising. Enterprising occupations frequently involve starting up and carrying out projects. These occupations can involve leading people and making many decisions. They sometimes require risk taking and often deal with business.

GOE—Interest Area: 12. Law and Public Safety. **Work Group:** 12.03. Legal Support. **Other Civilian Jobs in This Work Group:** Law Clerks; Title Examiners, Abstractors, and Searchers.

Skills—No data available.

Work Environment: Indoors; sitting; repetitive motions.

Paving, Surfacing, and Tamping Equipment Operators

- Annual Earnings: $30,320
- Growth: 15.6%
- Annual Job Openings: 7,000
- Self-Employed: 1.2%
- Part-Time: 6.3%
- Civilian Training Route: Moderate-term on-the-job training

Operate equipment used for applying concrete, asphalt, or other materials to road beds, parking lots, or airport runways and taxiways or equipment used for tamping gravel, dirt, or other materials. Includes concrete and asphalt paving machine operators, form tampers, tamping machine operators, and stone spreader operators. Start machine, engage clutch, and push and move levers to guide machine along forms or guidelines and to control the operation of machine attachments. Operate machines to spread, smooth, level, or steel-reinforce stone, concrete, or asphalt on road beds. Inspect, clean, maintain, and repair equipment, using mechanics' hand tools, or report malfunctions to supervisors. Operate oil distributors, loaders, chip spreaders, dump trucks, and snowplows. Coordinate truck dumping. Set up and tear down equipment. Operate tamping machines or manually roll surfaces to compact earth fills, foundation forms, and finished road materials according to grade specifications. Shovel blacktop. Drive machines onto truck trailers and drive trucks to transport machines and material to and from job sites. Observe distribution of paving material to adjust machine settings or material flow and indicate low spots for workers to add material. Light burners or start heating units of machines and regulate screed temperatures and asphalt flow rates. Control paving machines to push dump trucks and to maintain a constant flow of asphalt or other material into hoppers or screeds. Set up forms and lay out guidelines for curbs according to written specifications, using string, spray paint, and concrete/water mixes. Fill tanks, hoppers, or machines with paving materials. Drive and operate curbing machines to extrude concrete or asphalt curbing. Cut or break up pavement and drive guardrail posts, using machines equipped with interchangeable hammers. Install dies, cutters, and extensions to screeds onto machines, using hand tools. Operate machines that clean or cut expansion joints in concrete or asphalt and that rout out cracks in pavement. Place strips of material such as cork, asphalt, or steel into joints or place rolls of expansion-joint material on machines that automatically insert material.

Military Job That Provides Training for It (see the description in Part II): Construction Equipment Operators

Personality Type: Realistic. Realistic occupations frequently involve work activities that include practical, hands-on problems and solutions. They often deal with plants, animals, and real-world materials like wood, tools, and machinery. Many of the occupations require working outside and do not involve a lot of paperwork or working closely with others.

GOE—Interest Area: 02. Architecture and Construction. **Work Group:** 02.04. Construction Crafts. **Other Civilian Jobs in This Work Group:** Boilermakers; Brickmasons and Blockmasons; Carpet Installers; Cement Masons and Concrete Finishers; Commercial Divers; Construction Carpenters; Crane and Tower Operators; Drywall and Ceiling Tile Installers; Electricians; Fence Erectors; Floor Layers, Except Carpet, Wood, and Hard Tiles; Floor Sanders and Finishers; Glaziers; Hazardous Materials Removal Workers; Insulation Workers, Floor, Ceiling, and Wall; Insulation Workers, Mechani-cal; Manufactured Building and Mobile Home Installers; Operating Engineers and Other Construction Equipment Operators; Painters, Construction and Maintenance; Paperhangers; Pile-Driver Operators; Pipe Fitters and Steamfitters; Pipelayers; Plasterers and Stucco Masons; Plumbers; Plumbers, Pipefitters, and Steamfitters; Rail-Track Laying and Maintenance Equipment Operators; Refractory Materials Repairers, Except Brickmasons; Reinforcing Iron and Rebar Workers; Riggers; Roofers; Rough Carpenters; Security and Fire Alarm Systems Installers; Segmental Pavers; Sheet Metal Workers; Stone Cutters and Carvers, Manufacturing; Stonemasons; Structural Iron and Steel Workers; Tapers; Terrazzo Workers and Finishers; Tile and Marble Setters.

Skills—Operation Monitoring: Watching gauges, dials, or other indicators to make sure a machine is working properly. **Equipment Maintenance:** Performing routine maintenance on equipment and determining when and what kind of maintenance is needed. **Operation and Control:** Controlling operations of equipment or systems. **Repairing:** Repairing machines or systems, using the needed tools. **Installation:** Installing equipment, machines, wiring, or programs to meet specifications. **Equipment Selection:** Determining the kinds of tools and equipment needed to do a job. **Troubleshooting:** Determining causes of operating errors and deciding what to do about them. **Technology Design:** Generating or adapting equipment and technology to serve user needs.

Work Environment: Outdoors; noisy; very hot or cold; contaminants; hazardous equipment; using hands on objects, tools, or controls.

Payroll and Timekeeping Clerks

- Annual Earnings: $31,360
- Growth: 17.3%
- Annual Job Openings: 36,000
- Self-Employed: 1.1%
- Part-Time: 14.7%
- Civilian Training Route: Moderate-term on-the-job training

Compile and post employee time and payroll data. May compute employees' time worked, production, and commission. May compute

and post wages and deductions. May prepare paychecks. Process and issue employee paychecks and statements of earnings and deductions. Compute wages and deductions and enter data into computers. Compile employee time, production, and payroll data from time sheets and other records. Review time sheets, work charts, wage computation, and other information to detect and reconcile payroll discrepancies. Verify attendance, hours worked, and pay adjustments and post information onto designated records. Record employee information, such as exemptions, transfers, and resignations, to maintain and update payroll records. Keep informed about changes in tax and deduction laws that apply to the payroll process. Issue and record adjustments to pay related to previous errors or retroactive increases. Provide information to employees and managers on payroll matters, tax issues, benefit plans, and collective agreement provisions. Complete time sheets showing employees' arrival and departure times. Post relevant work hours to client files to bill clients properly. Distribute and collect timecards each pay period. Complete, verify, and process forms and documentation for administration of benefits such as pension plans and unemployment and medical insurance. Prepare and balance period-end reports and reconcile issued payrolls to bank statements. Compile statistical reports, statements, and summaries related to pay and benefits accounts and submit them to appropriate departments. Coordinate special programs, such as United Way campaigns, that involve payroll deductions.

Military Job That Provides Training for It (see the description in Part II): Finance and Accounting Specialists

Personality Type: Conventional. Conventional occupations frequently involve following set procedures and routines. These occupations can include working with data and details more than with ideas. Usually there is a clear line of authority to follow.

GOE—Interest Area: 04. Business and Administration. **Work Group:** 04.06. Mathematical Clerical Support. **Other Civilian Jobs in This Work Group:** Billing and Posting Clerks and Machine Operators; Billing, Cost, and Rate Clerks; Bookkeeping, Accounting, and Auditing Clerks; Brokerage Clerks; Statement Clerks; Tax Preparers.

Skills—Mathematics: Using mathematics to solve problems. **Time Management:** Managing one's own time and the time of others. **Active Listening:** Giving full attention to what other people are saying, taking time to understand the points being made, asking questions as appropriate, and not interrupting at inappropriate times. **Writing:** Communicating effectively in writing as appropriate for the needs of the audience. **Speaking:** Talking to others to convey information effectively. **Learning Strategies:** Selecting and using training/instructional methods and procedures appropriate for the situation when learning or teaching new things. **Judgment and Decision Making:** Considering the relative costs and benefits of potential actions to choose the most appropriate one. **Social Perceptiveness:** Being aware of others' reactions and understanding why they react as they do.

Work Environment: Indoors; noisy; sitting; repetitive motions.

Pest Control Workers

- Annual Earnings: $27,170
- Growth: 18.4%
- Annual Job Openings: 4,000
- Self-Employed: 9.7%
- Part-Time: 6.0%
- Civilian Training Route: Moderate-term on-the-job training

Spray or release chemical solutions or toxic gases and set traps to kill pests and vermin, such as mice, termites, and roaches, that infest buildings and surrounding areas. Record work activities performed. Inspect premises to identify infestation source and extent of damage to property, wall and roof porosity, and access to infested locations. Spray or dust chemical solutions, powders, or gases into rooms; onto clothing, furnishings, or wood; and over marshlands, ditches, and catch-basins. Clean work site after completion of job. Direct or assist other workers in treatment and extermination processes to eliminate and control rodents, insects, and weeds. Drive truck equipped with power spraying equipment. Measure area dimensions requiring treatment, using rule; calculate fumigant requirements; and estimate cost for service. Post warning signs and lock building doors to secure area to be fumigated. Cut or bore openings in building or surrounding concrete, access infested areas, insert nozzle, and inject pesticide to impregnate ground. Study preliminary reports and diagrams of infested area and determine treatment type required to eliminate and prevent recurrence of infestation. Dig up and burn or spray weeds with herbicides. Set mechanical traps and place poisonous paste or bait in sewers, burrows, and ditches. Clean and remove blockages from infested areas to facilitate spraying procedure and provide drainage, using broom, mop, shovel, and rake. Position and fasten edges of tarpaulins over building and tape vents to ensure airtight environment and check for leaks.

Military Job That Provides Training for It (see the description in Part II). Environmental Health and Safety Specialists

Personality Type: Realistic. Realistic occupations frequently involve work activities that include practical, hands-on problems and solutions. They often deal with plants, animals, and real-world materials like wood, tools, and machinery. Many of the occupations require working outside and do not involve a lot of paperwork or working closely with others.

GOE—Interest Area: 01. Agriculture and Natural Resources. **Work Group:** 01.05. Nursery, Groundskeeping, and Pest Control. **Other Civilian Jobs in This Work Group:** Landscaping and Groundskeeping Workers; Nursery Workers; Pesticide Handlers, Sprayers, and Applicators, Vegetation; Tree Trimmers and Pruners.

Skills—Persuasion: Persuading others to change their minds or behavior. **Service Orientation:** Actively looking for ways to help people. **Equipment Selection:** Determining the kinds of tools and equipment needed to do a job. **Social Perceptiveness:** Being aware of others' reactions and understanding why they react as they do. **Active Learning:** Understanding the implications of new information for both current and future problem-solving and decision-making. **Manage-ment of Material Resources:** Obtaining and seeing to the appropriate use of equipment, facilities, and materials needed to do certain work. **Coordination:** Adjusting actions in relation to others' actions. **Time Management:** Managing one's own time and the time of others.

Work Environment: More often outdoors than indoors; very hot or cold; contaminants; hazardous conditions; using hands on objects, tools, or controls.

Petroleum Pump System Operators, Refinery Operators, and Gaugers

- Annual Earnings: $51,060
- Growth: –8.6%
- Annual Job Openings: 6,000
- Self-Employed: 0.1%
- Part-Time: 0.8%
- Civilian Training Route: Long-term on-the-job training

Control the operation of petroleum-refining or -processing units. May specialize in controlling manifold and pumping systems, gauging or testing oil in storage tanks, or regulating the flow of oil into pipelines. Calculate test result values, using standard formulas. Clamp seals around valves to secure tanks. Signal other workers by telephone or radio to operate pumps, open and close valves, and check temperatures. Start pumps and open valves or use automated equipment to regulate the flow of oil in pipelines and into and out of tanks. Synchronize activities with other pumphouses to ensure a continuous flow of products and a minimum of contamination between products. Verify that incoming and outgoing products are moving through the correct meters and that meters are working properly. Prepare calculations for receipts and deliveries of oil and oil products. Read automatic gauges at specified intervals to determine the flow rate of oil into or from tanks and the amount of oil in tanks. Record and compile operating data, instrument readings, documentation, and results of laboratory analyses. Control or operate manifold and pumping systems to circulate liquids through a petroleum refinery. Monitor process indicators, instruments, gauges, and meters to detect and report any possible problems. Clean interiors of processing units by circulating chemicals and solvents within units. Operate control panels to coordinate and regulate process variables such as temperature and pressure and to direct product flow rate according to process schedules. Read and analyze specifications, schedules, logs, test results, and laboratory recommendations to determine how to set equipment controls to produce the required qualities and quantities of products. Perform tests to check the qualities and grades of products, such as assessing levels of bottom sediment, water, and foreign materials in oil samples, using centrifugal testers. Collect product samples by turning bleeder valves or by lowering containers into tanks to obtain oil samples. Patrol units to monitor the amount of oil in storage tanks and to verify that activities and operations are safe, efficient, and in compliance with regulations. Operate auxiliary equipment and control multiple processing units during distilling or treating operations, moving controls that regulate valves, pumps, compressors, and auxiliary equipment.

Military Jobs That Provide Training for It (see the descriptions in Part II): Non-Destructive Testers; Petroleum Supply Specialists

Personality Type: Realistic. Realistic occupations frequently involve work activities that include practical, hands-on problems and solutions. They often deal with plants, animals, and real-world materials like wood, tools, and machinery. Many of the occupations require working outside and do not involve a lot of paperwork or working closely with others.

GOE—Interest Area: 13. Manufacturing. **Work Group:** 13.16. Utility Operation and Energy Distribution. **Other Civilian Jobs in This Work Group:** Chemical Plant and System Operators; Gas Compressor and Gas Pumping Station Operators; Gas Plant Operators; Nuclear Power Reactor Operators; Power Distributors and Dispatchers; Power Plant Operators; Ship Engineers; Stationary Engineers and Boiler Operators; Water and Liquid Waste Treatment Plant and System Operators.

Skills—No data available.

Work Environment: Indoors; contaminants; hazardous conditions; standing; using hands on objects, tools, or controls.

Pharmacy Technicians

- Annual Earnings: $24,390
- Growth: 28.6%
- Annual Job Openings: 35,000
- Self-Employed: 0.3%
- Part-Time: 23.2%
- Civilian Training Route: Moderate-term on-the-job training

Prepare medications under the direction of a pharmacist. May measure, mix, count out, label, and record amounts and dosages of medications. Receive written prescription or refill requests and verify that information is complete and accurate. Maintain proper storage and security conditions for drugs. Answer telephones, responding to questions or requests. Fill bottles with prescribed medications and type and affix labels. Assist customers by answering simple questions, locating items, or referring them to the pharmacist for medication information. Price and file prescriptions that have been filled. Clean and help maintain equipment and work areas and sterilize glassware according to prescribed methods. Establish and maintain patient profiles, including lists of medications taken by individual patients. Order, label, and count stock of medications, chemicals, and supplies and enter inventory data into computer. Receive and store incoming supplies, verify quantities against invoices, and inform supervisors of stock needs and shortages. Transfer medication from vials to the appropriate number of sterile disposable syringes, using aseptic techniques. Under pharmacist supervision, add measured drugs or nutrients to intravenous solutions under sterile conditions to prepare intravenous (IV) packs. Supply and monitor robotic machines that dispense medicine into containers and label the containers. Prepare and process medical insurance claim forms and records. Mix pharmaceutical preparations according to written prescriptions. Operate cash registers to accept payment from customers. Compute charges for medication and equipment dispensed to hospital patients and enter data in computer. Deliver medications and pharmaceutical supplies to patients, nursing stations, or surgery. Price stock and mark items for sale. Maintain and merchandise home health-care products and services.

Military Job That Provides Training for It (see the description in Part II): Pharmacy Technicians

Personality Type: Conventional. Conventional occupations frequently involve following set procedures and routines. These occupations can include working with data and details more than with ideas. Usually there is a clear line of authority to follow.

GOE—Interest Area: 08. Health Science. **Work Group:** 08.02. Medicine and Surgery. **Other Civilian Jobs in This Work Group:** Anesthesiologists; Family and General

Practitioners; Internists, General; Medical Assistants; Medical Transcriptionists; Obstetricians and Gynecologists; Pediatricians, General; Pharmacists; Pharmacy Aides; Physician Assistants; Psychiatrists; Registered Nurses; Surgeons; Surgical Technologists.

Skills—No data available.

Work Environment: Indoors; standing; using hands on objects, tools, or controls; repetitive motions.

Photographers

- Annual Earnings: $26,100
- Growth: 12.3%
- Annual Job Openings: 23,000
- Self-Employed: 58.8%
- Part-Time: 28.9%
- Civilian Training Route: Long-term on-the-job training

Photograph persons, subjects, merchandise, or other commercial products. May develop negatives and produce finished prints. Take pictures of individuals, families, and small groups, either in studio or on location. Adjust apertures, shutter speeds, and camera focus based on a combination of factors such as lighting, field depth, subject motion, film type, and film speed. Use traditional or digital cameras, along with a variety of equipment such as tripods, filters, and flash attachments. Create artificial light, using flashes and reflectors. Determine desired images and picture composition; select and adjust subjects, equipment, and lighting to achieve desired effects. Scan photographs into computers for editing, storage, and electronic transmission. Test equipment prior to use to ensure that it is in good working order. Review sets of photographs to select the best work. Estimate or measure light levels, distances, and numbers of exposures needed, using measuring devices and formulas. Manipulate and enhance scanned or digital images to create desired effects, using computers and specialized software. Perform maintenance tasks necessary to keep equipment working properly. Perform general office duties such as scheduling appointments, keeping books, and ordering supplies. Consult with clients or advertising staff and study assignments to determine project goals, locations, and equipment needs. Select and assemble equipment and required background properties according to subjects, materials, and conditions. Enhance, retouch, and resize photographs and negatives, using airbrushing and other techniques. Set up, mount, or install photographic equipment and cameras. Produce computer-readable digital images from film, using flatbed scanners and photofinishing laboratories. Develop and print exposed film, using chemicals, touchup tools, and developing and printing equipment, or send film to photofinishing laboratories for processing. Direct activities of workers who are setting up photographic equipment. Employ a variety of specialized photographic materials and techniques, including infrared and ultraviolet films, macro-photography, photogrammetry, and sensitometry. Engage in research to develop new photographic procedures and materials.

Military Job That Provides Training for It (see the description in Part II): Photographic Specialists

Personality Type: Artistic. Artistic occupations frequently involve working with forms, designs, and patterns. They often require self-expression, and the work can be done without following a clear set of rules.

GOE—Interest Area: 03. Arts and Communication. **Work Group:** 03.09. Media

Technology. **Other Civilian Jobs in This Work Group:** Audio and Video Equipment Technicians; Broadcast Technicians; Camera Operators, Television, Video, and Motion Picture; Film and Video Editors; Multi-Media Artists and Animators; Radio Operators; Sound Engineering Technicians.

Skills—Persuasion: Persuading others to change their minds or behavior. **Equipment Maintenance:** Performing routine maintenance on equipment and determining when and what kind of maintenance is needed. **Management of Financial Resources:** Determining how money will be spent to get the work done and accounting for these expenditures. **Operation Monitoring:** Watching gauges, dials, or other indicators to make sure a machine is working properly. **Service Orientation:** Actively looking for ways to help people. **Monitoring:** Monitoring/assessing your performance or that of other individuals or organizations to make improvements or take corrective action. **Technology Design:** Generating or adapting equipment and technology to serve user needs. **Active Learning:** Understanding the implications of new information for both current and future problem-solving and decision-making.

Work Environment: More often indoors than outdoors; sitting; using hands on objects, tools, or controls.

Physical Therapist Assistants

- Annual Earnings: $39,490
- Growth: 44.2%
- Annual Job Openings: 7,000
- Self-Employed: 0.2%
- Part-Time: 28.6%
- Civilian Training Route: Associate degree

Assist physical therapists in providing physical therapy treatments and procedures. May, in accordance with state laws, assist in the development of treatment plans, carry out routine functions, document the progress of treatment, and modify specific treatments in accordance with patient status and within the scope of treatment plans established by a physical therapist. Generally requires formal training. Instruct, motivate, safeguard, and assist patients as they practice exercises and functional activities. Confer with physical therapy staff or others to discuss and evaluate patient information for planning, modifying, and coordinating treatment. Administer active and passive manual therapeutic exercises; therapeutic massage; and heat, light, sound, water, and electrical modality treatments such as ultrasound. Observe patients during treatments to compile and evaluate data on patients' responses and progress and report to physical therapist. Measure patients' range of joint motion, body parts, and vital signs to determine effects of treatments or for patient evaluations. Secure patients into or onto therapy equipment. Fit patients for orthopedic braces, prostheses, and supportive devices such as crutches. Train patients in the use of orthopedic braces, prostheses, or supportive devices. Transport patients to and from treatment areas, lifting and transferring them according to

P

positioning requirements. Monitor operation of equipment and record use of equipment and administration of treatment. Clean work area and check and store equipment after treatment. Assist patients to dress; undress; or put on and remove supportive devices such as braces, splints, and slings. Administer traction to relieve neck and back pain, using intermittent and static traction equipment. Perform clerical duties, such as taking inventory, ordering supplies, answering telephone, taking messages, and filling out forms. Prepare treatment areas and electrotherapy equipment for use by physiotherapists. Perform postural drainage, percussions, and vibrations and teach deep breathing exercises to treat respiratory conditions.

Military Job That Provides Training for It (see the description in Part II): Physical and Occupational Therapy Specialists

Personality Type: Social. Social occupations frequently involve working with, communicating with, and teaching people. These occupations often involve helping or providing service to others.

GOE—Interest Area: 08. Health Science. **Work Group:** 08.07. Medical Therapy. **Other Civilian Jobs in This Work Group:** Audiologists; Massage Therapists; Occupational Therapist Aides; Occupational Therapist Assistants; Occupational Therapists; Physical Therapist Aides; Physical Therapists; Radiation Therapists; Recreational Therapists; Respiratory Therapists; Respiratory Therapy Technicians; Speech-Language Pathologists.

Skills—Science: Using scientific rules and methods to solve problems. **Social Perceptiveness:** Being aware of others' reactions and understanding why they react as they do. **Service Orientation:** Actively looking for ways to help people. **Writing:** Communicating effectively in writing as appropriate for the needs of the audience. **Time Management:** Managing one's own time and the time of others. **Instructing:** Teaching others how to do something. **Speaking:** Talking to others to convey information effectively. **Reading Comprehension:** Understanding written sentences and paragraphs in work-related documents.

Work Environment: Indoors; disease or infections; standing; walking and running; using hands on objects, tools, or controls; bending or twisting the body.

Pilots, Ship

- Annual Earnings: $50,940
- Growth: 4.8%
- Annual Job Openings: 2,000
- Self-Employed: 5.4%
- Part-Time: 8.7%
- Civilian Training Route: Work experience in a related occupation

The job openings listed here are shared with Mates—Ship, Boat, and Barge and with Ship and Boat Captains.

Command ships to steer them into and out of harbors, estuaries, straits, and sounds and on rivers, lakes, and bays. Must be licensed by U.S. Coast Guard with limitations indicating class and tonnage of vessels for which license is valid and route and waters that may be piloted. Serve as a vessel's docking master upon arrival at a port and when at a berth. Prevent ships under their navigational control from engaging in unsafe operations. Provide assistance to vessels approaching or leaving seacoasts, navigating harbors, and docking and undocking. Steer ships into and out of berths or signal tugboat captains to berth and unberth ships. Advise ships' masters on harbor rules and customs procedures. Learn to operate new technology systems and procedures through the use of instruction, simulators, and models. Maintain and repair boats and equipment. Maintain ship logs. Oversee cargo storage on or below decks. Provide assistance in maritime rescue operations. Relieve crew members on tugs and launches. Report to appropriate authorities any violations of federal or state pilotage laws. Make nautical maps. Operate amphibious craft during troop landings. Operate ship-to-shore radios to exchange information needed for ship operations. Direct courses and speeds of ships based on specialized knowledge of local winds, weather, water depths, tides, currents, and hazards. Give directions to crew members who are steering ships. Set ships' courses that avoid reefs, outlying shoals, and other hazards, utilizing navigational aids such as lighthouses and buoys. Consult maps, charts, weather reports, and navigation equipment to determine and direct ship movements.

Military Jobs That Provide Training for It (see the descriptions in Part II): Quartermasters and Boat Operators; Ship and Submarine Officers

Personality Type: Realistic. Realistic occupations frequently involve work activities that include practical, hands-on problems and solutions. They often deal with plants, animals, and real-world materials like wood, tools, and machinery. Many of the occupations require working outside and do not involve a lot of paperwork or working closely with others.

GOE—Interest Area: 16. Transportation, Distribution, and Logistics. **Work Group:** 16.05. Water Vehicle Operation. **Other Civilian Jobs in This Work Group:** Captains, Mates, and Pilots of Water Vessels; Dredge Operators; Mates—Ship, Boat, and Barge; Motorboat Operators; Sailors and Marine Oilers; Ship and Boat Captains.

Skills—No data available.

Work Environment: More often indoors than outdoors; more often standing than sitting; keeping or regaining balance; using hands on objects, tools, or controls.

Pipe Fitters and Steamfitters

- Annual Earnings: $42,160
- Growth: 15.7%
- Annual Job Openings: 61,000
- Self-Employed: 13.3%
- Part-Time: 3.6%
- Civilian Training Route: Long-term on-the-job training

The job openings listed here are shared with Plumbers.

Lay out, assemble, install, and maintain pipe systems, pipe supports, and related hydraulic and pneumatic equipment for steam, hot water, heating, cooling, lubricating, sprinkling, and industrial production and processing systems. Cut, thread, and hammer pipe to specifications, using tools such as saws, cutting torches, and pipe threaders and benders. Assemble and secure pipes, tubes, fittings, and related equipment according to specifications by welding, brazing, cementing, soldering, and threading joints. Attach pipes to walls, structures, and fixtures, such as radiators or tanks, using brackets, clamps, tools, or welding equipment. Inspect, examine, and test installed systems and pipelines, using pressure gauge, hydrostatic testing, observation, or other methods. Measure and mark pipes for cutting and threading. Lay out full scale drawings of pipe systems, supports, and related equipment, following blueprints. Plan pipe system layout, installation, or repair according to specifications. Select pipe sizes and types and related materials, such as supports, hangers, and hydraulic cylinders, according to specifications. Cut and bore holes in structures such as bulkheads, decks, walls, and mains prior to pipe installation, using hand and power tools. Modify, clean, and maintain pipe systems, units, fittings, and related machines and equipment, following specifications and using hand and power tools. Install automatic controls used to regulate pipe systems. Turn valves to shut off steam, water, or other gases or liquids from pipe sections, using valve keys or wrenches. Remove and replace worn components. Prepare cost estimates for clients. Inspect work sites for obstructions and to ensure that holes will not cause structural weakness. Operate motorized pumps to remove water from flooded manholes, basements, or facility floors. Dip nonferrous piping materials in a mixture of molten tin and lead to obtain a coating that prevents erosion or galvanic and electrolytic action.

Military Job That Provides Training for It (see the description in Part II): Plumbers and Pipe Fitters

Personality Type: Realistic. Realistic occupations frequently involve work activities that include practical, hands-on problems and solutions. They often deal with plants, animals, and real-world materials like wood, tools, and machinery. Many of the occupations require working outside and do not involve a lot of paperwork or working closely with others.

GOE—Interest Area: 02. Architecture and Construction. **Work Group:** 02.04. Construction Crafts. **Other Civilian Jobs in This Work Group:** Boilermakers; Brickmasons and Blockmasons; Carpet Installers; Cement Masons and Concrete Finishers; Commercial Divers; Construction Carpenters; Crane and Tower Operators; Drywall and Ceiling Tile Installers; Electricians; Fence Erectors; Floor Layers, Except Carpet, Wood, and Hard Tiles; Floor Sanders and Finishers; Glaziers; Hazardous Materials Removal Workers; Insulation Workers, Floor, Ceiling, and Wall; Insulation Workers, Mechanical; Manufactured Building and Mobile Home Installers; Operating Engineers and Other Construction Equipment Operators; Painters, Construction and Maintenance; Paperhangers; Paving, Surfacing, and Tamping Equipment Operators; Pile-Driver Operators; Pipelayers; Plasterers and Stucco Masons; Plumbers; Plumbers, Pipefitters, and Steamfitters; Rail-Track Laying and Maintenance Equipment Operators; Refractory Materials Repairers, Except Brickmasons; Reinforcing Iron and Rebar Workers; Riggers; Roofers; Rough Carpenters; Security and Fire Alarm Systems Installers; Segmental Pavers; Sheet Metal Workers; Stone Cutters and Carvers, Manufacturing; Stonemasons; Structural Iron and Steel Workers; Tapers; Terrazzo Workers and Finishers; Tile and Marble Setters.

Skills—Installation: Installing equipment, machines, wiring, or programs to meet specifications. **Repairing:** Repairing machines or systems, using the needed tools. **Management of Personnel Resources:** Motivating, developing, and directing people as they work; identifying the best people for the job. **Systems Analysis:** Determining how a system should work and how changes in conditions, operations, and the environment will affect outcomes. **Equipment**

Maintenance: Performing routine maintenance on equipment and determining when and what kind of maintenance is needed. **Operation Monitoring:** Watching gauges, dials, or other indicators to make sure a machine is working properly. **Coordination:** Adjusting actions in relation to others' actions. **Technology Design:** Generating or adapting equipment and technology to serve user needs.

Work Environment: Outdoors; hazardous equipment; minor burns, cuts, bites, or stings; standing; using hands on objects, tools, or controls; repetitive motions.

Plumbers

- Annual Earnings: $42,160
- Growth: 15.7%
- Annual Job Openings: 61,000
- Self-Employed: 13.3%
- Part-Time: 3.6%
- Civilian Training Route: Long-term on-the-job training

The job openings listed here are shared with Pipe Fitters and Steamfitters.

Assemble, install, and repair pipes, fittings, and fixtures of heating, water, and drainage systems according to specifications and plumbing codes. Assemble pipe sections, tubing, and fittings, using couplings; clamps; screws; bolts; cement; plastic solvent; caulking; or soldering, brazing, and welding equipment. Fill pipes or plumbing fixtures with water or air and observe pressure gauges to detect and locate leaks. Review blueprints and building codes and specifications to determine work details and procedures. Prepare written work cost estimates and negotiate contracts. Study building plans and inspect structures to assess material and equipment needs, to establish the sequence of pipe installations, and to plan installation around obstructions such as electrical wiring. Keep records of assignments and produce detailed work reports. Perform complex calculations and planning for special or very large jobs. Locate and mark the position of pipe installations, connections, passage holes, and fixtures in structures, using measuring instruments such as rulers and levels. Measure, cut, thread, and bend pipe to required angle, using hand and power tools or machines such as pipe cutters, pipe-threading machines, and pipe-bending machines. Cut openings in structures to accommodate pipes and pipe fittings, using hand and power tools. Install pipe assemblies, fittings, valves, appliances such as dishwashers and water heaters, and fixtures such as sinks and toilets, using hand and power tools. Hang steel supports from ceiling joists to hold pipes in place. Repair and maintain plumbing, replacing defective washers, replacing or mending broken pipes, and opening clogged drains. Direct workers engaged in pipe cutting and preassembly and installation of plumbing systems and components. Install underground storm, sanitary, and water piping systems and extend piping to connect fixtures and plumbing to these systems. Clear away debris in a renovation. Install oxygen and medical gas in hospitals. Use specialized techniques, equipment, or materials, such as performing computer-assisted welding of small pipes or working with the special piping used in microchip fabrication.

Military Job That Provides Training for It (see the description in Part II): Plumbers and Pipe Fitters

Personality Type: Realistic. Realistic occupations frequently involve work activities that include practical, hands-on problems and solutions. They often deal with plants, animals, and real-world materials like wood, tools, and machinery. Many of the occupations require working outside and do not involve a lot of paperwork or working closely with others.

GOE—Interest Area: 02. Architecture and Construction. **Work Group:** 02.04. Construction Crafts. **Other Civilian Jobs in This Work Group:** Boilermakers; Brickmasons and Blockmasons; Carpet Installers; Cement Masons and Concrete Finishers; Commercial Divers; Construction Carpenters; Crane and Tower Operators; Drywall and Ceiling Tile Installers; Electricians; Fence Erectors; Floor Layers, Except Carpet, Wood, and Hard Tiles; Floor Sanders and Finishers; Glaziers; Hazardous Materials Removal Workers; Insulation Workers, Floor, Ceiling, and Wall; Insulation Workers, Mechanical; Manufactured Building and Mobile Home Installers; Operating Engineers and Other Construction Equipment Operators; Painters, Construction and Maintenance; Paperhangers; Paving, Surfacing, and Tamping Equipment Operators; Pile-Driver Operators; Pipe Fitters and Steamfitters; Pipelayers; Plasterers and Stucco Masons; Plumbers, Pipefitters, and Steamfitters; Rail-Track Laying and Maintenance Equipment Operators; Refractory Materials Repairers, Except Brickmasons; Reinforcing Iron and Rebar Workers; Riggers; Roofers; Rough Carpenters; Security and Fire Alarm Systems Installers; Segmental Pavers; Sheet Metal Workers; Stone Cutters and Carvers, Manufacturing; Stonemasons; Structural Iron and Steel Workers; Tapers; Terrazzo Workers and Finishers; Tile and Marble Setters.

Skills—Installation: Installing equipment, machines, wiring, or programs to meet specifications. **Repairing:** Repairing machines or systems, using the needed tools. **Systems Evaluation:** Identifying measures or indicators of system performance and the actions needed to improve or correct performance relative to the goals of the system. **Management of Material Resources:** Obtaining and seeing to the appropriate use of equipment, facilities, and materials needed to do certain work. **Science:** Using scientific rules and methods to solve problems. **Management of Financial Resources:** Determining how money will be spent to get the work done and accounting for these expenditures. **Equipment Selection:** Determining the kinds of tools and equipment needed to do a job. **Equipment Maintenance:** Performing routine maintenance on equipment and determining when and what kind of maintenance is needed.

Work Environment: Outdoors; contaminants; cramped work space, awkward positions; hazardous equipment; minor burns, cuts, bites, or stings; using hands on objects, tools, or controls.

Police Detectives

- Annual Earnings: $55,790
- Growth: 16.3%
- Annual Job Openings: 9,000
- Self-Employed: 0.0%
- Part-Time: 2.5%
- Civilian Training Route: Work experience in a related occupation

The job openings listed here are shared with Criminal Investigators and Special Agents; Immigration and Customs Inspectors; and Police Identification and Records Officers.

Conduct investigations to prevent crimes or solve criminal cases. Examine crime scenes to obtain clues and evidence, such as loose hairs, fibers, clothing, or weapons. Secure deceased body and obtain evidence from it, preventing bystanders from tampering with it prior to medical examiner's arrival. Obtain evidence from suspects. Provide testimony as a witness in court. Analyze completed police reports to determine what additional information and investigative work is needed. Prepare charges, responses to charges, or information for court cases according to formalized procedures. Note, mark, and photograph location of objects found, such as footprints, tire tracks, bullets, and bloodstains, and take measurements of the scene. Obtain facts or statements from complainants, witnesses, and accused persons and record interviews, using recording device. Obtain summary of incident from officer in charge at crime scene, taking care to avoid disturbing evidence. Examine records and governmental agency files to find identifying data about suspects. Prepare and serve search and arrest warrants. Block or rope off scene and check perimeter to ensure that entire scene is secured. Summon medical help for injured individuals and alert medical personnel to take statements from them. Provide information to lab personnel concerning the source of an item of evidence and tests to be performed. Monitor conditions of victims who are unconscious so that arrangements can be made to take statements if consciousness is regained. Secure persons at scene, keeping witnesses from conversing or leaving the scene before investigators arrive. Preserve, process, and analyze items of evidence obtained from crime scenes and suspects, placing them in proper containers and destroying evidence no longer needed. Record progress of investigation, maintain informational files on suspects, and submit reports to commanding officer or magistrate to authorize warrants. Organize scene search, assigning specific tasks and areas of search to individual officers and obtaining adequate lighting as necessary. Take photographs from all angles of relevant parts of a crime scene, including entrance and exit routes and streets and intersections.

Military Job That Provides Training for It (see the description in Part II): Law Enforcement and Security Specialists

Personality Type: Enterprising. Enterprising occupations frequently involve starting up and carrying out projects. These occupations can involve leading people and making many decisions. They sometimes require risk taking and often deal with business.

GOE—Interest Area: 12. Law and Public Safety. **Work Group:** 12.04. Law Enforcement and Public Safety. **Other Civilian Jobs in This Work Group:** Bailiffs; Correctional Officers and Jailers; Criminal Investigators and Special Agents; Detectives and Criminal Investigators; Fire Investigators; Forensic Science Technicians; Parking Enforcement Workers; Police and Sheriff's Patrol Officers; Police Identification and Records Officers; Police Patrol Officers; Sheriffs and Deputy Sheriffs; Transit and Railroad Police.

Skills—Persuasion: Persuading others to change their minds or behavior. **Negotiation:** Bringing others together and trying to reconcile differences. **Social Perceptiveness:** Being aware of others' reactions and understanding why they react as they do. **Coordination:** Adjusting actions in relation to others' actions. **Speaking:** Talking to others to convey information effectively. **Active Listening:** Giving full attention to what other people are saying, taking time to understand the points being made, asking questions as appropriate, and not interrupting at inappropriate times. **Service Orientation:**

Actively looking for ways to help people. **Writing:** Communicating effectively in writing as appropriate for the needs of the audience.

Work Environment: More often indoors than outdoors; very hot or cold; sitting.

Police Patrol Officers

- Annual Earnings: $46,290
- Growth: 15.5%
- Annual Job Openings: 47,000
- Self-Employed: 0.0%
- Part-Time: 1.4%
- Civilian Training Route: Long-term on-the-job training

The job openings listed here are shared with Sheriffs and Deputy Sheriffs.

Patrol assigned area to enforce laws and ordinances, regulate traffic, control crowds, prevent crime, and arrest violators. Provide for public safety by maintaining order, responding to emergencies, protecting people and property, enforcing motor vehicle and criminal laws, and promoting good community relations. Identify, pursue, and arrest suspects and perpetrators of criminal acts. Record facts to prepare reports that document incidents and activities. Review facts of incidents to determine if criminal act or statute violations were involved. Render aid to accident victims and other persons requiring first aid for physical injuries. Testify in court to present evidence or act as witness in traffic and criminal cases. Evaluate complaint and emergency-request information to determine response requirements. Patrol specific area on foot, horseback, or motorized conveyance, responding promptly to calls for assistance. Monitor, note, report, and investigate suspicious persons and situations, safety hazards, and unusual or illegal activity in patrol area. Investigate traffic accidents and other accidents to determine causes and to determine if a crime has been committed. Photograph or draw diagrams of crime or accident scenes and interview principals and eyewitnesses. Monitor traffic to ensure that motorists observe traffic regulations and exhibit safe driving procedures. Relay complaint and emergency-request information to appropriate agency dispatchers. Issue citations or warnings to violators of motor vehicle ordinances. Direct traffic flow and reroute traffic in case of emergencies. Inform citizens of community services and recommend options to facilitate longer-term problem resolution. Provide road information to assist motorists. Process prisoners and prepare and maintain records of prisoner bookings and prisoner status during booking and pre-trial process. Inspect public establishments to ensure compliance with rules and regulations. Act as official escorts, such as when leading funeral processions or firefighters.

Military Job That Provides Training for It (see the description in Part II): Law Enforcement and Security Specialists

Personality Type: Social. Social occupations frequently involve working with, communicating with, and teaching people. These occupations often involve helping or providing service to others.

GOE—Interest Area: 12. Law and Public Safety. **Work Group:** 12.04. Law Enforcement and Public Safety. **Other Civilian Jobs in This Work Group:** Bailiffs; Correctional Officers and Jailers; Criminal Investigators and Special Agents; Detectives and Criminal Investigators; Fire Investigators; Forensic Science Technicians; Parking Enforcement Workers; Police and

Sheriff's Patrol Officers; Police Detectives; Police Identification and Records Officers; Sheriffs and Deputy Sheriffs; Transit and Railroad Police.

Skills—Persuasion: Persuading others to change their minds or behavior. **Negotiation:** Bringing others together and trying to reconcile differences. **Judgment and Decision Making:** Considering the relative costs and benefits of potential actions to choose the most appropriate one. **Social Perceptiveness:** Being aware of others' reactions and understanding why they react as they do. **Service Orientation:** Actively looking for ways to help people. **Active Listening:** Giving full attention to what other people are saying, taking time to understand the points being made, asking questions as appropriate, and not interrupting at inappropriate times. **Complex Problem Solving:** Identifying complex problems and reviewing related information to develop and evaluate options and implement solutions. **Speaking:** Talking to others to convey information effectively.

Work Environment: Outdoors; noisy; very hot or cold; contaminants; hazardous equipment; using hands on objects, tools, or controls.

Postal Service Clerks

- Annual Earnings: $48,310
- Growth: 0.0%
- Annual Job Openings: 4,000
- Self-Employed: 0.0%
- Part-Time: 6.7%
- Civilian Training Route: Short-term on-the-job training

Perform any combination of tasks in a post office, such as receiving letters and parcels; selling postage and revenue stamps, postal cards, and stamped envelopes; filling out and selling money orders; placing mail in pigeonholes of mail rack or in bags according to state, address, or other scheme; and examining mail for correct postage. Keep money drawers in order and record and balance daily transactions. Weigh letters and parcels; compute mailing costs based on type, weight, and destination; and affix correct postage. Obtain signatures from recipients of registered or special delivery mail. Register, certify, and insure letters and parcels. Sell and collect payment for products such as stamps, prepaid mail envelopes, and money orders. Check mail to ensure correct postage and that packages and letters are in proper condition for mailing. Answer questions regarding mail regulations and procedures, postage rates, and post office boxes. Complete forms regarding changes of address or theft or loss of mail or for special services such as registered or priority mail. Provide assistance to the public in complying with federal regulations of Postal Service and other federal agencies. Sort incoming and outgoing mail according to type and destination by hand or by operating electronic mail-sorting and scanning devices. Cash money orders. Rent post office boxes to customers. Put undelivered parcels away, retrieve them when customers come to claim them, and complete any related documentation. Provide customers with assistance in filing claims for mail theft or lost or damaged mail. Respond to complaints regarding mail theft, delivery problems, and lost or damaged mail, filling out forms and making appropriate referrals for investigation. Receive letters and parcels and place mail into bags. Feed mail into postage-canceling devices or hand-stamp mail to cancel postage. Transport mail

P

from one workstation to another. Set postage meters and calibrate them to ensure correct operation. Post announcements or government information on public bulletin boards.

Military Jobs That Provide Training for It (see the descriptions in Part II): Administrative Support Specialists; Cargo Specialists; Warehousing and Distribution Specialists

Personality Type: Conventional. Conventional occupations frequently involve following set procedures and routines. These occupations can include working with data and details more than with ideas. Usually there is a clear line of authority to follow.

GOE—Interest Area: 04. Business and Administration. **Work Group:** 04.07. Records and Materials Processing. **Other Civilian Jobs in This Work Group:** Correspondence Clerks; File Clerks; Human Resources Assistants, Except Payroll and Timekeeping; Marking Clerks; Meter Readers, Utilities; Office Clerks, General; Order Fillers, Wholesale and Retail Sales; Postal Service Mail Sorters, Processors, and Processing Machine Operators; Procurement Clerks; Production, Planning, and Expediting Clerks; Shipping, Receiving, and Traffic Clerks; Stock Clerks and Order Fillers; Stock Clerks, Sales Floor; Stock Clerks—Stockroom, Warehouse, or Storage Yard; Weighers, Measurers, Checkers, and Samplers, Recordkeeping.

Skills—No data available.

Work Environment: Indoors; noisy; contaminants; standing; bending or twisting the body; repetitive motions.

Power Plant Operators

- Annual Earnings: $53,170
- Growth: –0.4%
- Annual Job Openings: 5,000
- Self-Employed: 0.0%
- Part-Time: 1.5%
- Civilian Training Route: Long-term on-the-job training

Control, operate, or maintain machinery to generate electric power. Includes auxiliary equipment operators. Monitor and inspect power plant equipment and indicators to detect evidence of operating problems. Adjust controls to generate specified electrical power or to regulate the flow of power between generating stations and substations. Operate or control power-generating equipment, including boilers, turbines, generators, and reactors, using control boards or semi-automatic equipment. Regulate equipment operations and conditions such as water levels based on data from recording and indicating instruments or from computers. Take readings from charts, meters, and gauges at established intervals and take corrective steps as necessary. Inspect records and logbook entries and communicate with other plant personnel to assess equipment operating status. Start or stop generators, auxiliary pumping equipment, turbines, and other power plant equipment and connect or disconnect equipment from circuits. Control and maintain auxiliary equipment, such as pumps, fans, compressors, condensers, feedwater heaters, filters, and chlorinators, to supply water, fuel, lubricants, air, and auxiliary power. Clean, lubricate, and maintain equipment such as generators, turbines, pumps, and compressors to prevent equipment failure or deterioration. Communicate with systems operators to regulate and coordinate transmission loads and frequencies and line voltages. Record and compile operational data, completing and maintaining forms, logs, and reports. Open and close valves and switches in sequence upon signals from other workers to start or shut down auxiliary units. Collect oil, water, and electrolyte samples for laboratory analysis. Make adjustments or minor repairs, such as tightening leaking gland and pipe joints; report any needs for major repairs. Control generator output to match the phase, frequency, and voltage of electricity supplied to panels. Place standby emergency electrical generators on line in emergencies and monitor the temperature, output, and lubrication of the system. Receive outage calls and call in necessary personnel during power outages and emergencies.

Military Jobs That Provide Training for It (see the descriptions in Part II): Power Plant Operators; Powerhouse Mechanics

Personality Type: Realistic. Realistic occupations frequently involve work activities that include practical, hands-on problems and solutions. They often deal with plants, animals, and real-world materials like wood, tools, and machinery. Many of the occupations require working outside and do not involve a lot of paperwork or working closely with others.

GOE—Interest Area: 13. Manufacturing. **Work Group:** 13.16. Utility Operation and Energy Distribution. **Other Civilian Jobs in This Work Group:** Chemical Plant and System Operators; Gas Compressor and Gas Pumping Station Operators; Gas Plant Operators; Nuclear Power Reactor Operators; Petroleum Pump System Operators, Refinery Operators, and Gaugers; Power Distributors and Dispatchers; Ship Engineers; Stationary Engineers and Boiler Operators; Water and Liquid Waste Treatment Plant and System Operators.

Skills—Operation Monitoring: Watching gauges, dials, or other indicators to make sure a machine is working properly. **Equipment Maintenance:** Performing routine maintenance on equipment and determining when and what kind of maintenance is needed. **Operation and Control:** Controlling operations of equipment or systems. **Technology Design:** Generating or adapting equipment and technology to serve user needs. **Systems Evaluation:** Identifying measures or indicators of system performance and the actions needed to improve or correct performance relative to the goals of the system. **Coordination:** Adjusting actions in relation to others' actions. **Troubleshooting:** Determining causes of operating errors and deciding what to do about them. **Science:** Using scientific rules and methods to solve problems.

Work Environment: Indoors; noisy; very hot or cold; contaminants; high places; hazardous conditions.

Printing Machine Operators

- Annual Earnings: $30,730
- Growth: 2.9%
- Annual Job Openings: 26,000
- Self-Employed: 3.2%
- Part-Time: 8.1%
- Civilian Training Route: Moderate-term on-the-job training

Set up or operate various types of printing machines, such as offset, letterset, intaglio, or gravure presses or screen printers, to produce print on paper or other materials. Inspect and examine printed products for print clarity, color accuracy, conformance to specifications, and external defects. Push buttons, turn handles, or move controls and levers to start and control printing machines. Reposition printing plates, adjust pressure rolls, or otherwise adjust machines to improve print quality, using knobs, handwheels, or hand tools. Set and adjust speed, temperature, ink flow, and positions and pressure tolerances of equipment. Examine job orders to determine details such as quantities to be printed, production times, stock specifications, colors, and color sequences. Select and install printing plates, rollers, feed guides, gauges, screens, stencils, type, dies, and cylinders in machines according to specifications, using hand tools. Monitor feeding, printing, and racking processes of presses to maintain specified operating levels and to detect malfunctions; make any necessary adjustments. Operate equipment at slow speed to ensure proper ink coverage, alignment, and registration. Load, position, and adjust unprinted materials on holding fixtures or in equipment loading and feeding mechanisms. Pour or spread paint, ink, color compounds, and other materials into reservoirs, troughs, hoppers, or color holders of printing units, making measurements and adjustments to control color and viscosity. Repair, maintain, or adjust equipment. Blend and test paint, inks, stains, and solvents according to types of material being printed and work order specifications. Clean and lubricate printing machines and components, using oil, solvents, brushes, rags, and hoses. Remove printed materials from presses, using handtrucks, electric lifts, or hoists, and transport them to drying, storage, or finishing areas. Input instructions to program automated machinery, using a computer keyboard. Place printed items in ovens to dry or set ink. Squeeze or spread ink on plates, pads, or rollers, using putty knives, brushes, or sponges. Measure screens and use measurements to center and align screens in proper positions and sequences on machines, using gauges and hand tools.

Military Job That Provides Training for It (see the description in Part II): Printing Specialists

Personality Type: Realistic. Realistic occupations frequently involve work activities that include practical, hands-on problems and solutions. They often deal with plants, animals, and real-world materials like wood, tools, and machinery. Many of the occupations require working outside and do not involve a lot of paperwork or working closely with others.

GOE—Interest Area: 13. Manufacturing. **Work Group:** 13.08. Graphic Arts Production. **Other Civilian Jobs in This Work Group:** Bindery Workers; Desktop Publishers; Etchers and Engravers; Job Printers; Photographic Process Workers; Photographic Processing Machine Operators; Prepress Technicians and Workers.

Skills—Operation Monitoring: Watching gauges, dials, or other indicators to make sure a machine is working properly. **Operation and Control:** Controlling operations of equipment or systems. **Equipment Maintenance:** Performing routine maintenance on equipment and determining when and what kind of maintenance is needed. **Repairing:** Repairing machines or systems, using the needed tools. **Quality Control Analysis:** Conducting tests and inspections of products, services, or processes to evaluate quality or performance. **Troubleshooting:** Determining causes of operating errors and deciding what to do about them. **Technology Design:** Generating or adapting equipment and technology to serve user needs. **Equipment Selection:** Determining the kinds of tools and equipment needed to do a job.

Work Environment: Noisy; contaminants; hazardous conditions; hazardous equipment; standing; using hands on objects, tools, or controls.

Production, Planning, and Expediting Clerks

- Annual Earnings: $37,590
- Growth: 7.7%
- Annual Job Openings: 24,000
- Self-Employed: 1.2%
- Part-Time: 6.1%
- Civilian Training Route: Short-term on-the-job training

Coordinate and expedite the flow of work and materials within or between departments of an establishment according to production schedule. Duties include reviewing and distributing production, work, and shipment schedules; conferring with department supervisors to determine progress of work and completion dates; and compiling reports on progress of work, inventory levels, costs, and production problems. Examine documents, materials, and products and monitor work processes to assess completeness, accuracy, and conformance to standards and specifications. Review documents such as production schedules, work orders, and staffing tables to determine personnel and materials requirements and material priorities. Revise production schedules when required due to design changes, labor or material shortages, backlogs, or other interruptions, collaborating with management, marketing, sales, production, and engineering. Confer with department supervisors and other personnel to assess progress and discuss needed changes. Confer with establishment personnel, vendors, and customers to coordinate production and shipping activities and to resolve complaints or eliminate delays. Record production data, including volume produced, consumption of raw materials, and quality control measures. Requisition and maintain inventories of materials and supplies necessary to meet production demands. Calculate figures such as required amounts of labor and materials, manufacturing costs, and wages, using pricing schedules, adding machines, calculators, or computers. Distribute production schedules and work orders to departments. Compile information, such as production rates and progress, materials inventories, materials used, and customer information, so that status reports can be completed. Arrange for delivery, assembly, and distribution of supplies and parts to expedite flow of materials and meet production schedules. Contact suppliers to verify shipment details. Maintain files such as maintenance records, bills of lading, and cost reports. Plan production commitments and timetables for business units, specific programs, or jobs, using sales forecasts. Establish and prepare product construction directions and locations and information on required tools, materials, and equipment; numbers of workers needed; and cost projections. Compile and prepare documentation related to production sequences; transportation; personnel schedules; and purchase, maintenance, and repair orders. Provide documentation and information to account for delays, difficulties, and changes to cost estimates.

Military Jobs That Provide Training for It (see the descriptions in Part II): Preventive Maintenance Analysts; Transportation Specialists; Warehousing and Distribution Specialists

Personality Type: Conventional. Conventional occupations frequently involve following set procedures and routines. These occupations can include working with data and details more than with ideas. Usually there is a clear line of authority to follow.

GOE—Interest Area: 04. Business and Administration. **Work Group:** 04.07. Records and Materials Processing. **Other Civilian Jobs in This Work Group:** Correspondence Clerks; File Clerks; Human Resources Assistants, Except Payroll and Timekeeping; Marking Clerks; Meter Readers, Utilities; Office Clerks, General; Order Fillers, Wholesale and Retail Sales; Postal Service Clerks; Postal Service Mail Sorters, Processors, and Processing Machine Operators; Procurement Clerks; Shipping, Receiving, and Traffic Clerks; Stock Clerks and Order Fillers; Stock Clerks, Sales Floor; Stock Clerks—Stockroom, Warehouse, or Storage Yard; Weighers, Measurers, Checkers, and Samplers, Recordkeeping.

Skills—Management of Material Resources: Obtaining and seeing to the appropriate use of equipment, facilities, and materials needed to do certain work. **Management of Financial Resources:** Determining how money will be spent to get the work done and accounting for these expenditures. **Systems Evaluation:** Identifying measures or indicators of system performance and the actions needed to improve or correct performance relative to the goals of the system. **Operations Analysis:** Analyzing needs and product requirements to create a design. **Negotiation:** Bringing others together and trying to reconcile differences. **Persuasion:** Persuading others to change their minds or behavior. **Coordination:** Adjusting actions in relation to others' actions. **Active Learning:** Understanding the implications of new information for both current and future problem-solving and decision-making.

Work Environment: Indoors; noisy; contaminants; sitting.

Purchasing Agents, Except Wholesale, Retail, and Farm Products

- Annual Earnings: $49,030
- Growth: 8.1%
- Annual Job Openings: 19,000
- Self-Employed: 3.5%
- Part-Time: 5.6%
- Civilian Training Route: Work experience in a related occupation

Purchase machinery, equipment, tools, parts, supplies, or services necessary for the operation of an establishment. Purchase raw or semi-finished materials for manufacturing. Purchase the highest-quality merchandise at the lowest possible price and in correct amounts. Prepare purchase orders, solicit bid proposals, and review requisitions for goods and services. Research and evaluate suppliers based on price, quality, selection, service, support, availability, reliability, production and distribution capabilities, and the supplier's reputation and history. Analyze price proposals, financial reports, and other data and information to determine reasonable prices. Monitor and follow applicable laws and regulations. Negotiate, or renegotiate, and administer contracts with suppliers, vendors, and other representatives. Monitor shipments to ensure that goods come in on time and trace shipments and follow up undelivered goods in the event of problems. Confer with staff, users, and vendors to discuss defective or unacceptable goods or services and determine corrective action. Evaluate and monitor contract performance to ensure compliance with contractual obligations and to determine need for changes. Maintain and review computerized or manual records of items purchased, costs, delivery, product performance, and inventories. Review catalogs, industry periodicals, directories, trade journals, and Internet sites and consult with other department personnel to locate necessary goods and services. Study sales records and inventory levels of current stock to develop strategic purchasing programs that facilitate employee access to supplies. Interview vendors and visit suppliers' plants and distribution centers to examine and learn about products, services, and prices. Arrange the payment of duty and freight charges. Hire, train, and/or supervise purchasing clerks, buyers, and expediters. Write and review product specifications, maintaining a working technical knowledge of the goods or services to be purchased. Monitor changes affecting supply and demand, tracking market conditions, price trends, or futures markets. Formulate policies and procedures for bid proposals and procurement of goods and services. Attend meetings, trade shows, conferences, conventions, and seminars to network with people in other purchasing departments.

Military Jobs That Provide Training for It (see the descriptions in Part II): Administrative Support Specialists; Finance and Accounting Specialists

Personality Type: Enterprising. Enterprising occupations frequently involve starting up and carrying out projects. These occupations can involve leading people and making many decisions. They sometimes require risk taking and often deal with business.

GOE—Interest Area: 14. Retail and Wholesale Sales and Service. **Work Group:** 14.05. Purchasing. **Other Civilian Jobs in This Work Group:** Wholesale and Retail Buyers, Except Farm Products.

Skills—Operations Analysis: Analyzing needs and product requirements to create a design. **Management of Financial Resources:** Determining how money will be spent to get the work done and accounting for these expenditures. **Management of Personnel Resources:** Motivating, developing, and directing people as they work; identifying the best people for the job. **Management of Material Resources:** Obtaining and seeing to the appropriate use of equipment, facilities, and materials needed to do certain work. **Speaking:** Talking to others to convey information effectively. **Writing:** Communicating effectively in writing as appropriate for the needs of the audience. **Mathematics:** Using mathematics to solve problems. **Judgment and Decision Making:** Considering the relative costs and benefits of potential actions to choose the most appropriate one.

Work Environment: Indoors; sitting; using hands on objects, tools, or controls; repetitive motions.

Radiologic Technicians

- Annual Earnings: $45,950
- Growth: 23.2%
- Annual Job Openings: 17,000
- Self-Employed: 0.4%
- Part-Time: 17.2%
- Civilian Training Route: Associate degree

The job openings listed here are shared with Radiologic Technologists.

Maintain and use equipment and supplies necessary to demonstrate portions of the human body on X-ray film or fluoroscopic screen for diagnostic purposes. Use beam-restrictive

R

devices and patient-shielding techniques to minimize radiation exposure to patient and staff. Position X-ray equipment and adjust controls to set exposure factors, such as time and distance. Position patient on examining table and set up and adjust equipment to obtain optimum view of specific body area as requested by physician. Determine patients' X-ray needs by reading requests or instructions from physicians. Make exposures necessary for the requested procedures, rejecting and repeating work that does not meet established standards. Process exposed radiographs, using film processors or computer-generated methods. Explain procedures to patients to reduce anxieties and obtain cooperation. Perform procedures such as linear tomography; mammography; sonograms; joint and cyst aspirations; routine contrast studies; routine fluoroscopy; and examinations of the head, trunk, and extremities under supervision of physician. Prepare and set up X-ray room for patient. Assure that sterile supplies, contrast materials, catheters, and other required equipment are present and in working order, requisitioning materials as necessary. Maintain records of patients examined, examinations performed, views taken, and technical factors used. Provide assistance to physicians or other technologists in the performance of more complex procedures. Monitor equipment operation and report malfunctioning equipment to supervisor. Provide students and other technologists with suggestions of additional views, alternate positioning, or improved techniques to ensure the images produced are of the highest quality. Coordinate work of other technicians or technologists when procedures require more than one person. Assist with on-the-job training of new employees and students and provide input to supervisors regarding training performance. Maintain a current file of examination protocols. Operate mobile X-ray equipment in operating room, in emergency room, or at patient's bedside. Provide assistance in radiopharmaceutical administration, monitoring patients' vital signs and notifying the radiologist of any relevant changes.

Military Job That Provides Training for It (see the description in Part II): Radiologic (X-Ray) Technicians

Personality Type: Realistic. Realistic occupations frequently involve work activities that include practical, hands-on problems and solutions. They often deal with plants, animals, and real-world materials like wood, tools, and machinery. Many of the occupations require working outside and do not involve a lot of paperwork or working closely with others.

GOE—Interest Area: 08. Health Science. **Work Group:** 08.06. Medical Technology. **Other Civilian Jobs in This Work Group:** Biological Technicians; Cardiovascular Technologists and Technicians; Diagnostic Medical Sonographers; Medical and Clinical Laboratory Technicians; Medical and Clinical Laboratory Technologists; Medical Equipment Preparers; Medical Records and Health Information Technicians; Nuclear Medicine Technologists; Opticians, Dispensing; Orthotists and Prosthetists; Radiologic Technologists; Radiologic Technologists and Technicians.

Skills—Science: Using scientific rules and methods to solve problems. **Operation Monitoring:** Watching gauges, dials, or other indicators to make sure a machine is working properly. **Operation and Control:** Controlling operations of equipment or systems. **Service Orientation:** Actively looking for ways to help people. **Equipment Selection:** Determining the kinds of tools and equipment needed to do a job. **Negotiation:** Bringing others together and trying to reconcile differences. **Active Listening:**

Giving full attention to what other people are saying, taking time to understand the points being made, asking questions as appropriate, and not interrupting at inappropriate times. **Speaking:** Talking to others to convey information effectively.

Work Environment: Indoors; radiation; disease or infections; standing; walking and running; using hands on objects, tools, or controls.

Radiologic Technologists

- Annual Earnings: $45,950
- Growth: 23.2%
- Annual Job Openings: 17,000
- Self-Employed: 0.4%
- Part-Time: 17.2%
- Civilian Training Route: Associate degree

The job openings listed here are shared with Radiologic Technicians.

Take X rays and Computerized Axial Tomography (CAT or CT) scans or administer nonradioactive materials into patient's bloodstream for diagnostic purposes. Includes technologists who specialize in other modalities, such as computed tomography, ultrasound, and magnetic resonance. Review and evaluate developed X rays, videotape, or computer-generated information to determine if images are satisfactory for diagnostic purposes. Use radiation safety measures and protection devices to comply with government regulations and to ensure safety of patients and staff. Explain procedures and observe patients to ensure safety and comfort during scan. Operate or oversee operation of radiologic and magnetic imaging equipment to produce images of the body for diagnostic purposes. Position and immobilize patient on examining table. Position imaging equipment and adjust controls to set exposure time and distance according to specification of examination. Key commands and data into computer to document and specify scan sequences, adjust transmitters and receivers, or photograph certain images. Monitor video display of area being scanned and adjust density or contrast to improve picture quality. Monitor patients' conditions and reactions, reporting abnormal signs to physician. Prepare and administer oral or injected contrast media to patients. Set up examination rooms, ensuring that all necessary equipment is ready. Take thorough and accurate patient medical histories. Remove and process film. Record, process, and maintain patient data and treatment records and prepare reports. Coordinate work with clerical personnel or other technologists. Demonstrate new equipment, procedures, and techniques to staff and provide technical assistance. Provide assistance in dressing or changing seriously ill, injured, or disabled patients. Move ultrasound scanner over patient's body and watch pattern produced on video screen. Measure thickness of section to be radiographed, using instruments similar to measuring tapes. Operate fluoroscope to aid physician to view and guide wire or catheter through blood vessels to area of interest. Assign duties to radiologic staff to maintain patient flows and achieve production goals. Collaborate with other medical team members, such as physicians and nurses, to conduct angiography or special vascular procedures. Perform administrative duties such as developing departmental operating budget, coordinating purchases of supplies and equipment, and preparing work schedules.

Military Job That Provides Training for It (see the description in Part II): Radiologic (X-Ray) Technicians

Personality Type: Realistic. Realistic occupations frequently involve work activities that include practical, hands-on problems and solutions. They often deal with plants, animals, and real-world materials like wood, tools, and machinery. Many of the occupations require working outside and do not involve a lot of paperwork or working closely with others.

GOE—Interest Area: 08. Health Science. **Work Group:** 08.06. Medical Technology. **Other Civilian Jobs in This Work Group:** Biological Technicians; Cardiovascular Technologists and Technicians; Diagnostic Medical Sonographers; Medical and Clinical Laboratory Technicians; Medical and Clinical Laboratory Technologists; Medical Equipment Preparers; Medical Records and Health Information Technicians; Nuclear Medicine Technologists; Opticians, Dispensing; Orthotists and Prosthetists; Radiologic Technicians; Radiologic Technologists and Technicians.

Skills—Operation Monitoring: Watching gauges, dials, or other indicators to make sure a machine is working properly. **Social Perceptiveness:** Being aware of others' reactions and understanding why they react as they do. **Instructing:** Teaching others how to do something. **Reading Comprehension:** Understanding written sentences and paragraphs in work-related documents. **Service Orientation:** Actively looking for ways to help people. **Active Listening:** Giving full attention to what other people are saying, taking time to understand the points being made, asking questions as appropriate, and not interrupting at inappropriate times. **Speaking:** Talking to others to convey information effectively. **Science:** Using scientific rules and methods to solve problems.

Work Environment: Indoors; disease or infections; standing; walking and running; using hands on objects, tools, or controls; repetitive motions.

Refrigeration Mechanics and Installers

- Annual Earnings: $37,040
- Growth: 19.0%
- Annual Job Openings: 33,000
- Self-Employed: 13.1%
- Part-Time: 3.6%
- Civilian Training Route: Long-term on-the-job training

The job openings listed here are shared with Heating and Air Conditioning Mechanics and Installers.

Install and repair industrial and commercial refrigerating systems. Braze or solder parts to repair defective joints and leaks. Observe and test system operation, using gauges and instruments. Test lines, components, and connections for leaks. Dismantle malfunctioning systems and test components, using electrical, mechanical, and pneumatic testing equipment. Adjust or replace worn or defective mechanisms and parts and reassemble repaired systems. Read blueprints to determine location, size, capacity, and type of components needed to build refrigeration system. Supervise and instruct assistants. Perform mechanical overhauls and refrigerant reclaiming. Install wiring to connect components to an electric power source. Cut, bend, thread, and connect pipe to functional components and water, power, or refrigeration system.

Adjust valves according to specifications and charge system with proper type of refrigerant by pumping the specified gas or fluid into the system. Estimate, order, pick up, deliver, and install materials and supplies needed to maintain equipment in good working condition. Install expansion and control valves, using acetylene torches and wrenches. Mount compressor, condenser, and other components in specified locations on frames, using hand tools and acetylene welding equipment. Keep records of repairs and replacements made and causes of malfunctions. Schedule work with customers and initiate work orders, house requisitions, and orders from stock. Lay out reference points for installation of structural and functional components, using measuring instruments. Fabricate and assemble structural and functional components of refrigeration system, using hand tools, power tools, and welding equipment. Lift and align components into position, using hoist or block and tackle. Drill holes and install mounting brackets and hangers into floor and walls of building. Insulate shells and cabinets of systems.

Military Job That Provides Training for It (see the description in Part II): Heating and Cooling Mechanics

Personality Type: Realistic. Realistic occupations frequently involve work activities that include practical, hands-on problems and solutions. They often deal with plants, animals, and real-world materials like wood, tools, and machinery. Many of the occupations require working outside and do not involve a lot of paperwork or working closely with others.

GOE—Interest Area: 02. Architecture and Construction. **Work Group:** 02.05. Systems and Equipment Installation, Maintenance, and Repair. **Other Civilian Jobs in This Work Group:** Electrical and Electronics Repairers, Powerhouse, Substation, and Relay; Electrical Power-Line Installers and Repairers; Elevator Installers and Repairers; Heating and Air Conditioning Mechanics and Installers; Maintenance and Repair Workers, General; Telecommunications Equipment Installers and Repairers, Except Line Installers; Telecommunications Line Installers and Repairers.

Skills—Installation: Installing equipment, machines, wiring, or programs to meet specifications. **Repairing:** Repairing machines or systems, using the needed tools. **Equipment Maintenance:** Performing routine maintenance on equipment and determining when and what kind of maintenance is needed. **Operation Monitoring:** Watching gauges, dials, or other indicators to make sure a machine is working properly. **Systems Evaluation:** Identifying measures or indicators of system performance and the actions needed to improve or correct performance relative to the goals of the system. **Systems Analysis:** Determining how a system should work and how changes in conditions, operations, and the environment will affect outcomes. **Science:** Using scientific rules and methods to solve problems. **Troubleshooting:** Determining causes of operating errors and deciding what to do about them.

Work Environment: Outdoors; very hot or cold; cramped work space, awkward positions; minor burns, cuts, bites, or stings; standing; using hands on objects, tools, or controls.

Retail Salespersons

- Annual Earnings: $19,140
- Growth: 17.3%
- Annual Job Openings: 1,350,000
- Self-Employed: 3.4%
- Part-Time: 36.7%
- Civilian Training Route: Short-term on-the-job training

Sell merchandise, such as furniture, motor vehicles, appliances, or apparel, in a retail establishment. Greet customers and ascertain what each customer wants or needs. Open and close cash registers, performing tasks such as counting money; separating charge slips, coupons, and vouchers; balancing cash drawers; and making deposits. Maintain knowledge of current sales and promotions, policies regarding payment and exchanges, and security practices. Compute sales prices and total purchases and receive and process cash or credit payment. Watch for and recognize security risks and thefts and know how to prevent or handle these situations. Maintain records related to sales. Recommend, select, and help locate or obtain merchandise based on customer needs and desires. Answer questions regarding the store and its merchandise. Describe merchandise and explain use, operation, and care of merchandise to customers. Prepare sales slips or sales contracts. Ticket, arrange, and display merchandise to promote sales. Place special orders or call other stores to find desired items. Demonstrate use or operation of merchandise. Clean shelves, counters, and tables. Exchange merchandise for customers and accept returns. Bag or package purchases and wrap gifts. Help customers try on or fit merchandise. Inventory stock and requisition new stock. Prepare merchandise for purchase or rental. Sell or arrange for delivery, insurance, financing, or service contracts for merchandise. Estimate and quote trade-in allowances. Estimate cost of repair or alteration of merchandise. Estimate quantity and cost of merchandise required, such as paint or floor covering. Rent merchandise to customers.

Military Jobs That Provide Training for It (see the descriptions in Part II): Recreation, Welfare, and Morale Specialists; Sales and Stock Specialists

Personality Type: Enterprising. Enterprising occupations frequently involve starting up and carrying out projects. These occupations can involve leading people and making many decisions. They sometimes require risk taking and often deal with business.

GOE—**Interest Area:** 14. Retail and Wholesale Sales and Service. **Work Group:** 14.03. General Sales. **Other Civilian Jobs in This Work Group:** Parts Salespersons; Real Estate Brokers; Real Estate Sales Agents; Sales Representatives, Wholesale and Manufacturing, Except Technical and Scientific Products; Service Station Attendants.

Skills—No data available.

Work Environment: Indoors; standing; walking and running; using hands on objects, tools, or controls; repetitive motions.

Riggers

- Annual Earnings: $37,010
- Growth: 13.9%
- Annual Job Openings: 2,000
- Self-Employed: 0.0%
- Part-Time: 1.9%
- Civilian Training Route: Short-term on-the-job training

Set up or repair rigging for construction projects, manufacturing plants, logging yards, ships and shipyards, or for the entertainment industry. Manipulate rigging lines, hoists, and pulling gear to move or support materials such as heavy equipment, ships, or theatrical sets. Signal or verbally direct workers engaged in hoisting and moving loads to ensure safety of workers and materials. Dismantle and store rigging equipment after use. Control movement of heavy equipment through narrow openings or confined spaces, using chainfalls, gin poles, gallows frames, and other equipment. Attach pulleys and blocks to fixed overhead structures such as beams, ceilings, and gin pole booms, using bolts and clamps. Attach loads to rigging to provide support or prepare them for moving, using hand and power tools. Align, level, and anchor machinery. Select gear such as cables, pulleys, and winches according to load weights and sizes, facilities, and work schedules. Tilt, dip, and turn suspended loads to maneuver over, under, or around obstacles, using multi-point suspension techniques. Test rigging to ensure safety and reliability. Fabricate, set up, and repair rigging, supporting structures, hoists, and pulling gear, using hand and power tools. Install ground rigging for yarding lines, attaching chokers to logs and then to the lines. Clean and dress machine surfaces and component parts.

Military Job That Provides Training for It (see the description in Part II): Survival Equipment Specialists

Personality Type: Realistic. Realistic occupations frequently involve work activities that include practical, hands-on problems and solutions. They often deal with plants, animals, and real-world materials like wood, tools, and machinery. Many of the occupations require working outside and do not involve a lot of paperwork or working closely with others.

GOE—Interest Area: 02. Architecture and Construction. **Work Group:** 02.04. Construction Crafts. **Other Civilian Jobs in This Work Group:** Boilermakers; Brickmasons and Blockmasons; Carpet Installers; Cement Masons and Concrete Finishers; Commercial Divers; Construction Carpenters; Crane and Tower Operators; Drywall and Ceiling Tile Installers; Electricians; Fence Erectors; Floor Layers, Except Carpet, Wood, and Hard Tiles; Floor Sanders and Finishers; Glaziers; Hazardous Materials Removal Workers; Insulation Workers, Floor, Ceiling, and Wall; Insulation Workers, Mechanical; Manufactured Building and Mobile Home Installers; Operating Engineers and Other Construction Equipment Operators; Painters, Construction and Maintenance; Paperhangers; Paving, Surfacing, and Tamping Equipment Operators; Pile-Driver Operators; Pipe Fitters and Steamfitters; Pipelayers; Plasterers and Stucco Masons; Plumbers; Plumbers, Pipefitters, and Steamfitters; Rail-Track Laying and Maintenance Equipment Operators; Refractory Materials Repairers, Except Brickmasons; Reinforcing Iron and Rebar Workers; Roofers; Rough Carpenters; Security and Fire Alarm Systems Installers; Segmental Pavers; Sheet Metal Workers; Stone Cutters and Carvers, Manufacturing; Stonemasons; Structural Iron and Steel Workers; Tapers; Terrazzo Workers and Finishers; Tile and Marble Setters.

Skills—Repairing: Repairing machines or systems, using the needed tools. **Technology Design:** Generating or adapting equipment and technology to serve user needs. **Operation and Control:** Controlling operations of equipment or systems. **Science:** Using scientific rules and methods to solve problems. **Operation Monitoring:** Watching gauges, dials, or other indicators to make sure a machine is working properly. **Installation:** Installing equipment, machines, wiring, or programs to meet specifications. **Management of Material Resources:** Obtaining and seeing to the appropriate use of equipment, facilities, and materials needed to do certain work. **Quality Control Analysis:** Conducting tests and inspections of products, services, or processes to evaluate quality or performance.

Work Environment: Outdoors; high places; standing; walking and running; climbing ladders, scaffolds, or poles; using hands on objects, tools, or controls.

Roofers

- Annual Earnings: $31,230
- Growth: 16.8%
- Annual Job Openings: 38,000
- Self-Employed: 23.8%
- Part-Time: 10.3%
- Civilian Training Route: Moderate-term on-the-job training

Cover roofs of structures with shingles, slate, asphalt, aluminum, wood, and related materials. May spray roofs, sidings, and walls with material to bind, seal, insulate, or soundproof sections of structures. Install, repair, or replace single-ply roofing systems, using waterproof sheet materials such as modified plastics, elastomeric, or other asphaltic compositions. Apply alternate layers of hot asphalt or tar and roofing paper to roofs according to specification. Apply gravel or pebbles over top layers of roofs, using rakes or stiff-bristled brooms. Cement or nail flashing-strips of metal or shingle over joints to make them watertight. Cut roofing paper to size, using knives, and nail or staple roofing paper to roofs in overlapping strips to form bases for other materials. Punch holes in slate, tile, terra cotta, or wooden shingles, using punches and hammers. Hammer and chisel away rough spots or remove them with rubbing bricks to prepare surfaces for waterproofing. Spray roofs, sidings, and walls with material to bind, seal, insulate, or soundproof sections of structures, using spray guns, air compressors, and heaters. Cover exposed nailheads with roofing cement or caulking to prevent water leakage and rust. Clean and maintain equipment. Cut felt, shingles, and strips of flashing and fit them into angles formed by walls, vents, and intersecting roof surfaces. Glaze top layers to make a smooth finish or embed gravel in the bitumen for rough surfaces. Inspect problem roofs to determine the best procedures for repairing them. Align roofing materials with edges of roofs. Mop or pour hot asphalt or tar onto roof bases. Apply plastic coatings and membranes, fiberglass, or felt over sloped roofs before applying shingles. Install vapor barriers or layers of insulation on the roof decks of flat roofs and seal the seams. Install partially overlapping layers of material over roof insulation surfaces, determining distance of roofing material overlap by using chalk lines, gauges on shingling hatchets, or lines on shingles. Cover roofs and exterior walls of structures with slate, asphalt, aluminum, wood, gravel, gypsum, and/or related materials, using brushes, knives, punches, hammers, and other tools. Waterproof and damp-proof walls, floors, roofs, foundations, and basements by painting or spraying surfaces with waterproof coatings, or by attaching waterproofing membranes to surfaces. Estimate roofing materials and labor required to complete jobs and provide price quotes.

Military Job That Provides Training for It (see the description in Part II): Construction Specialists

Personality Type: Realistic. Realistic occupations frequently involve work activities that include practical, hands-on problems and solutions. They often deal with plants, animals, and real-world materials like wood, tools, and machinery. Many of the occupations require working outside and do not involve a lot of paperwork or working closely with others.

GOE—Interest Area: 02. Architecture and Construction. **Work Group:** 02.04. Construction Crafts. **Other Civilian Jobs in This Work Group:** Boilermakers; Brickmasons and Blockmasons; Carpet Installers; Cement Masons and Concrete Finishers; Commercial Divers; Construction Carpenters; Crane and Tower Operators; Drywall and Ceiling Tile Installers; Electricians; Fence Erectors; Floor Layers, Except Carpet, Wood, and Hard Tiles; Floor Sanders and Finishers; Glaziers; Hazardous Materials Removal Workers; Insulation Workers, Floor, Ceiling, and Wall; Insulation Workers, Mechanical; Manufactured Building and Mobile Home Installers; Operating Engineers and Other Construction Equipment Operators; Painters, Construction and Maintenance; Paperhangers; Paving, Surfacing, and Tamping Equipment Operators; Pile-Driver Operators; Pipe Fitters and Steamfitters; Pipelayers; Plasterers and Stucco Masons; Plumbers; Plumbers, Pipefitters, and Steamfitters; Rail-Track Laying and Maintenance Equipment Operators; Refractory Materials Repairers, Except Brickmasons; Reinforcing Iron and Rebar Workers; Riggers; Rough Carpenters; Security and Fire Alarm Systems Installers; Segmental Pavers; Sheet Metal Workers; Stone Cutters and Carvers, Manufacturing; Stonemasons; Structural Iron and Steel Workers; Tapers; Terrazzo Workers and Finishers; Tile and Marble Setters.

Skills—No data available.

Work Environment: Outdoors; high places; minor burns, cuts, bites, or stings; kneeling, crouching, stooping, or crawling; keeping or regaining balance; using hands on objects, tools, or controls.

Rough Carpenters

- Annual Earnings: $35,580
- Growth: 13.8%
- Annual Job Openings: 210,000
- Self-Employed: 32.4%
- Part-Time: 8.2%
- Civilian Training Route: Long-term on-the-job training

The job openings listed here are shared with Construction Carpenters.

Build rough wooden structures, such as concrete forms, scaffolds, tunnel, bridge, or sewer supports, billboard signs, and temporary frame shelters, according to sketches, blueprints, or oral instructions. Study blueprints and diagrams to determine dimensions of structure or form to be constructed. Measure materials or distances, using square, measuring tape, or rule to lay out work. Cut or saw boards, timbers, or plywood to required size, using handsaw, power saw, or

R

woodworking machine. Assemble and fasten material together to construct wood or metal framework of structure, using bolts, nails, or screws. Anchor and brace forms and other structures in place, using nails, bolts, anchor rods, steel cables, planks, wedges, and timbers. Mark cutting lines on materials, using pencil and scriber. Erect forms, framework, scaffolds, hoists, roof supports, or chutes, using hand tools, plumb rule, and level. Install rough door and window frames, subflooring, fixtures, or temporary supports in structures undergoing construction or repair. Examine structural timbers and supports to detect decay and replace timbers as required, using hand tools, nuts, and bolts. Bore boltholes in timber, masonry, or concrete walls, using power drill. Fabricate parts, using woodworking and metalworking machines. Dig or direct digging of post holes and set poles to support structures. Build sleds from logs and timbers for use in hauling camp buildings and machinery through wooded areas. Build chutes for pouring concrete.

Military Job That Provides Training for It (see the description in Part II): Construction Specialists

Personality Type: Realistic. Realistic occupations frequently involve work activities that include practical, hands-on problems and solutions. They often deal with plants, animals, and real-world materials like wood, tools, and machinery. Many of the occupations require working outside and do not involve a lot of paperwork or working closely with others.

GOE—Interest Area: 02. Architecture and Construction. **Work Group:** 02.04. Construction Crafts. **Other Civilian Jobs in This Work Group:** Boilermakers; Brickmasons and Blockmasons; Carpet Installers; Cement Masons and Concrete Finishers; Commercial Divers; Construction Carpenters; Crane and Tower Operators; Drywall and Ceiling Tile Installers; Electricians; Fence Erectors; Floor Layers, Except Carpet, Wood, and Hard Tiles; Floor Sanders and Finishers; Glaziers; Hazar-dous Materials Removal Workers; Insulation Workers, Floor, Ceiling, and Wall; Insulation Workers, Mechanical; Manufactured Building and Mobile Home Installers; Operating Engineers and Other Construction Equipment Operators; Painters, Construction and Maintenance; Paperhangers; Paving, Surfacing, and Tamping Equipment Operators; Pile-Driver Operators; Pipe Fitters and Steamfitters; Pipelayers; Plasterers and Stucco Masons; Plumbers; Plumbers, Pipefitters, and Steamfitters; Rail-Track Laying and Maintenance Equipment Operators; Refractory Materials Repairers, Except Brickmasons; Reinforcing Iron and Rebar Workers; Riggers; Roofers; Security and Fire Alarm Systems Installers; Segmental Pavers; Sheet Metal Workers; Stone Cutters and Carvers, Manufacturing; Stonemasons; Structural Iron and Steel Workers; Tapers; Terrazzo Workers and Finishers; Tile and Marble Setters.

Skills—Repairing: Repairing machines or systems, using the needed tools. **Installation:** Installing equipment, machines, wiring, or programs to meet specifications. **Management of Personnel Resources:** Motivating, developing, and directing people as they work; identifying the best people for the job. **Equipment Selection:** Determining the kinds of tools and equipment needed to do a job. **Mathematics:** Using mathematics to solve problems. **Technology Design:** Generating or adapting equipment and technology to serve user needs. **Equipment Maintenance:** Performing routine maintenance on equipment and determining when and what kind of maintenance is needed. **Coordination:** Adjusting actions in relation to others' actions.

Work Environment: Outdoors; noisy; very hot or cold; contaminants; standing; using hands on objects, tools, or controls.

Secretaries, Except Legal, Medical, and Executive

- Annual Earnings: $26,670
- Growth: –2.4%
- Annual Job Openings: 231,000
- Self-Employed: 1.2%
- Part-Time: 20.3%
- Civilian Training Route: Moderate-term on-the-job training

Perform routine clerical and administrative functions such as drafting correspondence, scheduling appointments, organizing and maintaining paper and electronic files, or providing information to callers. Operate office equipment such as fax machines, copiers, and phone systems and use computers for spreadsheet, word-processing, database management, and other applications. Answer telephones and give information to callers, take messages, or transfer calls to appropriate individuals. Greet visitors and callers, handle their inquiries, and direct them to the appropriate persons according to their needs. Set up and maintain paper and electronic filing systems for records, correspondence, and other material. Locate and attach appropriate files to incoming correspondence requiring replies. Open, read, route, and distribute incoming mail and other material and prepare answers to routine letters. Complete forms in accordance with company procedures. Make copies of correspondence and other printed material. Review work done by others to check for correct spelling and grammar, ensure that company format policies are followed, and recommend revisions. Compose, type, and distribute meeting notes, routine correspondence, and reports. Learn to operate new office technologies as they are developed and implemented. Maintain scheduling and event calendars. Schedule and confirm appointments for clients, customers, or supervisors. Manage projects and contribute to committee and team work. Mail newsletters, promotional material, and other information. Order and dispense supplies. Conduct searches to find needed information, using such sources as the Internet. Provide services to customers, such as order placement and account information. Collect and disburse funds from cash accounts and keep records of collections and disbursements. Prepare and mail checks. Establish work procedures and schedules and keep track of the daily work of clerical staff. Coordinate conferences and meetings. Take dictation in shorthand or by machine and transcribe information. Arrange conferences, meetings, and travel reservations for office personnel. Operate electronic mail systems and coordinate the flow of information both internally and with other organizations. Supervise other clerical staff and provide training and orientation to new staff.

Military Job That Provides Training for It (see the description in Part II): Administrative Support Specialists

Personality Type: Conventional. Conventional occupations frequently involve following set procedures and routines. These occupations can include working with data and details more than with ideas. Usually there is a clear line of authority to follow.

GOE—Interest Area: 04. Business and Administration. **Work Group:** 04.04. Secretarial

Support. **Other Civilian Jobs in This Work Group:** Executive Secretaries and Administrative Assistants; Legal Secretaries; Medical Secretaries.

Skills—No data available.

Work Environment: Indoors; sitting; repetitive motions.

Security Guards

- Annual Earnings: $20,760
- Growth: 12.6%
- Annual Job Openings: 230,000
- Self-Employed: 0.7%
- Part-Time: 17.1%
- Civilian Training Route: Short-term on-the-job training

Guard, patrol, or monitor premises to prevent theft, violence, or infractions of rules. Patrol industrial or commercial premises to prevent and detect signs of intrusion and ensure security of doors, windows, and gates. Answer alarms and investigate disturbances. Monitor and authorize entrance and departure of employees, visitors, and other persons to guard against theft and maintain security of premises. Write reports of daily activities and irregularities such as equipment or property damage, theft, presence of unauthorized persons, or unusual occurrences. Call police or fire departments in cases of emergency, such as fire or presence of unauthorized persons. Circulate among visitors, patrons, or employees to preserve order and protect property. Answer telephone calls to take messages, answer questions, and provide information during non-business hours or when switchboard is closed. Warn persons of rule infractions or violations and apprehend or evict violators from premises, using force when necessary. Operate detecting devices to screen individuals and prevent passage of prohibited articles into restricted areas. Escort or drive motor vehicle to transport individuals to specified locations or to provide personal protection. Inspect and adjust security systems, equipment, or machinery to ensure operational use and to detect evidence of tampering. Drive or guard armored vehicle to transport money and valuables to prevent theft and ensure safe delivery. Monitor and adjust controls that regulate building systems, such as air conditioning, furnace, or boiler.

Military Job That Provides Training for It (see the description in Part II): Law Enforcement and Security Specialists

Personality Type: Social. Social occupations frequently involve working with, communicating with, and teaching people. These occupations often involve helping or providing service to others.

GOE—Interest Area: 12. Law and Public Safety. **Work Group:** 12.05. Safety and Security. **Other Civilian Jobs in This Work Group:** Animal Control Workers; Crossing Guards; Gaming Surveillance Officers and Gaming Investigators; Lifeguards, Ski Patrol, and Other Recreational Protective Service Workers; Private Detectives and Investigators; Transportation Security Screeners.

Skills—No data available.

Work Environment: More often outdoors than indoors; noisy; very hot or cold; more often sitting than standing.

S

Sheet Metal Workers

- Annual Earnings: $36,390
- Growth: 12.2%
- Annual Job Openings: 50,000
- Self-Employed: 4.9%
- Part-Time: 5.7%
- Civilian Training Route: Long-term on-the-job training

Fabricate, assemble, install, and repair sheet metal products and equipment, such as ducts, control boxes, drainpipes, and furnace casings. Work may involve any of the following: setting up and operating fabricating machines to cut, bend, and straighten sheet metal; shaping metal over anvils, blocks, or forms, using hammer; operating soldering and welding equipment to join sheet metal parts; and inspecting, assembling, and smoothing seams and joints of burred surfaces. Determine project requirements, including scope, assembly sequences, and required methods and materials, according to blueprints, drawings, and written or verbal instructions. Lay out, measure, and mark dimensions and reference lines on material such as roofing panels according to drawings or templates, using calculators, scribes, dividers, squares, and rulers. Maneuver completed units into position for installation and anchor the units. Convert blueprints into shop drawings to be followed in the construction and assembly of sheet metal products. Install assemblies such as flashing, pipes, tubes, heating and air conditioning ducts, furnace casings, rain gutters, and downspouts in supportive frameworks. Select gauges and types of sheet metal or non-metallic material according to product specifications. Drill and punch holes in metal for screws, bolts, and rivets. Fasten seams and joints together with welds, bolts, cement, rivets, solder, caulks, metal drive clips, and bonds to assemble components into products or to repair sheet metal items. Fabricate or alter parts at construction sites, using shears, hammers, punches, and drills. Finish parts, using hacksaws and hand, rotary, or squaring shears. Trim, file, grind, deburr, buff, and smooth surfaces, seams, and joints of assembled parts, using hand tools and portable power tools. Maintain equipment, making repairs and modifications when necessary. Shape metal material over anvils, blocks, or other forms, using hand tools. Transport prefabricated parts to construction sites for assembly and installation. Develop and lay out patterns that use materials most efficiently, using computerized metalworking equipment to experiment with different layouts. Inspect individual parts, assemblies, and installations for conformance to specifications and building codes, using measuring instruments such as calipers, scales, and micrometers. Secure metal roof panels in place and interlock and fasten grooved panel edges. Fasten roof panel edges and machine-made molding to structures, nailing or welding pieces into place.

Military Job That Provides Training for It (see the description in Part II): Welders and Metal Workers

Personality Type: Realistic. Realistic occupations frequently involve work activities that include practical, hands-on problems and solutions. They often deal with plants, animals, and real-world materials like wood, tools, and machinery. Many of the occupations require working outside and do not involve a lot of paperwork or working closely with others.

GOE—Interest Area: 02. Architecture and Construction. **Work Group:** 02.04. Construction Crafts. **Other Civilian Jobs in This Work**

Group: Boilermakers; Brickmasons and Blockmasons; Carpet Installers; Cement Masons and Concrete Finishers; Commercial Divers; Construction Carpenters; Crane and Tower Operators; Drywall and Ceiling Tile Installers; Electricians; Fence Erectors; Floor Layers, Except Carpet, Wood, and Hard Tiles; Floor Sanders and Finishers; Glaziers; Hazardous Materials Removal Workers; Insulation Workers, Floor, Ceiling, and Wall; Insulation Workers, Mechanical; Manufactured Building and Mobile Home Installers; Operating Engineers and Other Construction Equipment Operators; Painters, Construction and Maintenance; Paperhangers; Paving, Surfacing, and Tamping Equipment Operators; Pile-Driver Operators; Pipe Fitters and Steamfitters; Pipelayers; Plasterers and Stucco Masons; Plumbers; Plumbers, Pipefitters, and Steamfitters; Rail-Track Laying and Maintenance Equipment Operators; Refractory Materials Repairers, Except Brickmasons; Reinforcing Iron and Rebar Workers; Riggers; Roofers; Rough Carpenters; Security and Fire Alarm Systems Installers; Segmental Pavers; Stone Cutters and Carvers, Manufacturing; Stonemasons; Structural Iron and Steel Workers; Tapers; Terrazzo Workers and Finishers; Tile and Marble Setters.

Skills—Installation: Installing equipment, machines, wiring, or programs to meet specifications. **Repairing:** Repairing machines or systems, using the needed tools. **Equipment Maintenance:** Performing routine maintenance on equipment and determining when and what kind of maintenance is needed. **Mathematics:** Using mathematics to solve problems. **Technology Design:** Generating or adapting equipment and technology to serve user needs. **Troubleshooting:** Determining causes of operating errors and deciding what to do about them. **Coordination:** Adjusting actions in relation to others' actions. **Equipment Selection:** Determining the kinds of tools and equipment needed to do a job.

Work Environment: Noisy; contaminants; hazardous equipment; minor burns, cuts, bites, or stings; standing; using hands on objects, tools, or controls.

Sheriffs and Deputy Sheriffs

- Annual Earnings: $46,290
- Growth: 15.5%
- Annual Job Openings: 47,000
- Self-Employed: 0.0%
- Part-Time: 1.4%
- Civilian Training Route: Long-term on-the-job training

The job openings listed here are shared with Police Patrol Officers.

Enforce law and order in rural or unincorporated districts or serve legal processes of courts. May patrol courthouse, guard court or grand jury, or escort defendants. Drive vehicles or patrol specific areas to detect law violators, issue citations, and make arrests. Investigate illegal or suspicious activities. Verify that the proper legal charges have been made against law offenders. Execute arrest warrants, locating and taking persons into custody. Record daily activities and submit logs and other related reports and paperwork to appropriate authorities. Patrol and guard courthouses, grand jury rooms, or assigned areas to provide security, enforce laws, maintain order, and arrest violators. Notify patrol units to take violators into custody or to provide needed assistance or medical aid. Place people in protective custody. Serve statements of claims, subpoenas, summonses, jury summonses, orders to pay alimony, and other court orders. Take control of accident scenes to maintain traffic flow, to assist accident victims, and to investigate causes. Question individuals entering secured areas to determine their business, directing and rerouting individuals as necessary. Transport or escort prisoners and defendants en route to courtrooms, prisons or jails, attorneys' offices, or medical facilities. Locate and confiscate real or personal property, as directed by court order. Manage jail operations and tend to jail inmates.

Military Job That Provides Training for It (see the description in Part II): Law Enforcement and Security Specialists

Personality Type: Social. Social occupations frequently involve working with, communicating with, and teaching people. These occupations often involve helping or providing service to others.

GOE—Interest Area: 12. Law and Public Safety. **Work Group:** 12.04. Law Enforcement and Public Safety. **Other Civilian Jobs in This Work Group:** Bailiffs; Correctional Officers and Jailers; Criminal Investigators and Special Agents; Detectives and Criminal Investigators; Fire Investigators; Forensic Science Technicians; Parking Enforcement Workers; Police and Sheriff's Patrol Officers; Police Detectives; Police Identification and Records Officers; Police Patrol Officers; Transit and Railroad Police.

Skills—Negotiation: Bringing others together and trying to reconcile differences. **Persuasion:** Persuading others to change their minds or behavior. **Social Perceptiveness:** Being aware of others' reactions and understanding why they react as they do. **Service Orientation:** Actively looking for ways to help people. **Complex Problem Solving:** Identifying complex problems and reviewing related information to develop and evaluate options and implement solutions. **Judgment and Decision Making:** Considering the relative costs and benefits of potential actions to choose the most appropriate one. **Coordination:** Adjusting actions in relation to others' actions. **Equipment Selection:** Determining the kinds of tools and equipment needed to do a job.

Work Environment: More often outdoors than indoors; very hot or cold; contaminants; disease or infections; sitting.

Ship and Boat Captains

- Annual Earnings: $50,940
- Growth: 4.8%
- Annual Job Openings: 2,000
- Self-Employed: 5.4%
- Part-Time: 8.7%
- Civilian Training Route: Work experience in a related occupation

The job openings listed here are shared with Mates—Ship, Boat, and Barge and with Pilots, Ship.

Command vessels in oceans, bays, lakes, rivers, and coastal waters. Steer and operate vessels, using radios, depth finders, radars, lights, buoys, and lighthouses. Interview and hire crew members. Sort logs, form log booms, and salvage lost logs. Perform various marine duties such as checking for oil spills or other pollutants around ports and harbors and patrolling beaches. Contact buyers to sell cargo such as fish. Tow and maneuver barges or signal tugboats to tow barges to destinations. Signal passing vessels, using whistles, flashing lights, flags, and radios. Resolve questions or problems with customs officials. Read gauges to verify sufficient levels of hydraulic fluid, air pressure, and oxygen. Monitor the loading and discharging of cargo or passengers. Measure depths of water, using depth-measuring equipment. Calculate sightings of land, using electronic sounding devices and following contour lines on charts. Assign watches and living quarters to crew members. Arrange for ships to be fueled, restocked with supplies, or repaired. Collect fares from customers or signal ferryboat helpers to collect fares. Signal crew members or deckhands to rig tow lines, open or close gates and ramps, and pull guard chains across entries. Maintain records of daily activities, personnel reports, ship positions and movements, ports of call, weather and sea conditions, pollution control efforts, and cargo and passenger status. Inspect vessels to ensure efficient and safe operation of vessels and equipment and conformance to regulations. Direct and coordinate crew members or workers performing activities such as loading and unloading cargo; steering vessels; operating engines; and operating, maintaining, and repairing ship equipment. Compute positions, set courses, and determine speeds by using charts, area plotting sheets, compasses, sextants, and knowledge of local conditions. Purchase supplies and equipment. Maintain boats and equipment on board, such as engines, winches, navigational systems, fire extinguishers, and life preservers.

Military Jobs That Provide Training for It (see the descriptions in Part II): Quartermasters and Boat Operators; Ship and Submarine Officers

Personality Type: Enterprising. Enterprising occupations frequently involve starting up and carrying out projects. These occupations can involve leading people and making many decisions. They sometimes require risk taking and often deal with business.

GOE—Interest Area: 16. Transportation, Distribution, and Logistics. **Work Group:** 16.05. Water Vehicle Operation. **Other Civilian Jobs in This Work Group:** Captains, Mates, and Pilots of Water Vessels; Dredge Operators; Mates—Ship, Boat, and Barge; Motorboat Operators; Pilots, Ship; Sailors and Marine Oilers.

Skills—Management of Personnel Resources: Motivating, developing, and directing people as they work; identifying the best people for the job. **Operation Monitoring:** Watching gauges, dials, or other indicators to make sure a machine is working properly. **Operation and Control:** Controlling operations of equipment or systems. **Management of Material Resources:** Obtaining and seeing to the appropriate use of equipment, facilities, and materials needed to do certain work. **Systems Evaluation:** Identifying measures or indicators of system performance and the actions needed to improve or correct performance relative to the goals of the system. **Systems Analysis:** Determining how a system should work and how changes in conditions, operations, and the environment will affect outcomes. **Troubleshooting:** Determining causes of operating errors and deciding what to do about them. **Management of Financial Resources:** Determining how money will be spent to get the work done and accounting for these expenditures.

Work Environment: Outdoors; standing; using hands on objects, tools, or controls; repetitive motions.

Shipping, Receiving, and Traffic Clerks

- Annual Earnings: $25,180
- Growth: 3.7%
- Annual Job Openings: 121,000
- Self-Employed: 0.1%
- Part-Time: 11.0%
- Civilian Training Route: Short-term on-the-job training

Verify and keep records on incoming and outgoing shipments. Prepare items for shipment. Duties include assembling, addressing, stamping, and shipping merchandise or material; receiving, unpacking, verifying, and recording incoming merchandise or material; and arranging for the transportation of products. Examine contents and compare with records such as manifests, invoices, or orders to verify accuracy of incoming or outgoing shipment. Prepare documents such as work orders, bills of lading, and shipping orders to route materials. Determine shipping method for materials, using knowledge of shipping procedures, routes, and rates. Record shipment data such as weight, charges, space availability, and damages and discrepancies for reporting, accounting, and recordkeeping purposes. Contact carrier representative to make arrangements and to issue instructions for shipping and delivery of materials. Confer and correspond with establishment representatives to rectify problems such as damages, shortages, and nonconformance to specifications. Requisition and store shipping materials and supplies to maintain inventory of stock. Deliver or route materials to departments, using work devices such as handtruck, conveyor, or sorting bins. Compute amounts such as space available and shipping, storage, and demurrage charges, using calculator or price list. Pack, seal, label, and affix postage to prepare materials for shipping, using work devices such as hand tools, power tools, and postage meter.

Military Jobs That Provide Training for It (see the descriptions in Part II): Cargo Specialists; Sales and Stock Specialists; Transportation Specialists; Warehousing and Distribution Specialists

Personality Type: Conventional. Conventional occupations frequently involve following set procedures and routines. These occupations can include working with data and details more than with ideas. Usually there is a clear line of authority to follow.

GOE—Interest Area: 04. Business and Administration. **Work Group:** 04.07. Records and Materials Processing. **Other Civilian Jobs in This Work Group:** Correspondence Clerks; File Clerks; Human Resources Assistants, Except Payroll and Timekeeping; Marking Clerks; Meter Readers, Utilities; Office Clerks, General; Order Fillers, Wholesale and Retail Sales; Postal Service Clerks; Postal Service Mail Sorters, Processors, and Processing Machine Operators; Procurement Clerks; Production, Planning, and Expediting Clerks; Stock Clerks and Order Fillers; Stock Clerks, Sales Floor; Stock Clerks—Stockroom, Warehouse, or Storage Yard; Weighers, Measurers, Checkers, and Samplers, Recordkeeping.

Skills—Mathematics: Using mathematics to solve problems. **Learning Strategies:** Selecting and using training/instructional methods and procedures appropriate for the situation when learning or teaching new things. **Management of Financial Resources:** Determining how money will be spent to get the work done and accounting for these expenditures. **Negotiation:**

Bringing others together and trying to reconcile differences. **Speaking:** Talking to others to convey information effectively. **Time Management:** Managing one's own time and the time of others. **Social Perceptiveness:** Being aware of others' reactions and understanding why they react as they do. **Writing:** Communicating effectively in writing as appropriate for the needs of the audience.

Work Environment: Indoors; noisy; contaminants; sitting; walking and running; using hands on objects, tools, or controls.

Social and Human Service Assistants

- Annual Earnings: $25,030
- Growth: 29.7%
- Annual Job Openings: 61,000
- Self-Employed: 0.1%
- Part-Time: 16.0%
- Civilian Training Route: Moderate-term on-the-job training

Assist professionals from a wide variety of fields, such as psychology, rehabilitation, or social work, to provide client services, as well as support for families. May assist clients in identifying available benefits and social and community services and help clients obtain them. May assist social workers with developing, organizing, and conducting programs to prevent and resolve problems relevant to substance abuse, human relationships, rehabilitation, or adult daycare. Provide information and refer individuals to public or private agencies or community services for assistance. Keep records and prepare reports for owner or management concerning visits with clients. Visit individuals in homes or attend group meetings to provide information on agency services, requirements, and procedures. Advise clients regarding food stamps, child care, food, money management, sanitation, or housekeeping. Submit reports and review reports or problems with superior. Oversee day-to-day group activities of residents in institution. Interview individuals and family members to compile information on social, educational, criminal, institutional, or drug history. Meet with youth groups to acquaint them with consequences of delinquent acts. Transport and accompany clients to shopping areas or to appointments, using automobile. Explain rules established by owner or management, such as sanitation and maintenance requirements and parking regulations. Observe and discuss meal preparation and suggest alternate methods of food preparation. Demonstrate use and care of equipment for tenant use. Consult with supervisor concerning programs for individual families. Monitor free, supplementary meal program to ensure cleanliness of facility and that eligibility guidelines are met for persons receiving meals. Observe clients' food selections and recommend alternate economical and nutritional food choices. Inform tenants of facilities such as laundries and playgrounds. Care for children in client's home during client's appointments. Assist in locating housing for displaced individuals. Assist clients with preparation of forms, such as tax or rent forms. Assist in planning of food budget, using charts and sample budgets.

Military Job That Provides Training for It (see the description in Part II): Caseworkers and Counselors

Personality Type: Social. Social occupations frequently involve working with, communicating with, and teaching people. These occupations often involve helping or providing service to others.

GOE—Interest Area: 10. Human Service. **Work Group:** 10.01. Counseling and Social Work. **Other Civilian Jobs in This Work Group:** Child, Family, and School Social Workers; Clinical Psychologists; Clinical, Counseling, and School Psychologists; Counseling Psychologists; Marriage and Family Therapists; Medical and Public Health Social Workers; Mental Health and Substance Abuse Social Workers; Mental Health Counselors; Probation Officers and Correctional Treatment Specialists; Rehabilitation Counselors; Residential Advisors; Substance Abuse and Behavioral Disorder Counselors.

Skills—Social Perceptiveness: Being aware of others' reactions and understanding why they react as they do. **Management of Financial Resources:** Determining how money will be spent to get the work done and accounting for these expenditures. **Service Orientation:** Actively looking for ways to help people. **Speaking:** Talking to others to convey information effectively. **Judgment and Decision Making:** Considering the relative costs and benefits of potential actions to choose the most appropriate one. **Active Listening:** Giving full attention to what other people are saying, taking time to understand the points being made, asking questions as appropriate, and not interrupting at inappropriate times. **Time Management:** Managing one's own time and the time of others. **Learning Strategies:** Selecting and using training/instructional methods and procedures appropriate for the situation when learning or teaching new things.

Work Environment: Indoors; noisy; sitting.

Solderers and Brazers

- Annual Earnings: $30,990
- Growth: 5.0%
- Annual Job Openings: 52,000
- Self-Employed: 6.3%
- Part-Time: 1.7%
- Civilian Training Route: Long-term on-the-job training

The job openings listed here are shared with Welders, Cutters, and Welder Fitters.

Braze or solder together components to assemble fabricated metal parts, using soldering iron, torch, or welding machine and flux. Melt and apply solder along adjoining edges of workpieces to solder joints, using soldering irons, gas torches, or electric-ultrasonic equipment. Heat soldering irons or workpieces to specified temperatures for soldering, using gas flames or electric current. Examine seams for defects and rework defective joints or broken parts. Melt and separate brazed or soldered joints to remove and straighten damaged or misaligned components, using hand torches, irons, or furnaces. Melt and apply solder to fill holes, indentations, and seams of fabricated metal products, using soldering equipment. Clean workpieces to remove dirt and excess acid, using chemical solutions, files, wire brushes, or grinders. Guide torches and rods along joints of workpieces to heat them to brazing temperature, melt braze alloys, and bond workpieces together. Adjust electric current and timing cycles of resistance welding machines to heat metals to bonding temperature. Turn valves to start flow of gases and light flames and adjust valves to obtain desired colors and sizes of flames. Clean equipment parts, such as tips of soldering irons, using chemical solutions or cleaning compounds. Brush flux onto joints of workpieces or dip braze rods into flux to prevent oxidation of metal. Remove workpieces from fixtures, using tongs, and cool workpieces, using air or water. Align and clamp workpieces together, using rules, squares, or hand tools, or position items in fixtures, jigs, or vises. Sweat together workpieces coated with solder. Smooth soldered areas with alternate strokes of paddles and torches, leaving soldered sections slightly higher than surrounding areas for later filing. Remove workpieces from molten solder and hold parts together until color indicates that solder has set. Select torch tips, flux, and brazing alloys from data charts or work orders. Turn dials to set intensity and duration of ultrasonic impulses according to work order specifications. Dip workpieces into molten solder or place solder strips between seams and heat seams with irons to bond items together. Clean joints of workpieces with wire brushes or by dipping them into cleaning solutions.

Military Job That Provides Training for It (see the description in Part II): Welders and Metal Workers

Personality Type: Realistic. Realistic occupations frequently involve work activities that include practical, hands-on problems and solutions. They often deal with plants, animals, and real-world materials like wood, tools, and machinery. Many of the occupations require working outside and do not involve a lot of paperwork or working closely with others.

GOE—Interest Area: 13. Manufacturing. **Work Group:** 13.04. Welding, Brazing, and Soldering. **Other Civilian Jobs in This Work Group:** Structural Metal Fabricators and Fitters; Welders, Cutters, and Welder Fitters; Welders, Cutters, Solderers, and Brazers; Welding, Soldering, and Brazing Machine Setters, Operators, and Tenders.

Skills—Quality Control Analysis: Conducting tests and inspections of products, services, or processes to evaluate quality or performance. **Installation:** Installing equipment, machines, wiring, or programs to meet specifications. **Operation and Control:** Controlling operations of equipment or systems. **Troubleshooting:** Determining causes of operating errors and deciding what to do about them. **Equipment Selection:** Determining the kinds of tools and equipment needed to do a job. **Repairing:** Repairing machines or systems, using the needed tools. **Learning Strategies:** Selecting and using training/instructional methods and procedures appropriate for the situation when learning or teaching new things. **Equipment Maintenance:** Performing routine maintenance on equipment and determining when and what kind of maintenance is needed.

Work Environment: Indoors; noisy; contaminants; minor burns, cuts, bites, or stings; using hands on objects, tools, or controls; repetitive motions.

Stationary Engineers and Boiler Operators

- Annual Earnings: $44,600
- Growth: 3.4%
- Annual Job Openings: 5,000
- Self-Employed: 1.0%
- Part-Time: 3.5%
- Civilian Training Route: Long-term on-the-job training

Operate or maintain stationary engines, boilers, or other mechanical equipment to provide utilities for buildings or industrial processes.

Operate equipment such as steam engines, generators, motors, turbines, and steam boilers. Operate or tend stationary engines; boilers; and auxiliary equipment such as pumps, compressors and air-conditioning equipment to supply and maintain steam or heat for buildings, marine vessels, or pneumatic tools. Observe and interpret readings on gauges, meters, and charts registering various aspects of boiler operation to ensure that boilers are operating properly. Test boiler water quality or arrange for testing and take any necessary corrective action, such as adding chemicals to prevent corrosion and harmful deposits. Activate valves to maintain required amounts of water in boilers, to adjust supplies of combustion air, and to control the flow of fuel into burners. Monitor boiler water, chemical, and fuel levels and make adjustments to maintain required levels. Fire coal furnaces by hand or with stokers and gas- or oil-fed boilers, using automatic gas feeds or oil pumps. Monitor and inspect equipment, computer terminals, switches, valves, gauges, alarms, safety devices, and meters to detect leaks or malfunctions and to ensure that equipment is operating efficiently and safely. Analyze problems and take appropriate action to ensure continuous and reliable operation of equipment and systems. Maintain daily logs of operation, maintenance, and safety activities, including test results, instrument readings, and details of equipment malfunctions and maintenance work. Adjust controls or valves on equipment to provide power and to regulate and set operations of system or industrial processes. Switch from automatic controls to manual controls and isolate equipment mechanically and electrically to allow for safe inspection and repair work. Clean and lubricate boilers and auxiliary equipment and make minor adjustments as needed, using hand tools. Check the air quality of ventilation systems and make adjustments to ensure compliance with mandated safety codes. Perform or arrange for repairs, such as complete overhauls; replacement of defective valves, gaskets, or bearings; or fabrication of new parts. Weigh, measure, and record fuel used.

Military Jobs That Provide Training for It (see the descriptions in Part II): Power Plant Electricians; Power Plant Operators; Powerhouse Mechanics

Personality Type: Realistic. Realistic occupations frequently involve work activities that include practical, hands-on problems and solutions. They often deal with plants, animals, and real-world materials like wood, tools, and machinery. Many of the occupations require working outside and do not involve a lot of paperwork or working closely with others.

GOE—Interest Area: 13. Manufacturing. **Work Group:** 13.16. Utility Operation and Energy Distribution. **Other Civilian Jobs in This Work Group:** Chemical Plant and System Operators; Gas Compressor and Gas Pumping Station Operators; Gas Plant Operators; Nuclear Power Reactor Operators; Petroleum Pump System Operators, Refinery Operators, and Gaugers; Power Distributors and Dispatchers; Power Plant Operators; Ship Engineers; Water and Liquid Waste Treatment Plant and System Operators.

Skills—Repairing: Repairing machines or systems, using the needed tools. **Operation Monitoring:** Watching gauges, dials, or other indicators to make sure a machine is working properly. **Equipment Maintenance:** Performing routine maintenance on equipment and determining when and what kind of maintenance is needed. **Installation:** Installing equipment, machines, wiring, or programs to meet specifications. **Systems Analysis:** Determining how a system should work and how changes in conditions, operations, and the environment will affect outcomes. **Operation and Control:** Controlling operations of equipment or systems. **Operations Analysis:** Analyzing needs and product requirements to create a design. **Troubleshooting:** Determining causes of operating errors and deciding what to do about them.

Work Environment: Noisy; very hot or cold; very bright or dim lighting; contaminants; hazardous conditions; hazardous equipment.

Storage and Distribution Managers

- Annual Earnings: $69,120
- Growth: 12.7%
- Annual Job Openings: 15,000
- Self-Employed: 2.8%
- Part-Time: 4.0%
- Civilian Training Route: Work experience in a related occupation

The job openings listed here are shared with Transportation Managers.

Plan, direct, and coordinate the storage and distribution operations within an organization or the activities of organizations that are engaged in storing and distributing materials and products. Supervise the activities of workers engaged in receiving, storing, testing, and shipping products or materials. Plan, develop, and implement warehouse safety and security programs and activities. Review invoices, work orders, consumption reports, and demand forecasts to estimate peak delivery periods and to issue work assignments. Schedule and monitor air or surface pickup, delivery, or distribution of products or materials. Interview, select, and train warehouse and supervisory personnel. Confer with department heads to coordinate warehouse activities, such as production, sales, records control, and purchasing. Respond to customers' or shippers' questions and complaints regarding storage and distribution services. Inspect physical conditions of warehouses, vehicle fleets, and equipment and order testing, maintenance, repair, or replacement as necessary. Develop and document standard and emergency operating procedures for receiving, handling, storing, shipping, or salvaging products or materials. Examine products or materials to estimate quantities or weight and type of container required for storage or transport. Negotiate with carriers, warehouse operators, and insurance company representatives for services and preferential rates. Issue shipping instructions and provide routing information to ensure that delivery times and locations are coordinated. Examine invoices and shipping manifests for conformity to tariff and customs regulations. Prepare and manage departmental budgets. Prepare or direct preparation of correspondence; reports; and operations, maintenance, and safety manuals. Arrange for necessary shipping documentation and contact customs officials to effect release of shipments. Advise sales and billing departments of transportation charges for customers' accounts. Evaluate freight costs and the inventory costs associated with transit times to ensure that costs are appropriate. Participate in setting transportation and service rates. Track and trace goods while they are en route to their destinations, expediting orders when necessary. Arrange for storage facilities when required.

Military Jobs That Provide Training for It (see the descriptions in Part II): Cargo Specialists; Petroleum Supply Specialists

Personality Type: Enterprising. Enterprising occupations frequently involve starting up and carrying out projects. These occupations can involve leading people and making many decisions. They sometimes require risk taking and often deal with business.

GOE—Interest Area: 16. Transportation, Distribution, and Logistics. **Work Group:** 16.01. Managerial Work in Transportation. **Other Civilian Jobs in This Work Group:** Aircraft Cargo Handling Supervisors; First-Line Supervisors/Managers of Transportation and Material-Moving Machine and Vehicle Operators; Postmasters and Mail Superintendents; Railroad Conductors and Yardmasters; Transportation Managers; Transportation, Storage, and Distribution Managers.

Skills—Management of Personnel Resources: Motivating, developing, and directing people as they work; identifying the best people for the job. **Operations Analysis:** Analyzing needs and product requirements to create a design. **Monitoring:** Monitoring/assessing your performance or that of other individuals or organizations to make improvements or take corrective action. **Management of Material Resources:** Obtaining and seeing to the appropriate use of equipment, facilities, and materials needed to do certain work. **Systems Analysis:** Determining how a system should work and how changes in conditions, operations, and the environment will affect outcomes. **Systems Evaluation:** Identifying measures or indicators of system performance and the actions needed to improve or correct performance relative to the goals of the system. **Persuasion:** Persuading others to change their minds or behavior. **Service Orientation:** Actively looking for ways to help people.

Work Environment: Indoors; noisy; contaminants; more often standing than sitting.

Structural Iron and Steel Workers

- Annual Earnings: $40,580
- Growth: 15.0%
- Annual Job Openings: 13,000
- Self-Employed: 2.3%
- Part-Time: 5.8%
- Civilian Training Route: Long-term on-the-job training

Raise, place, and unite iron or steel girders, columns, and other structural members to form completed structures or structural frameworks. May erect metal storage tanks and assemble prefabricated metal buildings. Read specifications and blueprints to determine the locations, quantities, and sizes of materials required. Verify vertical and horizontal alignment of structural-steel members, using plumb bobs, laser equipment, transits, and/or levels. Connect columns, beams, and girders with bolts, following blueprints and instructions from supervisors. Hoist steel beams, girders, and columns into place, using cranes, or signal hoisting equipment operators to lift and position structural-steel members. Bolt aligned structural-steel members in position for permanent riveting, bolting, or welding into place. Ride on girders or other structural-steel members to position them or use rope to guide them into position. Fabricate metal parts such as steel frames, columns, beams, and girders according to blueprints or instructions from supervisors. Pull, push, or pry structural-steel members into approximate positions for bolting into place. Cut, bend, and weld steel pieces, using metal shears, torches, and welding equipment. Fasten structural-steel members to hoist cables, using chains, cables, or rope. Assemble hoisting equipment and rigging, such as cables, pulleys, and hooks, to move heavy equipment and materials. Force structural-steel members into final positions, using turnbuckles, crowbars, jacks, and hand tools. Erect metal and precast concrete components for structures such as buildings, bridges, dams, towers, storage tanks, fences, and highway guardrails. Unload and position prefabricated steel units for hoisting as needed. Drive drift pins through rivet holes to align rivet holes in structural-steel members with corresponding holes in previously placed members. Dismantle structures and equipment. Insert sealing strips, wiring, insulating material, ladders, flanges, gauges, and valves, depending on types of structures being assembled. Catch hot rivets in buckets and insert rivets in holes, using tongs. Place blocks under reinforcing bars used to reinforce floors. Hold rivets while riveters use air-hammers to form heads on rivets.

Military Jobs That Provide Training for It (see the descriptions in Part II): Construction Specialists; Welders and Metal Workers

Personality Type: Realistic. Realistic occupations frequently involve work activities that include practical, hands-on problems and solutions. They often deal with plants, animals, and real-world materials like wood, tools, and machinery. Many of the occupations require working outside and do not involve a lot of paperwork or working closely with others.

GOE—Interest Area: 02. Architecture and Construction. **Work Group:** 02.04. Construction Crafts. **Other Civilian Jobs in This Work Group:** Boilermakers; Brickmasons and Blockmasons; Carpet Installers; Cement Masons and Concrete Finishers; Commercial Divers; Construction Carpenters; Crane and Tower Operators; Drywall and Ceiling Tile Installers; Electricians; Fence Erectors; Floor Layers, Except Carpet, Wood, and Hard Tiles; Floor Sanders and Finishers; Glaziers; Hazardous Materials Removal Workers; Insulation Workers, Floor, Ceiling, and Wall; Insulation Workers, Mechanical; Manufactured Building and Mobile Home Installers; Operating Engineers and Other Construction Equipment Operators; Painters, Construction and Maintenance; Paperhangers; Paving, Surfacing, and Tamping Equipment Operators; Pile-Driver Operators; Pipe Fitters and Steamfitters; Pipelayers; Plasterers and Stucco Masons; Plumbers; Plumbers, Pipefitters, and Steamfitters; Rail-Track Laying and Maintenance Equipment Operators; Refractory Materials Repairers, Except Brickmasons; Reinforcing Iron and Rebar Workers; Riggers; Roofers; Rough Carpenters; Security and Fire Alarm Systems Installers; Segmental Pavers; Sheet Metal Workers; Stone Cutters and Carvers, Manufacturing; Stonemasons; Tapers; Terrazzo Workers and Finishers; Tile and Marble Setters.

Skills—Equipment Maintenance: Performing routine maintenance on equipment and determining when and what kind of maintenance is needed. **Installation:** Installing equipment, machines, wiring, or programs to meet specifications. **Troubleshooting:** Determining causes of operating errors and deciding what to do about them. **Coordination:** Adjusting actions in relation to others' actions. **Operation Monitoring:** Watching gauges, dials, or other indicators to make sure a machine is working properly. **Equipment Selection:** Determining the kinds of tools and equipment needed to do a job. **Technology Design:** Generating or adapting equipment and technology to serve user needs. **Repairing:** Repairing machines or systems, using the needed tools.

Work Environment: Outdoors; noisy; very hot or cold; high places; hazardous equipment; using hands on objects, tools, or controls.

Surgical Technologists

- Annual Earnings: $34,830
- Growth: 29.5%
- Annual Job Openings: 12,000
- Self-Employed: 0.3%
- Part-Time: 23.2%
- Civilian Training Route: Postsecondary vocational training

Assist in operations under the supervision of surgeons, registered nurses, or other surgical personnel. May help set up operating room; prepare and transport patients for surgery; adjust lights and equipment; pass instruments and other supplies to surgeons and surgeon's assistants; hold retractors; cut sutures; and help count sponges, needles, supplies, and instruments. Count sponges, needles, and instruments before and after operation. Hand instruments and supplies to surgeons and surgeons' assistants, hold retractors and cut sutures, and perform other tasks as directed by surgeon during operation. Scrub arms and hands and assist the surgical team in scrubbing and putting on gloves, masks, and surgical clothing. Position patients on the operating table and cover them with sterile surgical drapes to prevent exposure. Provide technical assistance to surgeons, surgical nurses, and anesthesiologists. Wash and sterilize equipment, using germicides and sterilizers. Prepare, care for, and dispose of tissue specimens taken for laboratory analysis. Clean and restock the operating room, placing equipment and supplies and arranging instruments according to instruction. Prepare dressings or bandages and apply or assist with their application following surgery. Operate, assemble, adjust, or monitor sterilizers, lights, suction machines, and diagnostic equipment to ensure proper operation. Monitor and continually assess operating room conditions, including patient and surgical team needs. Observe patients' vital signs to assess physical condition. Maintain supply of fluids, such as plasma, saline, blood, and glucose, for use during operations. Maintain files and records of surgical procedures.

Military Jobs That Provide Training for It (see the descriptions in Part II): Dental Specialists; Medical Care Technicians

Personality Type: Realistic. Realistic occupations frequently involve work activities that include practical, hands-on problems and solutions. They often deal with plants, animals, and real-world materials like wood, tools, and machinery. Many of the occupations require working outside and do not involve a lot of paperwork or working closely with others.

GOE—Interest Area: 08. Health Science. **Work Group:** 08.02. Medicine and Surgery. **Other Civilian Jobs in This Work Group:** Anesthesiologists; Family and General Practitioners; Internists, General; Medical Assistants; Medical Transcriptionists; Obstetricians and Gynecologists; Pediatricians, General; Pharmacists; Pharmacy Aides; Pharmacy Technicians; Physician Assistants; Psychiatrists; Registered Nurses; Surgeons.

Skills—Troubleshooting: Determining causes of operating errors and deciding what to do about them. **Equipment Selection:** Determining the kinds of tools and equipment needed to do a job. **Instructing:** Teaching others how to do something. **Operation Monitoring:** Watching gauges, dials, or other indicators to make sure a machine is working properly. **Science:** Using scientific rules and methods to solve problems. **Reading Comprehension:** Understanding written sentences and paragraphs in work-related documents. **Learning Strategies:** Selecting and using training/instructional methods and procedures appropriate for the situation when learning or teaching new things. **Active Learning:** Understanding the implications of new information for both current and future problem-solving and decision-making.

Work Environment: Indoors; contaminants; disease or infections; hazardous conditions; standing; using hands on objects, tools, or controls.

Surveying Technicians

- Annual Earnings: $31,290
- Growth: 9.6%
- Annual Job Openings: 9,000
- Self-Employed: 4.3%
- Part-Time: 4.3%
- Civilian Training Route: Moderate-term on-the-job training

The job openings listed here are shared with Mapping Technicians.

Adjust and operate surveying instruments, such as theodolite and electronic distance-measuring equipment, and compile notes, make sketches, and enter data into computers. Adjust and operate surveying instruments such as prisms, theodolites, and electronic distance-measuring equipment. Compile information necessary to stake projects for construction, using engineering plans. Run rods for benches and cross-section elevations. Position and hold the vertical rods, or targets, that theodolite operators use for sighting to measure angles, distances, and elevations. Record survey measurements and descriptive data, using notes, drawings, sketches, and inked tracings. Perform calculations to determine earth curvature corrections, atmospheric impacts on measurements, traverse closures and adjustments, azimuths, level runs, and placement of markers. Conduct surveys to ascertain the locations of natural features and man-made structures on the Earth's surface, underground, and underwater, using electronic distance-measuring equipment and other surveying instruments. Search for section corners, property irons, and survey points. Operate and manage land-information computer systems, performing tasks such as storing data, making inquiries, and producing plots and reports. Direct and supervise work of subordinate members of surveying parties. Set out and recover stakes, marks, and other monumentation. Lay out grids and determine horizontal and vertical controls. Compare survey computations with applicable standards to determine adequacy of data. Collect information needed to carry out new surveys, using source maps, previous survey data, photographs, computer records, and other relevant information. Prepare topographic and contour maps of land surveyed, including site features and other relevant information such as charts, drawings, and survey notes. Maintain equipment and vehicles used by surveying crews. Place and hold measuring tapes when electronic distance-measuring equipment is not used. Provide assistance in the development of methods and procedures for conducting field surveys. Perform manual labor, such as cutting brush for lines; carrying stakes, rebar, and other heavy items; and stacking rods.

Military Jobs That Provide Training for It (see the descriptions in Part II): Construction

Specialists; Surveying, Mapping, and Drafting Technicians

Personality Type: Realistic. Realistic occupations frequently involve work activities that include practical, hands-on problems and solutions. They often deal with plants, animals, and real-world materials like wood, tools, and machinery. Many of the occupations require working outside and do not involve a lot of paperwork or working closely with others.

GOE—Interest Area: 15. Scientific Research, Engineering, and Mathematics. **Work Group:** 15.09. Engineering Technology. **Other Civilian Jobs in This Work Group:** Aerospace Engineering and Operations Technicians; Cartographers and Photogrammetrists; Civil Engineering Technicians; Electrical and Electronic Engineering Technicians; Electrical and Electronics Drafters; Electrical Drafters; Electrical Engineering Technicians; Electro-Mechanical Technicians; Electronic Drafters; Electronics Engineering Technicians; Environmental Engineering Technicians; Mapping Technicians; Mechanical Drafters; Mechanical Engineering Technicians; Surveying and Mapping Technicians.

Skills—Mathematics: Using mathematics to solve problems. **Troubleshooting:** Determining causes of operating errors and deciding what to do about them. **Equipment Maintenance:** Performing routine maintenance on equipment and determining when and what kind of maintenance is needed. **Coordination:** Adjusting actions in relation to others' actions. **Equipment Selection:** Determining the kinds of tools and equipment needed to do a job. **Technology Design:** Generating or adapting equipment and technology to serve user needs. **Science:** Using scientific rules and methods to solve problems. **Quality Control Analysis:** Conducting tests and inspections of products, services, or processes to evaluate quality or performance.

Work Environment: Outdoors; very hot or cold; very bright or dim lighting; hazardous equipment; minor burns, cuts, bites, or stings; using hands on objects, tools, or controls.

Taxi Drivers and Chauffeurs

- Annual Earnings: $19,980
- Growth: 24.8%
- Annual Job Openings: 43,000
- Self-Employed: 25.7%
- Part-Time: 21.0%
- Civilian Training Route: Short-term on-the-job training

Drive automobiles, vans, or limousines to transport passengers. May occasionally carry cargo. Test vehicle equipment such as lights, brakes, horns, or windshield wipers to ensure proper operation. Notify dispatchers or company mechanics of vehicle problems. Drive taxicabs, limousines, company cars, or privately owned vehicles to transport passengers. Follow regulations governing taxi operation and ensure that passengers follow safety regulations. Pick up passengers at prearranged locations, at taxi stands, or by cruising streets in high-traffic areas. Perform routine vehicle maintenance such as regulating tire pressure and adding gasoline, oil, and water. Communicate with dispatchers by radio, telephone, or computer to exchange information and receive requests for passenger service. Record name, date, and taxi identification information on trip sheets, along with trip information such as time and place of pickup and dropoff and total fee. Complete accident reports when necessary. Provide passengers with assistance entering and exiting vehicles and help them with any luggage. Arrange to pick up particular customers or groups on a regular schedule. Vacuum and clean interiors and wash and polish exteriors of automobiles. Pick up or meet employers according to requests, appointments, or schedules. Operate vans with special equipment such as wheelchair lifts to transport people with special needs. Collect fares or vouchers from passengers and make change or issue receipts as necessary. Determine fares based on trip distances and times, using taximeters and fee schedules, and announce fares to passengers. Perform minor vehicle repairs such as cleaning spark plugs or take vehicles to mechanics for servicing. Turn the taximeter on when passengers enter the cab and turn it off when they reach the final destination. Report to taxicab services or garages to receive vehicle assignments. Perform errands for customers or employers, such as delivering or picking up mail and packages. Provide passengers with information about the local area and points of interest or give advice on hotels and restaurants.

Military Job That Provides Training for It (see the description in Part II): Vehicle Drivers

Personality Type: Realistic. Realistic occupations frequently involve work activities that include practical, hands-on problems and solutions. They often deal with plants, animals, and real-world materials like wood, tools, and machinery. Many of the occupations require working outside and do not involve a lot of paperwork or working closely with others.

GOE—Interest Area: 16. Transportation, Distribution, and Logistics. **Work Group:** 16.06. Other Services Requiring Driving. **Other Civilian Jobs in This Work Group:** Ambulance Drivers and Attendants, Except Emergency Medical Technicians; Bus Drivers, School; Bus Drivers, Transit and Intercity; Couriers and Messengers; Driver/Sales Workers; Parking Lot Attendants; Postal Service Mail Carriers.

Skills—No data available.

Work Environment: Outdoors; contaminants; sitting; using hands on objects, tools, or controls.

Technical Directors/Managers

- Annual Earnings: $53,860
- Growth: 16.6%
- Annual Job Openings: 11,000
- Self-Employed: 30.4%
- Part-Time: 8.1%
- Civilian Training Route: Long-term on-the-job training

The job openings listed here are shared with Directors—Stage, Motion Pictures, Television, and Radio; Producers; Program Directors; and Talent Directors.

Coordinate activities of technical departments, such as taping, editing, engineering, and maintenance, to produce radio or television programs. Direct technical aspects of newscasts and other productions, checking and switching between video sources and taking responsibility for the on-air product, including camera shots and graphics. Test equipment to ensure proper operation. Monitor broadcasts to ensure that programs conform to station or network policies and regulations. Observe pictures through monitors and direct camera and video staff concerning shading and composition. Act as liaisons between engineering and production departments. Supervise and assign duties to workers engaged in technical control and production of radio and television programs. Schedule use of studio and editing facilities for producers and engineering and maintenance staff. Confer with operations directors to formulate and maintain fair and attainable technical policies for programs. Operate equipment to produce programs or broadcast live programs from remote locations. Train workers in use of equipment such as switchers, cameras, monitors, microphones, and lights. Switch between video sources in a studio or on multi-camera remotes, using equipment such as switchers, video slide projectors, and video effects generators. Set up and execute video transitions and special effects such as fades, dissolves, cuts, keys, and supers, using computers to manipulate pictures as necessary. Collaborate with promotions directors to produce on-air station promotions. Discuss filter options, lens choices, and the visual effects of objects being filmed with photography directors and video operators. Follow instructions from production managers and directors during productions, such as commands for camera cuts, effects, graphics, and takes.

Military Job That Provides Training for It (see the description in Part II): Audiovisual and Broadcast Technicians

Personality Type: Realistic. Realistic occupations frequently involve work activities that include practical, hands-on problems and solutions. They often deal with plants, animals, and real-world materials like wood, tools, and machinery. Many of the occupations require working outside and do not involve a lot of paperwork or working closely with others.

GOE—Interest Area: 03. Arts and Communication. **Work Group:** 03.01. Managerial Work in Arts and Communication. **Other Civilian Jobs in This Work Group:** Agents and Business Managers of Artists, Performers, and Athletes; Art Directors; Producers; Producers and Directors; Program Directors; Public Relations Managers.

Skills—Operation and Control: Controlling operations of equipment or systems. **Operation Monitoring:** Watching gauges, dials, or other indicators to make sure a machine is working properly. **Monitoring:** Monitoring/assessing your performance or that of other individuals or organizations to make improvements or take corrective action. **Systems Analysis:** Determining how a system should work and how changes in conditions, operations, and the environment will affect outcomes. **Time Management:** Managing one's own time and the time of others. **Troubleshooting:** Determining causes of operating errors and deciding what to do about them. **Management of Personnel Resources:** Motivating, developing, and directing people as they work; identifying the best people for the job. **Installation:** Installing equipment, machines, wiring, or programs to meet specifications.

Work Environment: Indoors; noisy; sitting; using hands on objects, tools, or controls.

Telecommunications Equipment Installers and Repairers, Except Line Installers

- Annual Earnings: $50,620
- Growth: –4.9%
- Annual Job Openings: 21,000
- Self-Employed: 6.6%
- Part-Time: 4.9%
- Civilian Training Route: Long-term on-the-job training

Set up, rearrange, or remove switching and dialing equipment used in central offices. Service or repair telephones and other communication equipment on customers' property. May install equipment in new locations or install wiring and telephone jacks in buildings under construction. Note differences in wire and cable colors so that work can be performed correctly. Test circuits and components of malfunctioning telecommunications equipment to isolate sources of malfunctions, using test meters, circuit diagrams, polarity probes, and other hand tools. Test repaired, newly installed, or updated equipment to ensure that it functions properly and conforms to specifications, using test equipment and observation. Drive crew trucks to and from work areas. Inspect equipment on a regular basis to ensure proper functioning. Repair or replace faulty equipment such as defective and damaged telephones, wires, switching system components, and associated equipment. Remove and remake connections to change circuit layouts, following work orders or diagrams. Demonstrate equipment to customers, explain how it is to be used, and respond to any inquiries or complaints. Analyze test readings, computer printouts, and trouble reports to determine equipment repair needs and required repair methods. Adjust or modify equipment to enhance equipment performance or to respond to customer requests. Remove loose wires and other debris after work is completed. Request support from technical service centers when on-site procedures fail to solve installation or maintenance problems. Assemble and install communication equipment such as data and telephone communication lines, wiring, switching equipment, wiring frames, power apparatus, computer systems, and networks. Communicate with bases, using telephones or two-way radios to receive instructions or technical advice or to report equipment status. Collaborate with other workers to locate and correct malfunctions. Review manufacturer's instructions, manuals, technical specifications, building permits, and ordinances to determine communication equipment requirements and procedures. Test connections to ensure that power supplies are adequate and that communications links function. Refer to manufacturers' manuals to obtain maintenance instructions pertaining to specific malfunctions. Climb poles and ladders, use truck-mounted booms, and enter areas such as manholes and cable vaults to install, maintain, or inspect equipment.

Military Jobs That Provide Training for It (see the descriptions in Part II): Communications Equipment Operators; Electronic Instrument and Equipment Repairers; Ship Electricians

Personality Type: Realistic. Realistic occupations frequently involve work activities that include practical, hands-on problems and solutions. They often deal with plants, animals, and real-world materials like wood, tools, and machinery. Many of the occupations require working outside and do not involve a lot of paperwork or working closely with others.

GOE—Interest Area: 02. Architecture and Construction. **Work Group:** 02.05. Systems and Equipment Installation, Maintenance, and Repair. **Other Civilian Jobs in This Work Group:** Electrical and Electronics Repairers, Powerhouse, Substation, and Relay; Electrical Power-Line Installers and Repairers; Elevator Installers and Repairers; Heating and Air Conditioning Mechanics and Installers; Maintenance and Repair Workers, General; Refrigeration Mechanics and Installers; Telecommunications Line Installers and Repairers.

Skills—Installation: Installing equipment, machines, wiring, or programs to meet specifications. **Repairing:** Repairing machines or systems, using the needed tools. **Troubleshooting:** Determining causes of operating errors and deciding what to do about them. **Technology Design:** Generating or adapting equipment and technology to serve user needs. **Systems Analysis:** Determining how a system should work and how changes in conditions, operations, and the environment will affect outcomes. **Equipment Selection:** Determining the kinds of tools and equipment needed to do a job. **Quality Control Analysis:** Conducting tests and inspections of products, services, or processes to evaluate quality or performance. **Equipment Maintenance:** Performing routine maintenance on equipment and determining when and what kind of maintenance is needed.

Work Environment: Outdoors; noisy; very hot or cold; contaminants; cramped work space, awkward positions; using hands on objects, tools, or controls.

Telecommunications Line Installers and Repairers

- Annual Earnings: $42,410
- Growth: 10.8%
- Annual Job Openings: 23,000
- Self-Employed: 1.5%
- Part-Time: 2.5%
- Civilian Training Route: Long-term on-the-job training

String and repair telephone and television cable, including fiber optics and other equipment for transmitting messages or television programming. Travel to customers' premises to install, maintain, and repair audio and visual electronic reception equipment and accessories. Inspect and test lines and cables, recording and analyzing test results, to assess transmission characteristics and locate faults and malfunctions. Splice cables, using hand tools, epoxy, or mechanical equipment. Measure signal strength at utility poles, using electronic test equipment. Set up service for customers, installing, connecting, testing, and adjusting equipment. Place insulation over conductors and seal splices with moisture-proof covering. Access specific areas to string lines and install terminal boxes, auxiliary equipment, and appliances, using bucket trucks or by climbing poles and ladders or entering tunnels, trenches, or crawl spaces. String cables between structures and lines from poles, towers, or trenches and pull lines to proper tension. Install equipment such as amplifiers and repeaters to maintain the strength of communications transmissions. Lay underground cable directly in trenches or string it through conduits running through trenches. Pull up cable by hand

T

from large reels mounted on trucks; then pull lines through ducts by hand or with winches. Clean and maintain tools and test equipment. Explain cable service to subscribers after installation and collect any installation fees that are due. Compute impedance of wires from poles to houses to determine additional resistance needed for reducing signals to desired levels. Use a variety of construction equipment to complete installations, including digger derricks, trenchers, and cable plows. Dig trenches for underground wires and cables. Dig holes for power poles, using power augers or shovels; set poles in place with cranes; and hoist poles upright, using winches. Fill and tamp holes, using cement, earth, and tamping devices. Participate in the construction and removal of telecommunication towers and associated support structures.

Military Jobs That Provide Training for It (see the descriptions in Part II): Communications Equipment Operators; Electronic Instrument and Equipment Repairers; Ship Electricians

Personality Type: Realistic. Realistic occupations frequently involve work activities that include practical, hands-on problems and solutions. They often deal with plants, animals, and real-world materials like wood, tools, and machinery. Many of the occupations require working outside and do not involve a lot of paperwork or working closely with others.

GOE—Interest Area: 02. Architecture and Construction. **Work Group:** 02.05. Systems and Equipment Installation, Maintenance, and Repair. **Other Civilian Jobs in This Work Group:** Electrical and Electronics Repairers, Powerhouse, Substation, and Relay; Electrical Power-Line Installers and Repairers; Elevator Installers and Repairers; Heating and Air Conditioning Mechanics and Installers; Maintenance and Repair Workers, General; Refrigeration Mechanics and Installers; Telecommunications Equipment Installers and Repairers, Except Line Installers.

Skills—Installation: Installing equipment, machines, wiring, or programs to meet specifications. **Troubleshooting:** Determining causes of operating errors and deciding what to do about them. **Repairing:** Repairing machines or systems, using the needed tools. **Programming:** Writing computer programs for various purposes. **Equipment Maintenance:** Performing routine maintenance on equipment and determining when and what kind of maintenance is needed. **Technology Design:** Generating or adapting equipment and technology to serve user needs. **Systems Analysis:** Determining how a system should work and how changes in conditions, operations, and the environment will affect outcomes. **Quality Control Analysis:** Conducting tests and inspections of products, services, or processes to evaluate quality or performance.

Work Environment: Outdoors; very hot or cold; contaminants; cramped work space, awkward positions; hazardous equipment; using hands on objects, tools, or controls.

Tellers

- Annual Earnings: $21,300
- Growth: 6.8%
- Annual Job Openings: 108,000
- Self-Employed: 0.0%
- Part-Time: 26.6%
- Civilian Training Route: Short-term on-the-job training

Receive and pay out money. Keep records of money and negotiable instruments involved in a financial institution's various transactions.

Balance currency, coin, and checks in cash drawers at ends of shifts and calculate daily transactions, using computers, calculators, or adding machines. Cash checks and pay out money after verifying that signatures are correct, that written and numerical amounts agree, and that accounts have sufficient funds. Receive checks and cash for deposit, verify amounts, and check accuracy of deposit slips. Examine checks for endorsements and to verify other information such as dates, bank names, identification of the persons receiving payments, and the legality of the documents. Enter customers' transactions into computers to record transactions and issue computer-generated receipts. Count currency, coins, and checks received, by hand or using currency-counting machine, to prepare them for deposit or shipment to branch banks or the Federal Reserve Bank. Identify transaction mistakes when debits and credits do not balance. Prepare and verify cashier's checks. Arrange monies received in cash boxes and coin dispensers according to denomination. Process transactions such as term deposits, retirement savings plan contributions, automated teller transactions, night deposits, and mail deposits. Receive mortgage, loan, or public utility bill payments, verifying payment dates and amounts due. Resolve problems or discrepancies concerning customers' accounts. Explain, promote, or sell products or services such as travelers' checks, savings bonds, money orders, and cashier's checks, using computerized information about customers to tailor recommendations. Perform clerical tasks such as typing, filing, and microfilm photography. Monitor bank vaults to ensure cash balances are correct. Order a supply of cash to meet daily needs. Sort and file deposit slips and checks. Receive and count daily inventories of cash, drafts, and travelers' checks. Process and maintain records of customer loans. Count, verify, and post armored car deposits. Carry out special services for customers, such as ordering bank cards and checks. Compute financial fees, interest, and service charges. Obtain and process information required for the provision of services, such as opening accounts, savings plans, and purchasing bonds.

Military Job That Provides Training for It (see the description in Part II): Finance and Accounting Specialists

Personality Type: Conventional. Conventional occupations frequently involve following set procedures and routines. These occupations can include working with data and details more than with ideas. Usually there is a clear line of authority to follow.

GOE—Interest Area: 06. Finance and Insurance. **Work Group:** 06.04. Finance/Insurance Customer Service. **Other Civilian Jobs in This Work Group:** Bill and Account Collectors; Loan Interviewers and Clerks; New Accounts Clerks.

Skills—No data available.

Work Environment: Indoors; more often standing than sitting; using hands on objects, tools, or controls; repetitive motions.

Transit and Railroad Police

- Annual Earnings: $48,850
- Growth: 9.2%
- Annual Job Openings: Fewer than 500
- Self-Employed: 0.0%
- Part-Time: 1.4%
- Civilian Training Route: Long-term on-the-job training

Protect and police railroad and transit property, employees, or passengers. Patrol railroad yards, cars, stations, and other facilities to protect company property and shipments and to maintain order. Examine credentials of unauthorized persons attempting to enter secured areas. Apprehend or remove trespassers or thieves from railroad property or coordinate with law enforcement agencies in apprehensions and removals. Prepare reports documenting investigation activities and results. Investigate or direct investigations of freight theft, suspicious damage or loss of passengers' valuables, and other crimes on railroad property. Direct security activities at derailments, fires, floods, and strikes involving railroad property. Direct and coordinate the daily activities and training of security staff. Interview neighbors, associates, and former employers of job applicants to verify personal references and to obtain work history data. Record and verify seal numbers from boxcars containing frequently pilfered items, such as cigarettes and liquor, to detect tampering. Plan and implement special safety and preventive programs, such as fire and accident prevention. Seal empty boxcars by twisting nails in door hasps, using nail twisters.

Military Job That Provides Training for It (see the description in Part II): Law Enforcement and Security Specialists

Personality Type: Enterprising. Enterprising occupations frequently involve starting up and carrying out projects. These occupations can involve leading people and making many decisions. They sometimes require risk taking and often deal with business.

GOE—Interest Area: 12. Law and Public Safety. **Work Group:** 12.04. Law Enforcement and Public Safety. **Other Civilian Jobs in This Work Group:** Bailiffs; Correctional Officers and Jailers; Criminal Investigators and Special Agents; Detectives and Criminal Investigators; Fire Investigators; Forensic Science Technicians; Parking Enforcement Workers; Police and Sheriff's Patrol Officers; Police Detectives; Police Identification and Records Officers; Police Patrol Officers; Sheriffs and Deputy Sheriffs.

Skills—Persuasion: Persuading others to change their minds or behavior. **Service Orientation:** Actively looking for ways to help people. **Social Perceptiveness:** Being aware of others' reactions and understanding why they react as they do. **Negotiation:** Bringing others together and trying to reconcile differences. **Active Listening:** Giving full attention to what other people are saying, taking time to understand the points being made, asking questions as appropriate, and not interrupting at inappropriate times. **Writing:** Communicating effectively in writing as appropriate for the needs of the audience. **Complex Problem Solving:** Identifying complex problems and reviewing related information to develop and evaluate options and implement solutions. **Speaking:** Talking to others to convey information effectively.

Work Environment: More often indoors than outdoors; noisy; very hot or cold; very bright or dim lighting; hazardous conditions.

Truck Drivers, Heavy and Tractor-Trailer

- Annual Earnings: $34,280
- Growth: 12.9%
- Annual Job Openings: 274,000
- Self-Employed: 9.3%
- Part-Time: 9.1%
- Civilian Training Route: Moderate-term on-the-job training

Drive a tractor-trailer combination or a truck with a capacity of at least 26,000 GVW to transport and deliver goods, livestock, or materials in liquid, loose, or packaged form. May be required to unload truck. May require use of automated routing equipment. Requires commercial drivers' license. Follow appropriate safety procedures when transporting dangerous goods. Check vehicles before driving them to ensure that mechanical, safety, and emergency equipment is in good working order. Maintain logs of working hours and of vehicle service and repair status, following applicable state and federal regulations. Obtain receipts or signatures when loads are delivered and collect payment for services when required. Check all load-related documentation to ensure that it is complete and accurate. Maneuver trucks into loading or unloading positions, following signals from loading crew as needed; check that vehicle position is correct and any special loading equipment is properly positioned. Drive trucks with capacities greater than 3 tons, including tractor-trailer combinations, to transport and deliver products, livestock, or other materials. Secure cargo for transport, using ropes, blocks, chain, binders, or covers. Read bills of lading to determine assignment details. Report vehicle defects, accidents, traffic violations, or damage to the vehicles. Read and interpret maps to determine vehicle routes. Couple and uncouple trailers by changing trailer jack positions, connecting or disconnecting air and electrical lines, and manipulating fifth-wheel locks. Collect delivery instructions from appropriate sources, verifying instructions and routes. Drive trucks to weigh stations before and after loading and along routes to document weights and to comply with state regulations. Operate equipment such as truck cab computers, CB radios, and telephones to exchange necessary information with bases, supervisors, or other drivers. Check conditions of trailers after contents have been unloaded to ensure that there has been no damage. Crank trailer landing gear up and down to safely secure vehicles. Wrap goods, using pads, packing paper, and containers, and secure loads to trailer walls, using straps. Perform basic vehicle maintenance tasks such as adding oil, fuel, and radiator fluid or performing minor repairs. Load and unload trucks or help others with loading and unloading, operating any special loading-related equipment on vehicles and using other equipment as necessary.

Military Job That Provides Training for It (see the description in Part II): Vehicle Drivers

Personality Type: Realistic. Realistic occupations frequently involve work activities that include practical, hands-on problems and solutions. They often deal with plants, animals, and real-world materials like wood, tools, and machinery. Many of the occupations require working outside and do not involve a lot of paperwork or working closely with others.

GOE—Interest Area: 16. Transportation, Distribution, and Logistics. **Work Group:** 16.03. Truck Driving. **Other Civilian Jobs in This Work Group:** Truck Drivers, Light or Delivery Services.

Skills—No data available.

Work Environment: Outdoors; very hot or cold; contaminants; sitting; using hands on objects, tools, or controls; repetitive motions.

Truck Drivers, Light or Delivery Services

- Annual Earnings: $24,790
- Growth: 15.7%
- Annual Job Openings: 169,000
- Self-Employed: 8.9%
- Part-Time: 9.1%
- Civilian Training Route: Short-term on-the-job training

Drive a truck or van with a capacity of under 26,000 GVW primarily to deliver or pick up merchandise or to deliver packages within a specified area. May require use of automatic routing or location software. May load and unload truck. Obey traffic laws and follow established traffic and transportation procedures. Inspect and maintain vehicle supplies and equipment such as gas, oil, water, tires, lights, and brakes to ensure that vehicles are in proper working condition. Report any mechanical problems encountered with vehicles. Present bills and receipts and collect payments for goods delivered or loaded. Load and unload trucks, vans, or automobiles. Turn in receipts and money received from deliveries. Verify the contents of inventory loads against shipping papers. Maintain records such as vehicle logs, records of cargo, or billing statements in accordance with regulations. Read maps and follow written and verbal geographic directions. Report delays, accidents, or other traffic and transportation situations to bases or other vehicles, using telephones or mobile two-way radios. Sell and keep records of sales for products from truck inventory. Drive vehicles with capacities under three tons to transport materials to and from specified destinations such as railroad stations, plants, residences, and offices or within industrial yards. Drive trucks equipped with public address systems through city streets to broadcast announcements for advertising or publicity purposes. Use and maintain the tools and equipment found on commercial vehicles, such as weighing and measuring devices. Perform emergency repairs such as changing tires or installing light bulbs, fuses, tire chains, and spark plugs.

Military Job That Provides Training for It (see the description in Part II): Vehicle Drivers

Personality Type: Realistic. Realistic occupations frequently involve work activities that include practical, hands-on problems and solutions. They often deal with plants, animals, and real-world materials like wood, tools, and machinery. Many of the occupations require working outside and do not involve a lot of paperwork or working closely with others.

GOE—Interest Area: 16. Transportation, Distribution, and Logistics. **Work Group:** 16.03. Truck Driving. **Other Civilian Jobs in This Work Group:** Truck Drivers, Heavy and Tractor-Trailer.

Skills—No data available.

Work Environment: Outdoors; very hot or cold; contaminants; cramped work space, awkward positions; minor burns, cuts, bites, or stings; using hands on objects, tools, or controls.

Water and Liquid Waste Treatment Plant and System Operators

- Annual Earnings: $34,930
- Growth: 16.2%
- Annual Job Openings: 6,000
- Self-Employed: 0.0%
- Part-Time: 5.2%
- Civilian Training Route: Long-term on-the-job training

Operate or control an entire process or system of machines, often through the use of control boards, to transfer or treat water or liquid waste. Add chemicals such as ammonia, chlorine, or lime to disinfect and deodorize water and other liquids. Operate and adjust controls on equipment to purify and clarify water, process or dispose of sewage, and generate power. Inspect equipment or monitor operating conditions, meters, and gauges to determine load requirements and detect malfunctions. Collect and test water and sewage samples, using test equipment and color analysis standards. Record operational data, personnel attendance, or meter and gauge readings on specified forms. Maintain, repair, and lubricate equipment, using hand tools and power tools. Clean and maintain tanks and filter beds, using hand tools and power tools. Direct and coordinate plant workers engaged in routine operations and maintenance activities.

Military Job That Provides Training for It (see the description in Part II): Water and Sewage Treatment Plant Operators

Personality Type: Realistic. Realistic occupations frequently involve work activities that include practical, hands-on problems and solutions. They often deal with plants, animals, and real-world materials like wood, tools, and machinery. Many of the occupations require working outside and do not involve a lot of paperwork or working closely with others.

GOE—Interest Area: 13. Manufacturing. **Work Group:** 13.16. Utility Operation and Energy Distribution. **Other Civilian Jobs in This Work Group:** Chemical Plant and System Operators; Gas Compressor and Gas Pumping Station Operators; Gas Plant Operators; Nuclear Power Reactor Operators; Petroleum Pump System Operators, Refinery Operators, and Gaugers; Power Distributors and Dispatchers; Power Plant Operators; Ship Engineers; Stationary Engineers and Boiler Operators.

Skills—Operation Monitoring: Watching gauges, dials, or other indicators to make sure a machine is working properly. **Installation:** Installing equipment, machines, wiring, or programs to meet specifications. **Operation and Control:** Controlling operations of equipment or systems. **Troubleshooting:** Determining causes of operating errors and deciding what to do about them. **Management of Material Resources:** Obtaining and seeing to the appropriate use of equipment, facilities, and materials needed to do certain work. **Operations Analysis:** Analyzing needs and product requirements to create a design. **Equipment Maintenance:** Performing routine maintenance on equipment and determining when and what kind of maintenance is needed. **Mathematics:** Using mathematics to solve problems.

Work Environment: More often outdoors than indoors; noisy; very hot or cold; contaminants; minor burns, cuts, bites, or stings.

W

Welders, Cutters, and Welder Fitters

- Annual Earnings: $30,990
- Growth: 5.0%
- Annual Job Openings: 52,000
- Self-Employed: 6.3%
- Part-Time: 1.7%
- Civilian Training Route: Long-term on-the-job training

The job openings listed here are shared with Solderers and Brazers.

Use hand-welding or flame-cutting equipment to weld or join metal components or to fill holes, indentations, or seams of fabricated metal products. Operate safety equipment and use safe work habits. Weld components in flat, vertical, or overhead positions. Ignite torches or start power supplies and strike arcs by touching electrodes to metals being welded, completing electrical circuits. Clamp, hold, tack-weld, heat-bend, grind, or bolt component parts to obtain required configurations and positions for welding. Detect faulty operation of equipment or defective materials and notify supervisors. Operate manual or semi-automatic welding equipment to fuse metal segments, using processes such as gas tungsten arc, gas metal arc, flux-cored arc, plasma arc, shielded metal arc, resistance welding, and submerged arc welding. Monitor the fitting, burning, and welding processes to avoid overheating of parts or warping, shrinking, distortion, or expansion of material. Examine workpieces for defects and measure workpieces with straightedges or templates to ensure conformance with specifications. Recognize, set up, and operate hand and power tools common to the welding trade, such as shielded metal arc and gas metal arc welding equipment. Lay out, position, align, and secure parts and assemblies prior to assembly, using straightedges, combination squares, calipers, and rulers. Chip or grind off excess weld, slag, or spatter, using hand scrapers or power chippers, portable grinders, or arc-cutting equipment. Analyze engineering drawings, blueprints, specifications, sketches, work orders, and material safety data sheets to plan layout, assembly, and welding operations. Connect and turn regulator valves to activate and adjust gas flow and pressure so that desired flames are obtained. Weld separately or in combination, using aluminum, stainless steel, cast iron, and other alloys. Determine required equipment and welding methods, applying knowledge of metallurgy, geometry, and welding techniques. Mark or tag material with proper job number, piece marks, and other identifying marks as required. Prepare all material surfaces to be welded, ensuring that there is no loose or thick scale, slag, rust, moisture, grease, or other foreign matter.

Military Job That Provides Training for It (see the description in Part II): Welders and Metal Workers

Personality Type: Realistic. Realistic occupations frequently involve work activities that include practical, hands-on problems and solutions. They often deal with plants, animals, and real-world materials like wood, tools, and machinery. Many of the occupations require working outside and do not involve a lot of paperwork or working closely with others.

GOE—Interest Area: 13. Manufacturing. **Work Group:** 13.04. Welding, Brazing, and Soldering. **Other Civilian Jobs in This Work Group:** Solderers and Brazers; Structural Metal

Fabricators and Fitters; Welders, Cutters, Solderers, and Brazers; Welding, Soldering, and Brazing Machine Setters, Operators, and Tenders.

Skills—No data available.

Work Environment: Noisy; contaminants; minor burns, cuts, bites, or stings; standing; using hands on objects, tools, or controls; repetitive motions.

APPENDIX A

Resources for Further Exploration

The facts and pointers in this book provide a good beginning to the subject of preparing for a civilian job through military training. If you want additional details, we suggest you consult some of the resources listed here.

Military Careers and Military Life

An important resource provided by the Department of Defense is www.todaysmilitary.com. It has detailed information about military jobs and recruitment.

Another useful source is www.military.com, especially the features called "10 Steps to Joining the Military" (in the Join the Military section) and "Military-Friendly Employers" (in the Careers section).

Less gung-ho and perhaps more objective than the other sites, http://usmilitary.about.com has many informative articles, especially in the section called "Joining the United States Military." A good place to get expert answers is the Questions & Answers forum at http://usmilitary.about.com/mpboards.htm.

Transition to Civilian Life

When you're getting ready to leave the military, you may want to attend a three-day session given by the Transition Assistance Program (TAP). You'll learn about job searches; career decision making; labor market conditions; and how to succeed with resumes, cover letters, and interviews. You'll also get the most current information on veterans' benefits. Read about it at http://www.dol.gov/vets/programs/tap/main.htm and then sign up for a session at your military installation or one nearby.

The TAP session covers a lot of ground in three days. If you attend, be sure that they give you a Key to Career Success card, which helps you find the nearest One-Stop Career Center in your community and helps the staff there recognize your veteran status. At the One-Stop you can get additional assistance with the topics covered by TAP.

Many of the same topics are covered by the Key to Career Success Web site, http://www.careeronestop.org/MilitaryTransition/. For example, the site links to the Department of Defense's Military Resume Writer, which helps you produce a record of your military experience in terms (such as skills) that are useful in the civilian job market.

To learn what civilian jobs are related to your military job, go to the Military to Civilian Occupation Translator at http://www.acinet.org/acinet/moc/. You enter a Military Occupation Code (MOC) or some keywords and see a listing of related civilian jobs. Each job title links to detailed information about the job.

It's possible that your military experience gives you the credentials for a civilian job that normally requires a specialized certificate or other such entry ticket. Find out by visiting CareerOneStop's Workforce Credentials Information Center at http://www.careeronestop.org/Credentialing/.

If you are a disabled veteran with an honorable discharge, you may get preferential treatment when applying for a job, especially with the federal government. For information, see http://www.dodvets.com/ or http://www.federaljobs.net/veterans.htm.

Civilian Careers

Occupational Outlook Handbook (or the *OOH*) (JIST): Updated every two years by the U.S. Department of Labor, this book provides descriptions for almost 270 major jobs covering more than 85 percent of the workforce.

Enhanced Occupational Outlook Handbook (JIST): Includes all descriptions in the *OOH* plus descriptions of more than 6,300 more-specialized jobs related to them.

*O*NET Dictionary of Occupational Titles* (JIST): The only printed source of the nearly 950 jobs described in the U.S. Department of Labor's Occupational Information Network database. It covers all the jobs in the book you're now reading, but it offers more topics than we were able to fit here.

New Guide for Occupational Exploration (JIST): An important career reference that allows you to explore all major O*NET jobs based on your interests.

Career Decision-Making and Planning

Military-to-Civilian Career Transition Guide: The Essential Job Search Handbook for Service Members, by Janet I. Farley (JIST): This book provides step-by-step directions, checklists, worksheets, and sample resumes for military people who are considering transitioning to civilian life.

Expert Resumes for Military-to-Civilian Transitions, by Wendy S. Enelow and Louise M. Kursmark (JIST): This book gives strategies for successful resume writing as well as 180 pages of sample resumes specifically written for people making the leap back into the private sector.

Overnight Career Choice, by Michael Farr (JIST): This book can help you choose a career goal based on a variety of criteria, including skills, interests, and values. It is part of the Help in a Hurry series, so it is designed to produce quick results.

50 Best Jobs for Your Personality, by Michael Farr and Laurence Shatkin, Ph.D. (JIST): Built around the six Holland personality types, this book includes an assessment to help you identify your dominant and secondary personality types, plus lists and descriptions of high-paying and high-growth civilian jobs linked to those personality types.

College Credit for Military Experience

The American Council on Education has determined how many college credits you should get for your training (but it is up to individual colleges to decide how many credits they will grant). You can see their recommendations at their Web site, http://www.militaryguides.acenet.edu, but it is probably easier to request a transcript of your accumulated military training experiences showing the ACE's recommendations. Go to one of these sites to request a transcript:

Web Site	Service Branch
http://www.maxwell.af.mil/au/ccaf/transcripts.asp	Air Force
http://aarts.army.mil/Form.htm	Army
http://www.uscg.mil/hq/cgi/Institute_Forms/index.html	Coast Guard
https://smart.navy.mil/request.pdf	Navy or Marine Corps

Another way to prove your learning and get college credit is by taking a test. If you are planning to attend a particular college, you should find out which of the following widely accepted programs they favor:

Testing Program	Web Site
CLEP	http://www.collegeboard.com/clep
DSST	http://www.getcollegecredit.com
Excelsior College Examinations	http://www.excelsior.edu
TECEP	http://www.tesc.edu/students/tecep/tecep.php

Several "colleges without walls" specialize in granting credit for college-level learning that you gain through experience, including military work experience. You can get credit, even a degree, without visiting the college or residing in its state. But to prove you have learned at college level, you need to assemble a portfolio of your work, something a lot more detailed than a statement on a resume.

College	Web Site
Thomas Edison State College	http://www.tesc.edu
Charter Oak State College	http://www.charteroak.edu
Excelsior College	http://www.excelsior.edu

APPENDIX B

Military Jobs Not Described in This Book

This book covers 75 of the 141 major military job classifications (MOTDs). The following lists identify the military jobs that are *not* included in this book. Because these military jobs were ruled out, any civilian jobs they prepare for were not considered for inclusion among the 150 best civilian jobs.

You can find information about all of these military jobs at http://www.todaysmilitary.com.

Not Included Because There Is No Equivalent Civilian Job

Air Crew Members
Armored Assault Vehicle Crew Members
Armored Assault Vehicle Officers
Dental and Optical Laboratory Technicians
Divers
Infantry
Special Forces
Special Forces Officers

Not Included Because Civilian Jobs Lack Major Information Topics

Artillery and Missile Crew Members
Emergency Management Specialists
Flight Operations Specialists
Space Operations Specialists

Not Included Because They Are Officer-Level

Administrative Officers
Aerospace Engineers
Air Traffic Control Managers
Artillery and Missile Officers
Audiovisual and Broadcast Directors
Chaplains
Civil Engineers
Communications Managers
Computer Systems Officers
Dentists
Dietitians
Electrical and Electronics Engineers
Emergency Management Officers
Environmental Health and Safety Officers
Finance and Accounting Managers
Food Service Managers
Health Services Administrators
Industrial Engineers
Infantry Officers
Intelligence Officers
International Relations Officers
Law Enforcement and Security Officers
Lawyers and Judges
Life Scientists
Logisticians
Management Analysts and Planners
Marine Engineers
Music Directors
Nuclear Engineers
Optometrists
Ordnance Officers
Personnel Managers
Pharmacists
Physical and Occupational Therapists
Physical Scientists
Physician Assistants
Physicians and Surgeons
Psychologists
Public Information Officers
Purchasing and Contracting Managers
Recruiting Managers
Registered Nurses
Ship Engineers
Social Workers
Speech Therapists
Store Managers
Supply and Warehousing Managers
Teachers and Instructors
Training and Education Directors
Transportation Maintenance Managers
Transportation Managers

Not Included Because Considerable Additional Nonmilitary Training Is Required

Air Traffic Controllers
Training Specialists and Instructors
Meteorological Specialists

Index

A

B

C

D

E

F

G

H

I

J–K

L

M

N

O

P

Q–R

S

T

U–V

W–Z